J.K. LASSER PRO™

INTEGRATING INVESTMENTS AND THE TAX CODE

J.K. LASSER PRO™

INTEGRATING INVESTMENTS AND THE TAX CODE

Using the Tax Code to Enhance Returns and Add Value

William Reichenstein, CFA, PhD
William W. Jennings, CFA, PhD

John Wiley & Sons, Inc.

Published by John Wiley & Sons, Inc., Hoboken, New Jersey
Published simultaneously in Canada

For general information on our other products and services, or technical support, please contact our Cus-
tomer Care Department within the United States at 800-762-2974, outside the United States at 317-572-
3993 or fax 317-572-4002.

Wiley also publishes its books in a variety of electronic formats. Some content that appears in print may
not be available in electronic books.

Library of Congress Cataloging-in-Publication Data:

Reichenstein, William,
   Integrating Investments and the Tax Code. / William
Reichenstein, William W. Jennings.
      p. cm. —(J.K. Lasser Professional series)
   Includes bibliographic references and index.
   ISBN 0-471-21642-9
   1. Portfolio Management. 2. Asset Allocation. 3.
Financial Planners—United States. I. Jennings, William.
   HG4925   2003

Printed in the United States of America

10 9 8 7 6 5 4 3 2 1

Contents

Acknowledgments

With any large project, there are many people who deserve acknowledgment and our sincere thanks. We thank the Research Foundation of the Institute of Chartered Financial Analysts for funding part of this work. We thank Jean Brunel, Executive Editor of *Journal of Wealth Management,* for publishing earlier versions of six chapters in this journal. In addition, we thank *Financial Services Review, Journal of Financial Planning* and (American Association of Individual Investors) *AAII Journal* for publishing chapters and related articles. Karen Eilers Lahey and Conrad Ciccotello, Editors of *Financial Services Review,* Marvin W. Tuttle, Bruce W. Most, Mary Corbin, and the rest of the editorial team at the *Journal of Financial Planning,* and Maria Crawford Scott, Editor of *AAII Journal,* provided venues for our ideas. Kirsten Cook, Reichenstein's teacher's assistant, provided countless services, including manuscript editing, index organizing, writing most of the glossary, and joining us in authouring an article that formed the basis of Appendix 11.2. Without his assistance, the completion of the book would have been delayed by months. We owe a special thanks to David Pugh, our Editor at John Wiley & Sons, for his guidance at every step in the process. Ann Imhof, the Project Manager at Carlisle Publishers Services, remained cheery throughout the numerous revisions. The following individuals made valuable comments on one or more chapters: Steve Carney, Glenn Daily, Stephen P. Fraser, David R. King, and Moshe Milevsky. Patrick Reinkemeyer and Daniel Yeung provided complimentary copies of *Morningstar Principia Pro for Mutual Funds* and *Morningstar Principia Pro for Variable Annuities/Life.* In addition, we thank Barbara Wiedman at Baylor University for her patience with our endless revisions. Last but not least, we thank our wives, Mineva and Heather, for their love and patience.

Introduction

Major Themes

Three examples illustrate the major themes in this book.

Example 1. Tom and Frank are both age 30. They are currently in the 28 percent tax bracket, expect to remain in this bracket, and are saving for retirement 35 years hence. Tom invests $1,000 in a bond fund held in a taxable account. It earns 8 percent a year before taxes and 5.76 percent a year after taxes [8% • (1 − 0.28)]. In 35 years, it is worth $7,100 after taxes [$1,000 • $(1.0576)^{35}$]. Frank invests $1,000 in the same bond fund for 35 years but holds it in a Roth IRA. In this example, returns are tax-exempt in the Roth IRA. In 35 years, it is worth $14,785 after taxes [$1,000 • $(1.08)^{35}$]. They each invested the same amount of funds in the same investment for the same investment horizon. Yet, Frank ends up with more than twice the after-tax wealth. Taxes matter! Indeed, the choice of a savings vehicle (and its associated tax structure) matters a great deal. The first part of this book thoroughly examines savings vehicles in the United States. It models each savings vehicle's tax structure and thoroughly examines related investment implications. In addition, it examines tax-advantaged opportunities to save for education needs. This section helps individuals make the best use of the Tax Code and allows financial professionals to add value to client accounts by giving advice on the best use of the Tax Code.

Example 2. Steve and Teresa Adams, a 45-year-old couple, are currently in the 28 percent tax bracket and expect to remain there during retirement. They decide to reduce this year's consumption by $2,000 and save for retirement. Since purchases of goods and services are made with after-tax funds, they each need to save $1,000 *of after-tax funds.* Steve invests $1,000 in a Roth IRA. Teresa defers $1,389 in her 401(k) plan. The $1,389 contribution reduces taxable income by the same amount, which reduces taxes by $389 [$1,389 • 0.28]. The $1,389 of before-tax funds in the 401(k) represents $1,000 of after-tax funds plus the $389 tax savings.

They both invest in the same mutual fund. Assume it earns 9 percent a year for 30 years, at which time the funds are withdrawn and spent on retirement needs. Steve invests $1,000 of after-tax funds this year and it grows to $13,268 at age 75 [$1,000 • $(1.09)^{30}$]. Teresa invests $1,389 of before-tax funds this year. At age 75, it is worth $18,427 before taxes [$1,389 • $(1.09)^{30}$], and $13,268 after taxes [$18,427 • $(1 - 0.28)$]. At age 45, the $1,389 of before-tax funds in Teresa's 401(k) is equivalent to the $1,000 of after-tax funds in Steve's Roth IRA. At age 75, the $18,427 of before-tax funds in Teresa's 401(k) is equivalent to the $13,268 of after-tax funds in Steve's Roth IRA.

This example illustrates two important and related principles. First, when making the saving decision, the proper comparison is between a $1,389 investment in a 401(k) and a $1,000 investment in a Roth IRA (or any other nondeductible savings vehicle); we should compare investments that represent the same amount of *after-tax dollars*. Comparable investments reduce current-year consumption by the same amount.

Second, when calculating their asset allocation, $1,389 in a 401(k) must be considered equivalent to $1,000 in a Roth IRA, and, later, $18,427 in a 401(k) must be considered equivalent to $13,268 in a Roth IRA. They both buy the same amount of goods and services. Acceptable methods of calculating their asset allocation must compare *after-tax funds* to other *after-tax funds*. We should convert the $18,427 of before-tax funds in the 401(k) to $13,268 of after-tax funds and then compute the asset allocation based on after-tax dollars.

Suppose at age 75 Steve transfers the $13,268 in his Roth IRA into a stock fund, Teresa transfers the $18,427 in her 401(k) into a bond fund, and these are their only assets. What is the couple's current asset allocation? According to the traditional approach, it is 42 percent stocks [$13,268 / ($13,268 + $18,427)], and 58 percent bonds. The traditional approach is internally inconsistent in that it does not distinguish between before-tax funds and after-tax funds. The new approach first converts funds to after-tax values and then calculates the asset allocation based on these values. It says the Smiths have a 50 percent stock and 50 percent bond asset allocation. Unlike the traditional approach, this new approach recognizes the equivalence between the $13,268 in a Roth IRA and the $18,427 in a 401(k).

Example 3. A single woman just retired at age 65 and has $500,000 in a 401(k) invested in a stock fund and $500,000 in a taxable account invested in a bond fund. The market value and book value of the bond fund are $500,000. She expects to be in the 30 percent tax bracket during retirement. In addition, she receives monthly income totaling $1,250 from Social Security. What is her asset allocation? According to the traditional approach, it is 50 percent stocks and 50 percent bonds. We believe the traditional approach makes two mistakes. First, it makes no distinction between the before-tax funds in the 401(k) and the after-tax funds in the taxable account. Second, it ignores the value of the retirement income streams—Social Security benefits in this example. If she withdraws $1,000 from the 401(k), she pays $300 in taxes and can buy $700 of goods and services. If she withdraws $1,000 from the taxable account, she can buy $1,000 of goods and services. After conversion to after-tax values, her financial portfolio contains $350,000 in stocks—the after-tax value of the 401(k)—and $500,000 in bonds. For retirement planning, we advocate that she view Social Security payments and other retirement income streams (such as military retirement and company defined-benefit plans) as bonds in her extended portfolio and calculate the asset allocation of this extended portfolio. If the present value of Social Security payments is $150,000 after taxes, then her extended portfolio contains $350,000 after taxes in stocks and $650,000 in bonds, where the latter is the sum of the $500,000 in the bond fund and $150,000 in Social Security "bonds." For retirement planning, we contend that she should view her current asset allocation as 35 percent stocks [$350,000 / ($350,000 + $650,000)] and 65 percent bonds.

This book contains two parts: "Savings Vehicles" and "A New Approach to Calculating a Family's Asset Allocation." They both emphasize the need to distinguish before-tax funds and after-tax funds. After-tax funds should be compared to other after-tax funds when making saving decisions, when planning for retirement, and when calculating the asset allocation. The sections fit together like two gloves. A $1,000 contribution to a Roth IRA is a larger investment than a $1,000 contribution to a 401(k) because the Roth IRA contains after-tax funds. In retirement planning, $1,000 in a Roth IRA is larger than $1,000 in a 401(k) because the Roth IRA contains after-tax funds. Part I examines tax strategies when saving for retirement and education, which are the two most important goals for most people. It thoroughly examines the choice of savings vehicles and related investment implications. It helps financial professionals give advice to their clients. Should a client save in a Roth IRA or a 401(k) account with matching contributions? Should he or she save in a mutual fund or a non-qualified tax-deferred annuity? What are the advantages and disadvantages of a 529 plan and a Coverdell Savings Account? Part II presents a new approach to calculating a family's asset allocation. Unlike the traditional approach, the new approach distinguishes between before-tax and after-tax funds and includes the value of Social Security and other retirement income streams.

Investment Premise

John and Mary Smith have arranged an initial meeting with you, their prospective financial advisor. They are beginning to save for their retirement in 35 years and must make at least three decisions:

1. They must decide whether to save through a taxable account, a non-qualified tax-deferred annuity, or a 401(k) plan.
2. They must choose an asset mix.
3. They must select individual bonds and stocks or, more likely, bond and stock mutual funds.

The first half of this book looks primarily at the first decision. It asks which of these savings vehicles is best for accumulating retirement wealth. It shows that the Smiths' after-tax retirement income will probably be twice as large if they save through a 401(k) plan instead of a taxable account. The choice of a savings vehicle, and its associated tax structure, matters. In addition, the first half includes a chapter that examines tax-advantaged strategies for saving for education needs. The Economic Growth and Tax Relief Reconciliation Act of 2001 significantly increased the opportunities for individuals to save tax-efficiently for retirement and education needs. In short, the first half shows individuals and financial professionals how to best use the Tax Code when saving for retirement or education.

As noted earlier, the second half looks primarily at the asset allocation decision. It presents a new method of calculating a family's asset allocation that distinguishes before-tax and after-tax funds and considers the value of Social Security and other retirement income streams.

In addition, the book provides insight on the Smiths' third decision—at least, if they want to hold stocks in a taxable account. In a taxable account, the stocks' taxation depends upon the dividend yield and how quickly capital gains are realized. One good choice for the stock portion of their taxable account is thus to *passively* hold low-yield stocks. Another good choice is a stock index fund, especially one that has few stocks entering and leaving the index. We also make other recommendations.

A major theme of this book is the choice of savings vehicles for the Smiths and other people who are saving for retirement or, perhaps better stated, for the retirement portion of their savings. If the Smiths are saving for a new car or a vacation, this portion of their savings should be in a taxable account. The Smiths, however, can and should carefully choose the savings vehicles for the portion of their savings *intended to meet their retirement needs*.

This book examines the pros and cons of saving for retirement through the major savings vehicles in the United States. The major savings vehicles include (1) a taxable account, (2) a non-qualified tax-deferred annuity, (3) a deductible pension, such as a 401(k) plan, and (4) a Roth IRA. Chapter 2 discusses the characteristics of each of these vehicles extensively. It projects the ending after-tax wealth from investments in, respectively, bonds and stocks for a wide range of investment horizons. For the Smiths and others saving for retirement, the best savings vehicle is usually the one that maximizes the expected after-tax wealth. Other factors are considered, such as the 10 percent penalty tax that usually applies to withdrawals before age 59½ from a deductible pension. However, if the savings will be used during retirement, the penalty tax will not apply. Thus, the objective function—that is, the criterion used to define "best"—is the savings vehicle that maximizes after-tax retirement wealth.

This objective function points out the book's limitations. First, because it assumes savings will be used to meet retirement needs, it ignores issues related to estate taxes and bequests. Thus, the recommendations may or may not be "best" for someone facing estate taxes.

Second, the choice of savings vehicles relies on projected returns, projections of ending wealth, and thus the projected benefits of one savings vehicle over another. The first several chapters in this book project bond returns at 6 percent and stock returns at 11 percent. Taken at face value, the projections suggest no one should invest in bonds. That would be an inappropriate interpretation. They are point estimates and do not consider the range of possible outcomes; that is, they do not consider differences in risk. *Each individual should first determine whether he or she wants an investment in bonds or stocks, and then choose the appropriate savings vehicle.* We retain the 6 percent and 11 percent return assumptions to keep the analysis tractable. We also present the ending-wealth models so other return projections can easily be examined. One ending-wealth model is complex, and that is the model for stocks held in a taxable account. This model is available as an Excel spreadsheet at www.wiley.com/go/reichenstein. This model, as all models, is explained in an end-of-chapter appendix.

Suppose someone must decide whether to save in a Roth IRA or a taxable account. The Roth IRA provides a larger ending wealth when asset returns are positive. The Roth IRA should be chosen because the best prediction *before the fact* is that returns will be positive. *After the fact,* returns may be negative. However, this possibility *after the fact* does not negate the need to make decisions *before the fact.* In retirement planning the investment horizon almost always exceeds 10 years and is often 20 or 30 or 40 years. For these horizons we can be reasonably confident that returns will be positive and, therefore, that the advice to choose the Roth IRA is appropriate. In short, most of this book's advice prevails for a wide range of assumed returns and is not dependent upon the precise return projections.

Politicians forge tax laws in an environment of conflict and compromise. Thus, it is not surprising that tax laws produce an uneven playing field. It makes a big difference whether an investment is subject to tax structure A or tax structure B. Consequently, financial professionals can add value to their clients' portfolios by helping them choose the best combination of savings vehicles.

In the best of all worlds, the Smiths would choose the best bonds and stocks and hold them in the best savings vehicle. Financial analysts and financial planners may be able to add value by helping their clients choose good bonds and stocks. This study shows that they can also add value—probably more value—by helping their clients choose appropriate savings vehicles.

Tax and Investment Literature

This section briefly discusses two parts of the recent tax-investment literature. Then, it discusses tax topics considered in this book and topics ignored in this book.

History

Tax considerations have received increased attention in the investment literature. For the past several years, we have concentrated our research on the interaction between investments and tax considerations. This book combines much of that literature.

We wish to discuss two parts of the rest of the tax-and-investment literature. In *Integrated Wealth Management*, Jean L.P. Brunel discusses a range of tax-and-investment issues for the very wealthy. For example, this book discusses the types of trusts and their use in helping reduce estate taxes and in meeting multigenerational family needs. Also, it discusses the common problem among the very rich of a large portion of wealth being in a low-cost basis asset—often the founder's shares of a firm's common stock. *Integrated Wealth Management* is an excellent source of ideas, especially for professionals with very wealthy clients. In contrast, our book is much more narrowly focused, but the material applies to a broader spectrum of individuals.

We also wish to discuss the literature on the tax costs of realizing capital gains in a taxable account. Jeffrey and Arnott (1993) contributed the original work in this area. Their article spurred a series of articles that looks at these tax costs and asks whether active managers' alphas—a measure of value added—are sufficient to overcome these costs.[1] Jeffrey (1995) draws attention to two realities confronting investors and students of investing. First, *"Taxes are simply another item of expense"* which, like salaries and fees and commissions, should be evaluated and managed to insure that they are always adding value" (emphasis in the original). For taxable investors, taxes are usually the largest and most controllable of these transaction costs. Second, "few people in the money management business understand and articulate the first reality, i.e., that taxes *are* a very impor-tant item of expense" (emphasis in the original).

Taxes have been largely ignored for at least two reasons. First, they complicate performance analysis. Tax rates vary across investors. It is not easy to choose a representative tax rate. In the United States, the marginal federal tax rate in 2002 for individuals varied from zero to 38.6 percent. Considering state and local taxes would widen this range. While dividends are fully taxable to the individual investor, they are largely tax-exempt to the corporate investor. Moreover, money managers' largest customers have been tax-exempt defined-benefit pensions and endowments. A second reason for ignoring taxes is that it is in the best interest of many financial professionals to do so. As Jeffrey (1995) notes, "active managers are in the business of selling alpha"—a measure of value added—that is reduced by taxes, and "brokers are compensated by commissions on the trades that generate the taxes." So, there is every incentive on the "sell side" of Wall Street *not* to highlight tax considerations.

One thing is certain: Taxable investors notice and care about taxes. The outsized stock market returns in the 1980s and 1990s have given rise to outsized taxes and, naturally enough, attempts to reduce the tax drag. In response, in 1993

Morningstar Mutual Funds began reporting tax-adjusted returns, as well as the tax-efficiency of mutual funds. In 1994, the Association for Investment Management and Research (AIMR), which awards the Chartered Financial Analyst certification, released standards for after-tax performance measurement. Separately, mutual fund companies and investment advisors have introduced tax-managed funds that were explicitly designed to minimize the tax bite to taxable individual investors. It is safe to say taxes, and the desire to reduce them, will not go away.

Tax Topics Considered

This book examines the investment implications of the major savings vehicles in the United States. In addition, it examines tax-advantaged strategies when saving for education. Questions addressed include:

- Which savings vehicle provides the largest retirement income?
- When is it preferable to save in a non-qualified tax-deferred annuity instead of a taxable account?
- Should stocks be held in a pension and bonds in a taxable account, or vice versa?
- Should an individual convert funds from a traditional IRA to a Roth IRA—thus incurring an immediate tax liability—or retain funds in the traditional IRA?
- What factors should influence the decision to invest in the Roth IRA or the traditional IRA?
- What are the costs of realizing capital gains in a taxable account?
- What are good choices for the stock portion of a taxable account?
- What are the advantages and disadvantages of saving for a child's education in a 529 plan, a prepaid state tuition plan, and a Coverdell Savings Account?
- In education planning, what tax strategies best support college funding?

Tax Topic Ignored

In general, we ignore estate taxes. However, estate taxes remain a major issue to the wealthy. Individuals with estate planning needs should consult their tax specialist before implementing the strategies recommended in this book.

References

Brunel, Jean L.P. 2002. *Integrated wealth management: The new direction for portfolio managers.* London: Institutional Investor Books, Euromoney Institutional Investor Plc.

Hertog, Roger, and Mark R. Gordon. 1994a. Equity strategies for taxable investors. *Journal of Investing,* Fall, 91–94.

Hertog, Roger, and Mark R. Gordon. 1994b. Is your alpha big enough to cover its taxes?: Comment. *Journal of Portfolio Management,* Summer, 93–95.

Jeffrey, Robert H. 1995. Tax considerations in investing. In *The portable MBA in investments*, edited by Peter L. Bernstein. New York: John Wiley & Sons, Inc.

Jeffrey, Robert H., and Robert D. Arnott. 1993. Is your alpha big enough to cover its taxes? *Journal of Portfolio Management*, Spring, 15–25.

Jeffrey, Robert H., and Robert D. Arnott. 1994. Is your alpha big enough to cover its taxes?: Reply to comment. *Journal of Portfolio Management*, Summer, 96–97.

Notes

1. Related literature includes Hertog and Gordon (1994a and 1994b), Jeffrey and Arnott (1994), and Jeffrey (1995).

Part I

Savings Vehicles

Savings Vehicles: Structure and Ending-Wealth Models

Introduction

Let us return to our original setting. John and Mary Smith have arranged an initial meeting with you, their prospective financial advisor. They are beginning to save for their retirement in 35 years and must make at least three decisions:

1. They must decide whether to save through a taxable account, a non-qualified tax-deferred annuity, or a 401(k) plan.

2. They must choose an asset mix.

3. They must select individual bonds and stocks or, more likely, bond and stock mutual funds.

This chapter and, indeed, the first section of this book deal primarily with the first decision—the choice of savings vehicles.

The term "savings vehicle" refers to an entire legal structure within which someone can save, including applicable tax structures, liquidity restrictions, and other restrictions. When saving for retirement, five major savings vehicles are available in the United States: (1) a personal or taxable account, (2) a nondeductible IRA, (3) a non-qualified tax-deferred annuity, (4) a deductible pension (which we will define later), and (5) a Roth IRA. (In a later chapter, we discuss savings vehicles available when saving for educational needs.) The last four vehicles are "retirement savings vehicles." Congress has granted favored tax treatment, with concomitant restrictions, to savings intended for retirement that are held in these vehicles. For example, in a nondeductible IRA, the original investment contribution is not tax deductible, but taxes on investment returns are deferred until withdrawn, which is usually in retirement. This describes the *tax structure* of this savings vehicle. Other features of the *legal structure* of the nondeductible IRA influence its desirability, such as the 10 percent early distribution tax that usually applies to withdrawals before age 59½ (liquidity restriction) and the minimum withdrawal requirement after age 70½. Table 2.1 summarizes tax structures, liquidity restrictions, and other features of the five major savings vehicles.

To guide clients through the crucial selection of savings vehicles, the financial advisor needs to be familiar with the tax treatment of assets in each savings vehicle as well as the non-tax features of each vehicle. Given a projected rate of return, length of investment horizon, and the client's current tax rate and projected retirement tax rate, the financial advisor should be able to calculate the after-tax retirement wealth provided by each savings vehicle. In addition, he or she should be aware of how changes in each of these factors affect the desirability of one savings vehicle versus the others. This chapter provides a review of the features of the savings vehicles. It then presents an after-tax ending-wealth model for each vehicle.

Tax Structure of Five Savings Vehicles

Suppose a client invests in a bond fund and plans to liquidate and spend the funds during her retirement 30 years hence. Her after-tax wealth depends on the following:

1. The bond fund's rate of return,
2. Her tax rates each year, and
3. The tax treatment of the returns; that is, whether the returns are taxable each year or tax deferred or tax-exempt.

The client and her financial advisor have little control over the first two variables: financial markets largely determine whether the bond fund earns 6 percent or 8 percent a year, and governments set tax rates. Within limits, however, the tax treatment of the returns can be controlled. If the bond fund is held in a Roth IRA, its returns are generally tax-exempt. If the fund is held in a traditional IRA, its returns are tax deferred. If the fund is held in a taxable account, its returns are taxable each year, and her after-tax ending wealth is likely to be substantially less. This book is primarily concerned with this third variable—the one that is most within the control of the investor and her financial advisor.

For most clients, the tax structure is the most important part of a savings vehicle's legal structure because it has the greatest impact on ending wealth. When funds are actually used in retirement, many other features of savings vehicles, such as the 10 percent penalty tax for early withdrawals, will not apply. Thus, the choice of savings vehicles usually boils down to a choice of tax structures. Therefore, each vehicle's basic tax structure is considered first.

Taxable Account

In a taxable account, the individual invests after-tax dollars. The funds grow at the after-tax rate of return. Stated differently, the original investment amount (or principal) is not tax deductible and returns are generally not tax deferred. An exception exists for unrealized capital gains, which are tax deferred until realized through a sale or exchange. The investor owes taxes on interest and dividends for the year in which they are received; the applicable tax rate is the ordinary income tax rate. The investor owes taxes on capital gains for the year in which they are realized. If the asset is held for less than one year, it is considered a short-term capital gain, and the gain is taxed at the ordinary income tax rate. If the asset is held for more than one year, it is a long-term gain, and a preferential tax rate applies.

Nondeductible IRA

Technically, there are only two types of IRAs—traditional and Roth. When a lower-income individual contributes to a traditional IRA, the contribution amount is often deductible from that year's taxable income. This book refers to this use of a traditional IRA as a deductible IRA, and its tax structure is identical to any other deductible pension. When a higher-income individual contributes to a traditional IRA, the contribution amount may not be deductible. Nevertheless, these individuals may still contribute into a traditional IRA. Although the contribution amount is not deductible, returns are tax deferred until withdrawal. This book refers to this use of a traditional IRA as a nondeductible IRA.

In a nondeductible IRA, the individual invests after-tax dollars. The funds grow at the underlying asset's before-tax rate of return. That is, the returns are tax deferred. Accumulated returns are taxable in the year in which they are withdrawn, which is usually in retirement. The applicable rate is the ordinary income tax rate even if returns are in the form of capital gains. In determining the tax due, withdrawals are considered a pro-rata share of principal and interest or, more accurately, principal and deferred return.

Non-qualified Tax-deferred Annuity

The name of this savings vehicle reveals its tax structure. "Non-qualified" means the original investment does not qualify for tax deduction in the year of investment; that is, the original investment is made with after-tax funds. "Tax-deferred" means the returns accumulate tax deferred until withdrawn, which is usually in retirement. For tax computation, withdrawals are generally considered "interest first."[1] The term "interest first" means returns are first withdrawn, whether in the form of interest, dividends, or capital gains.

A non-qualified tax-deferred annuity is an insurance product. The annuity may be fixed or variable. In a fixed annuity, the insurance firm guarantees a fixed rate of return. In a variable annuity, the individual earns a return on a subaccount, which is structurally equivalent to a mutual fund.

The financial press often describes a non-qualified tax-deferred variable annuity as a mutual fund in a tax-deferred wrapper. The invested funds are managed in a subaccount, with investors sharing proportionately in the underlying asset's returns less the expenses of managing the account. In a variable annuity, the individual can choose to invest among various bond and stock subaccounts, and the individual's return depends on the performance of the subaccounts he selects.

The tax structure of a non-qualified tax-deferred annuity is the same as that of a mutual fund held in a nondeductible IRA. In both cases, the individual invests after-tax dollars, and the returns accumulate tax deferred. A key difference is that the total annual costs of an annuity exceed the total costs of a mutual fund due to the annuity's insurance fees. These annuities are examined in detail in Chapter 5.

Deductible Pension

In this book, "deductible pension" refers to any savings vehicles where both the investment amount and the investment returns are tax deferred. Included, among others, are deductible IRA, 401(k), 403(b), Keogh, and Simplified Employee Pension (SEP-IRA). Although differences exist in the amount of funds that can be invested in each type of deductible pension and in other details, they each face the same tax structure and similar liquidity restrictions.

In a deductible pension, an individual invests before-tax dollars that grow at the before-tax rate of return; both the principal and returns are tax deferred until withdrawal, which is usually in retirement. Withdrawals are fully taxable, and the ordinary income tax rate applies. Since all withdrawals are fully taxable, there is no need to distinguish between withdrawals of principal and withdrawals of interest.

Roth IRA

The Taxpayer Relief Act of 1997 introduced the Roth IRA. In a Roth IRA, the individual invests after-tax dollars, and the funds grow at the before-tax rate of return. The principal is not deductible in the contribution year but, in qualified withdrawals, investment returns are tax-exempt. In non-qualified withdrawals, investment returns are taxable. However, withdrawals from a Roth IRA are considered "principal first," which are tax-exempt.

Withdrawals are qualified if (1) the funds are invested for a minimum of five tax years and (2) the investor is at least age 59½. The five-year period begins with the tax year in which the Roth IRA is first established. For example, an individual invests $2,000 in a Roth IRA on April 15, 1999, for the 1998 tax year and he invests another $2,000 in each tax year from 1999 through 2002. If he is at least age 59½ on January 1, 2003, he could withdraw the *full account value* tax-free because the Roth IRA has been in existence for five tax years.

Qualified withdrawals from a Roth IRA are tax-exempt. Withdrawals are qualified if they meet the five-year holding period and the individual is at least age 59½. Withdrawals are also "qualified" if due to death, disability, or to help finance up to $10,000 of the cost of the principal residence of a first-time homebuyer. In all other situations, the accumulated returns (but not principal) are subject to ordinary income taxes and/or the 10 percent early withdrawal penalty.

As a rule, if neither the five-year holding period nor age 59½ requirement is met, the accumulated returns are subject to both ordinary income taxes and the 10 percent early withdrawal penalty tax. If the five-year holding period has been met but the individual is under age 59½, the penalty tax (but not income tax) is waived for withdrawals that are used to pay medical expenses exceeding 7.5 percent of adjusted gross income, qualified higher education expenses, or medical insurance premiums of the unemployed. If the investor meets the age requirement but not the five-year holding period, the penalty tax (but not income tax) is waived if the withdrawal is due to death, disability, or to pay for the principal residence of a first-time homebuyer, deductible medical expenses, higher education expenses, or medical insurance premiums of the unemployed.

Example: Sally contributes $2,000 a year for tax years 2001 through 2003 into a Roth IRA. In 2010, the $6,000 original investment is worth $8,400. Sally (then under age 59½) withdraws the full amount to pay her son's qualified education expenses. She does *not* owe a penalty tax but does owe income taxes on the $2,400 accumulated return. Alternatively, she could withdraw the $6,000 principal and retain the $2,400 in the account until after she reaches age 59½. In a Roth IRA, withdrawals are considered to come from principal first. So, she would owe no taxes on the $6,000 withdrawal.

As with any discussion of tax matters, financial advisors should seek expert advice. For example, the principal-first rule previously discussed applies to regular annual contributions, but it does not apply to qualified rollover contributions. Withdrawals come first from the regular annual contributions and then from rollover contributions. For the rollover contributions, withdrawals come first from the taxable portion.

Other Features of Savings Vehicles

Some non-tax-structure features of savings vehicles favor a taxable account, while others favor retirement accounts. For the client who is saving for retirement, however, liquidity restrictions and other non-tax-structure features should be of little importance. Table 2.1 lists features that may influence the choice of savings vehicles.

TABLE 2.1 A Summary of Five Savings Vehicles

	Taxable Account	Nondeductible IRA	Non-qualified Tax-deferred Annuity	Deductible Pension	Roth IRA
Tax Structure					
Original Investment	After-tax $	After-tax $	After-tax $	Before-tax $	After-tax $
Growth Rate	After-tax rate of return	Before-tax rate of return	Before-tax rate of return	Before-tax rate of return	Before-tax rate of return
Taxes:					
Tax-deferred	Unrealized capital gains	Returns	Net returns	Returns and principal	Returns are tax-exempt
When taxed interest, dividend	When paid	Withdrawal	Withdrawal	Withdrawal	Tax-exempt
capital gain	When realized	Withdrawal	Withdrawal	Withdrawal	Tax-exempt
Tax rate interest, dividends	Ordinary	Ordinary	Ordinary	Ordinary	Zero
capital gain	Preferential	Ordinary	Ordinary	Ordinary	Zero
Order of Withdrawals	N.A.	Pro-rata	Interest first	N.A.	Principal first
Liquidity Restrictions					
10% penalty tax rate on early withdrawals	No	Usually	Usually	Usually	Sometimes
Insurance Co. surrender penalty	No	No	Yes	No	No
Other Features					
Minimum distribution	No	Yes	No	Yes	No
Simplicity	No	Yes	Yes	Yes	Yes
Maximum Investment	No limit	Varies	No limit	Varies	Varies
Treatment at Death of Owner					
Death benefit	No	No	Yes	No	No
Stepped-up basis	Yes	No	No	No	No

N.A. Not applicable

Liquidity Restrictions

Savings in the retirement savings vehicles—nondeductible IRA, annuity, deductible pension, and Roth IRA—are less liquid than investments in a taxable account. A 10 percent early distribution tax usually applies to withdrawals before age 59½ from nondeductible IRAs, annuities, and deductible pensions. Exceptions to this penalty tax include withdrawals due to death or total disability, to pay medical expenses (exceeding 7.5 percent of adjusted gross income), or if part of a series of substantially equal periodic payments for the life or life expectancy of the owner. Chapter 6 provides additional detail for these and other exceptions. The 10 percent penalty tax applies less frequently to withdrawals from IRAs, including the Roth IRA. In particular, the penalty tax does not apply to IRA withdrawals to pay qualified education expenses or up to $10,000 to purchase the principal residence of a first-time homebuyer. In addition to this 10 percent tax, an annuity usually has a surrender penalty that further reduces its liquidity. A typical surrender penalty is 6 percent or 7 percent if the annuity is cancelled in the first year, with the penalty decreasing 1 percent each year thereafter.

Distribution Requirements

Minimum distribution requirements usually apply to savings in nondeductible IRAs and deductible pensions. In general, distributions must begin by April 1 of the calendar year following the year the account owner reaches age 70½. Among the retirement savings vehicles, the Roth IRA and annuity do not impose minimum distribution requirements during the owner's life. Thus, the taxable account, Roth IRA, and annuity provide the most flexibility in terms of withdrawals.

Tax Simplicity

Before retirement, the retirement accounts grow tax deferred. There are no Form 1099s associated with deductible pensions, annuities, and Roth IRAs, which means fewer headaches come tax season. One form must be filed whenever a new contribution is made to a nondeductible IRA; it tells the IRS that the cost basis has increased. Nevertheless, retirement accounts help simplify taxes before the retirement years. Of course, in a taxable account, taxable returns must be reported each year.

Treatment at Death of Owner

Investments in a taxable account receive the stepped-up basis at the owner's death. In community property states, upon the death of an owner or co-owner, an asset's cost basis is stepped-up to the market value at the date of death (or, if elected, six months later). In common law states, only half of the cost basis is stepped-up in value. For example, John and Mary live in a community property state and buy 1,000 shares of a stock at $10 per share. Years later, John dies when the stock is selling at $45 per share. At his death, the cost basis rises to $45,000. Mary could sell the 1,000 shares for $45,000 without incurring a capital gain tax. Investments in the retirement savings vehicles do not receive the benefit of stepped-up basis.

The annuity offers a death benefit that is unique to this savings vehicle. During the accumulation phase, a common type of death benefit guarantees that, if the annuity owner dies after investing, for example, $10,000, his beneficiary will receive the larger of $10,000 (less prior withdrawals and surrender charges) or the value of the annuity. In addition, some annuities offer a stepped-up death benefit; for example, after five years, the guaranteed amount is reset at the larger of the original amount or the then-current annuity value.

Limits on Contributions/Investments

There are no annual contribution or investment limits for taxable accounts and nonqualified annuities. If someone had the funds, he or she could invest $1 million or more in either type of account.

Someone could have more than one deductible pension. For example, suppose a 40-year-old university professor earns an annual salary of $80,000, and the university contributes an additional $8,000, or 10 percent, to a defined-contribution plan. She also earns $10,000 in royalties and consulting fees. She could tax defer $12,000 (in 2002) through a 403(b) plan, which is essentially a 401(k) plan for a not-for-profit business. In addition, she could tax defer $1,304 of her side business income through a SEP-IRA.[2] Moreover, the $8,000 defined contribution is like a deductible pension. It is non-taxable income returns grow tax deferred, and taxes are paid upon withdrawal at the ordinary income tax rate.

Eligibility Requirements

"Eligibility requirements" pertain to laws and regulations that determine whether contributions to a traditional IRA are deductible. They also determine whether contributions to a Roth IRA are allowed. We will postpone discussion of eligibility requirements until Chapter 4.

Ending-Wealth Models of Savings Vehicles

For the client saving for his or her retirement, the primary consideration in selecting savings vehicles should be the expected after-tax retirement wealth that each vehicle can provide. To facilitate comparison of the five savings vehicles, this section presents ending-wealth models for each vehicle. The models for the taxable account, nondeductible IRA, deductible pension, and Roth IRA reflect their respective tax structures. The model for the annuity reflects its tax structure adjusted to reflect its additional costs. The ending-wealth models express the value that an original investment of $1 of after-tax funds will grow to over n years in each savings vehicle. An understanding of the models allows a financial advisor to evaluate the inner workings of the various vehicles. What's more, they allow ready computation of the after-tax wealth for a range of assumptions. In addition, the models allow an advisor to quickly adapt to changes in tax laws.

To simplify the analysis, a number of assumptions are used throughout this chapter:

$1	The original investment of after-tax funds, which is made on January 1.
i	Annual rate of return on investment; $i = 6$ percent for bonds and 11 percent for stocks.
g	Return in the form of capital gains; $g = $ zero for bonds and 9 percent for stocks.
n	Length of the investment horizon; all funds are withdrawn n years after investment.
t	Combined federal-plus-state tax rate on ordinary income (i.e., dividends and interest) in all years before year n; $t = 35$ percent.
t_{cg}	Combined federal-plus-state tax rate on realized capital gains in all years; $t_{cg} = 35$ percent for assets held less than one year, 27 percent for assets held more than a year but not more than five years, and 25 percent for assets held more than five years.
t_n	Tax rate on ordinary income in year n; $t_n = 35$ percent or 28 percent.
f	Additional annual fees or costs on an annuity (expressed as a percent).

The tax rates are set at a common federal tax rate plus an assumed 7 percent extra for state and local taxes. For example, the 35 percent tax rate on ordinary income reflects a 28 percent federal tax rate plus 7 percent for state and local taxes. The 27 percent capital gain tax rate reflects the maximum federal rate of 20 percent for assets held more than one year plus 7 percent for state and local taxes. The 25 percent capital gain tax rate reflects the maximum federal rate of 18 percent for assets acquired after 2000 and held for more than five years plus 7 percent.[3]

The ending-wealth models assume that, after n years, all funds are completely liquidated, and taxes are paid. These simplifying assumptions allow most of the ending-wealth models to be expressed as simple algebraic models, which clearly point out important investment implications. (Chapter 4 relaxes the assumption that all funds are withdrawn at one time and assumes funds are withdrawn to provide a constant after-tax retirement income for 20 years.) Table 2.2 presents a summary of the after-tax ending-wealth models, except for the model when stocks are held in a taxable account. The end-of-chapter Appendix presents the ending-wealth model for stocks held in a taxable account.

Taxable Account

The ending-wealth model for bonds held in a personal or taxable account is:

$$[1 + i \bullet (1 - t)]^n \tag{Eq. 2.1}$$

Using the assumed values for i and t, this becomes:

$$[1 + 0.06 \bullet (1 - 0.35)]^n \text{ or } (1.039)^n$$

The original $1 earns 6 percent annually, of which 2.1 percent is paid in taxes [6% • 0.35]. The investment grows at the after-tax rate of return of 3.9 percent for the n-year investment horizon.

The ending-wealth model for stocks held in a taxable account is more complicated. The end-of-chapter Appendix presents this model. Stocks earn 11 percent annually—2 percent dividends and 9 percent capital gains. Taxes in any year are 35 percent of the 2 percent dividend plus t_{cg} percent of *realized* capital gains, where t_{cg}—the tax rate on capital gains—depends upon how long the asset is held. The slower capital gains are realized, the lower the taxes and the faster the growth rate of the stock portfolio.

The end-of-chapter Appendix presents and explains the ending-wealth model for stocks held in a taxable account. This model is available at www.wiley.com/go/reichenstein. There, the user can change the key assumptions to meet his or her needs—rate of return, dividend yield, and percent of capital gains realized annually.

Nondeductible IRA

The ending-wealth model for the nondeductible IRA is:

$$(1 + i)^n - t_n \bullet [(1 + i)^n - 1] \text{ or, equivalently, } (1 + i)^n \bullet (1 - t_n) + t_n \tag{Eq. 2.2}$$

While the second expression of Equation 2.2 is easier to calculate, the first and longer expression is easier to explain:

$(1 + i)^n$	The individual invests $1 of after-tax funds, which grows at the i percent before-tax rate of return for n years to produce this balance.
$t_n \bullet [(1 + i)^n - 1]$	In year n, the individual withdraws the account balance. The original $1 of after-tax funds is withdrawn tax-free. Taxes are paid on the accumulated *return* $[(1 + i)^n - 1]$ at the ordinary income tax rate t_n.

Notice that the capital gains tax rate is not part of this model because all returns —whether capital gains, dividends, or interest—are taxed at the ordinary income tax rate. In fact, the capital gain tax rate is not part of the ending-wealth model for any retirement account; the capital gain tax rate applies only to assets held in a taxable account.

Non-qualified Tax-deferred Annuity

The ending-wealth model for the non-qualified tax-deferred annuity is:

$(1 + i - f)^n - t_n \cdot [(1 + i - f)^n - 1]$ or,
equivalently, $(1 + i - f)^n \cdot (1 - t_n) + t_n$ (Eq. 2.3)

Comparing Equation 2.2 and Equation 2.3 reveals that the only difference is the subtraction of f, a fee. The non-qualified tax-deferred annuity faces the same *tax structure* as the nondeductible IRA: Investments are made with after-tax dollars, and returns accumulate tax deferred and are taxed upon withdrawal at the ordinary income tax rate. However, the individual's return in the nondeductible IRA is the return on the underlying asset, i, while the individual's return in the annuity is the underlying asset's return less the annuity's annual insurance fees, f.

Deductible Pension

The **general pension ending-wealth model** is:

$[(1 + mc) / (1 - t)] \cdot (1 + i)^n \cdot (1 - t_n)$ or,
equivalently, $[(1 + mc) \cdot (1 - t_n) / (1 - t)] \cdot (1 + i)^n$ (Eq. 2.4)

At first glance, this model may be intimidating, but it can be broken down into simple parts. Also, given two assumptions that are often appropriate, the model reduces to $(1 + i)^n$. The parts of this equation represent the major features of this model:

$(1 + mc)$	The individual's investment of $1 may be increased by the matching contribution, mc, that exists in some 401(k), 403(b), and 457 plans.
$1 / (1 - t)$	This amount is the before-tax dollars that are invested when the individual reduces consumption by $1 in the year of investment (as discussed later).
$(1 + i)^n$	The original investment grows at the i percent before-tax rate of return for n years.
$(1 - t_n)$	Taxes paid in year n decrease the ending value.

The second part, $1 / (1 - t)$, implies that an individual can invest more than $1 of before-tax funds in a deductible pension with the same net effect on his or her current year consumption as a $1 investment of after-tax funds in any other savings vehicle. For example, an individual in the 35 percent tax bracket can invest $1.54 of before-tax funds [$1 / (1 - 0.35)]. The tax deduction of $1.54 saves $0.54 in taxes [$1.54 • 0.35]. So, the $1.54 investment reduces his or her consumption this year by only $1.

The second version of Equation 2.4 consists of two parts: the scalar, $(1 + mc) \cdot (1 - t_n) / (1 - t)$, and the n-year compounding of the before-tax rate of return, $(1 + i)^n$. These parts are used in subsequent sections to illustrate pension advantages.

If there is no matching contribution ($mc = 0$), the model simplifies to:

$[1 / (1 - t)] \cdot (1 + i)^n \cdot (1 - t_n)$ or, equivalently, $[(1 - t_n) / (1 - t)] \cdot (1 + i)^n$ (Eq. 2.5)

When there is no matching contribution *and* the tax rates in the investment year and withdrawal year are the same ($mc = 0$ and $t = t_n$), the scalar becomes one, and the model simplifies to:

$$(1 + i)^n \tag{Eq. 2.6}$$

In this book, this is called the basic pension ending-wealth model or, simply, the **basic pension model.** In the basic pension model, *the effective tax rate is zero;* the investor earns after taxes the asset's before-tax rate of return.

Roth IRA

The tax features of the Roth IRA are distinct: contributions to the Roth IRA are not deductible in the investment year, but investment returns from qualified withdrawals are tax-exempt. With no taxes to consider, the ending-wealth model for the Roth IRA is simply $(1 + i)^n$, which is the basic pension model, Eq. 2.6. This again is the basic pension model. So, despite differences in their tax features, *for the purpose of building retirement wealth,* the Roth IRA is equivalent to a deductible pension for investors who expect to remain in their current tax bracket during retirement and do not receive matching contributions. Consequently, for many purposes, the Roth IRA can be viewed as a special type of deductible pension.

TABLE 2.2   A Summary of After-tax Ending-wealth Models for Each Savings Vehicle

---

Taxable Account

Bonds:	$[1 + i \cdot (1 - t)]^n$	(Eq. 2.1)
Stocks:	See end-of-chapter Appendix	

Nondeductible IRA

	$(1 + i)^n \cdot (1 - t_n) + t_n$	(Eq. 2.2)

Non-qualified Tax-deferred Annuity

	$(1 + i - f)^n \cdot (1 - t_n) + t_n$	(Eq. 2.3)

Deductible Pension

With matching contributions and tax timing:	$[(1 + mc) \cdot (1 - t_n)/(1 - t)] \cdot (1 + i)^n$	(Eq. 2.4)
With tax timing but without matching contributions:	$[(1 - t_n)/(1 - t)] \cdot (1 + i)^n$	(Eq. 2.5)
With matching contributions but without tax timing:	$(1 + mc) \cdot (1 + i)^n$	
Basic pension model, without matching contributions or tax timing:	$(1 + i)^n$	(Eq. 2.6)

Roth IRA

	$(1 + i)^n$	(Eq. 2.6)

Before continuing, it is important to clarify the terminology used in this book. Suppose a client has savings in (1) a 401(k) plan with matching contributions, (2) a deductible IRA, (3) a Roth IRA, and (4) a nondeductible IRA. *Legally,* all four are considered pensions. However, the general pension model, Equation 2.4, provides the ending wealth for the first three but not for the nondeductible IRA. In this book, the term "pension" refers to any savings vehicle whose ending wealth is given by the general pension model. Pension thus refers to all deductible pensions—401(k), deductible IRA, SEP-IRA, Keogh, and so on—as well as the Roth IRA. "Pension," in this book, does not refer to the nondeductible IRA. The term "deductible pension" refers to 401(k), deductible IRA, and so on, but not the Roth IRA.

Comparing the Savings Vehicles

The Roth IRA has generated widespread interest since its creation in 1997. Many investors view it as substantially better than anything previously available, so they are eager to open a Roth IRA. The financial advisor can seize on his or her client's interest in this vehicle as an opportunity to educate the client about all the available savings vehicles. The following comparisons are useful in this regard.

Deductible Pension versus Roth IRA

In a Roth IRA, all investment returns are tax-exempt. This concept is easy for the layman to understand; perhaps that accounts for much of the Roth IRA's appeal. But the basic pension ending-wealth model reveals that the Roth IRA and the deductible pension are equivalent given certain circumstances. In other circumstances, the deductible pension is superior.

As shown previously, the basic pension model, $(1 + i)^n$, applies to both (1) a deductible pension when tax timing and matching contributions are not present and (2) a Roth IRA. The only variables in this model are i, the rate of return, and n, the number of years the funds are invested. Taxes play no part in this model: in a Roth IRA, the tax rate is zero due to tax exemption, while in a deductible pension the tax deduction of the original investment—mathematically, $1 / (1 - t)$—cancels out the taxes paid on withdrawal—$(1 - t_n)$—when t is equal to t_n. As stated previously, the effective tax rate is zero. It is as if the investor legally avoids taxes!

For example, in a deductible pension, an individual in the 35 percent tax bracket invests $1.54. Although he actually writes a check for $1.54, it is useful to separate this amount into his contribution of $1 of after-tax funds and the tax savings of $0.54. His $1 grows to $1 • $(1 + i)^n$. The $0.54 tax saving grows to $0.54 • $(1 + i)^n$, which is precisely the tax liability in year n on the withdrawal of $1.54 • $(1 + i)^n$. In a Roth IRA, an individual invests $1 of after-tax funds, it grows tax exempt, and n years later it is worth $1 • $(1 + i)^n$ after taxes. In both the deductible pension (with scalar of 1.0) and the Roth IRA, the individual foregoes $1 of consumption and n years later has $1 • $(1 + i)^n$ of after-tax wealth.

The after-tax ending wealth (per \$1 of original after-tax investment) from a deductible pension is larger than that from a Roth IRA for individuals who receive matching contributions and/or expect to be in a lower tax bracket in retirement. These two advantages are reflected in the scalar of the general pension ending-wealth model, Equation 2.4. The scalar is $(1 + mc) \cdot (1 - t_n) / (1 - t)$.

The matching contribution produces $(1 + mc)$. For example, if the employer matches employee contributions dollar-for-dollar up to \$4,000, then $(1 + mc)$ is 2.0 for the first \$4,000 of savings and 1.0 for savings beyond this amount. Or, if the employer matches \$0.50 on the dollar, then $(1 + mc)$ is 1.5. Obviously, this factor is greater than 1.0 when there is any matching contribution. When $(1 + mc)$ is 2.0, it is like an instantaneous return of 100 percent.

The tax-timing advantage produces $(1 - t_n) / (1 - t)$, which is greater than 1.0 when the tax rate at withdrawal, t_n, is less than the tax rate at deposit, t. For example, an investor is in the 35 percent bracket in the investment year and the 28 percent bracket in the withdrawal year, and there is no matching contribution. The scalar is 1.1077 [0.72 / 0.65]. So, the individual who invests \$1 after taxes (or \$1.54 before taxes) in a deductible pension ends up with $\$1.1077 \cdot (1 + i)^n$ after taxes in n years. His or her ending wealth is 10.77 percent larger than the ending wealth from a Roth IRA. People who move to a state with no or low income taxes may have a lower federal-plus-state marginal tax rate during retirement even if their federal tax rate is unchanged.

Thus, the size of the scalar is determined by the amount of matching contributions and the individual's tax brackets in the years of deposit and withdrawal. When the scalar exceeds 1.0, the investor who saves through a deductible pension earns an after-tax rate of return that exceeds the underlying asset's before-tax rate of return; *the effective tax rate is negative.*

Note that the size of the scalar is independent of the investment horizon. The scalar is the same for a two-day investment horizon (i.e., deposit \$1 on December 31 and withdraw it on January 2) or a 35-year horizon. Consequently, for someone near retirement, the scalar's size should be a major factor influencing the attractiveness of a deductible pension. The following two examples illustrate this point.

Example: Jim will retire at the end of the year. He is in the 35 percent tax bracket this year but will be in the 28 percent bracket next year. He contributes \$1,000 to a deductible pension on December 31 and withdraws it on January 2. The \$1,000 is invested in a savings account for two days and earns no interest. The \$1,000 contribution and withdrawal represents a \$650 after-tax investment and a \$720 after-tax withdrawal. By shifting the \$1,000 into the retirement year, he earns 10.77 percent after taxes. Not a bad two-day return.

Example: Cathy will retire at the end of the year. She is in the 35 percent tax bracket this year and the 28 percent bracket next year, and her employer matches her 401(k) contributions dollar-for-dollar. She contributes \$1,000 of before-tax funds, which costs her \$650 after taxes. Due to the match, her account contains \$2,000 of before-tax funds on December 31 and January 2. It contains \$1,440 after taxes on January 2. By shifting income, the contribution cost her $650 after taxes on December 31 and it is worth $1,440 after taxes two days later. This represents a 122 percent after-tax return (in equation form $[2 \bullet 0.72 / 0.65 - 1]$, where $(1 + mc)$ is 2, $(1 - t_n)$ is 0.72, and $(1 - t)$ is 0.65).

In addition to these end-of-career tax-timing insights, the ending-wealth models are useful to people at the beginning of their career when their current tax rate is low. For example, the $(1 - t_n) / (1 - t)$ scalar shows that someone who expects his or her tax rate to rise should favor the Roth IRA over a deductible pension. This is handy advice to recent college graduates.

Although the ending wealth (per $1 of original after-tax investment) from saving in a deductible pension is greater when matching contributions and/or tax timing are available, some clients prefer to save in a Roth because of non-tax-structure features, such as the absence of minimum withdrawal requirements. Our ending-wealth models provide a way to "price" these features. Chapter 4 examines the specific decision to invest say $3,000 in a deductible IRA or a Roth IRA for those who are eligible to contribute to either type of account.

Deductible Pension versus Taxable Account

The analysis in the previous section showed that the effective tax rate on an investment in a deductible pension is zero or negative (assuming the scalar is 1.0 or higher). Why, then, would anyone choose to put savings in a *taxable* account?

There are two major disadvantages of saving through a deductible pension. First, withdrawals before age 59½ are generally subject to a 10 percent penalty tax. In practice, this restriction is not as severe as first appearances suggest for several reasons:

■ Many investors can rely on the liquidity of nonpension assets and their borrowing capacity to meet their liquidity needs.

■ Most pension plans with large employers allow participants to borrow against their account.

■ Withdrawals before age 59½ are not subject to the penalty tax if they are attributable to disability, major medical expenses (that can be itemized), and other special circumstances.

■ The advantages of the deductible pension are so strong that, after six years or so, the after-tax ending wealth from saving in a deductible pension, then withdrawing all funds and paying the 10 percent penalty, probably exceeds the ending wealth from saving in a taxable account.

■ If only part of the deductible pension funds are withdrawn, the penalty tax is assessed only on the amount withdrawn and not on all pension funds; the ending-wealth advantage from the remaining pension funds may exceed the 10 percent penalty tax on the withdrawn funds.

The second major disadvantage of deductible pensions is the fact that all withdrawals, including the portion of withdrawals representing capital gains, are taxed at the ordinary tax rate. In contrast, preferential capital gain tax rates apply to assets held more than one year in a taxable account. In 2002, the maximum federal tax rate on ordinary income is 38.6 percent, while federal tax rates on capital gains are generally lower.

Conversely, possible advantages of saving in the deductible pension include:

■ The tax deductibility of the investment amount—that is, the ability to begin with a $1 / (1 − t)$ investment while only reducing current-year consumption by $1.

■ The tax deferral of investment returns—that is, the investment grows at the before-tax rate of return.

■ Tax timing—the ability to withdraw funds in retirement when the investor may be in a lower tax bracket.

■ Matching contributions.

■ Simplicity in tax reporting—that is, returns on deductible pensions do not have to be reported annually before retirement.

■ Ability to trade—including trades to rebalance a family's asset allocation—with no tax consequences.

The financial advisor and clients need to understand that, in a deductible pension, the up-front deductibility of the investment amount allows more dollars to be invested for each dollar of deferred consumption than in the other savings vehicles. A recurring theme in this book is that it is important to distinguish before-tax and after-tax funds: it is inappropriate to compare a $1,000 investment in a taxable account to a $1,000 investment in a deductible pension because the latter requires less sacrifice in terms of reduced consumption. For example, if the client is in the 35 percent bracket, the proper comparison is between a $1,000 investment in a taxable account and a $1,538 investment in a deductible pension without matching contributions.

Table 2.3 demonstrates this important point. In this example, the Smiths have an $80,000 income subject to a 35 percent flat tax rate. (The same conclusion prevails with a progressive tax structure.) If they decide not to save anything, they could spend $52,000 of after-tax income. Suppose, instead, that they decide to reduce consumption this year by $1,000—that is, they will spend $51,000. Column A shows that they could achieve the $51,000 spending goal and save $1,000 of after-tax funds in a taxable account. Column B shows that they could save $1,538 in a deductible pension and still spend $51,000 this year; the $1,538 contribution reduces taxable income by a like amount, which reduces this year's taxes by $538. Moreover, they would not have to wait until next year to get the $538 tax savings; they could reduce tax withholdings this year by the same amount.

Tax deferral of investment returns allows the entire investment to grow at the before-tax rate of return, i, whereas, in a taxable account, the investment grows at the after-tax rate of return, $i \cdot (1 − t)$. Investments held in any deductible pension receive these first two tax advantages of deductibility and deferral, while the presence or absence of matching contributions and tax timing depends upon individual

TABLE 2.3   Amount of Initial Investment for $1,000 of Deferred Consumption

	A Taxable Account	B Deductible Pension (without matching contributions)	C Deductible Pension (with matching contributions[a])
1. Family Income	$80,000	$80,000	$80,000
2. Deductible Contributions	0	1,538	1,538
3. Taxable Income	80,000	78,462	78,462
4. Taxes (35%)	28,000	27,462	27,462
5. After-tax Income	52,000	51,000	51,000
6. After-tax Investments	1,000	0	0
7. Consumption	$51,000	$51,000	$51,000
8. Matching Contributions	0	0	$1,538
9. Total Investment[b]	$1,000	$1,538	$3,076

[a] Assumes the employer matches contributions dollar for dollar.
[b] Total investment is the sum of deductible contributions, after-tax investments, and dollar-for
 dollar matching contributions.

circumstances. Some individuals receive matching contributions and/or expect to be in a lower tax bracket in retirement, while others do not.

In the case of the Smiths, the effect of matching contributions on total investment is shown in Column C of Table 2.3. The Smiths contribute $1,538 to a 401(k) plan—a type of deductible pension—and the firm matches the contribution dollar-for-dollar. The Smiths' $1,538 reduces taxable income by the same amount and taxes by $538. They can spend $51,000 this year. Meanwhile, they begin with a $3,076 investment—their $1,538 contribution plus the company's matching contribution. All $3,076 grows tax deferred at the before-tax rate of return.

Nondeductible IRA versus Taxable Account

The nondeductible IRA and taxable account both require investments of after-tax dollars. The nondeductible IRA allows the funds to grow tax deferred. So, in the absence of tax timing and preferential capital gains tax treatment, the ending wealth from a nondeductible IRA exceeds the ending wealth from a taxable account for investment horizons longer than one year. With tax timing, the nondeductible IRA's advantage is even larger since the accumulated returns are taxed at the lower rate in retirement. We consider capital gains tax treatment in Chapter 3. Of course, the other factors listed in Table 2.1 could override the ending-wealth advantage of the nondeductible IRA. In particular, withdrawals from a nondeductible IRA are a pro-rata share of principal and deferred return. A series of partial withdrawals thus requires record-keeping. However, as discussed in Chapter 4, this task may be simplified by converting the nondeductible IRA to a Roth IRA.

Non-qualified Tax-deferred Annuity versus Taxable Account

For an individual who wants to save more than is allowed through pensions and nondeductible IRAs—a mean feat after the 2001 Tax Act—the choice comes down to a non-qualified tax-deferred annuity or a taxable account. Both savings vehicles require investments of after-tax funds. The annuity offers tax deferral on returns but charges an annual insurance fee for this privilege. A key question is whether the advantage of tax-deferred growth is sufficient to offset the annuity's higher costs. The ending-wealth models presented in this chapter can be used to address this question. Of course, the other factors listed in Table 2.1 also influence the decision to save in a taxable account or an annuity.

An apt comparison is between the after-tax ending wealth from investing in a mutual fund held in a taxable account and from investing in a non-qualified annuity. For example, if the mutual fund's assets earn 8 percent a year and expenses are 1 percent a year, the investor in a taxable account earns a *before-tax* net return of 7 percent a year. She pays taxes each year on the taxable portion of the return. Suppose the annuity is invested in the same mutual fund, but its expenses are 2 percent a year, with the difference due to the insurance fee. The investor in the annuity earns 6 percent a year, but taxes are deferred, probably until retirement. The annuity's accumulated net returns are taxable in the year of withdrawal, and the ordinary income tax rate applies. The individual who saves through the annuity pays higher annual expenses (and receives lower annual returns) but defers taxes on returns.

Whether the ability to defer taxes is worth the higher expenses (and lower returns) depends upon a variety of factors including length of investment horizon, tax brackets before and during retirement, the fees charged for the annuity, the investment return, and whether preferential capital gain rates apply to some of the mutual fund's returns in the taxable account. Chapter 5 presents a thorough analysis of this question, incorporating details of mutual fund and annuity cost structures. The ending-wealth models presented in this chapter, however, cover most of the investment implications.

Summary

Financial professionals can help clients choose the best savings vehicle or best set of savings vehicles for retirement savings. Helping a client make this choice requires comparisons of tax structures, liquidity restrictions, and other restrictions. However, the best vehicle is usually the one that produces the largest after-tax ending wealth, and the amount of ending wealth depends primarily upon the tax structure. Thus, the choice among savings vehicles is largely a choice among tax structures.

■ Care must be taken to compare after-tax funds to other after-tax funds. It is inappropriate to compare before-tax funds with after-tax funds. For example, it is inappropriate for a family to compare a $1,000 investment in a taxable account to a $1,000 investment in a deductible pension because the latter requires less sacrifice in terms of reduced consumption. Assuming the family is currently in the 35 percent tax bracket, the proper comparison is between a $1,000 investment in a taxable account or a $1,538 investment in a deductible pension without matching contributions.

■ The general pension ending-wealth model consists of two parts: the scalar, $(1 + mc) \bullet (1 - t_n) / (1 - t)$, and the n-year compounding of the before-tax rate of return, $(1 + i)^n$. The size of the scalar depends on factors specific to each individual investor: whether or not he receives matching contributions from his employer and his tax brackets in the years of deposit and withdrawal.

■ The basic pension model is $(1 + i)^n$. It applies to a deductible pension when the scalar is 1.0 (that is, tax-timing and matching-contributions advantages do not exist) and to a Roth IRA.

■ In a basic pension, the investor earns an asset's before-tax rate of return on an after-tax basis; the effective tax rate is zero.

■ When the scalar exceeds 1.0—that is, the employer at least partially matches or tax timing exists—the investor who saves through a deductible pension earns an after-tax rate of return that exceeds the underlying asset's before-tax rate of return; the effective tax rate is negative.

■ The size of the scalar is independent of the investment horizon. Consequently, for someone near retirement, the scalar's size should be a major factor influencing the attractiveness of a deductible pension.

■ The nondeductible IRA provides tax deferral of investment returns. If the individual will be in a lower tax bracket during retirement, it also offers the tax-timing advantage for the accumulated returns.

■ The non-qualified tax-deferred annuity provides the same tax-deferral benefits as the nondeductible IRA, but it imposes higher costs.

■ Individuals can choose between investing in a mutual fund held in a taxable account or investing in a non-qualified annuity. A key question is whether the advantage of the annuity's tax-deferred growth is sufficient to offset its higher costs.

Appendix 2.1: The Value of the $1 Stock Portfolio for a 10-year Investment Horizon

	1st Year	2nd Year	10th Year
1. Beginning Market Value	$1.0000	$1.0949	$2.0955
2. Return	0.1100	0.1204	0.2305
3. Ending Before-tax Value	1.1100	1.2153	2.3260
	1st Year	**2nd Year**	**10th Year**
4. Beginning Cost Base	1.0000	1.0349	1.7971
5. Capital Gain	0.0900	0.1585	0.4869
6. Realized Capital Gain	0.0300	0.0528	0.1623
7. Capital Gain Tax	0.0081	0.0143	0.0438
8. Capital Gain Reinvested	0.0219	0.0386	0.1185
9. Dividend	0.0200	0.0219	0.0419
10. Dividend Tax	0.0070	0.0077	0.0147
11. Dividend Reinvested	0.0130	0.0142	0.0272
12. Ending Cost Base	1.0349	1.0877	1.9429
13. Ending Market Value	1.0949	1.1934	2.2675

The beginning market value and beginning cost base are $1. The stock earns 11 percent—9 percent capital gain and 2 percent dividends. It is assumed that one-third of capital gains are realized each year. The 27 percent tax rate on capital gains produces the capital gain tax. Capital gain reinvested denotes realized gain less taxes on the gain. Dividends are 2 percent of beginning market value. The dividend tax rate is 35 percent. Ending cost base is beginning cost base plus the sum of capital gain reinvested and dividends reinvested. Ending market value is the ending before-tax value less the sum of capital gain tax and dividend tax. Capital gain in year 2 and beyond is 0.09 times beginning market value plus unrealized capital gain from the prior year, which is $(0.09 - 0.03)$ for year 2.

The $1 grows to $2.2675 in 10 years. If this amount is withdrawn, it produces a $0.0876 tax liability—a 27 percent capital gain tax on the difference between ending market value and ending cost base—and an ending after-tax value of $2.1799. The annual after-tax return after considering the liquidating tax liability is 8.10 percent $[2.1799^{(1/10)} - 1]$.

This model is available at www.wiley.com/go/reichenstein. The file name is Stocks in Taxable Account. The user may insert values in the Enter Values Below box. Entries include net rate of return (cell G19), tax rate on dividiends before retirement (G20), tax rate on dividends during retirement (G21), percent of capital gains realized each year (G22), tax rate on capital gains before retirement (G23), tax rate on capital gains during retirement (G24), and dividend yield (G25).

Notes

1. The interest-first rule applies to funds withdrawn when the annuity owner does not annuitize the contract; that is, when he does not cash-in the annuity for a guaranteed lifetime income. Only about 2 percent of annuity owners annuitize because, when they do, they lose complete control over the timing and amount of cash withdrawals. Different rules apply to funds withdrawn after an annuity contract has been annuitized. See Chapter 5 for more details.

2. The royalty and consulting income is a side business with one employee—the professor. This "business" sets up a SEP-IRA for this employee. The maximum contribution is 15 percent of *net income after the SEP-IRA contribution,* which is 13.04 percent of income before the contribution. She contributes $1,304, which is 15 percent of $8,696 net income after contribution. Mathematically, $10,000 / 1.15 is $8,696, and $8,696 • (0.15) is $1,304.

3. In most states and counties that tax income, realized capital gains are taxed at the state or county's ordinary income tax rate. State and local taxes are generally deductible from income before calculating federal income taxes. In chapters 2 through 4, we assume state and local income taxes raise marginal tax rates by 7 percent above the federal rate.

After-tax Wealth across Savings Vehicles

Introduction

For most clients, one question is paramount: How much money will I have when I retire? Using the ending-wealth models of the major savings vehicles introduced in Chapter 2, this chapter presents the ending-wealth values from saving in each vehicle, assuming all funds are withdrawn in one lump sum during retirement. Lump sum withdrawals are used for the sake of simplicity and clarity. Recognizing that most people withdraw their savings over time, Chapter 4 presents retirement incomes assuming the funds are withdrawn to provide a constant annual after-tax income during retirement. However, the major conclusions are the same whether funds are withdrawn all at once or slowly over time.

The projected investment horizon ranges from 1 year to 35 years. Many investors underestimate the length of their horizons. Suppose Mary and John Smith will retire in 35 years at age 67. If they expect to live until 87 and spend their funds evenly between ages 67 and 87, the average dollar will be spent at about age 77, or 45 years hence. Moreover, there is a good chance that one or both of them will live past age 87, and they should plan for such a possibility. About half the population outlives the average life expectancy. Generalizing, most individuals' investment horizons exceed by more than a decade the time until their planned retirement dates.

We begin this chapter by examining the importance of investment management style on the ending wealth from stocks invested in a taxable account. The taxable account has a different ending wealth for each stock investment management strategy. We then illustrate the tax burden of actively managing stocks in a taxable account. Next, we compare the ending wealth from saving in a taxable account to the ending wealth from saving in other savings vehicles. The comparisons emphasize the importance of the choice of savings vehicles. Finally, this chapter considers the implications for individuals who will be in the same tax bracket before and during retirement, and then extends the analysis to include individuals who will be in a lower tax bracket in retirement or who will receive a matching contribution.

Tax Consequences of Actively Trading Stocks in a Taxable Account

Investment management style—that is, trading frequency—does not affect the ending wealth on bond investments held in any savings vehicle, or the ending wealth on stock investments held in any savings vehicle except taxable accounts. This section considers the tax consequences of actively trading stocks held in taxable accounts. Chapter 7 presents a more detailed discussion of tax-efficient investing and related issues.

The top three rows in the bottom half of Table 3.1 present the after-tax ending wealth from stock investments in a taxable account for three hypothetical investors— passive investor, active investor, and trader. The key tax issue is how quickly the investor recognizes capital gains. We assume the "passive investor" realizes 5 percent of unrealized capital gains at the end of each year. He realizes capital gains, on average, in 20 years [1 / 0.05], and the gains are subject to a combined federal-plus-state tax rate of 25 percent. The "active investor" realizes one-third (33.3 percent) of capital gains as long-term gains each year. She realizes capital gains, on average, in three years [1 / 0.333], and the gains are subject to a combined federal-plus-state tax rate of 27 percent. The difference between the 25 percent and 27 percent combined federal-plus-state capital gain tax rates reflects the difference between the 18 percent federal rate on assets held more than five years and the 20 percent rate for assets held more than one year. The "trader" realizes all gains each year as short-term gains, and they are subject to the 35 percent tax rate on ordinary income. The 35 percent tax rate applies to dividends for all three investors. Note the non-linear relationship between average holding period and turnover ratio (i.e., percent of capital gains realized each year). An increase in turnover from 5 to 10 percent affects average holding period more than an increase in turnover from 50 to 100 percent.

How realistic are these hypothetical investors? The passive investor realizes 5 percent of gains each year. Some individuals manage their taxable stock portfolio this passively. Moreover, S&P 500 index funds generally realize less than 5 percent of gains each year. So, it is an attainable standard and one that we strongly encourage investors to consider. The active investor probably best represents the "typical" investor. Most individuals who manage their stock portfolio probably realize most capital gains within a few years. Most stock funds are actively managed, and they realize most capital gains within a few years. Therefore, the active investor is used

TABLE 3.1   After-tax Wealth for an Investor with an Average Tax Bracket
before and during Retirement

Savings Vehicle	Investment Horizon (years)				
	1	5	10	20	35
	Bonds				
Taxable Account	**$1.039**	**$1.211**	**$1.466**	**$2.149**	**$3.815**
Basic Pension	1.060	1.338	1.791	3.207	7.686
Nondeductible IRA	1.039	1.220	1.514	2.435	5.346
Non-qualified Annuity (low cost)	1.036	1.200	1.460	2.247	4.584
Non-qualified Annuity (avg. cost)	1.031	1.170	1.384	1.994	3.648
	Stocks				
Taxable Account					
Passive Investor	1.081	1.492	2.281	5.506	21.183
Active Investor	**1.079**	**1.472**	**2.180**	**4.789**	**15.596**
Trader	1.072	1.412	1.995	3.980	11.213
Basic Pension	1.110	1.685	3.839	8.062	38.575
Nondeductible IRA	1.072	1.445	2.196	5.591	25.424
Non-qualified Annuity (low cost)	1.068	1.421	2.114	5.138	21.759
Non-qualified Annuity (avg. cost)	1.063	1.385	1.998	4.528	17.218

Assumptions: The individual invests $1 of after-tax funds on January 1 and, after *n* years, withdraws all funds and pays taxes. Bonds earn 6 percent per year and stocks earn 11 percent, including 2 percent dividend yield and 9 percent capital gain. The investor has a combined federal-plus-state ordinary income tax rate of 35 percent before and during retirement. The passive investor, active investor, and trader realize, respectively, 5 percent, 33 percent, and 100 percent of capital gains annually. The combined federal-plus-state capital gain tax rate before and after retirement is 25 percent for the passive investor, 27 percent for the typical investor, and 35 percent for the active investor. The low-cost and average-cost tax-deferred annuities have additional annual insurance fees of 0.50 percent and 1.25 percent, respectively. Taxable account values for a "typical" active investor are highlighted in bold to provide benchmarks against which retirement account values can be compared.

as the benchmark when comparing the taxable account to the retirement accounts. The "trader" realizes all gains each year as short-term gains. This assumption may appear extreme, but it is clearly appropriate for day traders and is close to accurate for individuals and clients of stockbrokers who trade frequently. Henceforth, the term "turnover rate" refers to the longer but more accurate term "percent of capital gains realized each year by the taxable stock investor."[1]

In their classic article, Jeffrey and Arnott (1993) conclude, "passive indexing is a very difficult strategy to beat on an after-tax basis" (page 16). They believe few professional managers can overcome the *tax burden alone* from actively managing stocks in a taxable account. In practice, active investors and traders must overcome three burdens compared to passive investors: higher expense ratios, higher trading costs, and a higher tax burden. Trading costs include commissions and the potentially more significant bid-ask spread and market impact. Since our analysis only considers the tax burden, it implicitly assumes active investors and traders earn a sufficiently large gross return to just offset their additional expense, trading costs, and market impact.

Assume stocks earn 11 percent—9 percent capital gain and 2 percent dividend yield. The dollar value of a completely passive portfolio grows at 10.3 percent a year [9 + 2 • (1 − 0.35)]. An active investor's account—someone who realizes all gains each year or in one year and one day—grows at 7.97 percent a year [9 • (1 − 0.27) + 2 • (1 − 0.35)]. A trader's account grows at 7.15 percent a year [9 • (1 − 0.35) + 2 • (1 − 0.35)]. Jeffrey and Arnott conclude that, for long investment horizons, it is difficult for the trader to overcome a 3.15 percent growth disadvantage compared to the passive investor, and it is difficult for the active trader to overcome a 2.33 percent growth disadvantage compared to the passive investor. Thus, when stocks are held in taxable accounts, few professional managers can overcome the tax burden alone from actively managing stocks in a taxable account.

Table 3.1 shows the tax-related costs of actively managing stocks in a taxable account. The more quickly capital gains are realized, the lower the ending wealth. The lower ending wealth reflects two realities: Taxes are paid sooner when gains are realized more quickly, and the applicable tax rate tends to be higher. Compared to the passive investor, the trader must overcome two burdens: no benefit of tax deferral of unrealized gains and paying taxes on capital gains at the ordinary income tax rate. Compared to the passive investor, the active investor also has two burdens: a shorter deferral period on unrealized gains and paying a slightly higher capital gain tax rate.

The ending-wealth values under "taxable account" in the lower half of Table 3.1 repeat many of the lessons from Jeffrey and Arnott (1993). It is instructive to compare the ending-wealth values after 5 and 35 years. For traders, active investors, and passive investors, the applicable tax rates on capital gains are 35 percent, 27 percent, and 25 percent, while their average holding periods are less than a year, 3 years, and 20 years, respectively. As we go from the trader to the active investor, the increase in ending wealth is primarily due to this lower tax rate. As we go from the active investor to the passive investor, the increase in ending wealth is primarily due to the much-longer holding period. If the investment horizon is only five years, then the passive investor's ability to defer taxes on unrealized gains is small. Therefore, the ending-wealth values are similar for the active and passive investors. However, even after five years, the active investor has a substantial ending-wealth advantage compared to the trader; the active investor's preferential tax rate compared to the trader pays off handsomely as long as the investment horizon exceeds one year.

Next, consider the longer-term ending-wealth values. The passive investor has a substantial advantage compared to the active investor. Although there may be a difference of opinion about what constitutes a small or large advantage, the ending-wealth values in the table suggest that the passive investor's ability to defer taxes on unrealized gains is primarily important if the gains grow unharvested for at least 10 years.

After 35 years, the after-tax values of stocks are $21.183 for the passive investor, $15.596 for the active investor, and $11.213 for the trader. Clearly, tax-efficient investing makes a huge difference to the long-term investor. After 35 years, the passive investor's ending wealth is 36 percent larger than the active investor's wealth and 89 percent larger than the trader's wealth.

Moreover, these after-tax values may understate the passive investor's advantage. The $21.183 assumes the passive investor sold the stocks after 35 years and paid taxes on capital gains. If the gains are tax-exempt when sold, the passive investor's ending wealth will be $24,823. The gains are tax-exempt if the asset is donated to charity or the asset is liquidated after receiving a step up in basis at death.

To repeat, the ending-wealth values suggest that, when stocks are held in taxable accounts, passive indexing is a very difficult strategy to beat on an after-tax basis. Table 3.1 values indicate the burden of higher taxes alone. When the triple burdens of higher expenses, higher trading costs, and a higher tax burden are considered, passive investing is a more difficult strategy to beat. If an individual wants to actively manage stocks or select active stock funds, he should do so in a tax-deferred retirement account. There are no tax consequences to trading in a tax-deferred account. In contrast, passively managed stocks and passive stock funds are ideally suited to taxable accounts.

One implication from this section is that it makes no sense to be a trader in a taxable account. A trader must earn much higher gross returns to offset the triple burdens of higher expenses, higher trading costs, and a higher tax burden. Later in this chapter, we will compare the after-tax ending wealth from stock investments held in each savings vehicle, including taxable accounts. In these comparisons, we use the ending wealth for active investors and passive investors for the taxable account.

Investors in the Same Tax Bracket before and after Retirement

Contrary to popular belief, retirement does not always mean a lower tax bracket. Even when income declines, it may be offset by reduced deductions. The client is often in the same tax bracket before and during retirement.

Table 3.1 presents, for each savings vehicle, the after-tax ending wealth for an individual who is in the 35 percent tax bracket before and during retirement. He invests $1 of *after-tax funds* on January 1. On January 1, *n* years hence, all funds are withdrawn, and taxes are paid. The entry for "basic pension" presents the ending wealth for investments held in a deductible pension with a scalar of 1.0 or in a Roth IRA. Average-cost and low-cost annuities have additional annual costs (called "insurance fees") of 1.25 percent and 0.50 percent, respectively. (Appendix 3.1 discusses the estimates of average-cost and low-cost insurance fees.) As before, bond returns are 6 percent before taxes and stock returns are 11 percent, including 2 percent dividend yield. This book drops the repeated use of "expected return" in favor of "return." Nevertheless, it is important to remember that actual results may differ from the projected returns.

Many individuals, perhaps with the help of a financial advisor, first decide whether to invest in bonds or stocks and then choose the savings vehicle. To accommodate these individuals, we first compare the ending-wealth values for an investment in bonds and then compare the ending-wealth values for an investment in stocks.

Investment in Bonds

The top half of Table 3.1 presents after-tax ending-wealth values from an investment in bonds for horizons of 1 year through 35 years. This section compares ending-wealth values from:

1. A taxable account and a basic pension,
2. A taxable account and a nondeductible IRA, and
3. A taxable account and a tax-deferred annuity.

Taxable Account versus Basic Pension

From Chapter 2, an individual who places bonds earning 6 percent in a basic pension (scalar of 1.0) earns a 6 percent after-tax return; the effective tax rate is zero. The same bonds, when held in a taxable account, produce a 3.9 percent after-tax return. This pension advantage *in terms of annual return* is a constant 2.1 percent per year. This advantage *in terms of ending wealth* increases exponentially with the length of the investment horizon. The ending-wealth advantage is the more relevant criteria, because wealth determines someone's ability to consume.

After 35 years, the ending wealth from holding bonds in a basic pension is more than twice as large as the wealth from holding bonds in a taxable account! In the basic pension, the original $1 investment grows to $7.686, while it grows to $3.815 in the taxable account. The tax drag from saving in a taxable account imposes a relatively small ending-wealth disadvantage over short horizons but a huge disadvantage over long horizons. From Table 3.1, assuming a 6 percent annual return, the pension's ending wealth is $0.021 larger after 1 year, $0.325 larger after 10 years, $1.058 larger after 20 years, and $3.871 larger after 35 years. The precise advantage varies with the assumed return. It is smaller if returns are smaller and larger if returns are larger. But, as long as average bond returns are positive the basic pension provides a larger ending wealth.

Taxable Account versus Nondeductible IRA

In a nondeductible IRA, investment returns are tax deferred, an advantage that increases in importance with the length of the investment horizon. After one year, the ending wealth for a nondeductible IRA is the same as for a taxable account. The ending-wealth advantage of the nondeductible IRA is about $0.01 after 5 years, $0.05 after 10 years, $0.29 after 20 years, and $1.53 after 35 years. Figure 3.1 presents a graph of the *percentage* of ending-wealth advantage of the deductible IRA compared to the taxable account. This graph depicts the advantage of tax deferral alone. The values in Figure 3.1 and Table 3.1 show that the advantage of tax-deferred growth is relatively small for investment horizons of less than 10 years, but it is relatively large for horizons of 10 years or more.

Admittedly, "small" is a subjective term, and 10 years is a somewhat arbitrary investment horizon to separate a small change from a large change. One person may consider the less than $0.01 advantage after five years to be "large." Another person may consider the roughly $0.05 advantage after 10 years to be "small." This advantage of about $0.05 represents more than a 10 percent larger *return*: The taxable account provides a $0.466 return, while the nondeductible IRA provides a $0.514 return. Many investors would consider an extra 10 percent return from the same underlying asset to be a "large" advantage. Since tax deferral provides a relatively small advantage at short horizons and a relatively large advantage at very long horizons, tax deferral is especially important to investors with investment horizons of 20 years or longer.

Taxable Account versus Non-qualified Tax-deferred Annuity

For the average-cost annuity, it takes 45 years before the advantage of tax-deferred growth offsets the disadvantage of the 1.25 percent fee. The reason for the long breakeven period can be readily explained. The taxable account grows at 6 percent *before taxes*, while the annuity grows *tax deferred* at $(6 - f)$ percent, where f consists of the additional insurance fees. A 1.25 percent insurance fee is equivalent to a current-year tax rate of 25 percent [1.25% / 6%]. Meanwhile, the remaining 4.75 percent return is only tax deferred; it is not tax-exempt. Therefore, it takes 45 years before the benefit of tax-deferred growth at 4.75 percent offsets the 1.25 percent annual fee. For all but the youngest investors, the annuity's costs exceed its benefits.

The low-cost annuity provides better results. The advantage of tax-deferred growth offsets the disadvantage of the 0.5 percent annual fee after 12 years. Moreover, after 35 years, the ending wealth from the low-cost annuity is 20 percent larger than the ending wealth from the taxable account.

It is instructive to view the nondeductible IRA as an annuity with no insurance fee. As such, its breakeven period is always shorter than that of an annuity.

Investment in Stocks

This section compares the after-tax ending-wealth values from stock investments held in each savings vehicle. For the taxable account, there are different ending-

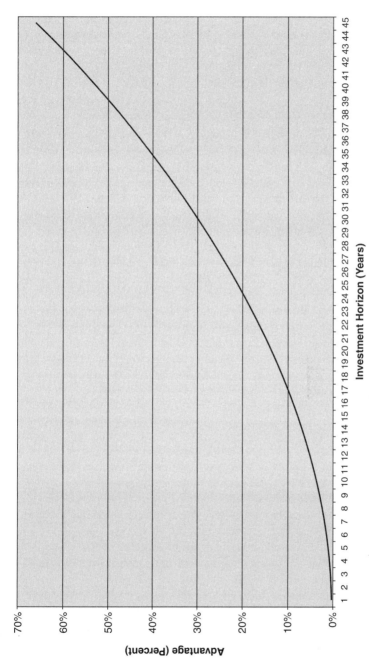

Percentage ending-wealth advantage from placing a 6% bond in a non-deductible IRA instead of a taxable account. The tax rate is 35%.

FIGURE 3.1 Advantage of Tax-deferred Growth

wealth values for the passive investor, active investor, and trader. As discussed in the previous section, it makes no sense to be a trader when managing stocks in a taxable account. Since the active investor probably best represents the "typical" investor, we generally use his ending wealth to represent the taxable account. However, the passive investor's ending wealth indicates the benefit of passively managing stocks in the taxable account.

Taxable Account versus Basic Pension

From Chapter 2, recall that an individual who places stocks in a basic pension earns an 11 percent annual after-tax return; the effective tax rate is zero. In contrast, stock returns are fully taxable when held in a taxable account. For the trader, all returns are taxed at 35 percent each year. Although active and passive investors receive more favorable tax treatment, they too must eventually pay taxes on returns. A financial reporter once said to one of the authors, "It is hard to imagine a better tax rate than the 20 percent capital gain tax rate." She missed the point. A zero percent tax rate beats a 20 percent rate. When realized in a taxable account, capital gains are usually taxed at preferential tax rates. But these preferential rates are above zero. Simply put, a tax rate of zero beats a reduced tax rate. Therefore, the ending wealth in the basic pension account always exceeds the ending wealth in a taxable account.

After 35 years, the basic pension's ending wealth of $38.575 is more than twice as large as the ending wealth for the active investor in a taxable account. The basic pension's ending wealth is more than three times as large as the ending wealth for the trader. While the passive investor benefits the most from the favored tax treatment of capital gains, the basic pension's ending wealth is 82 percent larger than this investor's ending wealth.

Taxable Account versus Nondeductible IRA

Preferential capital gains tax rates come into play when we compare stocks held in a taxable account to stocks held in a nondeductible IRA. In a nondeductible IRA, returns are tax deferred, but capital gains are eventually taxed at ordinary income tax rates. In a taxable account, *realized gains* are not tax deferred, but capital gains on assets held more than one year receive preferential tax rates. An active investor and a passive investor must weigh the trade-off between tax-deferred growth in the nondeductible IRA and preferential capital gain tax rates in the taxable account. The relative sizes of their ending-wealth values are explained by this trade-off.

For the active investor, it takes 10 years before the ending wealth in a nondeductible IRA exceeds the ending wealth in a taxable account. However, after 35 years the nondeductible IRA provides a 63 percent larger ending wealth. This reinforces the conclusion that tax-deferred growth is most important for the young.

For the passive investor, it takes 19 years before the ending wealth in a nondeductible IRA exceeds the ending wealth in a taxable account. The passive stock investor receives much of the benefit of tax deferral by realizing capital gains slowly. And, also, these gains, once realized, are subject to a lower tax rate.

Taxable Account versus Non-qualified Tax-deferred Annuity

While the nondeductible IRA has one strike against it, the annuity has two: Capital gains are eventually taxed at ordinary income tax rates, and the annuity charges higher annual fees.

From the perspective of the stock investor, the 1.25 percent annual fee of the average-cost annuity is equivalent to an 11.4 percent current-year "tax rate" [1.25% fee / 11% return]. Let us compare the after-tax wealth amounts for an average-cost annuity and an active investor in a taxable account. It takes 27 years for the annuity's tax-deferred-growth advantage to offset its two disadvantages. Even after 35 years, the average-cost annuity's ending-wealth advantage is a relatively modest 10 percent.

Next, we compare the after-tax wealth values for an average-cost annuity and passive investor in a taxable account. The passive investor's wealth is always larger. When compared to the passive investor, the average-cost annuity never offsets its disadvantages.

Not surprisingly, an annuity's prospects improve when its costs are low. For the active investor, the low-cost annuity offers a larger ending wealth than a taxable account after 15 years, and its wealth advantage after 35 years is 40 percent. For the passive investor, it takes 32 years before the low-cost annuity offers a larger ending wealth than a taxable account. Therefore, a low-cost variable annuity should be attractive to young, active stock investors. But it should appeal to few passive stock investors.

Tax Timing, Matching Contributions, and Other Cases

The last section compared after-tax ending-wealth values from each savings vehicle for individuals who are in the same tax bracket before and during retirement. This section extends the analysis to include individuals who (1) benefit from tax timing or (2) receive matching contributions. Tables 3.2 and 3.3 present ending-wealth values for, respectively, bond investors and stock investors. As before, $1 of after-tax funds is invested. At the end of the n-year investment horizon, the funds are withdrawn, and taxes are paid. The analysis compares investments in:

1. A taxable account and a deductible pension,
2. A taxable account and a nondeductible IRA, and
3. A taxable account and a non-qualified tax-deferred annuity.

Taxable Account versus Deductible Pension

In a deductible pension with a scalar that exceeds 1.0, the ending wealth is even larger than the ending wealth with a basic pension. The tax-timing cases under "deductible pension" in Tables 3.2 and 3.3 assume that the individual will be in a 28 percent tax bracket in retirement instead of the current 35 percent bracket. The ending wealth is always 10.77 percent larger with tax timing than without it [0.72 / 0.65 − 1].

The matching-contributions cases assume the employer matches the individual's investment contribution dollar for dollar; the scalar is 2.0. This individual will have twice the retirement wealth compared to the individual who does not receive matching contributions. She invests $1.54—the $1 of her funds and the $0.54 tax savings— and her employer kicks in an additional $1.54. She has a total of $3.08 invested compared to $1 if she invested in a savings vehicle other than a deductible pension.

In terms of ending wealth, the advantages of tax timing and matching contributions increase with the length of the investment horizon. For example, in the matching-contributions case in Table 3.2, the ending wealth after one year is $2.12 with matching contributions and $1.06 without them—a $1.06 advantage. After 35 years, the dollar advantage is $7.686.

The deductible pension could possibly have a tax-timing *disadvantage*. That is, the investor may be in a higher tax bracket in the year of withdrawal than in the year of investment. A higher income tax rate could occur if income increases (perhaps due to large retirement accounts), deductions decrease (such as mortgage interest payments), or Congress increases tax rates. However, for long investment horizons, the tax bracket must rise enormously to offset the other advantages of the deductible pension. Consider the bond investor in Table 3.2 who is in the 35 percent tax bracket today and does not receive matching contributions. For a 35-year investment horizon, this investor's retirement tax rate would have to be 68 percent to offset the other advantages. For a 20-year horizon, the tax rate would have to be 56 percent. For a 10-year horizon, it would have to be 47 percent. Thus, if someone is at least 10 years from retirement, the ending wealth from the deductible pension will likely exceed the ending wealth from a taxable account even if he expects to be in a higher tax bracket during retirement.

Taxable Account versus Nondeductible IRA

Tables 3.2 and 3.3 present the ending wealth for a nondeductible IRA with tax timing. It has two tax advantages: Growth is tax deferred, and returns are eventually taxed at a lower rate. It has one disadvantage when the underlying investment is stocks: Capital gains are eventually subject to the tax rate on ordinary income. For bonds in Table 3.2, the nondeductible IRA produces a small advantage compared to the taxable account after 1 year and a large advantage after 35 years. The advantage for the one-year horizon comes from the fact that the 6 percent interest is taxed at next year's 28 percent rate instead of this year's 35 percent rate. For the active investor in Table 3.3, the nondeductible IRA with tax timing produces a small

TABLE 3.2   After-tax Ending Wealth on Bonds

Savings Vehicle	Investment Horizon (years)				
	1	5	10	20	35
	After-tax Wealth				
Taxable Account	**$1.039**	**$1.211**	**$1.466**	**$2.149**	**$3.815**
Deductible Pension					
Basic Pension, $t_n = 35\%$	1.060	1.338	1.791	3.207	7.686
Tax Timing, $t_n = 28\%$	1.174	1.482	1.984	3.553	8.514
Matching Contributions	2.120	2.676	3.582	6.414	15.372
Nondeductible IRA					
No Tax Timing, $t_n = 35\%$	1.039	1.220	1.514	2.435	5.346
Tax Timing, $t_n = 28\%$	1.043	1.244	1.569	2.589	5.814
Non-qualified Annuity (avg. cost)					
No Tax Timing, $t_n = 35\%$	1.031	1.170	1.384	1.994	3.648
Tax Timing, $t_n = 28\%$	1.034	1.188	1.425	2.101	3.934
Non-qualified Annuity (low cost)					
No Tax Timing, $t_n = 35\%$	1.036	1.200	1.460	2.247	4.584
Tax Timing, $t_n = 28\%$	1.040	1.221	1.510	2.381	4.970

Assumptions: The individual invests $1 of after-tax funds on January 1 and, after *n* years, withdraws all funds and pays taxes. Bonds earn 6 percent per year. The investor is in the combined federal-plus-state ordinary income tax bracket of 35 percent in the investment year and in all years before year *n*. The tax rate in year *n* is t_n. The low-cost and average-cost non-qualified annuities have insurance fees of 0.5 percent and 1.25 percent. In matching contributions example, the individual receives dollar-for-dollar matching contributions from his or her employer and the tax rate in year *n* is 35 percent. The taxable account's values are highlighted in bold to provide a benchmark against which retirement accounts' values can be compared.

wealth advantage at short horizons (e.g., 1 percent after five years) and a large advantage at long horizons (e.g., 80 percent after 35 years). For the passive investor, the nondeductible IRA with tax timing produces a 32 percent ending-wealth advantage after 35 years.

Taxable Account versus Non-qualified Tax-deferred Annuity

The average-cost annuity with tax timing provides a larger ending wealth than this annuity without tax timing because returns are eventually taxed at lower tax rates during retirement. However, even with tax timing, it takes 28 years before the ending wealth from an average-cost annuity exceeds the ending wealth from holding a 6 percent bond in a taxable account (see Table 3.2). For the active stock investor in

TABLE 3.3 After-tax Ending Wealth on Stocks

Savings Vehicle	Investment Horizon (years)				
	1	5	10	20	35
	After-tax Wealth				
Taxable Account					
Passive Investor	$1.081	$1.492	$2.281	$5.506	$21.183
Active Investor	**1.079**	**1.472**	**2.180**	**4.789**	**15.596**
Trader	1.072	1.412	1.995	3.980	11.213
Deductible Pension					
Basic Pension, $t_n = 35\%$	1.110	1.685	2.839	8.062	38.575
Tax Timing, $t_n = 28\%$	1.230	1.867	3.145	8.931	42.729
Matching Contributions	2.220	3.370	5.679	16.125	77.150
Nondeductible IRA					
No Tax Timing, $t_n = 35\%$	1.072	1.445	2.196	5.591	25.424
Tax Timing, $t_n = 28\%$	1.079	1.493	2.324	6.085	28.054
Non-qualified					
Annuity (avg. cost)					
No Tax Timing, $t_n = 35\%$	1.063	1.385	1.998	4.528	17.218
Tax Timing, $t_n = 28\%$	1.070	1.426	2.105	4.908	18.965
Non-qualified (low cost)					
No Tax Timing, $t_n = 35\%$	1.068	1.421	2.114	5.138	21.759
Tax Timing, $t_n = 28\%$	1.076	1.466	2.234	5.584	23.994

Assumptions: The individual invests $1 of after-tax funds on January 1 and, after n years, withdraws all funds and pays taxes. Stocks earn 11 percent per year, including 2 percent dividend yield and 9 percent capital gain. The investor is in the combined federal-plus-state ordinary income tax bracket of 35 percent in the investment year and in all years before year n. The tax rate in year n is t_n. The passive investor, active investor, and trader realize, respectively, 5 percent, 33 percent, and 100 percent of capital gains annually. The combined federal-plus-state capital gain tax rate is 25 percent for the passive investor, 27 percent for the active investor, and 35 percent for the trader. The low-cost and average-cost non-qualified annuities have additional annual insurance fees of 0.5 percent and 1.25 percent. In matching contributions example, the individual receives dollar-for-dollar matching contributions from his or her employer, and the tax rate in year n is 35 percent. We highlighted in bold the values for an active investor in a taxable account to provide a benchmark against which retirement accounts' values can be compared.

Table 3.3, it takes 18 years before the average-cost annuity with tax timing produces the larger ending wealth.

Naturally, it takes fewer years for the low-cost annuity with tax timing to offset its cost disadvantage. It takes one year before the ending wealth from this annuity exceeds the ending wealth from holding a 6 percent bond in a taxable account. It takes six years before ending wealth from this annuity exceeds the ending wealth for the active stock investor.

Summary

Some generalized conclusions from this chapter follow:

- The basic pension model presents the after-tax ending wealth for savings held (1) in a deductible pension when neither tax timing nor matching contributions are available and (2) in a Roth IRA. These pension savings vehicles provide individuals with a larger ending wealth than the taxable account, and the wealth advantage increases with the underlying asset's rate of return and the length of the investment horizon. After 35 years, a typical investor can expect bonds or stocks held in a basic pension to provide more than twice the after-tax ending wealth compared to holding the same bonds or stocks in a taxable account. In addition, the deductible pension provides an even larger ending-wealth advantage for investors who will be in a lower tax bracket during retirement or who receive matching contributions.

- The advantage of tax-deferred growth increases with the length of the investment horizon. Therefore, compared to a taxable account, the nondeductible IRA and annuity's relative prospects tend to improve as the horizon lengthens.

- Holding bonds in a nondeductible IRA instead of a taxable account produces a small advantage at short horizons and a large advantage at long horizons. The nondeductible IRA's wealth advantage increases with the bond's rate of return, the length of the horizon, and if the individual is in a lower tax bracket during retirement.

- For stock investors, there is a trade-off between the tax-deferral feature of the nondeductible IRA and the lower tax rate on capital gains in a taxable account. For the typical active stock investor who will be in the same tax bracket before and during retirement, the taxable account produces the larger ending wealth for horizons less than 10 years and the nondeductible IRA produces the larger ending wealth for horizons of at least 10 years. The breakeven period is shorter when the individual will be in a lower tax bracket during retirement.

- Bond investors almost always receive a larger ending wealth from a taxable account than an average-cost annuity. The typical, active stock investor receives a larger wealth from a taxable account unless the investment horizon is at least 27 years. In general, the average-cost annuity should appeal to few active or passive stock investors. It should not appeal to bond investors. Naturally, a lower-cost annuity should be preferred to a higher-cost annuity.

- Non-qualified annuities should be most attractive to young stock investors, especially investors in their twenties and thirties. Yet, the latest industry statistics indicate that 53 percent are sold to individuals age 65 or older, 83 percent to those age 50 or older, and 93 percent to those age 40 or older.[2]

- Jeffrey and Arnott (1993) conclude few professional managers can overcome the tax burden alone from actively managing stocks in a taxable account. An examination of ending-wealth values for passive investors, active investors, and traders supports Jeffrey and Arnott's position. When stocks are held in a taxable account, active stock managers begin with three strikes against them compared to an index fund: higher expense ratios, higher trading costs, and a higher tax burden. Therefore, individuals who want to actively manage stocks or select active stock funds should hold these assets in tax-deferred retirement accounts. In contrast, passively managed stocks and passive stock funds are ideally suited to taxable accounts.

Appendix 3.1: Estimating the Additional Costs on Annuities[3]

The average total expense ratios for bond and stock subaccounts are:[4]

	Bonds	Stocks
Fund Expense	0.68%	0.77%
Insurance Expense	1.32	1.31
Total Expense	2.00	2.08

Subaccounts are essentially mutual funds held in an annuity, where the annuity is the savings vehicle sold through an insurance firm. Fund expense denotes the percent of subaccount assets deducted each year for fund operating expenses, management fees, and all other asset-based costs incurred by the fund, *except transaction costs*. Insurance expense is the sum of the mortality and expense (M&E) fee plus other miscellaneous administrative expenses. The total expense ratio does not include transaction costs. Total expense averages 2.00 percent and 2.08 percent on bond and stock subaccounts. In addition, there is an annual contract charge that averages $27 on bond and stock subaccounts. A few subaccounts also have an annual percentage contract charge and/or loads.

A key to estimating the additional costs on annuities is to determine the investment alternative. With few exceptions, individuals should invest all they can in deductible pensions and Roth IRAs before considering a non-qualified tax-deferred annuity. In practice, therefore, someone considering an annuity should be choosing between an annuity and a taxable account. In a taxable account, the individual who manages his or her funds has a total expense ratio (as defined above) of zero. He or she incurs transaction costs, but so does an annuity, and these costs are above and beyond the total expense ratio. Thus, someone could justify additional cost estimates of 2 percent and 2.08 percent for the average-cost bond and stock subaccounts. However, many individuals invest through mutual funds. Expense ratios on bond and stock funds (which also exclude transaction costs) average 1.15 percent and 1.40 percent, respectively.[5] These averages imply additional costs of 0.85 percent and 0.68 percent, respectively.

This study assumes the additional costs are 1.25 percent on average-cost annuities and 0.50 percent on low-cost annuities. For individuals who manage their funds, the average-cost fee of 1.25 percent is probably too low, while it is too high for someone who invests through an average-cost mutual fund. The low-cost fee of 0.50 percent is below average by any standard. However, there are a few annuties with such low costs. The low-cost annuity reflects their costs and advantages.

References

LIMRA International, Inc., 1999, *Deferred* Annuity Buyer Study: Profiles, LIMRA International, Inc.

Jeffrey, Robert H., and Robert D. Arnott. 1993. Is your alpha big enough to cover its taxes? *Journal of Portfolio Management*, Spring, 15–25.

Notes

1. The turnover rate of a mutual fund is the lesser of annual purchases or sales divided by average net assets. The turnover rate of the average stock fund is about 80 percent, but this does not mean it realizes 80 percent of net capital gains each year. By holding winners and selling losers, a fund can have a turnover rate in excess of 100 percent and still have no net realized gains.
2. Average costs come from the October 1998 version of *Morningstar Principia*. We thank Morningstar's Patrick Reinkemeyer for a complimentary copy of *Morningstar Principia Pro* and for his help. The estimates of additional average-cost and low-cost fees are our own.
3. The bond subaccount sample consists of all variable annuities, except qualified-only annuities, with a fixed-income Morningstar Category and net subaccount assets of at least $25 million. The minimum size constraint eliminates annuities with few assets, but does not appreciably affect the average costs. The stock subaccount sample consists of all variable annuities, except qualified-only annuities, with a domestic stock or international stock Morningstar Category and net assets of at least $50 million.
4. The mutual fund samples correspond to the variable annuity samples. The bond mutual fund sample consists of all funds with a Morningstar Category of taxable bonds that are not restricted to institutions or closed to new investments and have net assets of at least $25 million. The stock fund sample is similar except it includes domestic and international stock funds and has a $50 million size restriction.

Frequently Asked Questions Related to Savings Vehicles

Introduction

Given an original investment of $10,000 of after-tax funds in each savings vehicle, this chapter first projects constant annual after-tax retirement incomes for each of four representative investors. Each investor can save in any of five savings vehicles: deductible pension, Roth IRA, nondeductible IRA, non-qualified tax-deferred annuity, and taxable account. The analysis also considers projected retirement incomes for low-cost and average-cost annuities and three investors that differ in how quickly they realize capital gains in the taxable account. It then uses these projections of retirement incomes to answer frequently asked questions related to savings vehicles.

Representative Investors

Table 4.1 summarizes four representative investors with different tax rates. The first, Ave-Ave, is considered the "average" investor. He or she is in the 35 percent combined federal-plus-state tax bracket before and during retirement. The second, Ave-Low, is in the 35 percent tax bracket before retirement and the 28 percent bracket during retirement. The third, Hi-Hi, is in the 46.6 percent tax bracket before and during retirement. The fourth, Hi-Ave, is in the 46.6 percent tax bracket before retirement and the 35 percent bracket during retirement.

Tables 4.2 through 4.5 provide the levels of annual after-tax retirement income for these representative investors from an original investment of $10,000 of after-

	Ave-Ave Table 2	Ave-Low Table 3	Hi-Hi Table 4	Hi-Ave Table 5
TABLE 4.1 Four Representative Investors				
	Investor/Table			
	Tax Brackets			
Before Retirement				
Ordinary Income	35%	35%	46.6%	46.6%
Capital Gain-Passive	25	25	25	25
Capital Gain-Typical	27	27	27	27
Capital Gain-Active	35	35	46.6	46.6
During Retirement				
Ordinary Income	35%	28%	46.6%	35%
Capital Gain-Passive	25	18	25	25
Capital Gain-Typical	27	20	27	27
Capital Gain-Active	35	28	46.6	35

For Ave-Low, the capital gain tax rates are 7 percent lower during retirement. This assumption would be appropriate for someone who works in a state that imposes capital gain taxes, but chooses to retire in a state that does not impose capital gain taxes, such as Florida or Texas.

tax funds in each savings vehicle. The investment is made when the individual is age 30, 45, 55, 60, or immediately before retirement at age 65. Funds are withdrawn to provide a constant after-tax income for each year during a 20-year retirement period. The individual can invest in bonds or stocks. In the tables, we assume bonds earn 6 percent a year and stocks earn 11 percent, including a 2 percent dividend yield. Passive investors, active investors, and traders realize 5 percent, 33 percent, and 100 percent of capital gains each year. A passive stock investor is someone who either passively manages his own portfolio or selects a passively managed stock fund. Corresponding definitions apply to traders and active investors. Annual insurance fees are 1.25 percent on the average-cost non-qualified tax-deferred annuity and 0.50 percent on the low-cost annuity. The assumptions can be changed, and the models are available at http://www. wiley.com/go/reichenstein.

Frequently Asked Questions

Which Savings Vehicles Provide the Largest After-tax Retirement Income?

We first present rankings of the following five common savings vehicles in terms of their ability to provide retirement income: deductible pension (without an employer's matching contributions), Roth IRA, nondeductible IRA, average-cost non-qualified annuity, and taxable account for an active investor. As we shall see,

TABLE 4.2   Annual After-tax Income for an Investor with an Average Tax Bracket before and during Retirement (i.e., Ave-Ave)

Tax Structure	Horizon before Retirement (years)				
	0	5	10	20	35
			Bonds		
Taxable Account	$729	$883	$1,069	$1,568	$2,783
Deductible Pension	872	1,167	1,561	2,796	6,701
Roth IRA	872	1,167	1,561	2,796	6,701
Nondeductible IRA	756	949	1,206	2,010	4,549
Tax-def. Annuity (low cost)	708	857	1,062	1,704	3,649
Tax-def. Annuity (avg. cost)	678	797	955	1,419	2,707
			Stocks		
Taxable Accounts					
Passive Investor	$1,066	$1,636	$2,537	$6,198	$23,936
Active Investor	**1,026**	**1,519**	**2,251**	**4,947**	**16,110**
Trader	955	1,349	1,905	3,800	10,708
Deductible Pension	1,256	2,116	3,566	10,124	48,441
Roth IRA	1,256	2,116	3,566	10,124	48,441
Nondeductible IRA	1,040	1,603	2,547	6,813	31,720
Non-qualified Annuity (low cost)	931	1,391	2,216	5,818	26,068
Non-qualified Annuity (avg. cost)	896	1,294	1,983	4,891	19,539

Assumptions: The individual invests $10,000 of after-tax funds zero, 5, 10, 20, or 35 years before retirement. Funds are withdrawn to provide a constant after-tax income for 20 years. Bonds earn 6 percent per year and stocks earn 11 percent, including 2 percent dividend yield and 9 percent capital gain. The investor has a combined federal-plus-state ordinary income tax rate of 35 percent before and during retirement. The passive stock investor, active investor, and trader realize, respectively, 5 percent, 33 percent, and 100 percent of capital gains annually. The active investor is highlighted in bold because he is considered the "typical" taxable investor. The combined capital gain tax rate before and during retirement is 25 percent for the passive investor, 27 percent for the active investor, and 35 percent for the trader. The low-cost and average-cost non-qualified tax-deferred annuities have additional annual insurance fees of 0.50 percent and 1.25 percent, respectively.

for a given investment horizon, these vehicles' rankings are similar for each representative investor. The discussion for this question explains the reasons for these rankings. Later questions discuss the desirability of variations of these basic savings vehicles such as deductible pensions with matching contributions, passive investing in a taxable account, and low-cost non-qualified annuities.

Table 4.6 summarizes the general rankings of retirement incomes for the five common savings vehicles. For each of the four representative investors, the deductible pension and Roth IRA always provide a higher retirement income than any other savings vehicle. When the investor's tax rates are the same in the investment year and

TABLE 4.3 Annual After-tax Income for an Investor with an Average Tax Bracket before Retirement and Low Tax Bracket during Retirement (i.e., Ave-Low)

Tax Structure	Horizon before Retirement (years)				
	0	5	10	20	35
			Bonds		
Taxable Account	$757	$916	$1,110	$1,627	$2,888
Ded. Pension (with tax timing)	966	1,292	1,729	3,097	7,423
Roth IRA	872	1,167	1,561	2,796	6,701
Nondeductible IRA	780	993	1,278	2,168	4,980
Tax-def. Annuity (low cost)	733	903	1,134	1,850	4,009
Tax-def. Annuity (avg. cost)	699	834	1,012	1,532	2,962
			Stocks		
Taxable Account					
Passive Investor	$1,115	$1,736	$2,715	$6,672	$25,816
Active Investor	**1,081**	**1,614**	**2,394**	**5,261**	**17,135**
Trader	1,012	1,430	2,020	4,029	11,353
Ded. Pension (with tax timing)	1,391	2,344	3,950	11,215	53,657
Roth IRA	1,256	2,116	3,566	10,124	48,441
Nondeductible IRA	1,085	1,707	2,752	7,476	35,064
Non-qualified Annuity (low cost)	985	1,511	2,431	6,492	28,858
Non-qualified Annuity (avg. cost)	945	1,400	2,170	5,397	21,629

Assumptions: The individual invests $10,000 of after-tax funds zero, 5, 10, 20, or 35 years before retirement. Funds are withdrawn to provide a constant after-tax income for 20 years. Bonds earn 6 percent per year and stocks earn 11 percent, including 2 percent dividend yield and 9 percent capital gain. The investor has a combined federal-plus-state ordinary income tax rate of 35 percent before and 28 percent during retirement. The passive stock investor, active investor, and trader realize, respectively, 5 percent, 33 percent, and 100 percent of capital gains annually. The active investor is highlighted in bold because he is considered the "typical" taxable investor. The combined capital gain tax rate before retirement is 25 percent for the passive investor, 27 percent for the active investor, and 35 percent for the trader. The capital gain tax rate is 7 percent lower during retirement for each investor. The low-cost and average-cost non-qualified tax-deferred annuities have additional annual insurance fees of 0.50 percent and 1.25 percent, respectively.

withdrawal year, they are tied for first. When the investor is in a lower tax bracket during retirement, the deductible pension ranks ahead of the Roth IRA. The nondeductible IRA almost always ranks third. The major uncertainty is the relative rankings of the taxable account for an active investor and the average-cost annuity. For each representative investor, the taxable account ranks ahead of the average-cost annuity when the investment is made zero, 5, or 10 years before retirement. At 20

TABLE 4.4   Annual After-tax Income for an Investor with a High Tax Bracket before and during Retirement (i.e., Hi-Hi)

Tax Structure	Horizon before Retirement (years)				
	0	5	10	20	35
	Bonds				
Taxable Account	$685	$802	$939	$1,287	$2,065
Deductible Pension	872	1,167	1,561	2,796	6,701
Roth IRA	872	1,167	1,561	2,796	6,701
Nondeductible IRA	716	875	1,087	1,748	3,835
Tax-def. Annuity (low cost)	668	784	947	1,464	3,054
Tax-def. Annuity (avg. cost)	644	738	862	1,236	2,286
	Stocks				
Taxable Account					
Passive Investor	$1,047	$1,589	$2,437	$5,820	$21,732
Active Investor	**1,008**	**1,476**	**2,164**	**4,649**	**14,647**
Trader	863	1,148	1,527	2,703	6,362
Deductible Pension	1,256	2,116	3,566	10,124	48,441
Roth IRA	1,256	2,116	3,566	10,124	48,441
Nondeductible IRA	962	1,428	2,207	5,715	26,178
Non-qualified Annuity (low cost)	844	1,199	1,862	4,861	21,445
Non-qualified Annuity (avg. cost)	817	1,123	1,676	4,054	16,084

Assumptions: The individual invests $10,000 of after-tax funds zero, 5, 10, 20, or 35 years before retirement. Funds are withdrawn to provide a constant after-tax income for 20 years. Bonds earn 6 percent per year and stocks earn 11 percent, including 2 percent dividend yield and 9 percent capital gain. The investor has a combined federal-plus-state ordinary income tax rate of 46.6 percent before and during retirement. The passive stock investor, active investor, and trader realize, respectively, 5 percent, 33 percent, and 100 percent of capital gains annually. The active investor is highlighted in bold because he is considered the "typical" taxable investor. The combined capital gain tax rate before and during retirement is 25 percent for the passive investor, 27 percent for the typical investor, and 46.6 percent for the trader. The low-cost and average-cost non-qualified tax-deferred annuities have additional annual insurance fees of 0.50 percent and 1.25 percent, respectively.

years before retirement, the taxable account either provides a higher income or falls within a few percent of the income provided by the average-cost annuity. At 35 years, this annuity usually provides the higher retirement income.

Chapter 2 presented the ending-wealth models for an original investment of $1 of after-tax funds in each savings vehicle. A comparison of these models explains why the deductible pension and Roth IRA always rank above the others. In a Roth IRA, the individual invests $1 after taxes, it grows tax exempt at i percent for n years, and the ending-wealth model is $(1 + i)^n$. *The effective tax rate is zero.*

TABLE 4.5 Annual After-tax Income for an Investor with a High Tax Bracket before Retirement and Average Tax Bracket during Retirement (i.e., Hi-Ave)

Tax Structure	Horizon before Retirement (years)				
	0	**5**	**10**	**20**	**35**
			Bonds		
Taxable Account	$729	$854	$1,000	$1,370	$2,199
Ded. Pension (with tax timing)	1,061	1,420	1,901	3,404	8,157
Roth IRA	872	1,167	1,561	2,796	6,701
Nondeductible IRA	756	949	1,206	2,010	4,549
Tax-def. Annuity (low cost)	708	857	1,062	1,704	3,649
Tax-def. Annuity (avg. cost)	678	797	955	1,419	2,707
			Stocks		
Taxable Account					
Passive Investor	$1,066	$1,618	$2,482	$5,928	$22,134
Active Investor	**1,026**	**1,503**	**2,202**	**4,733**	**14,910**
Trader	955	1,270	1,690	2,991	7,041
Ded. Pension (with tax timing)	1,529	2,576	4,340	12,324	58,963
Roth IRA	1,256	2,116	3,566	10,124	48,441
Nondeductible IRA	1,040	1,603	2,547	6,813	31,720
Non-qualified Annuity (low cost)	931	1,391	2,216	5,878	26,068
Non-qualified Annuity (avg. cost)	896	1,294	1,983	4,891	19,539

Assumptions: The individual invests $10,000 of after-tax funds zero, 5, 10, 20, or 35 years before retirement. Funds are withdrawn to provide a constant after-tax income for 20 years. Bonds earn 6 percent per year and stocks earn 11 percent, including 2 percent dividend yield and 9 percent capital gain. The investor has a combined federal-plus-state ordinary income tax rate of 46.6 percent before retirement and 35 percent during retirement. The passive stock investor, active investor, and trader realize, respectively, 5 percent, 33 percent, and 100 percent of capital gains annually. The active investor is highlighted in bold because he is considered the "typical" taxable investor. The combined capital gain tax rate before and during retirement is 25 percent for the passive investor, 27 percent for the active investor, and the ordinary income tax rate for the trader. The low-cost and average-cost non-qualified tax-deferred annuities have additional annual insurance fees of 0.50 percent and 1.25 percent, respectively.

In a deductible pension, the individual invests $1 / (1 − t) *of before-tax funds*, where t is his tax bracket. If t is 35 percent, he invests $1.54 of before-tax funds [$1 / (1 − 0.35)], which is $1 of after-tax funds plus the $0.54 tax savings. The $1 investment in a Roth IRA and $1.54 investment in a deductible pension are equivalent because both reduce his current-year spending by $1. Many analysts miss this important point. In addition, he does not have to wait until next year to receive the $0.54 tax refund. He can reduce this year's tax withholding by $0.54. In the deductible pension, the funds grow tax deferred at i percent for n years and are taxed at withdrawal at the

TABLE 4.6   General Rankings of Retirement Incomes from Five Common
Savings Vehicles

	Horizon before Retirement		Horizon before Retirement
	0, 5, or 10 years		35 years
	Rank		Rank
	1. Deductible Pension		1. Deductible Pension
1(tied) or	2. Roth IRA	1(tied) or	2. Roth IRA
	3. Nondeductible IRA		3. Nondeductible IRA
	4. Active Taxable Account		4. Average-cost Annuity
	5. Average-cost Annuity		5. Active Taxable Account

For investors who have the same tax rate before and during retirement, the deductible pension
and Roth IRA tie for first. For investors who have a lower tax rate during retirement, deductible
pension ranks first and Roth IRA ranks second.

ordinary income tax rate during retirement, t_n. The after-tax ending-wealth model is
$[1 / (1 - t)] \cdot (1 + i)^n \cdot (1 - t_n)$ or, equivalently, $[(1 - t_n) / (1 - t)] \cdot (1 + i)^n$. When the
individual is in the same tax bracket before and during retirement (that is, $t = t_n$), the
model simplifies to $(1 + i)^n$. *The effective tax rate is zero.*

The effective tax rate is zero (1) in a Roth IRA and (2) in a deductible pension
(without matching contributions) when the individual is in the same tax bracket
before and during retirement. The effective tax rate is negative in a deductible pension
when the individual is in a lower tax bracket during retirement. In the other vehicles, returns may be deferred for years or taxed at favorable capital gain tax rates,
but they never have a zero (or negative) effective tax rate.

Not only do the deductible pension and Roth IRA always provide higher
retirement incomes than the other common savings vehicles, but their advantage is
also usually huge. For Ave-Ave in Table 4.2, the deductible pension and Roth IRA
provide a 15 percent higher retirement income than the next best savings vehicle for
someone retiring immediately and a 47 percent higher income for someone retiring
in 35 years. Their income advantage increases with the rate of return, the length of
the investment horizon, and the individual's tax rate.

The nondeductible IRA almost always provides the third-highest retirement
income. Its advantage compared to a bond investment in a taxable account is the tax
deferral of returns until withdrawal. The importance of tax-deferred growth
increases with the investment horizon. Thus, compared to bonds in a taxable account,
the nondeductible IRA provides a small income advantage to people who will retire
within five years and a much larger advantage to younger individuals.

Compared to an active stock portfolio held in a taxable account, the nondeductible IRA has one advantage and one disadvantage. Its advantage is tax-deferred
growth. Its disadvantage is the fact that long-term capital gains are eventually taxed
at the ordinary income tax rate in the nondeductible IRA instead of the lower capital

gain tax rate in the taxable account. For individuals retiring within five years, the two factors are usually roughly offsetting. The exception is Hi-Hi, the high-bracket individual before and during retirement, who should favor the taxable account. Active investors retiring in more than 10 years should favor the nondeductible IRA, and its advantage for these young investors is usually substantial.

Now, let us compare the retirement incomes in Table 4.2 through 4.5 from the taxable account for an active investor and the average-cost annuity. The annuity has the same tax structure as the nondeductible IRA but charges higher costs. For the bond investor, the annuity has the advantage of tax-deferred growth and the disadvantage of higher costs. Although differences exist across the tables, in general, the taxable account provides a higher income to bond investors who will retire within 20 years, and the annuity provides a higher income to bond investors who will retire in 35 years. From the bond investor's perspective, the annuity's higher costs are equivalent to a 25 percent current-year tax rate [1.25% / 6%]. The remaining 4.75 percent grows *tax deferred*. It takes a long time before the benefits of tax-deferred growth at 4.75 percent offset the cost disadvantage.

For the active stock investor, the annuity's advantage is tax-deferred growth, but it has two disadvantages: higher annual costs and the fact that capital gains in the taxable account are eventually taxed at preferential rates. If everything else remains the same, stocks' higher projected returns compared to projected bond returns would allow the annuity to more quickly offset its cost disadvantage. However, stocks' higher returns and the preferential capital gains tax treatment counter each other. The net effect is that, based on assumptions embedded in Tables 4.2 through 4.5, it generally takes more than 20 years before the average-cost annuity can overcome its cost disadvantage. For individuals 20 years from retirement, the annuity provides a small (less than 3 percent) income advantage for Ave-Low and Hi-Ave, the representative investors who will be in a lower tax bracket during retirement, but an income disadvantage to Ave-Ave and Hi-Hi. Moreover, Hi-Hi, the high-bracket investor before and during retirement, can expect a 15 percent higher retirement income from the active taxable account; the larger spread between ordinary income and capital gain tax rates favors the taxable account.

In summary, there is substantial agreement on the rankings of five common savings vehicles in terms of their ability to provide retirement income. *The deductible pension and Roth IRA are the best savings vehicles for bonds and for stocks, for all four investors, and for all investment horizons. Someone who is saving for retirement should save all he or she is allowed to save, or can afford to save, in deductible pensions and Roth IRAs.* Those wishing to save additional funds should first consider the nondeductible IRA. The benefits of tax-deferred growth can be substantial, especially to younger investors. The final choice is between saving in a taxable account for an active investor and an average-cost annuity. In general, individuals who are within 20 years of retiring should prefer the taxable account, while individuals who will not retire for more than 20 years should prefer the average-cost annuity. Chapter 5 presents a more detailed analysis of the decision to save in a non-qualified annuity or a taxable account.

Table 2.1 lists factors not appearing in ending-wealth and retirement income models that could influence the choice of savings vehicles. However, for someone saving to meet retirement income needs, maximizing ending wealth or projected retirement income is usually the dominant criterion for selecting a savings vehicle.

What Factors Limit the Attractiveness of the Nondeductible IRA?

Based on projected retirement income and projected ending wealth in Chapter 3, the nondeductible IRA is usually the third choice among savings vehicles. Why then has this savings vehicle not been particularly popular?

There are two factors not in the models that limit its attractiveness. First, before 2002, the maximum annual contribution to all IRAs was $2,000 per person, and the deductible IRA and Roth IRA are preferable to the nondeductible IRA. Since the Roth IRA is available to individuals and couples with adjusted gross incomes below $95,000 and $150,000, respectively, the nondeductible IRA should only be of interest to wealthy investors. Second, there are paperwork requirements associated with the nondeductible IRA. Some people consider the paperwork burden to exceed the nondeductible IRA's tax benefits. The good news is that many investors will be able to convert the nondeductible IRA to a Roth IRA after retirement and thus avoid the worst of these burdens.

Each year that a nondeductible IRA contribution is made, Form 8606 must be filed. It is a simple form that informs the IRS that a nondeductible IRA was made and the cumulative amount of nondeductible IRA contributions to date. The requirements upon withdrawal are more onerous. Legally, deductible and nondeductible IRAs are both traditional IRAs. The distinction is whether the original contribution is deductible. Suppose Mary has a traditional deductible IRA and a traditional nondeductible IRA in which she made one $2,000 contribution of after-tax funds. She withdraws $1,000 from *either* IRA during a year. The nontaxable portion of the withdrawal is:

$$\frac{\text{Unrecovered nondeductible contributions}}{\text{Total of all traditional IRA account balances at end of year} + \$1,000} \times \$1,000$$

The numerator is $2,000 the first year she withdraws funds but is less thereafter. She must maintain a record of the dwindling unrecovered after-tax contribution. The denominator also changes each year. Some people avoid the nondeductible IRA because of this paperwork hassle during their retirement years.[1]

Fortunately, many people can convert a nondeductible IRA to a Roth IRA soon after retiring and thus avoid this hassle. Suppose John earns too much income to qualify for a Roth IRA. He contributes $2,000 to a nondeductible IRA and will convert to a Roth IRA in 20 years when he retires and his income falls below $100,000. For simplicity, but without loss of generality, assume the funds are invested in bonds earning 8 percent, and he is in the combined federal-plus-state 43 percent tax bracket before retirement and 35 percent bracket during retirement. If the $2,000 is invested in a taxable account for 20 years, it is worth $4,879 after taxes [$2,000 • $(1.0456)^{20}$], where 4.56 percent is the after-tax rate of return. In 20 years, the $2,000 nondeductible IRA is worth $9,322 before taxes [$2,000 • $(1.08)^{20}$]. Suppose John, after age 59½, converts to a Roth IRA and pays taxes out of the nondeductible IRA. (When possible, he should pay taxes out of a separate taxable account. For simplicity, the example assumes taxes are paid with nondeductible IRA funds.) He pays taxes at 35 percent on the $7,322 deferred return. After conversion, he has $6,759 after taxes in a Roth IRA [$2,000 • $((1.08)^{20}$ • $(1 - 0.35) + 0.35)$]. Not only does he have more after-tax funds with the nondeductible IRA strategy, but the funds will also grow thereafter tax-exempt, while the funds in the taxable account will continue to grow at an after-tax rate of return.

Should Someone Save First in a Roth IRA, Deductible Pension with Matching Contributions, or Deductible Pension without Matching Contributions?

When possible, people should save the maximum allowable in a Roth IRA and deductible pensions. But what about someone who cannot save this amount? Should he save first in a Roth IRA, a deductible pension with matching contributions, or a deductible pension without matching contributions? To answer this question, we only need to compare the after-tax ending-wealth models, which were developed and discussed in Chapter 2. For the Roth IRA, it is $(1 + i)^n$. For the deductible pension without matching contributions, it is $[(1 - t_n) / (1 - t)]$ • $(1 + i)^n$. For the deductible pension with matching contributions, it is $[(1 + mc)$ • $(1 - t_n) / (1 - t)]$ • $(1 + i)^n$, where mc is the matching contributions. Each model contains $(1 + i)^n$. Their scalar values differ, where the scalar is the part of the models before $(1 + i)^n$. The scalar is 1.0 for the Roth, $(1 - t) / (1 - t_n)$ for the deductible pension without matching contributions, and $(1 + mc)$ • $(1 - t_n) / (1 - t)$ for the deductible pension with matching contributions. The scalars' sizes indicate the preference among these three choices per dollar of original after-tax investment.

Suppose Mary will forego $1,000 of spending this year; that is, she will save $1,000 of after-tax funds. She is in the 35 percent tax bracket before and during retirement. For simplicity, assume she invests in bonds that earn 8 percent before taxes and withdraws the funds during retirement in 20 years.[2] She can invest in a 401(k) with a 50 percent matching contributions, a deductible pension without matching contributions, or a Roth IRA. In 20 years, the after-tax value of the Roth is $4,661 [$1,000 • $(1.08)^{20}$]. The after-tax value of the deductible pension without matching contributions is $4,661 [$1,000 • $\{(1 - 0.35) / (1 - 0.35)$ • $(1.08)^{20}\}$] or [$1,000 • $(1.08)^{20}$]. The after-tax value of the 401(k) with matching contribution is $6,991 [$1,000 • $\{(1 + 0.5)$ • $(1 - 0.35) / (1 - 0.35)$ • $(1.08)^{20}\}$] or [$1,000 • (1.50) • $(1.08)^{20}$]. The scalars are 1.0 for the Roth IRA, 1.0 for the deductible pension without a match, and 1.5 for the deductible pension with a 50 percent match. Therefore, the latter should be preferred.

Unless the employee expects to change firms before any of the firm's contributions are vested, he or she should save first in the deductible pension with matching contributions. The 50-cent-on-the-dollar contributions mean the employee begins with a 50 percent larger investment portfolio than an employee without matching contributions and, for a given return and investment horizon, will end with a 50 percent larger retirement nest egg. An additional 50 percent guaranteed return is too good a deal to pass up. Dollar-for-dollar matching contributions should be even more difficult to pass up. Beg, borrow, or steal (from the "mad money" account) the funds necessary to obtain all matching contributions, but do not pass up free money.

The second choice is between the deductible pension without matching contributions and the Roth IRA. *For an equal investment of after-tax funds*, the key comparison is between the deductible pension's scalar of $(1 - t) / (1 - t_n)$ and the Roth IRA's scalar of 1.0. Individuals who will be in a lower tax bracket during retirement will receive a larger ending wealth *per after-tax dollar originally invested* if they save in the deductible pension. Individuals in the same tax bracket before and during retirement will receive the same ending wealth, while individuals in a lower bracket during retirement will receive a larger ending wealth if they save in the Roth IRA.

In practice, individuals in high tax brackets before retirement generally will prefer the deductible pension if they expect to be in a lower bracket during retirement. In contrast, individuals who are currently in a low tax bracket should favor the Roth IRA. Examples of the latter include recent college graduates and individuals coming off unemployment. For example, someone who graduates from college in May or is coming off unemployment may have only six months of income. He should save in a Roth IRA since he is likely to be in a low tax bracket. In addition, young workers may wish to save in a Roth IRA while they are establishing their careers until their incomes and tax brackets increase.

Factors not considered in the ending-wealth models could play an important role in the choice between a Roth IRA and a deductible pension, and they usually favor the Roth IRA. First, you usually cannot withdraw funds from a deductible pension before age 59½ without incurring the 10 percent penalty tax. In a Roth IRA, you can withdraw the principal (but not the accumulated returns) without incurring the penalty. Second, withdrawals from a deductible pension are part of adjusted gross income and, therefore, may increase taxes on Social Security benefits. In contrast, withdrawals from a Roth IRA do not affect Social Security taxes. Third, an individual must begin withdrawing funds from a deductible pension after age 70½, while there are no minimal withdrawal requirements for funds in a Roth IRA. Fourth, individuals with estates large enough to incur estate taxes have another reason to prefer the Roth IRA. Estate tax laws make no distinction between pre-tax and after-tax funds. For someone in the 35 percent tax bracket before and during retirement, the after-tax wealth is the same from investing $2,000 of before-tax funds in a deductible pension or $1,300 of after-tax funds in a Roth IRA. If returns average 8 percent for 20 years, the deductible pension is worth $9,322 before taxes [$2,000 $\bullet$ $(1.08)^{20}$], or $6,059 after taxes [$2,000 $\bullet$ $(1.08)^{20}$ $\bullet$ $(1 - 0.35)$], while the $1,300 in the Roth IRA is worth $6,059 after taxes. Even though both amounts represent $6,059 after taxes, if the individual dies in 20 years before withdrawing the funds, the IRS will treat the deductible pension as worth $9,322 and the Roth IRA as worth $6,059.

The problem is that estate-tax laws do not distinguish between pre-tax and after-tax funds.

Should Someone Who Qualifies for Both Save in a Deductible IRA or a Roth IRA?

This question differs from the prior question. For someone in the 35 percent tax bracket before and during retirement, the ending after-tax wealth is the same from investing $1,300 of after-tax funds in a Roth or $2,000 of before-tax funds in a deductible pension (without matching contributions). If the individual will only save $1,300 after taxes, then, as previously discussed, the choice between the deductible IRA (or any other deductible pension without a match) and the Roth IRA depends upon the expected tax rates in the contribution year, t, and withdrawal year, t_n.

If, however, the investor wants to invest more than $1,300 after taxes, the analysis is different. Jonathan Clements (1997) recognized this key distinction. He compared a $2,000 investment in a Roth IRA to a $2,000 investment in a deductible IRA *plus* a separate investment of $700 in a taxable account. Both strategies require $2,000 of after-tax funds. He concludes that investors should prefer the Roth IRA.

Continuing with the prior example, assume someone is in the 35 percent tax bracket before and during retirement. *In the absence of taxation*, the $700 in the separate taxable account would become $700 • $(1.08)^{20}$, which would precisely pay the taxes on the withdrawal of $2,000 • $(1.08)^{20}$ from the deductible IRA in 20 years. However, because returns on the $700 side account will be taxed each year, it will be insufficient to pay all taxes on the withdrawal of the deductible IRA. Thus, the $2,000 • $(1.08)^{20}$ after taxes in the Roth IRA is preferred.

The analysis is more complex for someone who expects to be in a lower tax bracket in retirement. Suppose Ann is in the 35 percent tax bracket today but expects to be in the 28 percent bracket when she retires. Continuing with the same assumptions, a $2,000 investment in the Roth IRA will be worth $9,322 after taxes in 20 years [$2,000 • $(1.08)^{20}$]. After taxes, the deductible IRA and $700 side account will be worth $8,641 [$2,000 • $(1.08)^{20}$ • $(1 - 0.28) + $700 • $\{1 + 0.08 • (1 - 0.35)\}^{20}$]. This analytic framework shows that unless the tax bracket falls sharply and the investment horizon is short—probably five years or less—individuals should prefer the Roth IRA to the deductible IRA. *When someone qualifies for a Roth IRA or a deductible IRA, he or she should almost always choose the Roth IRA.*

Should Someone Convert Funds from a Traditional IRA to a Roth IRA?

Individuals can convert a traditional IRA to a Roth IRA subject to an income limitation. In a conversion, there is a *direct transfer* of funds from the trustee of a non-Roth IRA to the trustee of a Roth IRA, or the redesignation of a non-Roth IRA as a Roth IRA maintained by the same trustee.

Recall that a traditional IRA can be a deductible IRA or a nondeductible IRA. If the taxpayer—individual or couple—has an adjusted gross income less than $100,000 and the taxpayer is not married filing separately, the traditional IRA can be fully or partially converted to a Roth IRA. The full amount of the converted

deductible IRA funds (or the amount of converted nondeductible IRA funds representing accumulated return) counts as income for the year, but it does not count
against the adjusted gross income limit. A couple with $90,000 adjusted income
could convert all or part of a $40,000 deductible IRA to a Roth IRA. If they convert
the entire IRA, they would owe taxes on $130,000.

Most people with traditional IRAs have a deductible IRA. We will discuss
deductible IRAs first, followed by a discussion of converting nondeductible IRA funds.

Deductible IRA Conversions

In general, converting deductible IRA funds makes sense if and only if the taxes
associated with the conversion will be paid from funds in a separate taxable account.
Converting to the Roth IRA and paying the associated taxes from a taxable account
effectively allows a larger investment in the favored pension tax structure.

Suppose Mary has $10,000 in a deductible IRA plus $3,500 in a separate taxable account, and she is in the 35 percent tax bracket before and during retirement.
She invests in bonds earning 8 percent and will use the funds for consumption in 20
years. If she converts to the Roth IRA and uses the $3,500 in the taxable account to
pay the taxes, she will have $46,610 after taxes in 20 years [$10,000 $\bullet$ $(1.08)^{20}$].
If she does not convert, she will have $39,943 after taxes [$10,000 $\bullet$ $(1 - 0.35)$ $\bullet$
$(1.08)^{20}$ + $3,500 $\bullet$ $(1.052)^{20}$], where 5.2 percent is the after-tax return on bonds in
the taxable account. The latter total fails to keep up with the Roth IRA's total because
taxes must be paid on the taxable account. If the $3,500 earned 8 percent *after taxes*,
the latter sum would have been $46,610. Since taxes are paid on the taxable account
whether the underlying asset is bonds or stocks, the conversion also makes sense if
the taxable account contains stocks.

Another perspective may clarify the advantage of converting when taxes upon
conversion are paid from a taxable account. Before conversion, Mary has $10,000
of after-tax funds in the two accounts: $6,500 of after-tax funds ($10,000 of before-
tax funds) in the deductible IRA plus $3,500 in the taxable account. After convert-
ing and paying taxes, she still has $10,000 of after-tax funds, but now all $10,000
is in the tax-sheltered Roth IRA. Conversion effectively moves the $3,500 from the
taxable account into the tax-exempt Roth IRA. The ending-wealth advantage from
converting is precisely the difference between the $3,500 earning 8 percent tax-
exempt in the Roth IRA instead of 5.2 percent after taxes in the taxable account.

Conversion can also be desirable even if the tax rate in retirement is lower. Suppose the tax rate is 35 percent before retirement and 28 percent after. The Roth IRA
would be worth $46,610, as before, while the sum of the separate accounts would
be worth $43,206 [$10,000 $\bullet$ $(1.08)^{20}$ $\bullet$ $(1 - 0.28)$ + $3,500 $\bullet$ $(1.052)^{20}$].

What if taxes are paid from the funds withdrawn from the deductible IRA, so only
the after-tax amount of the conversion is rolled into the Roth IRA? In this case, Mary
has $10,000 in the deductible IRA, but she does not have the taxable side account.
Without conversion, the deductible IRA will be worth $10,000 $\bullet$ $(1 + i)^n$ before taxes
and $10,000 $\bullet$ $(1 - t_n)$ $\bullet$ $(1 + i)^n$ after taxes in year n, where t_n is the year n tax rate.

With conversion to a Roth IRA and withdrawing funds to pay taxes, the funds will be worth $10,000 \cdot (1 - t - \text{penalty}) \cdot (1 + i)^n$ after taxes in year n, where t is the current year's tax rate and penalty denotes the 10 percent penalty tax rate on early withdrawals, if applicable. An individual can *convert* $10,000 from a deductible IRA into a Roth IRA without incurring the penalty tax. However, if $3,500 is *withdrawn* from the deductible IRA to pay taxes, these funds are subject to the penalty tax if the individual is younger than age 59½. Therefore, someone younger than 59½ would not likely want to convert and withdraw funds from the deductible IRA to pay taxes. If the penalty tax does not apply and taxes are paid out of the deductible IRA, then conversion makes sense only if the expected tax rate in retirement is *higher* than the current tax rate. That is not the usual situation. *In general, it makes sense to convert a deductible IRA to a Roth IRA if and only if the associated taxes will be paid from funds in a taxable account.*

Other factors could affect the decision to convert, but most of these other factors also favor conversion. First, unlike a deductible IRA, in a Roth IRA, an investor is not required to take minimum distributions after age 70½. In the Roth IRA, the funds can continue to grow tax-exempt. Second, withdrawals from a deductible IRA are part of adjusted gross income and, therefore, may increase taxes on Social Security benefits. In contrast, withdrawals from a Roth IRA do not affect Social Security taxes. Third, conversion may reduce estate taxes, since tax laws do not distinguish between the before-tax dollars of the traditional IRA and the after-tax dollars of the Roth IRA. In short, there are additional, less obvious, tax incentives to convert to a Roth IRA.

Finally, we have a suggestion concerning (1) timing of conversions of nondeductible IRAs to a Roth IRA and (2) rollovers of 401(k) and other retirement accounts into a traditional deductible IRA. Suppose someone just retired and has $25,000 of nondeductible IRAs and $500,000 of 401(k) balances. First, convert the nondeductible IRA into a Roth IRA as soon as possible after retirement. Then, at least one tax year later, roll the 401(k) into a traditional deductible IRA. This allows all nondeductible IRA funds to be converted first. In contrast, if the 401(k) funds are rolled first and then $25,000 converted to a Roth IRA, the conversion would be a pro-rata share of funds in the nondeductible and deductible IRAs—with correspondingly higher taxes on the conversion. Of course, additional amounts could be subsequently converted to a Roth IRA, but converting the undiluted basis of the nondeductible IRA first saves taxes.

Nondeductible IRA Conversions

In general, someone should convert a nondeductible IRA to a Roth IRA as soon as possible. However, conversion is not always possible.

As discussed earlier, the nondeductible IRA should only be attractive to high-income individuals and married couples who do not qualify for the Roth IRA. A nondeductible IRA can be converted to a Roth IRA if *the taxpayer*—individual or couple—has adjusted gross income less than $100,000. Before retirement, few high-income taxpayers will have a low enough income to convert a nondeductible

IRA, but many high-income taxpayers will be able to convert the nondeductible IRA soon after retirement. As we shall see, there is a significant advantage to converting funds from the tax-deferred status of the nondeductible IRA to the tax-exempt status of the Roth IRA.

This first example assumes the associated taxes will be paid from a taxable side account. Suppose John, age 45, made one $2,000 nondeductible IRA contribution five years ago, the funds have earned 8 percent a year, and they are currently worth $2,939 [$2,000 • $(1.08)^5$]. He is in the 35 percent tax bracket before and during retirement. The underlying investment is in bonds earning 8 percent, and he will use the funds for consumption in 20 years. He has a taxable side account worth $329, which is also the tax bill if he immediately converts to a Roth IRA [$939 • 0.35]. If he converts, the $329 side account pays the taxes. After conversion, the Roth IRA has $2,939 of after-tax funds. In 20 years, the after-tax value of the Roth IRA will be $13,697 [$2,000 • $(1.08)^{25}$] or [$2,939 • $(1.08)^{20}$]. If he does not convert, he begins with $2,939 in the nondeductible IRA and $329 after taxes in the taxable account. In 20 years, the after-tax sum of the nondeductible IRA and side account will be $10,510 [$2,000 • $\{(1.08)^{25}$ • $(1 - 0.35) + 0.35\}$ + $329 • $(1.052)^{20}$].

The advantage from converting a nondeductible IRA is substantially larger than the advantage from converting a deductible IRA. After the nondeductible IRA conversion, the remaining funds grow *tax-exempt* in the Roth IRA, which is much better than the *tax-deferred* growth in the nondeductible IRA. Think of the $2,939 of funds in the nondeductible IRA as $2,610 of after-tax funds [$2,000 + $939(1 - 0.35)]. Before conversion, the investor had $2,939 of after-tax funds: the $2,610 in the nondeductible IRA and $329 in the side account. The $2,939 grows tax deferred and the side account grows at the after-tax rate. After conversion, the $2,939 of after-tax funds in the Roth IRA grows tax-exempt. In a nondeductible IRA conversion, the tax status improves for the funds in both the nondeductible IRA and taxable account. In a deductible IRA conversion, in contrast, the tax status improves only for the funds in the taxable account.

Converting a nondeductible IRA to a Roth IRA usually makes sense even if taxes, including the penalty tax, must be paid from funds withdrawn from the nondeductible IRA. Let us retain the prior assumptions except assume that there is not a separate side account. If John does not convert, in 20 years the nondeductible IRA will be worth $13,697 *before taxes* [$2,000 • $(1.08)^{25}$] and $9,603 *after taxes* [$2,000 • $\{(1.08)^{25}$ • $(1 - 0.35) + 0.35\}$]. If he withdraws funds today to pay taxes, including a 10 percent penalty tax on the taxable portion of the distribution, he must withdraw $340.[3] The Roth IRA begins with a balance of $2,599 [$2,939 - $340]. In 20 years, it is worth $12,114 after taxes [$2,599 • $(1.08)^{20}$]. Converting the nondeductible IRA to a Roth IRA produces a $2,511 net advantage despite the penalty tax. Moreover, most individuals can pay the taxes with other funds and avoid the penalty. The longer the investment horizon, the larger will be the advantage to converting the nondeductible IRA.

Finally, recall the example from the discussion for this section entitled "What Factors Limit the Attractiveness of the Nondeductible IRA?". John earns too much income during his working years to contribute to a Roth IRA. Therefore, he contributes to a nondeductible IRA and, soon after retiring, converts the funds to a Roth IRA. This use of the nondeductible IRA provides far more after-tax wealth than saving in a taxable account.

In short, a good rule of thumb is someone should convert a nondeductible IRA to a Roth IRA as soon as possible, even if a penalty tax must be paid, because of the huge advantage to having funds grow tax-exempt instead of tax deferred.

Should Someone Save in a Taxable Account or a Non-qualified Tax-deferred Annuity?

This question is examined thoroughly in Chapter 5. It presents more detailed models than the models presented here. It compares the income available from non-qualified annuities and mutual funds held in taxable accounts. However, as we shall see, the conclusions are the same whether the income numbers come from these more detailed models or the models in this chapter.

Summary

Some generalized conclusions from this chapter follow:

■ Deductible pensions and Roth IRAs are the best savings vehicles for bonds and stocks, for all four hypothetical investors, and for all investment horizons. Someone who is saving for retirement should save all he or she is allowed to save, or can afford to save, in pensions.

■ Individuals who save less than they are allowed to save in deductible pensions and Roth IRAs should save first in pension plans where the employer matches or partially matches the contribution.

■ The nondeductible IRA usually promises the next highest level of retirement income. Individuals should weigh the tax benefits of this savings vehicle against its paperwork burdens. The burden will be minimal if the individual can convert this IRA to a Roth IRA before or shortly after retiring.

■ It generally makes sense to convert a deductible IRA to a Roth IRA if and only if the associated taxes will be paid from a taxable account. It generally makes sense to convert a nondeductible IRA to a Roth IRA as soon as possible.

References

Clements, Jonathan. 1997. Jam today or jam tomorrow? Roth IRA will show many investors it pays to wait. *The Wall Street Journal*, September 16, C1.

Clements, Jonathan. 1998. *25 myths you've got to avoid if you want to manage your money right*. New York: Simon & Schuster.

Notes

1. Clements (1998) expressed the sentiment of many when he wrote, "If the Internal Revenue Service had an ounce of kindness and common sense, it would allow you to pull these nondeductible contributions out of your retirement account as soon as you retire, thereby eliminating all hassles. Instead, the IRS, in its infinite wisdom, insists that every dollar withdrawn from your [traditional IRA] is a mix of taxable and nontaxable money."
2. The ending-wealth model for stocks in a taxable account is complex, while the model for bonds is simple. We assume a bond investment so we can present simply and clearly the tax issues involved. The same conclusions prevail for investments in stocks.
3. The math gets nasty, but the key point is that the advantage of growing tax-exempt instead of tax deferred exceeds the disadvantage of the penalty tax. The penalty tax is 10 percent of the taxable portion of the withdrawal. The taxable portion is 0.3172 [$939 / $2,939]. To pay all taxes from withdrawal, $340 must be withdrawn [$329 / {1 − (0.3172 • 0.1)}]. The penalty tax is about $11 [0.10 • $340 • 0.3172].

Who Should Buy a Non-qualified Tax-deferred Annuity?

Introduction

What is a non-qualified tax-deferred annuity? Who should buy one? The goal of this chapter is to provide a rigorous framework to answer these questions *from the investor's perspective*. As explained later, we believe non-qualified annuities tend to be *sold* by some professionals because of their high commissions. The analysis in this chapter is for the investor.

The short answer to the first question is that a non-qualified annuity is a mutual fund held in a tax-deferred wrapper. The original investment amount is not deductible from income in the contribution year. Returns accumulate tax deferred until withdrawal, at which time they are taxable at ordinary income tax rates. The annuity is *not* the investment; it is the wrapper.

Part A of Figure 5.1 illustrates the distinction. Joe decides to invest in the XYZ mutual fund. The mutual fund is the investment. Also, he must choose the savings vehicle. For now, assume he is deciding between two savings vehicles: a taxable account and a non-qualified tax-deferred annuity. If the mutual fund is held in a taxable account, he pays taxes each year on distributions. If held in an annuity, the returns accumulate tax deferred. Obviously, the tax-deferral feature favors the annuity. However, annuities generally have higher expenses than taxable accounts. A key question addressed in this study is when are the benefits of tax deferral worth the annuity's generally higher costs?

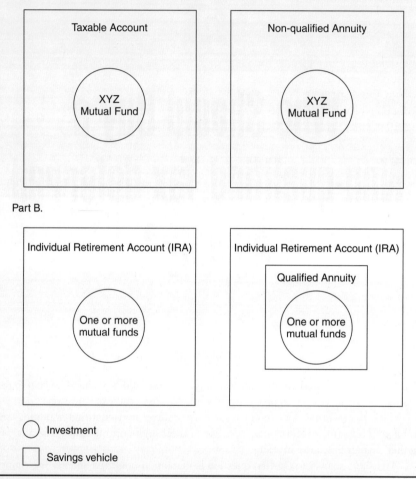

FIGURE 5.1   The Distinction between Investments and Savings Vehicles

The longer answer to the first question is a non-qualified annuity is a complex insurance product. It is a savings vehicle with its own set of tax rules and other legal requirements. Inside this legal structure, an individual can invest in stock funds, bond funds, balanced funds, and other mutual funds. (Technically, mutual funds held inside an annuity are called subaccounts. Since they are functionally identical to mutual funds, we call them mutual funds in this book.) Since an annuity includes an insurance feature, it must be sold through an insurance company.

The second question is "Who should buy a non-qualified annuity?" Some people should be interested in a non-qualified annuity for its investment feature—

Question 1. Is the investor saving to meet preretirement needs?

Yes	No

She should save in a taxable account. Withdrawals before age 59½ from a non-qualified annuity, Roth IRA, or deductible pension are usually subject to a 10 percent penalty tax.

Go to Question 2.

Question 2. The investor is saving to meet postretirement needs and she is not concerned about protection from creditors. Which savings vehicles are best?

Top Choices

Roth IRAs and Deductible Pensions

Secondary Choices

Taxable Accounts Non-qualified Annuities

Roth IRAs and deductible pensions are best for accumulating retirement wealth. She should first fully fund these two savings vehicles. Go to Question 3.

Question 3. The investor has fully funded Roth IRAs and deductible pensions and wishes to invest additional funds to meet her postretirement needs. Should she save in taxable accounts or non-qualified annuities?

Taxable Accounts	Non-qualified Annuities

This decision is examined in this chapter.

FIGURE 5.2   Jane's Decisions

that is, tax-deferred growth—and others for its creditor-protection feature. In some states, an annuity provides protection from creditors. Thus, a medical doctor may prefer to save in an annuity instead of a taxable account. What about individuals who are not concerned about creditor protection? They should invest in the best savings vehicle for acquiring after-tax wealth.

Figure 5.2 illustrates this decision for Jane, our hypothetical investor, who is not concerned about creditor protection. She must first decide whether she is saving to meet preretirement needs or postretirement needs. If she is saving to meet preretirement needs such as the purchase of a car or an unexpected expense, then she should save in a taxable account. We call all other savings vehicles retirement savings vehicles. Since withdrawals from them before age 59½ are generally subject to a 10 percent penalty tax, they are inappropriate for someone saving for preretirement needs.[1]

If Jane is saving for postretirement needs, she can invest in any of four savings vehicles—taxable account, non-qualified annuity, Roth IRA, or deductible pension.[2] A deductible pension is any savings vehicle where the investment amount is deductible in the contribution year, returns accrue tax deferred, and withdrawals are taxed at ordinary income tax rates. Examples include 401(k), 403(b), 457, Keogh, SEP-IRA, and deductible IRA. As we shall see, the Roth IRA and the deductible pension are much more tax-favored savings vehicles than the other two for accumulating retirement wealth. Therefore, Jane should first fully fund Roth IRAs and deductible pensions. Then, if she wants to save additional funds for retirement, she should decide between saving in an annuity or a taxable account. As discussed in Chapter 6, the Economic Growth and Tax Relief Reconciliation Act of 2001 (henceforth, the Tax Act) substantially increased investment opportunities in these savings vehicles. Therefore, this decision should apply to few individuals.

We examine in detail the decision to save in an annuity or a taxable account. This decision depends upon the comparative costs of the annuity and the taxable account. This chapter considers average-cost and low-cost annuities and, not only average-cost and low-cost mutual funds, but also tax-inefficient and tax-efficient mutual funds. The first conclusion to emerge from this analysis is that costs matter a great deal. Knowledgeable investors should only consider buying a low-cost non-qualified annuity or a low-cost mutual fund. In general, a low-cost annuity makes sense for individuals concerned about protection from creditors and individuals with long investment horizons.

Some individuals want to invest in bond funds. Assuming gross bond returns of 5.5 percent and 25 percent tax brackets before and during retirement, the low-cost annuity should be preferred by individuals with horizons exceeding 17 years. The breakeven period is less than 10 years if returns average 8 percent or the investor is in a 33 percent tax bracket before retirement and 25 percent bracket during retirement.

Other individuals want to invest in stock funds. The analysis implies that a *passive,* low-cost stock fund always provides a larger ending wealth than a low-cost annuity. However, most individuals actively manage their stock portfolio or select an active stock fund. Assuming 8 percent gross stock returns and 25 percent tax brackets before and during retirement, the breakeven period for the low-cost annuity compared to a low-cost active stock fund is 15 years. The breakeven period is eight years if gross returns average 12 percent. The big loser in the analysis is the insurance industry's staple—annuities with annual expenses around 2 percent. These products are not in the best interest of investors.

The next section explains why few individuals should have to make the decision to save in a non-qualified annuity or a mutual fund held in a taxable account. Before making this decision, they should first fully fund deductible pensions and Roth IRAs. In addition, individuals who want to provide for their children's education needs will probably fund these needs before making this decision. Later, we will present the analysis for the relatively few people who should decide between saving in a non-qualified annuity or a mutual fund held in a taxable account. We then present the incentive structures that explain why annuities are usually pushed by commission-based professionals and discouraged by fee-only professionals.

Terminology, Tax Structures, and More

We begin this section with a discussion of annuity terminology. Then, we discuss tax structures for four savings vehicles and their implications for saving in annuities. Finally, we discuss differences in levels of creditor protection across savings vehicles.

Terminology

The three major retirement markets for tax-deferred annuities are (1) employer-sponsored markets such as 403(b), SEP-IRA, Keogh, and 401(k) plans; (2) direct IRA rollovers; and (3) the non-qualified market. To repeat, in a non-qualified annuity, the original investment is not deductible, but returns accumulate tax deferred until withdrawal, which is usually in retirement. The other two markets deal with qualified annuities, which means the original investment contributions are tax deductible.

Part B of Figure 5.1 illustrates a qualified annuity held in a direct IRA rollover. George recently retired and wants to rollover his $1 million in 401(k) funds into a traditional IRA. In the left-hand picture of Part B, he rolls the $1 million into an IRA. Inside the IRA, he selects one or more mutual funds. Since they are held in a traditional IRA, returns on the mutual funds are tax deferred. In the right-hand picture, he rolls the $1 million into an IRA. Inside the IRA, he buys a qualified annuity. Inside the annuity, he selects one or more mutual funds. Since the IRA already provides tax deferral, the annuity's higher costs cannot be justified as the cost of providing tax-deferred growth. It is difficult to justify placing an annuity inside a qualified plan. In fact, there are currently multiple class-action lawsuits against firms that sold annuities inside qualified plans. See Geer (1998) and Panko (2000) for related discussion.

Tax Structures

If Jane, our hypothetical investor, wants to save for preretirement income needs, she should save in a taxable account. When saving for retirement, saving in a non-qualified annuity must compete against saving in taxable accounts, Roth IRAs, and deductible pensions. This section compares tax structures facing savings in each of four savings vehicles. It demonstrates that when saving for retirement individuals (who are not concerned about creditor protection) should save all they are allowed to save (or all they can afford to save) in Roth IRAs and deductible pensions before they save in either taxable accounts or non-qualified tax-deferred annuities.

Table 5.1 presents the ending wealth from investing the same amount of after-tax funds in the same mutual fund in each of four savings vehicles. Jane decides to forego $1,000 of spending this year and to withdraw the funds in 15 years during her retirement. She invests in a bond or stock mutual fund that returns 8 percent a year. She is

---

TABLE 5.1   Four Different Tax Structures: After-tax Amounts after 15 Years

---

Assumptions:

Initial investment of $1,000 of after-tax income
8 percent pretax return
28 percent tax rate on ordinary income both now and in 15 years
20 percent capital gain tax rate

1. Taxable Account

Bonds =	$1,000 \bullet [1 + 0.08 \bullet (1 - 0.28)]^{15}$
=	$1,000 \bullet (1.0576)^{15}$
=	$2,316$ after taxes
Stocks =	$1,000 \bullet [1 + 0.01 \bullet (1 - 0.28) + 0.07 \bullet (1 - 0.20)]^{15}$
=	$1,000 \bullet (1.0632)^{15}$
=	$2,507$ after taxes

2. Roth IRA

=	$1,000 \bullet [(1 + 0.08)^{15}]$
=	$1,000 \bullet (1.08)^{15}$
=	$3,172$ after taxes

3. Deductible Pension
Deductible Pension (without matching contributions*):

=	$1,000 \bullet [1/(1 - 0.28)] \bullet (1 + 0.08)^{15} \bullet (1 - 0.28)]$
=	$1,000 \bullet (1.08)^{15}$
=	$3,172$ after taxes

Deductible Pension (with matching contributions*):

=	$1,000 \bullet [2/(1 - 0.28) \bullet (1 + 0.08)^{15} \bullet (1 - 0.28)]$
=	$1,000 \bullet [2 \bullet (1.08)^{15}]$
=	$6,344$ after taxes

4. Nondeductible IRA and Non-qualified Tax-deferred Annuity:

=	$1,000 \bullet (1 + 0.08)^{15} - 0.28 \bullet [\$1,000 \bullet (1 + 0.08)^{15} - \$1,000]$
=	$1,000 \bullet (1.08)^{15} - 0.28 \bullet [\$1,000 \bullet (1.08)^{15} - \$1,000]$
=	$3,172 - 0.28 \bullet (\$2,172)$
=	$2,564$ after taxes

---

* Multiplying the $1,000 after-tax investment by $[1/(1 - 0.28)]$ converts it to a pre-tax equivalent. In the deductible pension with matching contributions, we multiply that amount by 2 to adjust for the company's matching contributions.

currently in the 20 percent capital gain tax bracket and 28 percent ordinary income tax bracket, and she will remain in these brackets before and during retirement.

If Jane saves in a taxable account, she begins with a $1,000 investment of after-tax funds. If it is invested in a bond mutual fund, she will earn 8 percent a year before taxes and 5.76 percent after taxes [8% $\bullet$ (1 − 0.28)]. In 15 years, she will have $2,316 of after-tax funds [$1,000 $\bullet$ $(1.0576)^{15}$]. Suppose the assets are stocks earning 8 percent per year. The tax consequences depend upon how much of the return is capital gains and how quickly the gains are realized. For now, assume 1 percent of the return is dividends taxed at 28 percent and 7 percent is capital gains that are realized each year (technically, in one year plus one day) and taxed at 20 percent. After-tax returns are 6.32 percent per year [1% • (1 − 0.28) + 7% • (1 − 0.20)]. In 15 years, she will have $2,507 [$1,000 • $(1.0632)^{15}$]. The tax structures are different for bond funds and stock funds held in a taxable account. In this example, capital gains enjoy the preferential 20 percent tax rate. In contrast, the other savings vehicles have the same tax structure whether the investment is a bond fund or a stock fund.

If Jane saves in a Roth IRA, she begins with a $1,000 investment of after-tax funds. If she withdraws the funds at least five years hence when she will be at least age 59½, returns are tax-exempt. For someone saving for retirement, these two qualifications are almost always met. Henceforth, we consider returns in the Roth IRA to be tax-exempt. In 15 years, she will have $3,172 after taxes [$1,000 • $(1.08)^{15}$].

The next savings vehicle is a deductible pension such as 401(k) or Keogh. If Jane saves in a deductible pension, she would be able to invest $1,389 of pretax funds, which is the equivalent of $1,000 of after-tax funds. In other words, the $1,389 contribution reduces taxes by $389 [$1,389 • 0.28]. Recall that Jane will forego $1,000 of spending this year. If she invests in one of the other savings vehicles, she invests $1,000 of after-tax funds this year. The appropriate comparison for a deductible pension is an initial investment of $1,389, since this also reduces this year's spending by $1,000. The $1,389 invested at 8 percent for 15 years turns into $4,406. If she withdraws the entire amount, she will owe taxes of 28 percent for an after-tax amount of $3,172. This is the same amount as the Roth IRA. Economically, the $1,389 investment of before-tax funds can be separated into $1,000 of Jane's after-tax funds plus $389 in tax savings. The tax savings grow to precisely satisfy the tax bill on withdrawal. The simple algebra demonstrates that this deductible pension and Roth IRA always provide the same after-tax wealth when the tax rates in the contribution and withdrawal years are the same.

Employers sometimes match or partially match employee contributions to deductible pensions. The next example assumes the employer matches employee contributions dollar-for-dollar. Jane contributes $1,389 of pre-tax funds, which is $1,000 of after-tax funds. The employer matches the $1,389 contribution. Due to the match, Jane begins with twice as many dollars and ends with twice as many dollars. In 15 years, she will have $6,344 after taxes.

Examples of the fourth savings vehicle are nondeductible IRA and non-qualified tax-deferred annuity. They have the same tax structure, but the annuity has higher costs.[3] Therefore, this annuity is essentially a higher-cost nondeductible IRA. If Jane saves in a nondeductible IRA, she begins with a $1,000 investment of after-tax funds. The funds grow tax deferred at 8 percent for 15 years. After 15 years, the account is worth $3,172, which consists of $2,172 of tax-deferred returns plus the original $1,000 of after-tax funds. At withdrawal, she pays taxes at 28 percent on the $2,172 of deferred returns. The original $1,000 can be withdrawn tax-free. She has $2,564 of after-tax funds. To repeat, the annuity provides less wealth due to its higher costs.

These examples are sufficient to illustrate the points of this section. When saving for retirement, the Tax Code treats savings in Roth IRAs and deductible pensions much more favorably than savings in taxable accounts and annuities. In a Roth IRA, returns are tax-exempt. In a deductible pension (without matching contributions), returns are effectively tax-exempt when the tax rates are the same in the contribution and withdrawal years. The deductible pension offers an even better deal when the tax rate in the withdrawal year is lower than the tax rate in the contribution year or there is even a partial matching contribution. Moreover, the typical assumption is people will be in the same or a lower tax bracket during retirement. Under typical circumstances, returns in Roth IRAs and deductible pensions are effectively *tax-exempt* or better. In contrast, returns are taxable in taxable accounts and annuities. In annuities, returns are *tax deferred* but eventually taxed. As these examples show, there is a big difference between tax-exemption and tax deferral.

Therefore, when saving for retirement, individuals (who are not worried about creditor protection) should save all they are allowed to save (or all they can afford to save) in Roth IRAs and deductible pensions before they save in either taxable accounts or non-qualified tax-deferred annuities.

Importance of 2001 Tax Act

The 2001 Tax Act significantly increased the opportunities for individuals to invest funds more tax-efficiently than in a taxable account or non-qualified annuity. Returns in a Roth IRA are generally tax-exempt. In a deductible pension (without matching contributions), returns are effectively tax-exempt when the tax rates are the same in the contribution and withdrawal years. The deductible pension offers an even better deal when the tax rate in the withdrawal year is lower than the tax rate in the contribution year or there is even a partial matching contribution. In addition, parents can save tax-exempt for their children's education in 529 plans and Coverdell Education Savings Accounts. Individuals typically have more than one investment goal. If their only goal is retirement savings then they should fully fund Roth IRAs and deductible pensions before choosing to save additional funds in an annuity or a taxable account. If their goals include retirement savings and meeting children's education needs, then they should fund Roth IRAs, deductible pensions, and 529 plans before choosing to save additional funds in an annuity or a taxable account. Consequently, it is important to note how the Tax Act affects contribution limits to retirement accounts and 529 plans.

The Tax Act increases the annual Roth IRA contribution limit from $2,000 in 2001 to $5,000 in 2008. Thereafter, the limit will be indexed to inflation. Beginning in 2002, a special catch-up provision allows larger contributions for people age 50 or older. A similar story applies to most deductible pensions. By 2006, the maximum contribution rises to $15,000 in 401(k), 403(b), and 457 plans, and to $10,000 in SIMPLE plans. Beginning in 2002, 401(k), 403(b), and SIMPLE plans allow larger catch-up contributions to people age 50 and older, and contribution limits are indexed to inflation after 2006.

To put these numbers in perspective, consider a married couple, both age 50 by 2008. They have 401(k) plans and qualify for Roth IRA contributions. In 2008, they could each contribute $20,000 to a 401(k)—regular contribution of $15,000 plus $5,000 catch up—plus $6,000 to a Roth IRA—regular contribution of $5,000 plus $1,000 catch up. As a couple, they could invest up to $52,000 in these most-favored savings vehicles. In addition, in 2002, parents can contribute up to $11,000 each to each child's 529 plan (this contribution limit is indexed for inflation).

Creditor Protection across Savings Vehicles

There are differences in levels of creditor protection across savings vehicles. Funds in most deductible pensions offer the best protection; ERISA-qualified and profit-sharing plans are protected from creditors (see Patterson v. Shumate, 1992). Taxable accounts are not protected. The level of protection provided by IRAs and annuities varies by state, and is addressed later.

Summary thus Far

To summarize the conclusions thus far, if someone is saving for preretirement income needs, the non-qualified annuity is not an appropriate savings vehicle. If saving for retirement income needs, with few exceptions, individuals should save all they can in Roth IRAs and deductible pensions before considering a non-qualified annuity. An exception applies to individuals who need creditor protection; depending upon the state, they may choose to avoid IRAs. Since the 2001 Tax Act substantially increases the amount of funds that can be invested in deductible pensions and Roth IRAs, few individuals should consider non-qualified annuities. Of those few, some will prefer to save tax-exempt in 529 plans for children's education before saving in either an annuity or a taxable account. After fully funding deductible pensions and Roth IRAs, someone wanting to save additional funds for retirement should decide between saving in a non-qualified annuity and a taxable account. We examine this decision in the next section.

Non-qualified Annuity or Mutual Fund Held in Taxable Account?

In this section, we compare mutual funds held in non-qualified annuities and taxable accounts. We compare differences in their tax structures and other factors that may affect the choice between these two savings vehicles. The analysis considers low-cost and average-cost annuities and, not only low-cost and average-cost mutual funds, but also tax-efficient and tax-inefficient mutual funds.

Comparing Features of Annuities and Taxable Accounts

Table 5.2 presents factors that should influence the decision to save for retirement in a non-qualified annuity (henceforth, annuity) or taxable account. The annuity has one major advantage and up to two major disadvantages. The advantage is the

TABLE 5.2   Factors Affecting the Decision to Save Through a Non-qualified
Annuity or a Taxable Account

	Annuity	Taxable Account
Major Factors		
Tax-deferred Growth	Yes	No
Costs	Higher	Lower
Preferential Capital Gain Tax Rate	No	Usually
Other Factors		
Liquidity:		
—10 percent Early Withdrawal Penalty Tax Rate	Usually	No
—Insurance Company—Surrender Penalty	Usually	No
Step-up in Basis	No	Yes
Death Benefit	Yes	No
Real Option to Harvest Losses	No	Yes
Protection from Creditors, Including Lawsuits	Sometimes	No

ability to grow tax deferred. One disadvantage is its typically higher costs. The second disadvantage, which applies if the investor wants an underlying stock exposure, is that capital gains are eventually taxed at the ordinary income tax rate. In a taxable account, capital gains are usually taxed at preferential rates.

Table 5.2 also lists other factors that should influence the decision. Liquidity favors the taxable account. Withdrawals from an annuity before age 59½ are generally subject to a 10 percent penalty tax. In addition, the insurance firm usually imposes a surrender penalty. A typical surrender fee is 5 percent to 7 percent if liquidated in the first year, with the fee decreasing 1 percent per year.

The next three factors are (1) step-up in basis, (2) death benefit, and (3) real option to harvest losses. The first and third favor the taxable account, while the death benefit favors the annuity. Assets held in a taxable account receive a stepped-up basis at date of death. Suppose a husband and wife jointly own 100 shares of Microsoft purchased at $20 per share. In a community property state, the full property value receives a step-up in basis at the death of the first. For example, in Texas, a community property state, if the husband dies when the stock is selling at $70 per share the surviving wife's cost basis rises to $7,000. So, she could sell the 100 shares for $7,000 without incurring a capital gain tax. In a common law state, like Iowa, the step-up applies to half the property value. In the prior example, the wife's cost basis rises to $4,500 at her husband's death. Beginning in 2010 the step-up in basis for the surviving spouse will be limited to $4.3 million.[4] Investments do not receive the step-up in basis when held in any retirement account including an annuity.

The annuity offers a death benefit that is unique to this savings vehicle. This benefit makes the annuity an insurance product, and thus it can only be sold through an insurance firm. During the accumulation phase, a Minimum Guaranteed Death Benefit (MGDB) promises that if the investor dies after investing, say, $40,000, her beneficiary will receive the larger of $40,000 (less prior withdrawals and surrender charges) or the value of the annuity. The next section discusses the value of the death benefit.

Value of Death Benefit

This section discusses the value of an annuity's death benefit, based on the work of Milevsky and Posner (2001). It first discusses the types of death benefit and then discusses factors that should affect the value (and, hence, cost) of insurance. Finally, it summarizes Milevsky and Posner's estimates of the fair insurance values of two popular types of death benefits.

Variable annuity contracts offer several types of death benefits. The simplest type is Accumulated-value Death Benefit, where the beneficiary receives the value of the contract as of the death of the policyholder. This type, which is in approximately 20 percent of annuity contracts, merely says the beneficiary receives the value of the contract at death. It has no insurance value.

A second type, which is in about 28 percent of contracts, is a Guaranteed Minimum Death Benefit. The GMDB promises that upon the investor's involuntary death the beneficiary will receive the larger of the ending investment value and the original investment amount (reduced for subsequent withdrawals). Suppose Jane invests $40,000 in an annuity at age 50. At her death, the beneficiary receives the larger of the ending account value or $40,000 (less withdrawals).[5]

The roll-up type of death benefit guarantees that the account value will increase by at least some minimum guaranteed rate for a limited number of years. If the guaranteed rate is 5 percent then, at death, the beneficiary receives the larger of the ending account value or the original investment amount accrued at 5 percent a year (up to twice the original investment amount); the 5 percent guarantee lasts until the floor value is twice the original investment amount, or for about 14 years in this example. However, any death benefit other than the account value typically ends at age 75 or 80. Since the floor value is sometimes larger, this death benefit is clearly more valuable—and should be more costly—than the GMDB.

A step-up type of death benefit is based on a highest anniversary account value. For example, suppose Luke invests $40,000 on January 10, 2003. The contract may call for the minimum floor value to be reset at the higher of $40,000 or the value on January 10, 2008. In January 2013, the floor is reset at the higher of the floor in January 2008 or the value in January 2013.

The Accumulated-value Death Benefit has no insurance value and, henceforth, is not considered a death benefit. The other death benefits can be valued as the value of a put option with the payoff contingent upon *both* death and a decrease in the account's value. Rational pricing requires that the insurance costs vary with the insured's age, sex, and the volatility of the underlying investments. Consider the value of the GMDB to a 50-year-old male. It pays off if he dies *and* the value of the investments decreases. His annuity account—that is, the portfolio of one or more mutual funds in Figure 5.1—may consist of (1) only a money market fund, (2) only a high-grade bond fund, (3) only a stock fund, or (4) a combination of money market, bond, and stock funds. If it consists of only a money market fund, the guarantee has no value because money market funds do not lose money. If it consists of only high-grade bond funds, the death benefit has little value because there is little chance that he will die within a few years *and* high-grade bond funds will experience a loss. There is a negligible chance that a high-grade bond fund will experience a loss over horizons exceeding a few years. If it consists of a portfolio of money market, bond, and stock funds, the death benefit has little value because the annuity contract only insures the value of the entire portfolio, and not each mutual fund; thus, if one stock fund in the annuity portfolio loses $5,000 but all other funds collectively gain at least $5,000, there is no payout from the insurance company. The death benefit has its highest value when the annuity portfolio consists of one volatile fund. Milevsky and Posner estimate the fair insurance value of the death benefit when the annuity portfolio consists of one stock fund. [Technically, the value of the death benefit depends upon the volatility of the portfolio, and not on whether it consists of a stock fund or a bond fund. The authors estimated the death benefit's value for a fund with a level of volatility of 20% because it slightly exceeds the volatility of stock funds. Consequently, we refer to it as a stock fund in our analysis.] Their value estimates are too high when the portfolio contains a money market fund, a bond fund, or multiple stock funds.

Milevsky and Posner estimate the values of two types of death benefits: GMDB and roll-up with a 5 percent guaranteed interest rate. Their estimates rely on 1994 mortality tables and assume an all-stock annuity portfolio with a 20 percent annual volatility (standard deviation). A sample of the estimates of fair insurance value follows:

		Type of Death Benefit	
Age	Sex	GMDB[*]	5 percent Guaranteed Interest
50	m	0.035%	0.192%
50	f	0.02%	0.1084%
60	m	0.087%	0.375%
60	f	0.05%	0.216%

[*]GMDB denotes Guaranteed Minimum Death Benefit.

These fair insurance values are a small portion of average and median mortality and expense (M&E) fees in annuity contracts. In September 1999, the average and median M&E fees were, respectively, 1.04 percent and 1.15 percent for annuity contracts with Guaranteed Minimum Death Benefits, while the estimated fair insurance value for someone age 60 or younger was, at most, 0.087 percent. In reality, M&E fees do not vary by age, by sex, or by volatility of underlying investment. Milevsky and Posner ask, "If indeed the M&E risk charge is meant to cover mortality risk, why is it not based on mortality risk?" Also, they "detect a very strong 'clustering' effect in the M&E risk charge. . . . [A] full 40% of policies impose an M&E risk charge of exactly 125 basis points. This is regardless of age, volatility or guarantee structure. This appears to be a relic of previous regulations that capped the M&E risk charge at exactly 125 basis points." In short, M&E fees far exceed the fair insurance value of the death benefit and, in fact, are set with a complete disregard for mortality risk factors.

Assuming the annuity portfolio contains only one stock fund, Milevsky and Posner estimate that the GMDB is worth less than 10 basis points for individuals who are age 60 or less. It is less valuable if the portfolio contains a money market fund, a bond fund, or multiple stock funds. It tends to be more valuable if the individual is older than 60 or if the death benefit contains a minimum return guarantee. However, the reality is that M&E fees are not priced to reflect mortality risk and far exceed the fair insurance value of the death benefit.

Let us return to the "Other Factors" in Table 5.2. Milevsky and Panyagometh (2001) examine the role of return uncertainty on the choice between an annuity and a mutual fund held in a taxable account. The investor in a mutual fund held in a taxable account has the real option to harvest losses; if the account value declines, the investor can recognize the loss, which effectively creates a tax refund. This real option is not available on an annuity. They conclude that this real option, which is not considered in this chapter, lengthens the breakeven period—that is, the length of time before the annuity's tax-deferral benefit offsets its cost disadvantage.

The last factor is protection from creditors. Assets in mutual funds held in taxable accounts are not protected. Depending upon the state, assets in an annuity are sometimes protected. Based on Rothschild and Rubin (1999), some 32 states and the District of Columbia appear to provide no protection or limited creditor protection to annuities, while 18 states provide strong protection. Of those providing limited protection, six states protect proceeds of annuity policies only to the extent they are necessary for the reasonable support of debtor and dependents. Fifteen states and D.C. place dollar limits on assets exempt from creditors; most exempt a monthly total with a frequent exemption amount being $350 per month under all annuity contracts, while others have a maximum total-dollar exemption of say $10,000. Eleven states provide no creditor protection or protection that is limited to one or more sections of the Tax Code such as 408 that applies to IRAs. Of the 18 that appear to provide strong protection, two limit protection on contributions made shortly before filing bankruptcy. For additional information, see Fair (1993) and Spero (2001).

"Guaranteed lifetime income" is often considered an annuity benefit. It is not listed in the table because it is not unique to the annuity. The investor could save in a taxable account and, at retirement, cash it in and buy an immediate annuity with a lifetime income guarantee. Both savings vehicles provide the option of a lifetime income guarantee.[6]

Since annuities are designed for someone saving for postretirement needs, their liquidity impairments should seldom come into play. The stepped-up basis and real option to harvest losses favor the taxable account, while the death benefit and protection from creditors favor the annuity. These factors are at least partially offsetting. Most individuals should choose between an annuity and taxable account based on these savings vehicles' abilities to provide after-tax wealth. The analysis that follows is for these individuals. Therefore, it concentrates on the three major factors.

Accumulation and Distribution Phases

Annuitization is a unique feature of the distribution phase. When an annuity is annuitized, it is exchanged for a guaranteed monthly income for the rest of the contract owner's life or, more commonly, the rest of the contract owner and his or her spouse's lives. At the death of the last to survive, the investment usually has no remaining value. A major benefit of annuitization is the guarantee that the holder will never run out of money.

Some 98 percent of individuals who invest in non-qualified annuities do *not* annuitize.[7] When it is not annuitized, the individual decides when, and how much, to withdraw during retirement. Once annuitized, the investor loses control over the amount of funds that can be withdrawn each year. Few investors appear willing to give up that control. When it is not annuitized and funds remain after death, they are bequeathed to the spouse, children, or whomever. Annuity buyers who do not annuitize are interested in the annuity's accumulation feature—tax-deferred growth—but they are not interested in its unique distribution feature—annuitization. The remaining 2 percent of annuity buyers are interested in both features. As we shall see, an *average-cost* annuity is not an optimal accumulation vehicle. As a distribution vehicle, annuitization provides a guaranteed lifetime income. It provides a unique hedge against longevity risk—the risk, in terms of running out of money, of living longer than expected.

Cost Structures

Table 5.3 presents average expenses on annuities and mutual funds held in taxable accounts. For annuities, fund expense denotes the annual expense ratio on the underlying mutual funds. Insurance expense is the sum of the mortality and expense (M&E) fee plus all other administrative and distribution expenses. Annuities' total expense averages 2 percent a year on bond funds and 2.1 percent a year on stock funds. In addition, annuities impose an annual fixed-dollar contract charge on 86 percent of bond funds that averages $26 per year across all bond funds. The same percentage and average cost apply to stock funds. Only 2 percent to 3 percent of annuities charge a front-end load, but over 90 percent have a contingent surrender fee. Annuities typically allow penalty-free withdrawals of up to 10 percent of principal each year. Withdrawals beyond this amount are subject to the surrender fee. A typical surrender fee is 6 percent of withdrawals beyond

TABLE 5.3 Average Costs of Variable Annuities and Mutual Funds Held in Taxable Accounts ·

	Variable Annuity[2]		Mutual Fund[2]	
	Bonds	Stocks	Bonds	Stocks
Fund Expense	0.69%	0.79%	1.12%	1.43%
Insurance Expense	1.31%	1.31%	NA	NA
Total Expense	2.00%	2.10%	1.12%	1.43%
Contract Charge	$26	$26	NA	NA
Front-load	0.05%	0.10%	1.44%	1.73%
Deferred Load	6.29% cont.[1]	6.27% cont.[1]	1.01%	1.12%

[1]Cont. denotes a load that is contingent upon the time between investment and withdrawal of funds.

[2]For annuities, the bond fund sample consists of mutual funds in all variable annuities, except qualified-only annuities, with a fixed-income Morningstar Category and net assets of at least $25 million. The minimum size constraint eliminates funds with few assets but does not appreciably affect average costs. The stock fund sample consists of mutual funds in all variable annuities, except qualified-only annuities, with a domestic stock or international stock Morningstar Category and net assets of at least $50 million. For taxable accounts, the mutual fund samples correspond to the annuity samples. The bond fund sample consists of all funds with Morningstar Category of taxable bonds that are not restricted to institutions or closed to new investments and have net assets of at least $25 million. The stock fund sample is similar except it includes domestic and international stock funds and has a $50 million size restriction. *Sources:* January 2001 versions of *Morningstar's Principia Pro for Variable Annuities/Life* and *Morningstar Principia Pro for Mutual Funds.*

the free-withdrawal amount in the first year of the contract, with the penalty rate decreasing 1 percent a year.

For mutual funds held in taxable accounts, the annual expense ratio averages 1.12 percent on bond funds and 1.43 percent on stock funds. Mutual funds do not charge an annual contract fee. Some 63 percent of mutual funds do not have a front-end load, but it averages 1.44 percent on all bond funds and 1.73 percent on all stock funds. Some 68 percent of mutual funds do not have a deferred load, but it averages a little over 1 percent on all funds.

This study assumes the following cost structures. An average-cost annuity has a 2 percent total expense ratio when the underlying asset is a bond fund and a 2.1 percent expense ratio when the asset is a stock fund. In addition, each has a contract charge of $26 a year. A low-cost annuity has a 0.6 percent expense ratio and no annual contract charge. By intent, this chapter's low-cost annuity reflects the opportunities that are available to knowledgeable investors. Table 5.4 presents a list of low-cost annuities. The average-cost bond mutual fund has a 1.1 percent expense ratio, a 1.4 percent front-end load, and a 1 percent deferred load. The average-cost active stock fund has a 1.4 percent expense ratio, a 1.7 percent front-end load, and

TABLE 5.4 Low-cost Variable Annuities

TIAA-CREF Life Funds: DCR Rating: AAA, AM Best Rating: A++, (800) 223–1200

Subaccount Name	Total Expense Ratio[1]	Annual Contract Charge	Morningstar Category[2]	Benchmark	Minimum Initial Purchase
Growth Equity	0.55%	None	Large Growth	Russell 3000 Growth Index	$250
Growth & Income	0.53	None	Large Blend	S&P 500 Index	250
International Equity	0.59	None	Foreign Stock	MSCI EAFE Index[3]	250
Stock Index	0.37	None	Large Blend	Russell 3000 Index	250
Social Choice Equity	0.48	None	Large Blend	Russell 3000 Index	250

Vanguard Variable Annuity Funds: DCR Rating: AA, AM Best Rating: A+, (800) 523–9954

Subaccount Name	Total Expense Ratio	Annual Contract Charge[4]	Morningstar Category	Benchmark	Minimum Initial Purchase
Money Market	0.53%	$25	Money Market		$5,000
Total Bond Market	0.57	25	Inter-term Bond	Lehman Aggregate Bond Index	5,000
High Yield Bond	0.63	25	High Yield Bond		5,000
Short-term Corporate	0.56	25	Short-term Bond		5,000
Balanced	0.65	25	Domestic Hybrid		5,000
Diversified Value	0.83	25	Large Value		5,000
Equity Income	0.67	25	Large Value		5,000
Equity Index	0.53	25	Large Blend	S&P 500 Index	5,000
Growth	0.74	25	Large Growth		5,000
Mid-cap Index	0.65	25	Medium Blend	S&P MidCap 400 Index	5,000
REIT Index	0.74	25	Small Value	Morgan Stanley REIT Index	5,000
Small Comp. Growth	0.86	25	Small Growth		5,000
International	0.78	25	Foreign Stock		5,000

[1] These are the expense ratios for a recent year. TIAA-CREF Life and the funds advisor currently waive certain fees.
[2] Morningstar Categories are set consistent with the benchmark portfolio.
[3] Morgan Stanley Capital International—Europe, Australasia, Far East Index
[4] Applies to contracts valued at less than $25,000 at the time of purchase and on the last business day of each year. None of these variable annuities has either a front-end load or a surrender charge.
Source: http://www.tiaa-cref.org; http://www.vanguard.com; and *Morningstar's Principia Pro for Variable Annuities/Life* (January 2001).

a 1.1 percent deferred load. Low-cost bond and stock funds have 0.30 percent expense ratios and no loads. The low-cost active stock fund realizes all capital gains after one year and one day, while the passive stock fund realizes 5 percent of capital gains each year. Cost structures are remarkably stable at annuities and mutual funds. Thus, an average-cost or a low-cost alternative will likely remain, respectively, average cost or low cost.

The analysis assumes that 1 percent higher costs reduce net returns—the returns that investors receive—by 1 percent. For money market funds, Domian and Reichenstein (1997) conclude that each 1 percent of expense reduces net returns by 1 percent. For bond funds, Blake, Elton, and Gruber (1993), Reichenstein (1999a), and Domian and Reichenstein (2002) conclude that each 1 percent of expense reduces net returns by, on average, about 1 percent. For stock funds, Bogle (1998) and Peterson, Pietranico, Riepe, and Xu (2001) conclude that each 1 percent of expense reduces net returns by, respectively, 1.30 percent and 1.15 percent. Furthermore, most of annuities' higher expenses are associated with sales commissions. It is difficult to understand how a commission paid to a salesman is supposed to raise the gross return on a mutual fund held within an annuity. How does the salesman's commission make someone else—the fund manager—a better investor?

In addition, the analysis assumes there is no relationship between turnover ratio and net return. For the samples in Table 5.3, the average turnover ratio is lower in annuities than in mutual funds. Among bond funds, it is 120 percent at annuities and 143 percent at mutual funds. Among stock funds, it is 76 percent and 99 percent, respectively. If a lower turnover ratio raises net returns, then an annuity's lower turnover ratios would partially offset its higher costs. If true, this would improve the relative prospects of an average-cost annuity compared to an average-cost mutual fund. However, low-cost annuities and low-cost mutual funds have lower turnover ratios than average-cost annuities. For example, average turnover ratios for bond and stock mutual funds with expense ratios of 0.4 percent or lower are 97 percent and 35 percent, respectively. Thus, if turnover affects net returns, this study understates the relative advantage of both a low-cost annuity and a low-cost mutual fund compared to an average-cost annuity. In short, if higher turnover reduces net returns, then this study makes average-cost annuities look too good, and knowledgeable investors have yet another reason to invest in low-cost annuities and low-cost mutual funds.

Comparing Retirement Incomes

Jane, the representative investor, has already saved all she is allowed to save in Roth IRAs and deductible pensions. Moreover, if she has children with education needs, she would probably want to fund these needs before deciding between a non-qualified annuity and a mutual fund held in a taxable account. She invests $40,000 of additional funds in a non-qualified tax-deferred annuity or a mutual fund held in a taxable account.[8] Figure 5.3 presents the investment possibilities. The underlying

Investment	Bond Fund	Stock Fund
Saving	Average-cost annuity	Average-cost annuity
vehicles	Low-cost annuity	Low-cost annuity
	Average-cost bond fund	Average-cost active stock fund
	Low-cost bond fund	Low-cost active stock fund
		Low-cost passive stock fund

FIGURE 5.3:   Jane's Investment Choices after Fully Funding Roth IRAs and Deductible Pensions

asset can be a bond fund or a stock fund. The bond fund can be held in one of four savings vehicles: average-cost annuity, low-cost annuity, average-cost bond fund, or low-cost bond fund. The stock fund can be held in one of five savings vehicles: average-cost annuity, low-cost annuity, average-cost active stock fund, low-cost active stock fund, or low-cost passive stock fund.

Gross bond returns average 5.5 percent or 8 percent. On August 26, 2002, yields to maturity on 5-, 10-, and 30-year Treasury securities were 3.28 percent, 4.22 percent, and 5.01 percent. Therefore, for the next decade, returns on the benchmark 10-year Treasury will be below 5 percent. High-grade corporate bond returns will probably be somewhat higher, perhaps 5.5 percent. Gross stock returns average 8 percent or 12 percent. Due to today's lofty stock market multiples, several experts conclude that long-horizon stock returns will likely average 8 percent or less.[9] The 12 percent exceeds the historic geometric average return on the S&P 500 since 1926.

The analysis considers two sets of tax rates. In the first set, Jane's ordinary income tax rate is 25 percent both before and during retirement. In the second set, her ordinary income tax rate falls from 33 percent before retirement to 25 percent after retirement. This set is appropriate for individuals in high tax brackets before retirement. Due to the 2001 Tax Act, people with real incomes subject to the 28 percent marginal tax bracket in 2000 will be in the 25 percent bracket by 2006. In both sets of tax rates, she pays taxes at 20 percent on realized capital gains held more than one year but less than five and at 18 percent on realized gains held more than five years. These capital gain tax rates are the current rates and apply before and during retirement.

Bond interest is tax deferred in annuities and taxed each year in taxable accounts. Stock returns are tax deferred in annuities. The tax treatment of stock returns in taxable accounts is more complex. For the two active stock funds, we assume 2 percent of each year's gross return is dividends plus short-term capital gains that are taxed at 25 percent, and the remainder is capital gains that are realized in one year and one day and taxed at 20 percent. If gross stock returns are 8 percent, each year the average-cost active stock fund distributes net income of 0.6 percent—the 2 percent less 1.4 percent expense ratio—and the 6 percent capital gain is realized and taxed at 20 percent. It grows at a 5.25 percent after-tax rate of return $[0.6\% \cdot (1 - 0.25) + 6\% \cdot (1 - 0.20)]$. The low-cost active stock fund has a 0.3 percent expense ratio and grows at a 6.075 percent after-tax rate of return $[1.7\% \cdot (1 - 0.25) + 6\% \cdot (1 - 0.20)]$. These active stock funds are not tax efficient; they realize some short-term capital gains each year and never benefit from the tax deferral of unrealized gains. The passive stock index fund is tax efficient. Each year it distributes little net income—only 0.9 percent—and realizes few capital gains—5 percent of capital gains. Therefore, most of the passive fund's returns grow unrealized—just like the annuity—but it avoids the annuity's higher costs.

In each case, the original $40,000 investment provides a constant after-tax retirement income for 25 years. Jane does not annuitize. The level of retirement income depends upon several factors: bond or stock fund, rate of return, and tax rates. For each savings vehicle, Tables 5.4 through 5.7 present levels of after-tax retirement incomes for combinations of these factors. They will help us determine when it makes sense to save in a non-qualified annuity. Appendices 5.1, 5.2, and 5.3 demonstrate the calculations of the constant after-tax retirement income. The models are available for download at www.wiley.com/go/reichenstein.

Same Tax Bracket before and during Retirement

Tables 5.5 and 5.6 compare after-tax retirement incomes from each savings vehicle when the individual is in the same tax bracket before and during retirement. Table 5.5 presents retirement incomes when the underlying assets are bonds. The major lessons from this table are:

■ Costs matter! The low-cost savings vehicles always provide the highest after-tax retirement incomes. The low-cost annuity and low-cost bond fund always provide more retirement income than the average-cost annuity and average-cost bond fund.

■ Knowledgeable investors who want a bond investment should compare the low-cost annuity to the low-cost bond fund. Based on current bond yields, gross returns on high-grade bonds will average about 5.5 percent. Assuming 5.5 percent returns, the breakeven period for the low-cost annuity (compared to the low-cost bond fund) is 12 years; that is, it takes 12 years (rounded to the nearest year) for the benefit of tax deferral to offset the low-cost annuity's 0.3 percent cost disadvantage.

■ If interest rates rise on high-grade bonds to 8 percent, the incomes for 8 percent gross returns will prove useful for comparing new investments at that time. The low-cost annuity's breakeven period (compared to the low-cost bond fund) is six years. If everything else remains the same, a higher interest rate favors the annuity and lowers the breakeven period.

■ The income from the average-cost annuity never matches the income from the low-cost bond fund. The annuity's tax-deferral advantage never offsets its cost disadvantage.

■ Some individuals buy an annuity for its protection against lawsuits. They should first fully fund ERISA-qualified plans. Annuities may offer the next-best protection. If so, investors should next compare low-cost and average-cost annuities. A low-cost annuity provides substantially higher income than an average-cost annuity. Assuming 5.5 percent gross returns, the low-cost annuity provides 27 percent more retirement income for someone retiring in 10 years and 46 percent more for someone retiring in 20 years.

■ Some prior studies only compare incomes or ending wealth from an average-cost annuity and an average-cost mutual fund. At 5.5 percent gross returns, the average-cost annuity never offsets its higher costs compared to an average-cost bond fund. Even at 8 percent gross returns, the breakeven period exceeds 20 years. However, studies that ignore the low-cost alternatives ignore the relevant comparison for knowledgeable investors.

It is easy to explain the importance of costs. Suppose gross returns average 5.5 percent. *Ignoring the $26 annual contract charge,* the average-cost annuity provides a 3.5 percent tax-deferred net return. From the investor's perspective, its 2 percent expense ratio is like a 36.4 percent tax rate [2% / 5.5%]. Meanwhile, the 3.5 percent is not tax-exempt; it is merely tax deferred. The low-cost bond fund pro-

---

TABLE 5.5   After-tax Retirement Incomes from Bond Funds Held in Annuities and Taxable Accounts: Same Tax Bracket before and during Retirement*

Years until Age 65	Gross Bond Returns	Average-cost Annuity	Low-cost Annuity	Average-cost Bond Fund	Low-cost Bond Fund
0	5.5%	$2,127	$2,386	$2,244	$2,438
	8.0	2,563	2,839	2,680	2,895
10	5.5	2,791	3,534	3,105	3,575
	8.0	4,181	5,276	4,440	5,076
20	5.5	3,761	5,484	4,295	5,241
	8.0	7,243	10,525	7,353	8,899
30	5.5	5,152	8,672	5,943	7,684
	8.0	12,780	21,303	12,178	15,602

*Zero, 10, 20, or 30 years before retirement, the individual invests $40,000 in either a non-qualified annuity or a mutual fund held in a taxable account. The dollar amounts are the constant annual after-tax incomes she can withdraw each year for 25 years during retirement. Gross bond returns are 5.5 percent or 8 percent. The average-cost annuity has a 2 percent annual expense ratio and $26 annual contract fee. The low-cost annuity has a 0.6 percent expense ratio and no contract fee. The average-cost bond fund has a 1.1 percent expense ratio, 1.4 percent front-end load, and 1 percent deferred load. The low-cost bond fund has a 0.3 percent expense ratio and no loads. Tax rates on ordinary income are 25 percent before and during retirement.

vides a 5.2 percent net return and a 3.90 percent after-tax return [5.2% • (1 − 0.25)]. Obviously, the low-cost bond fund's 3.90 percent *after-tax return* beats the average-cost annuity's 3.5 percent *tax-deferred return,* and the longer the investment horizon, the larger the ending-wealth advantage. The average-cost annuity's advantage of tax-deferred growth never offsets its 1.7 percent cost disadvantage.

Now compare the low-cost annuity and low-cost bond fund. The low-cost annuity provides a 4.9 percent tax-deferred return, while the low-cost bond fund provides a 3.90 percent after-tax return. It takes 12 years for the advantage of tax-deferred growth to offset the low-cost mutual fund's 0.3 percent cost advantage.

Many financial advisors have read Huggard (1999 and 2001), which compare investments in annuities and average-cost mutual funds (held in taxable accounts). His work consistently favors annuities over mutual funds. It is important, therefore, to point out problems in his analyses. Critiques of his work are available under "Research" at http://finance.baylor.edu/reichenstein.

Table 5.6 presents the retirement incomes when the underlying investment is a stock fund. The major lessons of this table can be quickly covered:

■ Again, costs matter! The three best savings vehicles are the low-cost ones.

■ Knowledgeable investors who want a stock investment, and who can and will passively manage stocks, should compare the low-cost annuity to the low-cost passive stock fund. The low-cost passive stock fund almost always provides the higher retirement income. Investors who can and will allow capital gains to accrue unrealized will fare better by *passively* managing stocks in a taxable account. Passive investors as defined here are those who passively manage a portfolio of individual stocks or invest in a passively managed stock fund, such as many index funds. However, the key is to allow unrealized gains to grow unharvested for many, many years.

■ Many knowledgeable investors cannot or will not passively manage stocks. They should compare the low-cost annuity to the low-cost active stock fund. Assuming 8 percent returns, it takes 12 years for this annuity's tax-deferral benefit to offset the active fund's cost advantage. Assuming 12 percent returns, the breakeven period is seven years.

■ Some individuals buy an annuity for its protection against lawsuits. They should first fully fund ERISA-qualified plans. Annuities may offer the next-best protection. If so, they should next compare low-cost and average-cost annuities. A low-cost annuity provides substantially higher income than an average-cost annuity. Assuming 8 percent gross returns, the low-cost annuity provides 28 percent more retirement income for someone retiring in 10 years and 49 percent more for someone retiring in 20 years.

■ Some prior studies compare an average-cost active annuity and an average-cost active mutual fund. At 8 percent gross returns, the average-cost annuity does not offset its higher costs even for someone retiring in 30 years. At 12 percent returns, the average-cost annuity offsets its higher costs after about 11 years.

However, studies that ignore the low-cost alternatives ignore the relevant comparison for knowledgeable investors.

Recall that when the investments are bonds, the low-cost annuity provides more income than the low-cost bond fund at sufficiently long investment horizons. When the investments are passively held stocks, it takes 30 years and a 12 percent return for the low-cost annuity to provide as high an income as the low-cost passive stock fund. It is easy to explain why. Bond interest is tax deferred in the annuity and fully taxable in the taxable bond fund. Thus, the benefit of tax deferral eventually exceeds the annuity's higher cost. When the assets are stocks held passively, net returns are tax deferred in the annuity, but most returns are tax deferred in a passive stock fund, too. In addition, capital gains are eventually taxed at 25 percent in the annuity and 18 percent in the passive index fund.

TABLE 5.6   After-tax Retirement Incomes from Stock Funds Held in Annuities and Taxable Accounts: Same Tax Bracket before and during Retirement*

Years until Age 65	Gross Stock Returns	Average-cost Annuity	Low-cost Annuity	Average-cost Active Stock Fund	Low-cost Active Stock Fund	Low-cost Passive Stock Fund
0	8%	$2,545	$2,839	$2,688	$2,971	$3,090
	12	3,301	3,616	3,489	3,810	4,036
10	8	4,114	5,276	4,483	5,358	5,919
	12	7,756	9,791	7,853	9,250	10,897
20	8	7,055	10,525	7,478	9,664	11,488
	12	19,697	28,602	17,673	22,456	30,141
30	8	12,326	21,303	12,475	17,429	22,396
	12	50,444	84,017	39,774	54,519	83,855

*Zero, 10, 20, or 30 years before retirement, the individual invests $40,000 in either a non-qualified annuity or a mutual fund held in a taxable account. The dollar amounts are the constant annual after-tax incomes she can withdraw each year for 25 years during retirement. Gross stock returns are 8 percent or 12 percent. The average-cost annuity has a 2.1 percent annual expense ratio and $26 annual contract fee. The low-cost annuity has a 0.6 percent expense ratio and no contract fee. The average-cost stock fund has a 1.4 percent expense ratio, 1.7 percent front-end load, and 1.1 percent deferred load. The low-cost stock funds have a 0.3 percent expense ratio and no loads. The active stock funds generate 2 percent gross dividends plus short-term gains each year, while the remainder is long-term capital gains that are realized in one year and one day. The passive fund generates 1.2 percent gross dividends and realizes 5 percent of unrealized capital gains each year. Tax rates on ordinary income are 25 percent before retirement and during retirement. Capital gains tax rates are 20 percent for active stock funds and 18 percent for the passive fund.

Lower Tax Bracket during Retirement

Tables 5.7 and 5.8 compare after-tax retirement incomes from each savings vehicle when the individual is in the 33 percent tax bracket before retirement and the 25 percent bracket during retirement. The assumed 8 percent decrease in tax bracket at retirement is a hefty decrease. This improves the comparative position of annuities since their returns are not only tax deferred, but they are also taxed at a lower rate. Tables 5.7 and 5.8 present the retirement incomes when the underlying assets are, respectively, bonds and stocks. The major points from these tables are:

- Again, costs matter! The low-cost vehicles always provide the highest retirement incomes.

- When the underlying assets are bonds, the low-cost annuity often provides a higher retirement income than the low-cost bond fund. At 5.5 percent gross returns, the breakeven period is six years. At 8 percent, it is three years. At today's yields, knowledgeable investors more than six years from retirement should prefer the low-cost annuity, while investors within six years of retirement should prefer the low-cost bond fund.

TABLE 5.7   After-tax Retirement Incomes from Bond Funds Held in Annuities and Taxable Accounts: Lower Tax Bracket during Retirement than before Retirement*

Years until Age 65	Gross Bond Returns	Average-cost Annuity	Low-cost Annuity	Average-cost Bond Fund	Low-cost Bond Fund
0	5.5%	$2,127	$2,386	$2,244	$2,438
	8	2,563	2,839	2,680	2,895
10	5.5	2,791	3,534	3,000	3,434
	8	4,181	5,276	4,212	4,788
20	5.5	3,761	5,484	4,012	4,837
	8	7,243	10,525	6,618	7,918
30	5.5	5,152	8,672	5,365	6,812
	8	12,780	21,303	10,400	13,094

*Zero, 10, 20, or 30 years before retirement, the individual invests $40,000 in either a non-qualified annuity or a mutual fund held in a taxable account. The dollar amounts are the constant annual after-tax incomes she can withdraw each year for 25 years during retirement. Gross bond returns are 5.5 percent or 8 percent. The average-cost annuity has a 2 percent annual expense ratio and $26 annual contract fee. The low-cost annuity has a 0.6 percent expense ratio and no contract fee. The average-cost bond fund has a 1.1 percent expense ratio, 1.4 percent front-end load, and 1 percent deferred load. The low-cost bond fund has a 0.3 percent expense ratio and no loads. Tax rates on ordinary income are 33 percent before retirement and 25 percent during retirement.

■ When the underlying assets are stocks and the investment horizon is less than 30 years, the low-cost passive stock fund continues to beat the low-cost annuity. At 30 years, the amounts are comparable.

■ Many individuals cannot or will not passively manage stocks. They should compare the low-cost annuity to the low-cost active stock fund. At 8 percent gross returns, the breakeven period is about 10 years. At 12 percent, it is six years.

■ Some individuals buy an annuity for its protection against lawsuits. They should first fully fund ERISA-qualified plans. If annuities provide the next-best protection then they should compare low-cost and average-cost annuities. As before, the low-cost annuity provides substantially higher incomes than the average-cost annuity.

■ Some prior studies only compare an average-cost annuity and an average-cost mutual fund. Assuming 5.5 percent gross bond returns, the average-cost annuity does not offset its higher costs even for someone retiring in 30 years. Assuming

TABLE 5.8   After-tax Retirement Incomes from Stock Funds Held in Annuities and Taxable Accounts: Lower Tax Bracket during Retirement than before Retirement*

Years until Age 65	Gross Stock Returns	Average-cost Annuity	Low-cost Annuity	Average-cost Stock Fund	Low-cost Active Stock Fund	Low-cost Passive Stock Fund
0	8%	$2,545	$2,839	$2,688	$2,971	$3,090
	12	3,301	3,616	3,489	3,810	4,036
10	8	4,114	5,276	4,463	5,290	5,878
	12	7,756	9,791	7,818	9,135	10,824
20	8	7,055	10,525	7,410	9,419	11,329
	12	19,697	28,602	17,517	21,904	29,737
30	8	12,326	21,303	12,305	16,771	21,931
	12	50,444	84,017	39,250	52,519	82,172

*Zero, 10, 20, or 30 years before retirement, the individual invests $40,000 in either a non-qualified annuity or a mutual fund held in a taxable account. The dollar amounts are the constant annual after-tax incomes she can withdraw each year for 25 years during retirement. Gross stock returns are 8 percent or 12 percent. The average-cost annuity has a 2.1 percent annual expense ratio and $26 annual contract fee. The low-cost annuity has a 0.6 percent expense ratio and no contract fee. The average-cost stock fund has a 1.4 percent expense ratio, 1.7 percent front-end load, and 1.1 percent deferred load. The low-cost stock funds have a 0.3 percent expense ratio and no loads. The active stock funds generate 2 percent gross dividends plus short-term gains each year, while the remainder is long-term capital gains that are realized in one year and one day. The passive fund generates 1.2 percent gross dividends and realizes 5 percent of unrealized capital gains each year. Tax rates on ordinary income are 33 percent before retirement and 25 percent during retirement. Capital gains tax rates are 20 percent for active stock funds and 18 percent for the passive fund.

8 percent stock returns, the average-cost annuity barely offsets its higher costs after 30 years. However, studies that ignore the low-cost alternatives ignore the relevant comparison for knowledgeable investors.

Advocates of non-qualified annuities like to point out that, when the individual will be in a lower tax bracket during retirement, the annuity not only provides tax deferral but also returns are eventually taxed at lower rates. In this example, returns are deferred and eventually taxed at 25 percent instead of 33 percent. This gives annuities an important advantage compared to bond mutual funds because bond interest is passed through to the mutual fund investor. However, the 33 percent tax rate before retirement does little to improve annuities compared to active or passive stock funds. Since only a small portion of stock fund returns is taxed at the higher 33 percent rate, there is little difference between their retirement incomes in Tables 5.6 and 5.8. For example, only 1.7 percent of the low-cost active fund's returns is taxed at 33 percent, where 1.7 percent is 2 percent dividend plus short-term capital gain less 0.3 percent expense ratio. The remainder of its returns is taxed at 20 percent, which is less than the 25 percent tax rate annuities eventually pay on gains.

Distribution Phase

The purpose of this section is to explain what it means to annuitize an annuity and to discuss its pros and cons. Suppose Jane, age 65, invested $40,000 20 years ago in a non-qualified annuity. Today, it is worth $100,000, the original $40,000 of principal plus $60,000 of tax-deferred returns. How can she use the annuity to finance her retirement needs?

She has two choices. She can annuitize the annuity or simply withdraw funds as needed from the annuity. Suppose she annuitizes and exchanges the $100,000 for a lifetime guaranteed income (with no period-certain guarantee). Depending upon the levels of current interest rates, she may receive $637 a month for the rest of her life. However, when she dies, there is no remaining value for her beneficiaries. Alternatively, if she does not annuitize, she can withdraw as much or as little of the funds as she wishes whenever she wishes. Obviously, if she does not annuitize, she could exhaust the value of the annuity before her death. But if funds remain after her death, they are available to her beneficiaries. Some 98 percent of people prefer the flexibility of not annuitizing.

We discuss two advantages and one disadvantage of annuitization. The advantages include a guaranteed lifetime income and tax advantages. Concerning the tax advantage, if Jane does not annuitize, withdrawals are considered "interest first" and are thus fully taxable.[10] If she annuitizes, part of each monthly payment for 20 years—her approximate life expectancy—is considered a tax-exempt return of principal. The disadvantage of annuitization is that the annuity usually has no remaining value upon her death. To partially offset this disadvantage, Jane could exchange the annuity for a lower guaranteed monthly income but with the guarantee that she or her beneficiary will receive the monthly income for a minimum of, say, 20 years. The remainder of this section examines the advantage of the lifetime income guarantee, an advantage that, we believe, is not fully appreciated. The numbers are based on a study by Ameriks, Veres, and Warshawsky (2001).

Jane, age 65, has financial assets worth $1 million. Her goal is to withdraw $45,000 the first year of retirement and an inflation-adjusted $45,000 each year thereafter. What is the probability that she will not be able to withdraw an inflation-adjusted $45,000 a year for the rest of her life? To answer this question, consider the following three portfolios. In the first, she invests the $1 million in a 40 percent stocks, 40 percent bonds, and 20 percent cash portfolio. In the second, she uses $250,000 to buy a single premium immediate fixed annuity, which is immediately annuitized. The remaining $750,000 is invested in a 60 percent stocks, 30 percent bonds, and 10 percent cash portfolio. The third portfolio uses $500,000 to buy an immediate fixed annuity, and the remaining $500,000 is invested in an 85 percent stocks and 15 percent bonds portfolio. The annuitized annuity can be thought of as a "bond" in that it provides a fixed payment, but in this case for the rest of her life. Each portfolio contains a similar amount of stocks and fixed-income securities when the annuity is considered a bond.

Portfolio	SPIA* "Bond"	Stocks	Bonds	Cash	Stocks	Fixed Income
Balanced	$ 0	$400,000	$400,000	$200,000	$400,000	$600,000
Growth	250,000	450,000	225,000	75,000	450,000	550,000
Aggressive	500,000	425,000	75,000	0	425,000	575,000

*SPIA stands for single premium immediate annuity.

Ameriks, Veres, and Warshawsky estimate the probability that she will not be able to withdraw an inflation-adjusted $45,000 a year for the rest of her life. Table 5.9 indicates the failure rate; that is, the probability of not being able to maintain a $45,000 a year real income for the rest of her life. Their estimation procedure uses Monte Carlo simulation. The simulations are based on 1946 to 1999 monthly returns on S&P 500, five-year Treasury notes, and one-month Treasury bills reduced by 1 percent to reflect management fees. They simulate 10,000 separate 50-year periods. For each simulation, the future is simulated by randomly drawing return and inflation data one month at a time, with replacement, from the 1946 to 1999 historical monthly data. They then record the failure rates after 20, 25, 30, 35, 40, 45, and 50 years for each portfolio. Table 5.9 summarizes the key comparisons.

The balanced portfolio with none of the portfolio annuitized failed 8.1 percent of the time after 25 years, 23.7 percent after 30 years, and 41.1 percent after 35 years. The growth portfolio with $250,000 annuitized failed 2.6 percent of the time after 25 years, 7.8 percent after 30 years, and 14.3 percent after 35 years. The

TABLE 5.9   Failure Rates When Withdrawing 4.5 Percent of the Portfolio the First Year and an Inflation-Adjusted Equivalent Amount Each Year Thereafter

Lifetime	Balanced Portfolio and None Annuitized	Growth Portfolio and 25% Annuitized	Aggressive Portfolio and 50% Annuitized
20 years	0.9%	0.4%	0.1%
25	8.1	2.6	0.9
30	23.7	7.8	2.5
35	41.1	14.3	5.0
40	55.4	21.2	7.4

Source: Ameriks, Veres, and Warshawsky (2001).

aggressive portfolio with $500,000 annuitized failed 0.9 percent of the time after 25 years, 2.5 percent after 30 years, and 5.0 percent after 35 years. Since the portfolios have similar stock exposures, the decrease in failure rates is primarily attributable to the benefits of annuitization.

If the 65-year-old knew she would only live 20 more years, there is little chance of her running out of money with any of the three combined portfolios previously discussed. However, she may live longer. If she lives to age 95, her failure rate is 23.7 percent if she invests the $1 million in the balanced portfolio. The failure rate falls to 7.8 percent if she buys a $250,000 immediate fixed annuity and invests the remainder in the growth portfolio. The failure rate drops to 2.5 percent if she buys a $500,000 annuity and invests the remainder in the aggressive portfolio.

There are two reasons for these dramatic decreases in failure rate. First, annuitization provides a natural hedge against longevity risk; by design, the longer someone lives, the higher is its total return. Second, annuitization allows someone to receive more income from bonds than would be available without annuitization. Suppose long-term interest rates are 5.5 percent, and a 65-year-old single female is considering annuitizing a $100,000 bond portfolio. If she does not annuitize, the only way she can be sure of not outliving the bonds' value is to live on interest only. She could consume the $5,500 a year in interest income. In contrast, if she annuitizes, the $100,000 may provide $7,932 a year for the rest of her life.[11] If she withdrew this amount without annuitizing, the funds would be exhausted after 20 years, her life expectancy. Due to the pooling of risk, an insurance firm can guarantee her $7,932 a year for the rest of her life. In essence, the insurance firm uses funds remaining from those who die sooner than expected to pay those who live longer than expected.

Since many scholars predict long-run stock returns will be below historic levels, future failure rates for an initial 4.5 percent withdrawal may exceed those estimated by Ameriks, Veres, and Warshawsky. Perhaps a 4 percent withdrawal rate may be advisable today. Nevertheless, annuitizing part of the portfolio should continue to enhance people's ability to maintain a desired standard of living for the rest of their lives.

Incentives

The analysis in the prior sections implies that few individuals should buy a non-qualified annuity. Before buying this annuity, at a minimum, they should first fully fund deductible pensions and Roth IRAs. The analysis implies that these annuities make the most sense for individuals concerned about creditor protection and the young. Average-cost annuities are never in the best interest of the investor. Yet, LIMRA International (1999) reports non-qualified annuity sales of $66 billion, the average age of buyers is 63, and only 11 percent are bought by individuals younger than 45. Moreover, Reichenstein (2000b) reports that 95 percent of stock funds in annuities have annual expenses of at least 1.5 percent. This section tries to explain why the profile of non-qualified annuity buyers is so different from the profile of buyers for whom they are best suited.

Non-qualified annuities are complex contracts. Few individuals walk into a broker's office saying "I want to buy a non-qualified annuity." They are *sold* and, in our opinion, the incentive structures surrounding annuity sales best explain why commission-based professionals frequently push an annuity even when it is not in the client's best interest. Also, incentive structures explain why fee-only professionals sometimes discourage clients from buying an annuity when it is in the client's best interest.

Suppose a client asks a commission-based broker to help her invest $40,000. The broker gets no commission if she does any of the following: increases her 401(k) or Roth IRA contribution, buys a no-load low-cost annuity, or buys a no-load mutual fund. If she buys an average-cost mutual fund with a 3 percent front-end load, the broker and his or her firm share $1,200. If she buys an average-cost annuity, the broker and his or her firm may share a 6 percent commission or $2,400. It is in the broker's interest to recommend the high-commission annuity.

This average-cost annuity will probably have a 6 percent surrender fee, since the insurance company needs to cover the sales commission. If the client opts out of the contract within one year, she owes the 6 percent surrender fee, which allows the insurance firm to cover the commission. The surrender fee typically falls 1 percent a year. If the client opts out after one year, she owes a 5 percent surrender fee. Since the average annual insurance fee is 1.31 percent, the insurance firm more than makes up for the 1 percent lower surrender fee.

In contrast, the income of a fee-only professional is not based on commissions. Rather, he typically charges 1 percent per year on assets *under management*. If a client buys a $40,000 annuity, the professional will likely get $400 less in fees the first year and less in fees in each subsequent year. It is not in the fee-only professional's self-interest to recommend the annuity.

Summary

The first paragraph of this chapter posed the question, "Who should buy a non-qualified tax-deferred annuity?" The first conclusion is that, unless they have creditor-protection concerns, few individuals should have to decide between buying a non-qualified annuity or a mutual fund held in a taxable account. Annuities are not appropriate for individuals who are saving for preretirement needs, because there is usually a 10 percent penalty tax for withdrawals before age 59½. Individuals who are saving for retirement needs and are not concerned about creditor-protection issues should, at a minimum, fully fund Roth IRAs and deductible pensions before deciding between saving in an annuity or a taxable account. In addition, before making this decision, many individuals will first wish to take advantage of the tax-free investment opportunities for funding their children's education needs. Due to changes made by the 2001 Tax Act, few individuals should ever reach the point that they should decide between saving in the annuity or taxable account.

A non-qualified annuity makes sense for some individuals who are in one of the following three groups:

1. They are concerned about protection from creditors.
2. They have long investment horizons and are in the accumulation stage of life.
3. They favor annuitization's ability to reduce longevity risk during the distribution stage of life.

A section on the distribution stage, which is based on a study by Ameriks, Veres, and Warshawsky (2001), addresses the third group.

Individuals may seek an annuity for its creditor-protection feature. Since creditor protection is strongest on funds in ERISA-qualified plans, these individuals should first fully fund their ERISA-qualified plans before buying an annuity. ERISA-qualified plans not only provide better creditor protection, but they are also more tax favored. Depending upon the state, the annuity may offer the next-best protection. If they buy an annuity for its creditor protection, then they should seek a low-cost annuity.

The second group of investors that should be interested in annuities is individuals with long investment horizons who have, at a minimum, fully funded their Roth IRAs and deductible pensions. If they have fully funded these savings vehicles and are looking to save additional funds for retirement, then they must choose between saving in an annuity and saving in a mutual fund held in a taxable account. The major conclusions from analysis of this choice are as follows.

■ Costs matter a great deal. Knowledgeable investors should compare a low-cost non-qualified annuity to a low-cost mutual fund.
■ Some individuals want an investment in bond funds. Assuming 5.5 percent gross bond returns and 25 percent tax brackets before and during retirement, the low-cost annuity should be preferred by individuals with investment horizons

exceeding 12 years. The breakeven period is about six years if gross returns average 8 percent or if the investor is in a 33 percent tax bracket before retirement and 25 percent during retirement.

■ The choice between a low-cost annuity and a stock fund held in a taxable account is more complex because of the tax treatment of the stock fund in the taxable account. Individuals who will buy and retain a low-cost passive stock fund for at least a decade should favor this stock fund to the low-cost annuity. In the passive stock fund, most capital gains accumulate tax deferred—just like in the annuity. In addition, this passive fund has two advantages: It has lower costs, and capital gains are eventually taxed at preferential rates.

■ Many investors will not passively manage individual stocks or hold a passive stock fund. These investors should compare a low-cost annuity to a low-cost active stock fund. Assuming 8 percent gross stock returns and 25 percent tax brackets before and during retirement, the breakeven period is 12 years. The breakeven period is seven years if gross returns average 12 percent. The breakeven period is only slightly shorter for someone in a higher preretirement tax bracket.

■ The big loser in the analyses is the insurance industry's staple—annuities with expense ratios around 2 percent and with annual contract fees. These products are not in the best interest of investors.

Finally, incentive structures explain why commission-based financial advisors usually push average-cost annuities, while fee-only advisors usually discourage the purchase of any annuity. Unfortunately, it appears that the advice frequently is not in the best interest of the client.

Appendix 5.1: Calculation of Constant After-tax Retirement Incomes from a Bond Fund or a Stock Fund Held in an Annuity

Year	Wbefore	Principal	Acc. Interest	WD after-tax	WD interest	WD prin	WD before	Wafter
1	$56,118.93	$40,000.00	$16,118.93	$2,790.53	$3,720.70	$0.00	$3,720.70	$52,398.23
2	54,206.17	40,000.00	14,206.17	2,790.53	3,720.70	0.00	3,720.70	50,485.47
24	5,569.48	5,406.26	163.22	2,790.53	163.22	2,668.11	2,831.33	2,738.15
25	2,807.98	2,738.15	69.84	2,790.53	69.84	2,738.15	2,807.98	0.00

Example: Someone invests $40,000 in a bond fund held in an average-cost non-qualified tax-deferred annuity at age 55. Gross bond return averages 5.5 percent a year. The annuity earns 3.5 percent return net of its 2 percent expense ratio but before the annual contract charge of $26. At age 65, her account value or wealth before withdrawal (Wbefore) is $56,118.93. This amount is in cell M10 in the model. It is $40,000(1.035) - \$26 = \$41,374$ at age 56, $\$41,374(1.035) - \$26 = \$42,796.09$ at age 57, and this pattern repeats until age 65. Principal at age 65 (in year 1 of the retirement period) is \$40,000. Accrued interest is Wbefore − principal. WD after-tax denotes the constant annual after-tax income that is withdrawn each year. WD interest denotes withdrawn interest. It is WD after-tax / $(1 - 0.25)$ if this amount is greater than accrued interest, and accrued interest otherwise, where 0.25 is the marginal tax rate. Withdrawal of principal, WD prin, is WD after-tax − WD interest $(1 - 0.25)$; for example, in year 24, withdrawn interest is \$163.22 before taxes (and \$122.42 after taxes), so withdrawal of principal is \$2,668.11, or $\$2,790.53 - \$122.42$. Withdrawal before tax, WD before, is the sum of WD interest and WD prin. Wafter denotes the wealth after the withdrawal and is Wbefore − WD before. Wbefore in year $t + 1$, $\text{Wbefore}_{t+1} = \text{Wafter}_t (1.035) - \$26$. Principal in year $t + 1$ is principal$_t$ − WD prin$_t$. The constant after-tax retirement income is the value of WD aftertax that makes Wafter in year 25 equal zero.

This model is available for download at www.wiley.com/go/reichenstein. The file named App 5.1 Bond Fund or Stock Fund Held in Annuity contains the above worksheet. In order to use the model, enter values in the Input cells in the Enter Values Below box. If the investor will retire and begin withdrawals in, say, 20 years, set cell B6 equal to the value in cell K24. Then, press the "Ctrl" and "t" keys simultaneously to run the macro. An alternative approach is to change the value in cell E6, WDaftertax in Year 1," until the value in I30 is zero. To have Excel do this, place the cursor on I30, "Wafter in Year 25," and go to "Tools" then "Goal Seek." "Set cell" is I30, "To value" is 0, and "By changing cell" is E6. With these commands, Excel changes the value in E6 until the value in I30 is zero.

Appendix 5.2: Calculation of Constant After-tax Retirement Incomes from a Bond Fund or an Active Stock Fund Held in a Taxable Account

Example: Someone deposits \$40,000 at age 55 in an average-cost bond mutual fund held in a taxable account. Gross bond return averages 5.5 percent, bond fund expense is 1.1 percent, so net bond returns average 4.4 percent a year before taxes and 3.3 percent a year after paying taxes at 25 percent. Ignoring loads, account value at age 65 is $\$55,343.06 = \$40,000 (1.033)^{10}$. Considering the loads it is $\$54,022.58 = 0.986 (\$55,343.06) (0.99)$, where 0.986 and 0.99 represent the 1.4 percent front-end load and 1 percent deferred load. Then, calculate the payment for a 25-year annuity due by dividing by the annuity due factor of 17.401. Equivalently, insert in a financial calculator PV = \$54,022.58, FV = 0, $n = 25$, $i = 3.3$ percent, and calculate the PMT *for an annuity due* of \$3,105 (rounded to the nearest dollar). For the low-cost bond fund, divide wealth before loads by the annuity due factor.

Next consider the average-cost, active stock fund. Assume gross returns average 8 percent. Dividends plus short-term capital gains are 2 percent, so 0.6 percent

(2 percent less 1.4 percent expense ratio) is distributed annually and taxed at 25 percent. The 6 percent long-term capital gain is realized in one year and one day and taxed at 20 percent. The net return after taxes is 5.25 percent, 0.6 percent (1 − 0.25) + 6 percent (1 − 0.20). Ignoring loads, account value in 10 years at age 65 is $66,723.84 = $40,000(1.0525)^{10}$. Considering the loads it is $64,868.05 = 0.983($51,134.92)(0.989), where 0.983 and 0.989 represent the 1.7 percent and 1.1 percent loads. Then, calculate the payment for a 25-year annuity due of $4,483 (rounded to the nearest dollar). For the low-cost stock fund, divide wealth before loads by the annuity due factor.

This model is available at www.wiley.com/go/reichenstein. The file is named Appendix 5.2 Calculation of Constant Annual Income from Bond Fund and Active Stock Fund Held in Taxable Account. In order to use the model, insert *Input* values in the Enter Values Below box. The Derived Series and payments automatically change.

Appendix 5.3: Calculation of Constant After-tax Retirement Income from a Passive Stock Fund Held in a Taxable Account

Year	1st	10th	11th	34th
Beginning Market Value	$40,000.00	$75,073.40	$74,058.82	$6,118.94
Return	3,080.00	5,780.65	5,702.53	471.16
Ending Before-tax Value	43,080.00	80,854.06	79,761.35	6,590.10
Beginning Cost Base	40,000.00	48,708.14	46,520.70	2,880.62
Capital Gain	2,720.00	31,470.25	32,574.12	3,654.42
Realized Capital Gain	136.00	1,573.51	1,628.71	182.72
Capital Gain Tax	24.48	283.23	293.17	32.89
Capital Gain Reinvested	111.52	1,290.28	1,335.54	149.83
Dividends	360.00	675.66	666.53	55.07
Dividends Tax	90.00	168.92	166.63	13.77
Dividends Reinvested	270.00	506.75	499.90	41.30
Ending Cost Base (before distribution)	40,381.52	50,505.17	48,356.13	3,071.75
Ending Market Value (before distribution)	42,965.52	80,401.91	79,301.55	6,543.44
Ending Cost Base (after distribution)		46,520.70	44,474.51	0.00
Ending Market Value (after distribution)		74,058.82	72,935.88	0.00
Before-tax Withdrawal		6,343.09	6,365.67	6,543.44
After-tax Withdrawal		5,918.54	5,918.54	5,918.54

Beginning market value and beginning cost base are $40,000. Gross stock return is 8 percent, including 1.2 percent dividend yield and 6.8 percent capital gain. After 0.3 percent expenses, net return is 7.7 percent and net dividend yield is 0.9 percent. Five percent of capital gains are realized each year and the capital gain tax rate is 18 percent. Dividends are taxed at 25 percent. Capital gain reinvested denotes realized gain less taxes on the gain. Ending cost base is beginning cost base plus the sum of capital gain reinvested and dividends reinvested. Ending market value is the ending before-tax value less the sum of capital gain tax and dividends tax. Capital gain in years 2 through 10 is 0.068 times beginning market value plus unrealized capital gain from the prior year, which is ($2,720 − $136) for year 2. The $40,000 grows to $80,401.91 in 10 years (but before the year-end distribution).

The investment provides $5,918.54 after taxes each year for 25 years with the first payment occurring after year 10. After year 10, she withdraws $6,343.09 = $5,918.54 / (1 − [0.18(Ending market value − ending cost base) / Ending market value]). Taxes on liquidation of $6,343.09 is 18 percent of realized capital gain, and realized capital gain is the product $6,343.09 times (Ending market value − ending cost base) / Ending market value. The constant after-tax income of $5,918.54 is the value that makes ending value after distribution after year 34 equal zero. Capital gain in years 11 through 34 is 0.068 times beginning market value plus (Capital gain − realized gain) from the prior year less capital gain realized at the prior year's year-end distribution; for year 11 the latter is $6,343.09 times [(Ending market value − ending cost base) / Ending market value] in year 10.

This model is available at www.wiley.com/go/reichenstein. The file named is App 2.1 & 5.3 Passive Stock Fund in Taxable Account. This worksheet is named App. 5.3. To calculate the constant annual after-tax withdrawal amount, change the value in cell L20 until the value in AJ17, "Ending Market Value (after distribution) in 34th Year," is zero. To have Excel do this, place the cursor on AJ17, "market value after withdrawal" in year 25, and go to "Tools" then "Goal Seek." "Set cell" is AJ17, "To value" is 0, and "By changing cell" is L20. With these commands, Excel changes the value in L20 until the value in AJ17 is zero.

References

Ameriks, John, Robert Veres, and Mark J. Warshawsky. 2001. Making retirement income Last a Lifetime. *Journal of Financial Planning,* December, 60–74.

Arnott, Robert D., and Ronald J. Ryan. 2001. The death of the risk premium. *Journal of Portfolio Management,* Summer, 61–74.

Blake, Christopher R., Edwin J. Elton, and Martin J. Gruber. 1993. The performance of bond mutual funds. *Journal of Business,* July, 371–403.

Bogle, John C. 1998. The implications of style analysis for mutual fund performance evaluation. *Journal of Portfolio Management,* Summer, 34–42.

Brown, Anthony. 2000. What's next for the S&P 500? *Journal of Investing,* Winter, 60–66.

Domian, Dale, and William Reichenstein. 1997. Performance and persistence in money market fund returns. *Financial Services Review,* vol. 6, no. 3, 169–183.

Domian, Dale, and William Reichenstein. 2002. Predicting municipal bond fund returns. *Journal of Investing,* Fall 2002, 53–65.

Fair, Andrew J. 1993. Qualified plans, IRAs, your creditors, and you. *The CPA Journal,* January, 71–74.

Fama, Eugene F., and Kenneth R. French. 2001. The equity premium. Working Paper No. 522, The Center for Research in Security Prices, Graduate School of Business, University of Chicago, January.

Geer, Carolyn T. 1998. The great annuity rip-off. *Forbes,* February 9, 106–110.

Hube, K. 1998. Annuity companies pitch 'Annuitization' to recover their appeal. *The Wall Street Journal,* June 8, C1.

Huggard, John P. 1999. Variables claim victory: Clients with excess funds available for retirement are often better off purchasing variable annuities than mutual funds. *Financial Planning,* March.

Huggard, John P. 2001. VA's victorious at tax time. *Financial Planning,* October, 119–130.

Jagannathan, Ravi, Ellen R. McGrattan, and Anna Scherbina. 2000. The declining U.S. equity premium. *Quarterly Review of Federal Reserve Bank of Minneapolis,* Fall, 3–19.

LIMRA International. 1999. Deferred annuity buyer study: Profiles. 1999 Report.

Milevsky, Moshe Arye, & Kamphol Panyagometh. 2001. Variable annuities versus mutual funds: A Monte Carlo analysis of the options. Working Paper, York University, Toronto, Canada.

Milevsky, Moshe Arye, and Steven E. Posner. 2001. The titanic option: Valuation of a Guaranteed Minimum Death Benefit in variable annuities and mutual funds. *Journal of Risk and Insurance,* Vol. 68, No. 1, March, 93–128.

Panko, Ron. 2000. Can annuities pass muster? *Best's Review,* July, 103–109.

Patterson v. Shumate. 1992. Supreme Court of the U.S. (91–913), 504 U.S. 753.

Peterson, James D., Paul A. Pietranico, Mark W. Riepe, and Fran Xu. 2001. Explaining the performance of domestic equity mutual funds. *Journal of Investing,* Fall, 81–91.

Reichenstein, William. 1999a. Bond fund returns and expenses: A study of bond market efficiency. *Journal of Investing,* Winter, 8–16.

Reichenstein, William. 1999b. Savings vehicles and the taxation of individual investors. *Journal of Private Portfolio Management* (since renamed, *Journal of Wealth Management*), Winter, 15–26.

Reichenstein, William. 2000a. After-tax wealth and returns across savings vehicles. *Journal of Private Portfolio Management* (since renamed, *Journal of Wealth Management*), Spring, 9–19.

Reichenstein, William. 2000b. An analysis of non-qualified tax-deferred annuities. *Journal of Investing,* Summer, 73–85.

Rothschild, Gideon, and Daniel S. Rubin. 1999. Creditor protection for life insurance and annuities. *The Journal of Asset Protection,* May.

Shiller, Robert J. 2000. *Irrational exuberance.* New York: Broadway Books.

Siegel, Jeremy J. 1999. The shrinking equity premium. *Journal of Portfolio Management,* Fall, 10–17.

Sondergeld, E. 1997. Annuity persistence study. LIMRA International and the Society of
Actuaries.
Spero, Peter. 2001. Using life insurance and annuities for asset protection. *Estate Planning,*
January, 12–18.

Notes

1. For long investment horizons, the tax benefits of especially Roth IRAs and deductible
   pensions may be strong enough to more than offset the 10 percent penalty tax. Nevertheless, annuities are seldom appropriate for someone saving for retirement needs.
2. A nondeductible IRA is not considered separately since it is essentially a non-qualified
   annuity without insurance fees.
3. Technically, there are only two IRAs—the Roth IRA and traditional IRA. In a traditional
   IRA, the investment amount may or may not be deductible in the contribution year. If it
   is deductible, it is a deductible pension as defined here. If it is not deductible, it has the
   nondeductible IRA tax structure.
4. Based on the 2001 Tax Act, beginning in 2010, there will be limits on the amount of
   basis step-up at death. An estate can give up to $1.3 million in step-up to one or more
   beneficiaries. In addition, an estate can give up to $3 million in step-up to a surviving
   spouse. In total, a spouse could receive $4.3 million in step-up. Therefore, the 2001 Tax
   Act will not restrict the benefit of the step-up in basis at death except for the very
   wealthy.
5. Annuities are a tax-inefficient way to buy life insurance. Suppose Jane dies when her
   account value is $36,000. Although her beneficiary receives, a death benefit of $4,000,
   it is taxable. In contrast, traditional life insurance benefits are tax-exempt.
6. The annuity contract provides a guaranteed minimum annuitization rate. Annuitization
   is discussed in the next section. If the investor annuitizes, it typically guarantees a minimum interest rate of about 3 percent. According to Milevsky and Posner (2001), this
   option has had so little value that it has been ignored by pricing actuaries, valuation
   actuaries, regulators, and the reinsurer. Its value is ignored here.
7. According to the Annuity Persistence Study of LIMRA (see Sondergeld, 1997),
   2 percent to 3 percent of annuities are annuitized. Hube (1998) estimates that 1 percent
   of annuity buyers annuitize. The 1 percent figure comes from the Life Insurance Market-
   ing and Research Association.
8. In 1997, the average non-qualified annuity contract was for $39,700 according to
   LIMRA International (1999).
9. See Arnott and Ryan (2001), Brown (2000), Fama and French (2001), Jagannathan,
   McGrattan, and Scherbina (2000), Shiller (2000), and Siegel (1999).
10. Withdrawals are considered "interest first" for annuities on contributions after August 13,
    1982. Withdrawals are considered "principal first" for withdrawals from annuities
    in which the entire investment was made before August 14, 1982.
11. The present value of a $7,932 annuity due for 20 years when discounted at 5.5 percent
    a year is $100,000.

Saving Opportunities in Deductible Pensions and Roth IRAs after the 2001 Tax Act

Introduction

Deductible pensions and the Roth IRA provide the most tax-advantaged savings vehicles when saving for retirement. Deductible pensions include deductible IRA, 401(k), 403(b), 457, SIMPLE, SEP-IRA, and Keogh plans. For each savings vehicle, this chapter summarizes the rules governing the size of contributions, income limits, and restrictions on withdrawals, including when funds can be withdrawn before age 59½ without paying the 10 percent penalty tax. The next section discusses contribution limits for the Roth IRA and each deductible pension as well as the income limits on IRA contributions. We also discuss issues related to withdrawals, including minimum withdrawal requirements and withdrawals that are not subject to the 10 percent penalty tax if withdrawn before age 59½.

Contribution Limits and Income Limits

This section presents the maximum contribution limits to IRAs, 401(k), 403(b), Keogh, and other deductible pensions. It also presents income limits that determine eligibility for contributions to the deductible IRA and the Roth IRA.

Contribution Limits

Table 6.1 presents the maximum contribution limits to IRAs and deductible pensions by year for people with at least that level of earned income. For example, in 2002, the maximum annual contribution limit for someone under age 50 to a 401(k) is the larger of $11,000 per person or earned income. Generally, we drop the constant reminder that the individual can only contribute up to his or her level of earned income. Earned income includes wages, salary, and tips but does not include interest, dividends, and capital gains.

There is, however, an exception to the "or earned income" limitation. A stay-at-home spouse with no earned income can, in essence, use the other spouse's earned income for a contribution to a Roth or traditional IRA. For example, suppose Jim has an adjusted gross income of $148,000 and Mary, his wife, works as a stay-at-home mother. If they file jointly, Mary can make a $3,000 (in 2002) contribution to a Roth or traditional IRA even though she has no earned income. This is sometimes referred to as a spousal IRA, but the contribution for Mary will either be a traditional IRA or a Roth IRA.

Table 6.1 presents the contribution limits to the other deductible pensions. A 401(k) plan provides employees in for-profit corporations the opportunity to defer income. A 403(b) plan is essentially a 401(k) plan for employees of nonprofit firms such as universities and some hospitals. The 457 plans typically exist for employees at local governments and school districts. The maximum annual *regular* contribution in 401(k), 403(b), and 457 plans is $11,000 in 2002, but it increases $1,000 a year until reaching $15,000 in 2006. After 2006, the $15,000 contribution limit will be indexed for inflation in $500 increments.

Furthermore, individuals age 50 or older can make additional *catch-up* contributions totaling $1,000 in 2002. The size of the catch-up contribution increases by $1,000 a year until it reaches $5,000 in 2006. After 2006, the maximum catch-up contribution will be indexed for inflation in $500 increments. The name "catch-up contribution" is a bit of a misnomer, as it seems to suggest that only individuals who have not maximized prior contributions can catch up by making larger contributions after age 50. This is not the law. Everyone age 50 or over as of the end of the year can make catch-up contributions—even individuals who have made maximum contributions to deductible pensions in all prior years.

SIMPLE plans are available at many smaller corporations. Employees in these plans may make a maximum regular contribution of $7,000 in 2002, $8,000 in 2003,

TABLE 6.1 Contribution Limits to Deductible Pensions and Roth IRAs under 2001 Tax Act

Year	Traditional and Roth IRAs		401(k), 403(b), and 457 Plans		SIMPLE Plans		Keogh Plans	SEP-IRA Plans
	Regular	Catch-up	Regular	Catch-up	Regular	Catch-up	Regular	Regular
2002	$3,000	$ 500	$11,000	$1,000	$ 7,000	$ 500	$40,000	15%
2003	3,000	500	12,000	2,000	8,000	1,000	Indexed	15
2004	3,000	500	13,000	3,000	9,000	1,500		15
2005	4,000	500	14,000	4,000	10,000	2,000		15
2006	4,000	1,000	15,000	5,000	Indexed	2,500		15
2007	4,000	1,000	Indexed	Indexed		Indexed		15
2008	5,000	1,000						15
2009	Indexed	1,000						15

Anyone age 50 or over as of the end of the year can make catch-up contributions, even if he or she has made maximum contributions in all prior years.

$9,000 in 2004, and $10,000 in 2005. In addition, employees age 50 or over may make additional catch-up contributions up to $500 in 2002, $1,000 in 2003, $1,500 in 2004, $2,000 in 2005, and $2,500 in 2006. After 2005, the maximum regular contribution will be indexed for inflation in $500 increments; indexing for the maximum catch-up contribution begins after 2006.

Keogh and SEP-IRAs are available to self-employed individuals. Medical doctors and other well-to-do self-employed individuals typically have a Keogh plan. It allows regular annual contributions up to $40,000. The $40,000 limit will be indexed for inflation beginning in 2002 in $1,000 increments.

Less-wealthy self-employed individuals or individuals with unpredictable compensation often prefer a Simplified Employee Pension—Individual Retirement Account or SEP-IRA. The paperwork requirements are substantially easier for the SEP-IRA than the Keogh. For example, consider an author or consultant who has irregular income from this part-time job and who also has a full-time job. If he establishes a SEP-IRA for this side business, he may contribute and thus tax-defer each year a portion of income from this part-time job. Furthermore, contributions to a SEP-IRA do not affect contribution limits to Roth IRAs or qualified plans such as 401(k)s or 403(b)s at his regular, full-time job.

The maximum contribution limit for the SEP-IRA is 15 percent of income, and it is scheduled to remain at 15 percent. The 15 percent limit is somewhat misleading, however. It is 13.04 percent of income before the contribution, which corresponds to 15 percent of income after the contribution. For simplicity, suppose income before the contribution is $100. The maximum contribution is $13.04. Thus, after deducting this contribution, taxable income is $86.96. The 15 percent is $13.04 / $86.96.

Income Limits

Each individual can make a maximum contribution to all IRAs—traditional and Roth—of $3,000 per year in 2002. (Self-employed individuals may be able to make contributions to a SEP-IRA. If so, SEP-IRA contributions do not apply to this limit.)

The traditional IRA includes the deductible IRA and the nondeductible IRA. In both cases, it is a traditional IRA. The only difference is whether the contribution is deductible in the contribution year. Deductible and Roth IRAs are clearly preferable to the nondeductible IRA. This section addresses income limits that determine the eligibility to make traditional and Roth IRA contributions. It also explains when a contribution to a traditional IRA is deductible.

Rules affecting eligibility to contribute to a Roth IRA are relatively simple. Contributions to a Roth IRA are subject to income limits. For single taxpayers, the $3,000 contribution limit (in 2002) is phased out between adjusted gross income of $95,000 and $110,000. For joint filers, contributions are phased out between adjusted gross income of $150,000 and $160,000.

Unfortunately, the rules governing the eligibility to make a deductible contribution to a traditional IRA are not simple. Eligibility rules depend upon whether the individual (or his or her spouse, if applicable) is an active participant in an employer-sponsored retirement plan.

Single taxpayers who are not active participants can make a maximum deductible contribution each year. There is no income limit. Similarly, if *neither* spouse of a couple filing jointly is an active participant then they may each make a deductible contribution up to the maximum contribution level each year.

Active participants below a threshold level of income may make a deductible contribution. The deductible portion of the contribution is phased out between the lower threshold level and a higher income level, and the contribution is nondeductible above the higher income level. For single taxpayers, the threshold income level for the year 2002 is $34,000, and the deductible portion phases out between adjusted gross incomes of $34,000 and $44,000. The phase-out range is scheduled to increase each year until it settles at $50,000 to $60,000 for year 2005 and thereafter. For married taxpayers filing jointly, the threshold income level for year 2002 is $54,000, and the deductible portion phases out between $54,000 and $64,000. The phase-out range is scheduled to gradually increase to between $80,000 to $100,000 for year 2007 thereafter. Tables 6.2 and 6.3 summarize income limits that determine the eligibility to make IRA contributions for singles and married couples, respectively.

For example, suppose Brad is a single taxpayer under age 50 who actively participates in an employer-sponsored retirement plan. In 2002, Brad's adjusted gross income is $35,700. His income exceeds the threshold level by $1,700, and his deductible IRA contribution is subject to a phase-out. His maximum deductible contribution is reduced by 17 percent ($1,700 / $10,000). He may only contribute and deduct $2,490 in 2002 [$3,000 • (1 − 0.17)]. He can still contribute the full $3,000, but the last $510 is nondeductible. If Brad were not an active participant in an employer-sponsored plan or other qualified plan, the phase-out would not apply, and he could contribute and deduct the maximum of $3,000.

TABLE 6.2   IRA Eligibility for Singles

How much can you contribute to an IRA?

| Your 2002 AGI is . . . | Traditional IRA (deductible) | | Traditional IRA | Roth IRA |
	Active[1]	Not active[2]	(nondeductible)	
Less than $34,000	Maximum	Maximum	Maximum	Maximum
$34,000–$44,000	Phase-out	Maximum	Maximum	Maximum
$44,000–$95,000	None	Maximum	Maximum	Maximum
$95,000–$110,000	None	Maximum	Maximum	Phase-out
More than $110,000	None	Maximum	Maximum	None

[1]**Active:** This column applies to active participants in an employer-sponsored plan.
[2]**Not active:** This column applies to single taxpayers who are not active participants in an employer-sponsored plan.

TABLE 6.3 IRA Eligibility for Married Couples Filing Joint Returns

How much can you contribute to an IRA?

Your 2002 AGI is . . .	Traditional IRA (deductible)			Traditional IRA (nondeductible)	Roth IRA
	Active[1]	Not active[2]	Neither active[3]		
Less than $54,000	Maximum	Maximum	Maximum	Maximum	Maximum
$54,000–$64,000	Phase-out	Maximum	Maximum	Maximum	Maximum
$64,000–$150,000	None	Maximum	Maximum	Maximum	Maximum
$150,000–$160,000	None	Phase-out	Maximum	Maximum	Phase-out
More than $160,000	None	None	Maximum	Maximum	None

[1] **Active:** This column applies to active participants in an employer-sponsored plan. It applies to both members of the couple if both are active participants, and to the active member of the couple if one member is an active participant and the other is not.

[2] **Not active:** If one member of the couple is an active participant and the other is not, this column applies to the non-active member.

[3] **Neither active:** If neither member of the couple is active participant in an employer-sponsored plan, this column applies to both members.

Next, consider a married couple filing jointly, when one spouse is an active participant but the other spouse is not. Prior to the Tax Reform Act of 1997, the nonactive spouse was considered an active participant in an employer-sponsored plan merely because his or her spouse was an active participant. Now, subject to income limits, the couple can make a deductible contribution for the non-participating spouse. The phase-out occurs between adjusted gross incomes of $150,000 and $160,000. Thus, under the new regulations most homemakers can now make a contribution to a traditional (deductible) IRA or to a Roth IRA.

For example, suppose John and Wendy are married, and both are under age 50. John actively participates in a qualified retirement plan at his job, but Wendy does not. In 2002, the couple's adjusted gross income is $140,000. Since their income does not exceed the threshold income level, Wendy may contribute up to $3,000 to either a traditional IRA or a Roth IRA. Since John is covered under the qualified plan and the couple's income exceeds $64,000, he cannot make a deductible contribution. However, John can contribute up to $3,000 to a Roth IRA.

Most taxpayers living in states that assess and collect income taxes can deduct their contributions to traditional, deductible IRAs on their state income tax returns. However, New Jersey, Massachusetts, and Pennsylvania disallow these deductions. Residents of these states should consider this fact when deciding between the traditional and Roth IRAs.

Finally, if the couple's adjusted gross income exceeds $160,000, each spouse may make a contribution to a traditional (nondeductible) IRA. Although the contribution is not deductible, returns accumulate tax deferred. See Chapter 4 for a discussion of the pros and cons of a traditional nondeductible IRA.

Lower-income Credit for Retirement Contributions

To encourage lower-income taxpayers to save for retirement, the Economic Growth and Tax Relief Reconciliation Act of 2001 (henceforth, 2001 Tax Act) includes a new tax credit for contributions to traditional and Roth IRAs, 401(k)s, 403(b)s, SIMPLEs, 457s, and SEP-IRAs. A tax credit is a dollar-for-dollar reduction in the final income tax liability. Depending on the taxpayer's adjusted gross income, the credit ranges from 10 percent to 50 percent of the contribution as indicated in Table 6.4. The maximum annual contribution eligible for the credit is $2,000, and the credit only applies in years 2002 through 2006. The credit cannot be claimed by anyone under age 18, by a full-time student, or by a person who can be claimed as a dependent on another taxpayer's return.

For example, assume Tiffany, a 22-year-old single taxpayer, graduates from college in May of 2002 and enters the work force in June. She earns $2,500 per month, totaling $17,500 for the final seven months of the year. If Tiffany contributes at least $2,000 to a Roth IRA in 2002, she is eligible for a $200 credit. The credit is 10 percent of the first $2,000 of her contribution. If Tiffany only contributes $1,500 to the IRA, the credit is $150.

TABLE 6.4   Income Limits that Apply to the Tax Credit

Joint Filers	Heads of Households	Other Filers	Tax Credit Rate
$0–$30,000	$0–$22,500	$0–$15,000	50%
$30,000–$32,500	$22,500–$24,375	$15,000–$16,250	20%
$32,500–$50,000	$24,375–$37,500	$16,250–$25,000	10%
$50,000 +	$37,500 +	$25,000 +	None

Ability to Obtain Funds before Retirement

Deductible pensions and Roth IRAs are retirement accounts, and the government places restrictions that are intended to encourage funds to remain in these savings vehicles until retirement. This section reviews the rules affecting the ability to obtain funds before retirement. First, it notes that individuals can borrow from some accounts and discusses this use of funds. Second, the Treasury usually imposes a 10 percent penalty tax on withdrawals before age 59½ This section issues a warning and reviews exceptions to the 10 percent penalty tax.

Exceptions to the 10 Percent Penalty Tax on Distributions before Age 59½

Subject to the exceptions listed below, distributions from deductible pensions, nondeductible IRAs, and non-qualified annuities before the owner reaches age 59½ are subject to a 10 percent early withdrawal penalty. This penalty tax applies only to the portion of the distribution that represents taxable income; it does not apply to the return of principal (or cost basis).

Exceptions [See IRC § 72(t)]:

- Distributions at the death of the owner.
- Distributions due to disability.
- Distributions that are part of a series of substantially equal periodic payments for the life or life expectancy of the recipient. Also, this exception applies to substantially equal periodic payments for the joint lives or joint life expectancies of the recipient and beneficiary.
- Distributions to an employee who is at least age 55, separates from the service of his employer, and receives the distribution upon separation from the service of the employer.
- Distributions to pay deductible medical expenses. Medical expenses are deductible to the degree they exceed 7.5 percent of adjusted gross income.
- Distributions to someone other than the employee under a Qualified Domestic Relations Order.

- Distributions to unemployed persons for health insurance premiums.
- If the employee rolls the distribution over to an IRA.
- Distributions from a traditional or Roth IRA to pay qualified higher education expenses of the owner, his or her spouse, or their children or grandchildren.
- Distributions from a traditional or Roth IRA of up to $10,000 to pay for the principal residence of a first-time homebuyer.

These are the rules. Below we provide additional detail about the 10 percent penalty tax and specific terms such as first-time homebuyer and qualified higher education expense.

Let us clarify the nature of the 10 percent penalty tax. It applies only to the taxable portion of the withdrawal; it does not apply to the portion, if any, representing the return of principal. Withdrawals from 401(k), 403(b), 457, Keogh, SEP-IRA, and deductible IRAs are fully taxable. Therefore, if the 10 percent penalty tax applies, it applies to the full amount of the withdrawal. Withdrawals from non-qualified annuities (that are not annuitized) are considered interest-first. Therefore, if the 10 percent penalty tax applies, it usually applies to the full amount of the withdrawal. Withdrawals from a Roth IRA are considered principal-first and, therefore, potentially avoid the penalty tax.

Let us consider an example of a withdrawal from a Roth IRA. Jessica is 25 and contributed $2,000 of after-tax funds to a Roth IRA in each of the last three years. The value of the Roth IRA is currently $8,500. Jessica can withdraw $6,000 from the Roth IRA without paying regular income taxes or the 10 percent penalty tax. If she withdraws the full $8,500, she would owe regular tax and the penalty tax on the $2,500 of deferred return; the penalty tax is $250, 10 percent of $2,500, not 10 percent of the $8,500 withdrawal.

Continue to assume that Jessica made three separate $2,000 contributions to a Roth IRA that is currently worth $8,500. She purchases her first home, withdrawing all $8,500 from the Roth IRA and using the funds as a down payment. Jessica avoids the 10 percent penalty tax if she makes the down payment within 120 days of receiving the distribution. However, she owes regular taxes on the $2,500 of earnings.

Now, let us examine a different scenario. Jessica meets Mark, and they marry. Jessica and Mark purchase a new home. It is Jessica's first house, but Mark still owns the house he lived in before their marriage. Jessica cannot withdraw funds from her Roth IRA and use them as a down payment on their new home without incurring the 10 percent penalty tax. IRC Section 72(t)(8)(D)(i) defines a first-time homebuyer as "any individual if such individual (and if married, such individual's spouse) had no present ownership interest in a principal residence during the 2-year period ending on the date of acquisition of the principal residence to which this paragraph applies." Because Mark still owns the house he lived in before their marriage, neither Mark nor Jessica qualifies as a first-time homebuyer.

Qualified higher education expenses include tuition, fees, books, supplies, and equipment required for enrollment at an eligible educational institution. If the student is enrolled at least half-time, room and board expenses also qualify. An eligible educational institution is any college, university, vocational school, or other postsecondary educational institution that is described in Section 481 of the Higher Education Act of 1965 (20 U.S.C. 1088). This category includes virtually all accredited public, nonprofit, and proprietary postsecondary institutions. The same eligibility requirements for institutions apply for the Hope scholarship credit, the lifetime learning credit, and Coverdell Education Savings Accounts.

Warning

Usually, individuals may borrow against or withdraw funds from retirement accounts. However, if the funds are intended for retirement, we discourage individuals from using these funds for other reasons. The tax advantages of retirement accounts, especially deductible pensions and Roth IRAs, are substantial. Moreover, since these tax advantages increase with the length of the investment horizon, they are especially strong when held until retirement. Nevertheless, there are opportunities to gain access to funds previously contributed to retirement accounts. Individuals should view the potential to access funds as an inducement to save in these savings vehicles. That is, since individuals will have access to the funds in dire circumstances, they should not hesitate to save all they think they can. Absent the dire circumstances, however, the funds should be retained within these advantaged savings vehicles.

Summary

Deductible pensions and the Roth IRA are the most tax-advantaged savings vehicles. Consequently, it is important that the 2001 Tax Act significantly increased contribution limits to these savings vehicles. This chapter summarized the size of contribution, income limits, and restrictions on withdrawals, including when funds can be withdrawn before age 59½ without incurring the 10 percent penalty tax.

By 2006, an individual's maximum regular contribution to 401(k), 403(b), and 457 plans will be $15,000. Additional catch-up contributions of $5,000 will be available to individuals who are age 50 or older. Furthermore, by 2008 individuals will be able to make regular contributions to IRAs of $5,000 and, if over age 50, catch-up contributions of $1,000. The bottom line is most people will be able to save all the funds they can afford to save in these most-favored vehicles.

Income limits affect the eligibility to contribute to a Roth IRA. For single taxpayers, the maximum contribution limit is phased out between adjusted gross income of $95,000 and $110,000. For joint filers, contributions are phased out between adjusted gross income of $150,000 and $160,000. Although more complex, this chapter presented the rules governing eligibility to make a deductible contribution to a traditional IRA. In addition, it presented rules governing the tax credits that are designed to encourage lower-income individuals to save for retirement. This credit should be of special interest to lower-income taxpayers, new college grads, and individuals coming off lengthy unemployment. Finally, it discussed exceptions to the general rule that withdrawals from retirement accounts before age $59\frac{1}{2}$ are subject to a 10 percent penalty tax. One recent change of note is that distributions are not subject to the penalty tax if used to pay qualified higher education expenses for family members or to pay for up to $10,000 for the principal residence of a first-time homebuyer.

CHAPTER

7

Tax-Efficient Investing

Introduction

The tax-efficient-investing literature is primarily concerned with the management of stocks in taxable accounts. In the first half of this book, we extended this literature to include the importance of choosing savings vehicles. When saving for retirement, individuals should save all they are allowed to save, or all they can afford to save, in deductible pensions and Roth IRAs before investing in either taxable accounts or non-qualified annuities. In practice, deductible pensions and Roth IRAs usually offer returns that are tax-exempt or better. They are the most tax-efficient savings vehicles.

In this chapter, we concentrate on the tax-efficiency literature, primarily that concerned with the management of stocks in taxable accounts.[1] When held in taxable accounts, it can make a big difference whether stock returns are in the form of dividends or capital gains and how quickly the capital gains are realized. In contrast, when held in a tax-deferred account, all stock returns—whether dividends, short-term capital gains, or long-term capital gains—are eventually taxed at ordinary income tax rates.

It is well known that, in the battle of active management versus passive management, active managers have a hard time overcoming the twin burdens of additional management costs and additional trading costs. In their seminal study, Jeffrey and Arnott (1993) go one step further. They conclude that, for stocks held in taxable accounts, it is virtually impossible for active managers to overcome the *tax burden alone* of active trading. The combination of additional management fees, trading costs, and tax burden represent a formidable trio of burdens.

Allow Capital Gains to Grow Unharvested

Table 7.1 presents the ending after-tax wealth of three hypothetical individual investors after 5 and 30 years. Each individual invests in the same stock fund that earns an annual net return of 11 percent before taxes. Notice that this example assumes that active management raises gross returns sufficiently to offset the additional management fees and trading costs. That is, this example only considers the tax burden of trading. The example assumes an original investment of $1,000 that earns 11 percent per year. The combined federal-plus-state tax rate on net dividend income is 35 percent, and the rate on capital gains is 27 percent in all years. The investment horizon is 5 or 30 years.

The trader invests in a stock fund that realizes all gains as short-term gains each year. He pays taxes at 35 percent on the full 11 percent. The after-tax value grows at 7.15 percent per year $[11\% \bullet (1 - 0.35)]$, and the ending wealth after n years is $\$1,000 \bullet (1.0715)^n$. The active investor buys a stock fund that realizes all gains in one year and one day and, therefore, pays the preferential capital gain tax rate of 27 percent. Assume the dividend yield (net of fund costs) is 1 percent, and capital gains are 10 percent. The after-tax value grows at 7.95 percent per year $[1\% \bullet (1 - 0.35) + 10\% \bullet (1 - 0.27)]$, and the ending wealth after n years is $\$1,000 \bullet (1.0795)^n$. The passive investor buys a stock fund that favors low-yield stocks and, therefore, the net dividend yield on this fund is zero. The fund grows at 11 percent per year before taxes. Capital gains are deferred until sold after 5 or 30 years.[2] The ending after-tax wealth is $\$1,000 \bullet [(1.11)^n - 0.27 \bullet \{(1.11)^n - 1\}]$, where the amount in braces is capital gains (per $1 original investment) that are realized after n years. Table 7.1 presents each investor's after-tax wealth after, respectively, 5 and 30 years.

Let us first consider the five-year investment horizon. Compared to the trader, the active investor benefits from preferential capital gain tax rates. This active trader

TABLE 7.1   Tax Efficiency of Stock Management Styles

Management Style	Investment Horizon	
	5 years	30 years
Trader	$1,412	$7,939
Active Investor	$1,466	$9,924
Passive Investor	$1,500	$16,981

Assumptions: Each individual invests $1,000 for 5 or 30 years. The stock fund earns 11 percent per year, and combined state-plus-federal tax rates are 35 percent on ordinary income and 27 percent on capital gains. The trader buys a fund that realizes all gains within a year and thus earns 7.15 percent a year after taxes $[11\% \bullet (1 - 0.35)]$. The active investor realizes all gains in one year and one day. The stock fund earns 1 percent net dividend yield plus 10 percent capital gain. After-tax returns are 7.95 percent $[1\% \bullet (1 - 0.35) + 10\% \bullet (1 - 0.27)]$. The passive investor passively holds a stock fund that pays no net dividends. It grows tax deferred at 11 percent but pays taxes at 27 percent on accumulated gains at the end of the investment horizon.

does not benefit from allowing gains to grow unharvested. After five years, the active investor has $1,466 after taxes, which is 3.8 percent more than the trader's $1,412.

Compared to the active investor, the passive investor benefits from allowing gains to grow unharvested for five years. Recall from Chapter 3 that the benefit of tax deferral alone is small at relatively short horizons. After five years, the passive investor has 2.3 percent more than the active investor. For the five-year horizon, the benefit of preferential tax rates exceeds the benefit of tax deferral.

Next, let us consider the 30-year horizon that is representative of many individuals' horizons when investing for retirement. After 30 years, the active investor has 25 percent more than the trader. However, after 30 years, the passive investor's advantage compared to the active investor has grown to 71.1 percent. For the 30-year horizon, the benefit of tax deferral far exceeds the benefit of preferential capital gain tax rates. This reinforces the lesson that the benefit of tax deferral is most important when the horizon is very long.

Comparing the ending-wealth values for the trader and the passive investor indicates the total tax burden that the trader must overcome to match the after-tax performance of the passive investor. After five years, this burden is 6.2 percent, while, after 30 years, it is 113.9 percent.

Furthermore, the ending-wealth values in Table 7.1 assume that the passive investor sold the fund at the end of the investment horizon and paid taxes on accumulated capital gains. In practice, passive investors sometimes can avoid paying taxes on accumulated gains, in which case the advantage of passive investing is much larger. The individual can avoid paying taxes on the accumulated gain in two ways. First, he can give the appreciated asset to charity. In the previous example, the market value of the passive fund in 30 years is $22,892 [$1,000 • $(1.11)^{30}$]. If he donates the stock fund after 30 years, he can deduct from taxable income the $22,892 market value. Meanwhile, due to its tax-exempt status, the charity can sell the stock without paying taxes. Second, he can await the step-up in basis at death. Assume a couple holds the stock jointly and the husband dies after 30 years. In a community property state, the wife's cost basis rises to $22,892, the market value at death. In a common-law state, the cost basis is adjusted to market value on half the stock. After the husband's death, the wife's cost basis rises to $11,946 [$22,892 / 2 + $500], where $500 is the cost basis on the half that does not receive the step-up in basis.

Harvesting Capital Losses

In a taxable account, realized capital losses can be used to reduce taxes. This provides a value that the prior example ignores. Suppose Cliff, an investor in his working years, follows the recommendations in Part I of this book. He saves all he is allowed in deductible pensions and Roth IRAs. He has $10,000 extra to invest, and he decides to save in a low-cost stock index fund. He invests the $10,000 in early 2000 and, by December 2001, it is worth $7,000. He sells this index fund and invests in another stock index fund. Meanwhile, he uses the $3,000 loss to reduce 2001 taxes by $1,050 [$3,000 • 0.35]. In essence, the government refunds part of the loss.

Selling one stock index fund and buying another one that targets the same index is an example of a tax swap. Although it is not always easy to find a close substitute for an individual stock, it is usually easy to find a close substitute for a high-grade individual bond or a mutual fund.

Loss harvesting should be a year-round program. It is not necessary to wait until December to harvest losses. In fact, investors who wait until December may miss opportunities to harvest losses during the year.

Behavioral-finance scholars tell us that many individuals hesitate to realize a capital loss. Apparently, they feel that selling at a loss is an admission that they made a mistake; for them, realizing an actual loss is more painful than suffering years of the opportunity cost of a bad investment. The realized loss appears on Schedule D of the Form 1040 for all (spouse, accountant, etc.) to see; an opportunity cost is much less visible. Financial advisors perform a valuable service by educating their clients about the advantages of loss harvesting and the need to overcome any psychological barrier to selling losers.

Two Lessons in Managing Taxable Accounts

The two prior sections illustrated two lessons when managing taxable accounts. First, allow capital gains to grow unharvested. Second, harvest capital losses. We believe these are the two most important tax-efficiency lessons when managing taxable accounts. Arnott, Berkin, and Ye (2001) list and discuss what they believe are the three main errors in the management of taxable assets. Their first two errors are unnecessary realization of capital gains and failure to harvest capital losses. The third error, according to these authors, is failure to take an appropriate yield tilt. Recall that the passive investor in Table 7.1 invests in a stock fund that favors low-yield stocks. This is an example of a yield tilt. Since dividends do not receive favorable tax treatment, stocks held in the taxable account should be low-yield stocks. We prefer to list only two main lessons when managing taxable accounts because we believe these are the most important.

Good Choices for Stocks Held in Taxable Accounts

When stocks are held in taxable accounts, it makes a big difference whether the returns are in the form of dividends or capital gains and how quickly the capital gains are realized. At one extreme is the trader who pays taxes each year at the ordinary income tax rate on all returns. At the other extreme is the passive investor in zero-yield stocks. All returns are tax deferred. It is a waste of the tax-deferral feature to passively hold zero-yield stocks in retirement accounts. These two extreme examples provide insights into the type of stocks and stock funds that best fit the taxable account. These include: (1) zero-yield or low-yield individual stocks that will be passively held, (2) stock index funds that should realize minimal capital gains, (3) exchange traded funds (ETFs), and (4) tax-managed stock funds. Table 7.2 provides a list of tax-efficient stock funds.

One good choice for the stock portion of a taxable account is zero-yield (or low-yield) individual stocks that will be passively held for a few decades. Recall that the benefits of tax deferral are minimal unless the taxes are deferred for at least a decade.

A second good choice is stock index funds that realize minimal capital gains. However, not all stock index funds realize minimal gains. Consider a small-cap index fund that follows the Russell 2000. The Russell 2000 consists of the 2,000 stocks from the 1,001st to 3,000th largest in market capitalization. It is updated once a year to reflect the new market valuations. A Russell 2000 index fund will not be tax-efficient because it will be forced to sell and realize gains on the best perform-ing stocks that grow too large for this small-cap index. A mid-cap index fund has the same problem. Some index funds consist of the value half or growth half of an index, say the value half of the S&P 500. These index funds will be forced to real-ize gains as stocks migrate from the value half to the growth half. To achieve the degree of tax efficiency desired, we need an index fund that is tied to large-cap stocks or the total stock market.

For example, an S&P 500 index fund will buy and hold the 500 stocks in pro-portion to their index weight. Even a large-cap fund will be forced to realize some gains. Each year a few stocks leave the S&P 500, which may cause some capital gains to be realized. If an S&P 500 firm is acquired for cash, the index fund is forced to realize gains. However, most stocks that are dropped have experienced rough times and are replaced by larger stocks. Consequently, when an index fund sells these losers, it usually will result in capital losses that can be used to offset the minor gains. Large-cap index funds have been around for a while now. It is clear that cap-ital gains can grow virtually unharvested in these index funds. Similarly, capital gains can grow virtually unharvested in total stock market index funds. Table 7.2 presents a list of low-cost index funds tied to various stock indexes. The S&P 500 is a large-cap index, the Russell 1000 is a large- and mid-cap index, and the Russell 3000 and Wilshire 5000 are total U.S. stock market indexes.

Some professionals express concern about a potential problem with index funds—most of which had sizable unrealized gains in early 2000. Suppose there is a market correction and, in panic, many investors exit the index fund. The portfolio manager would have to sell existing stock, thus realizing gains and saddling remain-ing investors with a large capital gain distribution. After the bear market that began in March 2000, we believe we can now put this concern to rest. Even after the sharp market correction, index funds were not forced to realize and distribute sizable gains. These fears—probably installed by active managers—proved to be false alarms.

ETFs are another good choice for the stock portion of taxable accounts. To be more specific, we recommend ETFs that track a large-cap or a total stock market index. ETFs that track small-cap or value or growth halves of indexes should be less tax-efficient due to the reason previously discussed for index funds. One example of an ETF is a SPDR—pronounced spider—or Standard & Poors' Depository Receipt. SPDRs are units in a trust that holds the stocks in the S&P 500 in proportion to their index weight. Even though they pay a small dividend yield, the passive investor can defer capital gains indefinitely; thus, they are tax-efficient. The units sell on the American Stock Exchange just like any other stock shares. Arbitrage assures that they sell at approximately one-tenth the value of the index. So, if the S&P 500 index is at 900, the units will sell for approximately $90. Let us consider the choice between an investment in the Vanguard 500 Index Fund—the largest index fund—and an investment in SPDRs.

Both investments should produce gross returns that virtually replicate the total return on the S&P 500. The SPDR has an annual expense ratio of 0.12 percent, while the expense ratio on the Vanguard index fund varies from 0.12 percent for some large investors to 0.18 percent for smaller investors. The SPDR and index fund pay small but comparable dividend yields. Investing through SPDRs, however, requires paying commissions to buy and sell the trust units. For practical purposes, therefore, tax-conscious investors must decide whether it is worthwhile to pay commissions on the SPDRs to obtain a potential small annual expense advantage and ensure against the possibility of getting saddled with realized capital gains.

Finally, tax-managed mutual funds are a good choice for the stock portion of taxable accounts. The bottom of Table 7.2 presents a list of low-cost tax-managed mutual funds offered by Vanguard Group. Its Tax-managed Growth and Income, Tax-managed Capital Appreciation, Tax-managed Small-cap, and Tax-managed International funds buy and passively manage a selection of stocks in, respectively, the S&P 500, Russell 1000, S&P SmallCap 600, and MSCI-EAFE (Morgan Stanley Capital International—Europe, Australasia, Far East Index). Its Tax-managed Balanced Fund invests about 50 percent to 55 percent of assets in intermediate-term tax-exempt municipal bonds and 45 percent to 50 percent in stocks in the Russell 1000 Index. To encourage only long-term passive investors in its tax-managed accounts, Vanguard charges a 2 percent redemption fee on shares held less than one year and a 1 percent fee on shares held between one and five years. Other mutual fund families offer tax-managed funds. Although they have not had a long history, it is reasonable to assume that they will allow capital gains to grow unharvested.

A key point about each of the recommended choices for taxable accounts is they are all broad-based, core portfolios. This may be important when it comes to rebalancing. Suppose an individual has a long-run strategic asset allocations that calls for 50 percent U.S. stocks, 10 percent international stocks, and 40 percent bonds, with the U.S. stock portion consisting of 70 percent large-cap and 30 percent small-cap stocks and balanced between value and growth stocks. He holds some stocks in taxable accounts and some in tax-deferred accounts. One good choice for the stock portion of the taxable account would be a total (U.S.) stock market index fund. If he and his financial advisor decide to tilt the portfolio toward say value stocks or small-cap stocks, they can do so by tranferring funds in tax-deferred stock funds. Meanwhile, there are no

TABLE 7.2   List of Tax-efficient Funds

Tax-efficient Index Funds

S&P 500 Index Funds—This index contains primarily large-cap U.S. stocks.

Fund Name	Total Expense Ratio	Minimum Initial Investment
Vanguard 500 Index[*]	0.18%	$ 3,000
USAA S&P 500 Index	0.18	3,000
Fidelity Spartan 500 Index	0.19	10,000
California Investment S&P 500 Index	0.20	5,000
Dreyfus Basic S&P 500 Stock Index	0.20	10,000

Russell 1000 Index Funds—This index contains the 1,000 largest market-cap U.S. stocks, which include both large- and mid-cap stocks.

Fund Name	Total Expense Ratio	Minimum Initial Investment
Schwab 1000[*]	0.46%	$2,500

Russell 3000 or Wilshire 5000 Index Funds—These indexes follow the total U.S. stock market.

Fund Name	Total Expense Ratio	Minimum Initial Investment
Vanguard Total Stock Market Index[*]	0.20%	$ 3,000
Fidelity Spartan Total Market Index	0.26	15,000
Schwab Total Stock Market Index[*]	0.40	2,500

International Index Funds—These funds follow various international stock indexes.

Fund Name	Total Expense Ratio	Minimum Initial Investment
Vanguard Total International Stock Index	0.35%	$ 3,000
Fidelity Spartan International Index	0.35	15,000
Schwab International Index[*]	0.58	2,500
Dreyfus International Stock Index	0.60	2,500

(continued)

TABLE 7.2   (*continued*)

Balanced Index Funds—This fund contains approximately 60 percent stocks (which follow the Wilshire 5000 Index) and 40 percent bonds (which follow the Lehman Aggregate Bond Index).

Fund Name	Total Expense Ratio	Minimum Initial Investment
Vanguard Balanced Index*	0.20%	$3,000

Tax-managed Mutual Funds

Fund Name	Total Expense Ratio	Minimum Initial Purchase
Vanguard's Tax-managed Growth and Income	0.19%	$10,000
Vanguard's Tax-managed Capital Appreciation	0.19	10,000
Vanguard's Tax-managed International	0.35	10,000
Vanguard's Tax-managed Small-cap	0.20	10,000
Vanguard's Tax-managed Balanced	0.20	10,000

These Vanguard funds impose a 2 percent fee on shares redeemed before one year and a 1 percent fee on shares redeemed between one and five years.

* There is a special class of this fund with a significantly reduced expense ratio for investors who make a minimum initial investment or have a current balance of $50,000 or more. For Schwab funds, see their Select Shares and, for Vanguard funds, see their Admiral Shares. None of the funds has a front-end load.
Source: Morningstar Principia Pro for Mutual Funds, January 2001.

transactions in, and thus no tax consequences for, the core stock fund in the taxable account. Similarly, another good choice for the stock portion of the taxable account would be a broad-based international stock index fund. This would satisfy the permanent need for an international exposure, and there should be no need to transfer funds from this account during rebalancing.

Investment Implications

This book takes a broad view of tax-efficient investing. When saving for retirement, individuals should save all they are allowed to save, or all they can afford to save, in deductible pensions and Roth IRAs before saving in either taxable accounts or nonqualified tax-deferred annuities. They are the most tax-efficient savings vehicles. This chapter, however, concentrates on the narrower topic of tax-efficient investing in taxable accounts. The main issue is the management of stocks in taxable accounts. Two key lessons are, allow capital gains to grow unharvested and realize capital losses.

As a preview, Chapter 14 will examine the asset-location question. That is, to the degree possible, should stocks be located in taxable accounts, and bonds in tax-deferred retirement accounts, or vice versa? As we shall see, the best solution is to hold stocks in taxable accounts and to manage them tax efficiently, while holding bonds in retirement accounts. Tax-efficient management allows most of stocks' returns to benefit from tax deferral—just like the retirement account. Moreover, in a taxable account, the capital gains are eventually taxed at preferential tax rates (or tax-exempt rates if given to charity or held until receiving the step-up in basis at death). In contrast, in a retirement account, the gains are eventually taxed at ordinary income tax rates. It is thus a waste of the retirement account's tax shelter to passively hold stocks in them.

Many individuals actively manage a portion of their stock portfolio and passively manage the rest. The actively managed portion—whether due to active management of individual stocks or selecting actively managed stock funds—should be held in retirement accounts, while the passive portion should be located in taxable accounts.

Good choices for the stock portion of taxable accounts include: (1) zero-yield or low-yield individual stocks that will be passively held, (2) large-cap or total stock market index funds, (3) tax-efficient exchange traded funds, such as SPDRs, and (4) tax-managed stock funds.

References

Arnott, Robert D., Andrew L. Berkin, and Jia Ye. 2001. The management and mismanagement of taxable assets. *Journal of Investing,* Spring, 15–21.
Jeffrey, Robert H., and Robert D. Arnott. 1993. Is your alpha big enough to cover its taxes? *Journal of Portfolio Management,* Spring, 15–25.

Notes

1. Tax-efficient investing also means comparing the tax-exempt yield on a tax-exempt bond to the after-tax yield on a taxable bond when the bond is held in a taxable account. This topic is covered by every investment text, and there is no need to discuss it here.
2. Many passive stock funds pay a dividend yield of perhaps 1 percent. The ending wealth from such a fund would be similar to the ending wealth for the zero-yield fund. We assume a zero yield to keep the analysis simple. Suppose a mutual fund pays a 1 percent dividend yield. Each year the investor would reinvest the dividends after paying taxes in new shares of the mutual fund. This would increase the number of shares and raise the cost basis. After 30 years, he would sell the fund's shares, including the shares purchased each year, and pay taxes on the realized gains. The realized gain would have to reflect the ending cost basis after 30 years of reinvested dividends. Assuming a zero yield thus simplifies the calculation of the after-tax ending wealth without affecting the relative rankings of the trader, active investor, and passive investor.

CHAPTER

8

College Savings Strategies

Introduction

Prior chapters have examined the choice of savings vehicles and related tax strategies to satisfy the goal of meeting retirement needs. Another goal of many families is to accumulate savings for education needs. This chapter discusses savings strategies to finance these education needs.

Tax incentives for college savings continue to evolve. The Economic Growth and Tax Relief Reconciliation Act of 2001 (henceforth, 2001 Tax Act) enhanced the tax advantages of many savings vehicles designed to fund higher education. The Taxpayer Relief Act of 1997 introduced the Hope scholarship credit, the lifetime learning credit, and the education IRA. In addition, the Tax Code permits shifting assets from individuals in higher tax brackets to individuals in lower brackets. In this chapter, we compare and contrast several savings strategies that are available to finance the education needs of middle- and high-income families. In general, these strategies reduce the tax burden on savings intended for higher education. Although we briefly discuss financial aid implications, our focus is not on strategies designed to maximize need-based grants, which are likely to interest lower-income families. Similarly, we do not consider loan-based strategies, which are also likely to interest lower-income families.

The chapter first presents background information, followed by a discussion of savings vehicles that can be used to finance education. The chapter then discusses tax strategies, such as income shifting and the use of the Hope and lifetime learning credits. These are followed by an analysis of these strategies and a discussion of the basics of financial aid, including examples.

Background

We first define two terms used throughout the analysis: qualified higher education expenses and modified adjusted gross income (MAGI). Their definitions vary across strategies. We then discuss sunset provisions associated with the 2001 Tax Act.

Qualified Higher Education Expenses

Under the Internal Revenue Code, the definition of qualified higher education expenses (henceforth, qualified expenses) varies from strategy to strategy. For all savings vehicles and for all tax strategies, qualified expenses include tuition and fees required as a condition of enrollment. They may or may not include textbooks, supplies, and room and board. Textbooks and supplies required as a condition of enrollment and paid directly from the educational institution are typically considered qualified expenses. For example, science and art classes typically have lab or studio fees. Textbooks and supplies purchased from a third party are qualified expenses under Coverdell Education Savings Accounts, IRAs, and 529 savings plans, but not under the savings bond, Hope credit, or lifetime learning credit strategies.

Qualified expenses are reduced by the amount of scholarships and grants received by the student. If a student "spends" $25,000 on qualified education expenses, but receives a $10,000 scholarship, qualified expenses are only $15,000. Although a student must incur the qualified expenses while attending an eligible institution, most universities, colleges, junior colleges, and vocational schools are eligible institutions.

Modified Adjusted Gross Income

Income tests affect families' eligibility for several of the savings vehicles and tax strategies. For each strategy, benefits phase-out at different levels of modified adjusted gross income (MAGI). Further, the definition of MAGI varies across strategies. However, it is always a variant of adjusted gross income (AGI), which is income before standard or itemized deductions and personal and dependency exemptions. Table 8.1 summarizes the 2002 phase-out limits for each strategy. The income limits depend upon whether the tax filer is single, married filing jointly, or married filing separately. With the possible exception of Coverdell Education Savings Accounts, when an income limit exists, the strategy is not available to married couples filing separately.[1]

Sunset Provisions

The intent of this chapter is to provide a broad overview of the college funding strategies currently available. As previously indicated, this means incorporating the changes included in the 2001 Tax Act; however, an automatic sunset provision repeals all features of this Act after 2010 unless Congress acts (H.R. 1836, §901).

TABLE 8.1 Highlights of Tax Strategies for Financing Higher Education

	529 Prepaid QTP	529 Savings QTP	Coverdell ESA	IRA	Savings Bond	Gifting	Above-the-line Deduction	Hope Credit	Lifetime Learning Credit
Tax Benefit	Tax-exempt returns; possibly state income tax credit	Tax-exempt returns; possibly state income tax credit	Tax-exempt returns	Low effective tax rate	Interest is excludable from income	Shifting investment income into child's name	Reduce taxable income	Non-refundable tax credit	Non-refundable tax credit
Annual Contribution Limit	Varies by state but large	Varies by state but large	$2,000 per child under 18	$3,000 per person, more if over 50; amounts increase after 2003	$30,000, in face value	None	$3,000 in 2002–2003 $4,000 in 2004–2005	First $1,000 and 50% of second $1,000; up to $1,500 per student	Beginning in 2003, 20% of expenses; up to $2,000 per family
Single Taxpayer Modified AGI Phase-out Levels	NA	NA	$95,000–$110,000	Range varies[1]	$57,600–$72,600	NA	$65,000	$41,000–$51,000	$41,000–$51,000
Married Taxpayer Modified AGI Phase-out Levels	NA	NA	$190,000–$220,000	Range varies[1]	$86,400–$116,400	NA	$130,000	$82,000–$102,000	$82,000–$102,000
Phase-out Inflation Adjustment	NA	NA	No	Yes	Yes	NA	No[2]	Yes	Yes

Adult Control?	Yes	Yes	Yes	Yes	Yes	Before majority	NA	NA	NA
Asset Flexibility?	No	Limited	Yes	Yes	No	Yes	NA	NA	NA
Gift to Child?	Yes	Yes	Yes	No	No	Yes	NA	NA	NA
Levels of Education Covered	Undergrad and grad	Undergrad and grad	Elem & Sec, undergrad, and grad	Undergrad and grad	Undergrad and grad	Elem, Sec, undergrad and grad	Undergrad and grad	First two years of undergrad, if at least half-time student	Undergrad, grad, & to acquire or improve skills
Tuition Covered?	Yes	Yes	Yes	Yes	Yes	Yes	Yes	Yes	Yes
Books, Supplies, and Equipment Covered?	Yes	Yes	Yes	Yes	If paid to the college	Yes	No	If paid to the college	If paid to the college
Room & Board Covered?	If > half-time attendance	If > half-time attendance	If > half-time attendance	If > half-time attendance	No	Yes	No	No	No
What Other Conditions Apply?	Subject to gift tax reporting conventions; five-year "pre-gifting" allowed	Subject to gift tax reporting conventions; five-year "pre-gifting" allowed	Must use by age 30	Required minimum distribution rules	Series I and post-1989 Series EE bonds; purchaser must be 24	UGMA/ UTMA rules apply; Kiddie Tax applies		Can be claimed only two tax years	

[1] Chapter 6 explains who can make deductible contributions to a traditional IRA and the maximum size of the contributions.

[2] For 2004 and 2005, a $4,000 above-the-line deduction is available to singles with adjusted gross income at or below $65,000 and married couples filing jointly with AGI at or below $130,000. A $2,000 deduction is available to singles with AGI between $65,000 and $80,000 and married couples filing jointly with AGI between $130,000 and $160,000.

Since the relevant provisions of the 2001 Tax Act were specifically designed to foster college savings and since large amounts of money have gone into the savings vehicles affected by these provisions, there will be significant pressure for extension. Nevertheless, those who are investing for educational expenses to be incurred after 2010 should be aware of the sunset provision and plan accordingly. For a survey of tax-wise education savings strategies prior to the 2001 Act, see Marks and Reichenstein (2000).

Savings Vehicles

This section discusses strategies associated with savings vehicles. These include the use of 529 prepaid qualified tuition plans (QTPs), 529 savings QTPs, Coverdell Education Savings Accounts, IRAs, and U.S. savings bonds. For each strategy, we discuss the tax benefit. Table 8.1 summarizes other criteria affecting the strategies' desirability such as applicable income tests, whether the student gains control of the funds, and the flexibility in choosing the underlying investment asset.

529 Qualified Tuition Plans

The 529 qualified tuition plans are named after Internal Revenue Code Sec. 529. They come in two styles—prepaid tuition plans and savings plans. Under the 2001 Tax Act, returns in these savings vehicles are now tax-exempt if used to finance qualified expenses. Additionally, the 2001 Tax Act allows private universities and colleges, beginning in 2003, to offer prepaid tuition plans. For this reason, the nomenclature "qualified tuition plans" replaces "qualified state tuition plans."

The contribution limit varies by state, but generally exceeds $100,000 per beneficiary. Suppose a grandmother is trying to reduce the size of her taxable estate. She can give up to $55,000 (in 2002) in one calendar year to each child/student she wishes to help; for estate planning, it is viewed as a gift of $11,000 per year for the next five years, so it does not use part of her lifetime gift and estate tax exemption.

Prepaid Qualified Tuition Plans

Prepaid QTPs generally allow people to prepay tuition (and often room and board) at today's prices at state universities for a specific beneficiary. The "return" earned is the difference between the eventual tuition cost when the child is enrolled and the prepaid cost.[2] For example, suppose a grandfather prepays one year of undergraduate tuition for his granddaughter for $3,500. Ten years later, she redeems the one-year credit when the cost of tuition is $5,000; under the 2001 Tax Act, the $1,500 of deferred "return" is tax-free.

There are several minor differences among state plans. Some plans allow prepaid QTPs to pay for out-of-state or private school tuition. Some state plans offer bonuses or guarantees. Colorado, for example, guarantees a 4 percent return when the funds are used to meet qualified expenses. Some plans guarantee the child in-state tuition rates even if he or she subsequently moves to another state. This should be particularly attractive to those moving from a state with high-quality universities. It should also be attractive to parents who wish to send their children to their alma mater, but are leaving the state.

We believe most investors will prefer the expected returns from other savings vehicles where the returns are tied to market-based returns on stocks and bonds. However, before dismissing prepaid tuition plans, it is worth considering some aspects of their return. First, college costs have historically increased more rapidly than general inflation. If this trend continues, prepaid tuition plans will offer a positive real return when compared to general inflation. These plans may be particularly attractive in states with low current in-state tuition if their tuition level is expected to converge to the national average. Second, the prepaid tuition plans offer liability matching in that the underlying asset—prepaid tuition—exactly matches the college funding liability. Third, they avoid reinvestment risk.

Table 8.1 presents other criteria affecting prepaid QTPs. The investor has no control over the asset choice; he or she receives a return equal to the tuition inflation rate. However, the minor cannot gain control of the funds; that is, the student cannot withdraw the funds and spend them as he or she wishes. There are no income tests. The funds are available to finance undergraduate and graduate years, but not private high school. The funds cover tuition and may cover room and board. If the funds are not used, the owner-parent may transfer them to another family member. Under the 2001 Tax Act, the definition of family members for the transfer of funds has been expanded to include first cousins, half-siblings, and stepsiblings. This expanded definition increases the attractiveness of 529 plans.

529 Savings Qualified Tuition Plans

In savings QTPs, an individual invests in a portfolio of mutual funds that offers the market-based returns of the underlying stocks and bonds. The key characteristic of this savings vehicle is that returns are tax-exempt if used to meet qualified expenses.

Although federal tax exemption is the key characteristic, some states (for example, Colorado, Illinois, and Iowa) offer a state income tax deduction for new contributions. Some states limit the amount of the deduction, while others do not. Taking the deduction generally requires using that state's 529 savings QTP. (Some states also allow deductions for contributions to 529 prepaid QTPs, but deductions for 529 savings QTPs are more prevalent.)

This savings vehicle offers limited asset flexibility. The investor cannot direct the investment policy of a specific 529 plan. However, he or she can shop around for a plan that has his or her desired asset mix. The portfolios' asset mixes vary sharply across plans. Some portfolios contain 100 percent bonds. Others contain 100 percent stocks. Many maintain a prespecified asset mix, where the stock allocation slowly decreases as the student approaches postsecondary education. Most states are liberalizing residency requirements so nonresidents can open an account in their

TABLE 8.2   A List of Low-cost 529 Savings Qualified Tuition Plans

State	Investment Manager	Expense Level	Separate Mutual Fund Expenses?*	Web site
Connecticut	TIAA-CREF	0.81%	No	www.aboutchet.com
Illinois	Salomon	0.99	No	www.brightstartsavings.com
Iowa	Vanguard	0.65	No	www.collegesavingsiowa.com
Maryland	T. Rowe Price	0.38	Yes	www.collegesavingsmd.org
Michigan	TIAA-CREF	0.65	No	www.misaves.com
Minnesota	TIAA-CREF	0.65	No	www.mnsaves.org
Missouri	TIAA-CREF	0.65	No	www.missourimost.com
New Hampshire	Fidelity	0.30	Yes	www.fidelity.com/unique
New York	TIAA-CREF	0.65	No	www.nysaves.org
Ohio	Putnam	0.99	No	www.collegeadvantage.com

*For example, in the Maryland plan, T. Rowe Price charges 0.38 percent, but this does not include the cost of the underlying mutual fund's expense ratio. In the Connecticut plan, TIAA-CREF charges 0.81 percent, which includes the underlying mutual fund's expense ratio.

savings plan. From the investors' perspective, this means that their investment options are not limited to the 529 plan adopted by their state.

The other criteria affecting the desirability of this savings vehicle are the same as for the 529 prepaid plans. There are no loss-of-control issues or income tests. The funds are available to finance undergraduate and graduate school, but not private high school. They cover tuition and, if at least a half-time student, room and board.

Finally, we encourage financial professionals to search for plans with low expense ratios and, as a second criterion, a desirable asset allocation. Expenses for 529 plans are often considerably higher than expenses on low-cost mutual funds. Not surprisingly, expenses vary substantially across plans. Planners should seek a low-cost plan, whether housed in the home state or another state. (State income tax deductions may offset the higher expenses of the in-state plan.) Table 8.2 presents a selection of low-cost 529 savings plans. Usually, the plan's asset allocation should be less of a concern than the expense ratio because the other assets in the family's portfolio can be reallocated to meet the family's target asset allocation.

Coverdell Education Savings Accounts

After the 2001 Tax Act, the misnomer "*education* individual *retirement* accounts" became known as Coverdell Education Savings Accounts. Contributions to Education Savings Accounts are not deductible, but the returns are tax-exempt when funds pay for qualified expenses. Because Education Savings Accounts are typically invested in mutual funds, they earn market-based returns of the underlying stocks and bonds.

Various restrictions limit the usefulness of this strategy. We outline some here and in Table 8.1. First, contributions can be made to a child's Education Savings Account only if the child is under age 18. Second, an income test may bar contributions; for a married couple filing jointly, the ability to fund an Education Savings Account is phased out at MAGI between $190,000 and $220,000. Third, subject to the income test, anyone (e.g., parent, grandparent, or friend) can contribute to a child's Education Savings Account, but the total annual contribution from all donors cannot exceed $2,000. Fourth, there are control issues since the beneficiary obtains control of the funds at the age of majority, which is usually 18 or 21. On a positive note, this savings vehicle provides excellent asset flexibility.

The 2001 Tax Act removed or mitigated several hindrances to Education Savings Accounts. Now, contributions to and withdrawals from 529 QTPs are allowed concurrently with contributions to and withdrawals from Education Savings Accounts. Further, withdrawals from Education Savings Accounts no longer eliminate the opportunity to use Hope or lifetime learning credits. Finally, prior-year contributions are allowed through April 15 of the following year. The planned sunset of these provisions in 2010 could be a problem for those caught unaware. See Internal Revenue Service Publication 590 (2001) and Internal Revenue Code Sec. 530 for additional details.

Individual Retirement Accounts

This section discusses the use of IRAs to fund qualified expenses.

Traditional (Deductible) IRAs

In earlier chapters, we encouraged individuals who are saving for retirement to save all they are allowed to save, or all they can afford to save, in Roth IRAs and deductible pensions including deductible IRAs. Our recommendation has not changed. However, suppose parents are eligible to contribute, but do not plan to make the maximum contribution to a traditional deductible IRA. As discussed in Chapter 6, the 2001 Tax Act substantially increased contribution limits to 401(k) and other qualified plans. Therefore, many people will not be able to fully fund their deductible IRAs. Assume the parents previously discussed want to invest $3,000 for their child's education needs. A parent could contribute to his or her deductible IRA and, years later, withdraw the funds to finance the child's education needs. The effective tax rate is low—often zero. A key to this strategy is that the 10 percent penalty tax that usually applies to IRA withdrawals before age 59½ does not apply when the withdrawal pays for qualified expenses.

Table 8.1 lists other criteria that favor this strategy. IRAs offer excellent asset flexibility. Also, there are no control issues. Since the funds are in the parent's IRA, the child has no legal claim to the funds. The IRA is particularly useful when the level of education expenses is unknown. Suppose the student decides to attend a public college instead of a private college and, therefore, the IRA funds are not needed for education. The parent can retain the funds in his or her IRA, while preserving its tax-advantaged character. IRA contributions are deductible *above the line;* consequently, they reduce modified adjusted gross income and may allow individuals to qualify for additional savings strategies. Qualified expenses for IRA withdrawals are broadly defined to include tuition, books and supplies, and, if the student is at least half-time, room and board. Although income tests restrict some individuals from making deductible IRA contributions, a nonworking spouse can make a deductible contribution as long as the couple files jointly and has AGI of $150,000 or less.

Roth IRAs

As with traditional IRAs, parents who do not plan to fully fund Roth IRAs for their retirement needs may want to use this savings vehicle to finance education. Suppose a mother invests $3,000 in a Roth IRA. Seven years later, when her child is entering college, the Roth IRA is worth $4,900. If withdrawals pay for qualified expenses, she may withdraw any or all of the $4,900 without paying the 10 percent penalty tax. However, she would owe regular income taxes on the $1,900 of deferred returns unless she withdraws the funds after age 59½. We encourage her to limit the withdrawal to $3,000—the principal. As discussed in Chapter 6, withdrawals from a Roth IRA are principal first. Therefore, she could withdraw $3,000 and pay no taxes. If possible, she should not withdraw any of the $1,900 return until after turning 59½, at which time all withdrawals would be tax-free.

Table 8.1 lists other favorable criteria. They are the same for the Roth IRA as for the traditional IRA and include asset flexibility, parental control, flexibility when the level of educational expenses is unknown, and broadly defined qualified expenses.

U.S. Savings Bonds

Interest income on Series EE and Series I U.S. savings bonds is potentially tax-exempt if redemption proceeds pay for qualified expenses. Before detailing their educational use, we will provide background information.

Funds invested in savings bonds receive the interest rate specified by the applicable contract at that time of investment. On a few occasions in years past, Series EE bond contracts offered interest rates that were higher than current market yields. The current Series EE contract offers a floating rate that is set at 90 percent of the average market yield on five-year Treasury notes over the preceding six months. This interest rate is currently 4.07 percent (May 2002). Series EE bonds are issued at half of face value. Newly issued savings bonds are guaranteed to reach face value in 17 years—essentially guaranteeing a minimum 4.16 percent effective annual return if held that long. Except when market rates are falling fast, the current series EE contract offers below market rates.

The interest rate on Series I bonds is composed of two components: a rate that remains constant for the length of the contract and a component that varies with the consumer inflation rate. The current (May 2002) Series I contract has a fixed rate of

2.00 percent, and the inflation-linked rate is 2.38 percent. After adjusting for inter-actions and compounding, it offers a 4.40 percent interest rate.[3] Since marketable Treasury Inflation Protection Securities (TIPS) currently (October 2002) offer fixed real yields exceeding 2 percent, the Series I bonds offer below-market interest rates.

The Department of Treasury can change the contract terms on Savings Bonds on May 1 and November 1 each year; the new rates apply only to new investments. The Treasury credits interest monthly, and interest compounds semi-annually. Each tax-payer may purchase savings bonds up to $30,000 in face value each year. The maxi-mum term on Series EE and Series I bonds is 30 years. Investors can redeem bonds after the first six months, and a three-month interest penalty applies to bonds redeemed within the first five years. Since they are Treasury securities, interest is exempt from state and local taxation. With respect to federal taxation, owners may elect to recognize interest income each year or defer it. Naturally, most prefer to defer taxes.

Series EE bonds issued after January 1990 and all Series I bonds are eligible for the Education Bond Program under Internal Revenue Code Sec. 135. Suppose a father purchases a savings bond. Subject to an income test, he can use the proceeds to pay qualified expenses in the redemption year for himself, his spouse, or his dependents. However, there are several disadvantages to these savings bonds.

First, as previously noted, they generally provide below-market returns. Sec-ond, the interest exclusion tends to be small. Suppose a parent invested $5,000 in an EE bond eight years ago, and it is worth $8,000 today. If qualified expenses total $6,000, the interest exclusion would apply to $2,250 [($6,000 / $8,000) • $3,000], where $3,000 is deferred interest. Third, severe income tests apply. In 2002, educa-tional use of savings bonds is phased out for MAGIs between $57,600 and $72,600 for single taxpayers and between $86,400 and $116,400 for married filing jointly taxpayers. These limits are adjusted annually for inflation. Fourth, the income limit applies to income in the distribution year. Many couples do not know if their income many years hence will exceed the then inflation-adjusted limits. Fifth, there is no asset flexibility.

On a positive note, there are no management costs on these bonds. This cost advantage may exceed the disadvantage of their typical below-market yields.[4] In addition, they provide flexibility when the level of educational expenses is uncer-tain; that is, savings bonds can be freely diverted to other savings goals should educational costs prove lower than anticipated. There is no control issue with these bonds. Further, they avoid reinvestment risk. Finally, savings bonds offer a tax-timing advantage; the owner can time the realization of the deferred interest for a low tax-rate year.

Individuals wishing to implement this strategy should buy many small denomina-tion bonds instead of a few large denomination bonds. This allows the redemption of savings bonds to be scaled to the qualified expenses. For example, if qualified expenses total $5,000, it is better to liquidate four small bonds for $5,000, including $1,000 in interest, than one large bond for $12,500 including $2,500 in interest. Since the proceeds are prorated, in both cases $1,000 of interest is tax-exempt; the exemption for the large bond is $1,000 [($5,000 / $12,500) • $2,500]. Therefore, buying 30 $1,000 savings bonds provides more flexibility than buying three $10,000 bonds.

Other Tax Strategies

This section discusses several tax strategies including those based on shifting interest or capital gains into a child/student's name, shifting wage income, and the Hope and lifetime's learning credits.

Gifting Strategies

Parents, grandparents, and friends can give assets to children under the Uniform Gift to Minors Act (UGMA) and the Uniform Transfer to Minors Act (UTMA). The minor owns the assets, but an adult custodian controls the account until the minor attains the state-specified age of majority.[5] After reaching the age of majority, the child obtains control of the asset. (Of course, some parents do not inform their children of their legal rights.)

There are two separate gifting strategies. The first is to shift an asset's earnings into the child's lower tax rate. The second is to shift unrealized capital gains into the child's name. Shifting earnings involves shifting *future* returns, while shifting capital gains involves shifting *past* unrealized returns. Details are in Internal Revenue Code Sec. 2503.

In practice, the donor is usually a grandparent or parent. If the donor is a grandparent, the goals are usually to reduce estate taxes as well as income taxes. The grandparent should give the asset to a grandchild through UGMA or UTMA and name a parent as the custodian. This would remove the assets from the grandparent's estate. If the grandparent is the custodian, the underlying assets would belong to his or her estate until the child reaches majority age. If the parent gives the asset, usually the sole goal is to reduce income taxes.

The so-called Kiddie Tax rules apply to shifting earnings to children under age 14. Under the Kiddie Tax, there are three tiers of tax rates on unearned income, which consists of dividends, interest, and capital gains. The first $750 (in 2002) is tax-free. The next $750 is taxed at the child's rate. Unearned income above $1,500 is taxed at the parents' rate. Once the child reaches 14, potential tax savings are much higher. Assuming all income is unearned, the standard deduction applies to the first $750 of income. Additional income through $6,000 is taxed at 10 percent, while additional income up to $27,950 is taxed at 15 percent.

The other gifting strategy is to shift low-basis assets to children. This strategy transfers the unrealized capital gains into the child's name. To avoid estate and gift tax implications, the transferred assets should be worth less than $11,000 (in 2002) per donor or $22,000 per couple; higher amounts can be given, but they eat into the lifetime gift and estate tax exemption. The key to this strategy is that the child donee retains the donor's cost basis. The child's long-term capital gain tax rate would probably be 8 percent or 10 percent, instead of the donor's 20 percent.[6]

There are positive and negative aspects to gifting strategies. First, on the positive side, parents can delay giving low-basis assets to a child until it is clear that the child will need (and not misuse) the funds. Suppose parents have two children approaching college. The parents could plan to give some of the low-basis asset to the first child as needed, but refrain from doing so if he receives a scholarship. Second, gifting strategies can be used to finance any education expense, including fraternity dues. Third, there are no income limits.

Three main drawbacks exist. First, the child obtains control of the funds at the age of majority. Some will view the risk of the child misappropriating education funds as a significant negative. Parents can retain low-basis assets in their names until the child needs the funds and shows sufficient maturity. However, this wait-and-see option is not available to a grandmother who is trying to reduce her estate or a parent who is considering shifting an asset's future earnings into the child's name. Second, there is no ability to use the funds' flexibility to meet multiple children's education needs. Suppose parents give equal amounts to two children. Years later, the first child enters the (free) U.S. Air Force Academy and the second attends (high-cost) Notre Dame. Since the funds given to the first child belong to this child, the parents cannot use these funds to meet the second child's educational needs. Third, suppose the goal is to shift an asset's future earnings into the child's name. Unless the child has little income, the future earnings will still be taxable, albeit at a lower rate. In contrast, 529 QTPs and Education Savings Accounts offer tax-exempt returns.

Shifting Wage Income

Some parents may be able to shift earned income into a child's name. Business owners and professionals will find this to be an attractive strategy. Naturally, the pay must be for real work and cannot exceed market wages for comparable work. In 2002, a child's standard deduction is the greater of $750 or $250 plus *earned income* up to a total of $4,700. Consequently, this strategy must be coordinated with gifting strategies.

If the business is in the 40 percent combined income tax bracket, each $1,000 in wages reduces the business' income by $600 after taxes. If the child's income is below the standard deduction, he or she pays no income taxes. Payroll taxes like Social Security and unemployment insurance add some complexity, but income shifting like this typically produces substantial tax savings. While this strategy can continue through the college years, there are financial aid implications. Each dollar of student earnings reduces aid by up to 50 percent.

Hope Credit

The Hope scholarship credit is a 100 percent credit for the first $1,000 and 50 percent credit for the second $1,000 of qualified expenses. These amounts are indexed for inflation. Since credits are dollar-for-dollar reductions in taxes, they are generally preferable to deductions. The Hope credit is available only for the first two years of undergraduate school. The student must be enrolled at least half-time in a degree program and cannot have a felony drug conviction. A family can claim more than one student per year.

Qualified expenses are those paid during two *calendar* tax years before the student completes the first two years of undergraduate work. This provision may be a problem for a traditional student who begins college in the fall semester and finishes the sophomore year of school in the third calendar year. A special rule allows tuition for next year's spring semester to be prepaid. To fully use the Hope credit for a student living at home and attending a local college, the parents should prepay spring-term tuition bills in December of the freshman year and December of the sophomore year.

The income limits on the Hope credit are strict. The ability to use a Hope credit is phased out for MAGIs between $41,000 and $51,000 if single, or $82,000 and $102,000 if married filing jointly.

Lifetime Learning Credit

Beginning in 2003, the lifetime learning credit provides a tax credit of 20 percent of up to $10,000 of qualified expenses for a maximum credit of $2,000.[7] (Before 2003, this credit was 20 percent of up to $5,000 of qualified expenses.) This credit applies to any year of undergraduate or graduate school; in addition, it can be used for any course of instruction from an eligible institution that improves the student's job skills. The income limits are the same as for the Hope credit.

The lifetime learning credit differs in many aspects from the Hope credit. There is no limit on the number of years a family can claim this credit. The student may be a full-time student, a part-time student, or taking courses on an *ad hoc* basis. The maximum credit applies *per family,* not per student. Further, felony drug use does not disqualify one from the lifetime learning credit. The Hope and lifetime learning credits may not be taken in the same tax year with respect to the same student's tuition and related expenses.

Above-the-line Deductions

Before the 2001 Tax Act, the major deductions for educational expenses were those authorized under Internal Revenue Code Sec. 162. To be eligible for deduction, educational expenses (1) must maintain or improve skills in the individual's current trade or business or (2) must be required by the individual's employer. The deduction is not allowed if the education qualifies the individual for a new trade or business (as an undergraduate degree would likely do). Further, the deduction falls under miscellaneous itemized deductions. This means the deduction applies to individuals who itemize, and the deductible amount is limited to amounts in excess of 2 percent of AGI. (The requirement to itemize makes these Sec. 162 provisions a "below-the-line" deduction.) In short, before the 2001 Tax Act, educational expenses provided tax savings to few individuals, and then the tax savings were usually modest.

The 2001 Tax Act authorized a new above-the-line deduction for qualified expenses in 2002 through 2005. ("Above-the-line" means itemizing is not required to claim the deduction, and the 2 percent-of-AGI miscellaneous-deductions provision does not apply.) The Act authorizes a deduction of up to $3,000 in 2002 and 2003, and up to $4,000 in 2004 and 2005. The deduction applies to undergraduate and graduate tuition expenses paid in a calendar year. The tuition must be for enrollment during that calendar year or for a term that begins in the first three months of the following year.

Income limits apply. For 2002 and 2003, the $3,000 above-the-line deduction is available to singles with adjusted gross income at or below $65,000 and married couples filing jointly with AGI at or below $130,000. For 2004 and 2005, a $4,000 above-the-line deduction is available to singles with AGI at or below $65,000 and married couples filing jointly with AGI at or below $130,000. A $2,000 deduction is available to singles with AGI between $65,000 and $80,000 and married couples filing jointly with AGI between $130,000 and $160,000. Finally, as its name states, this is an above-the-line deduction. For taxpayers just over a MAGI threshold, this deduction could make them eligible for additional education savings strategies.

Not Claiming a Child as a Dependent

This section asks if parents should claim a child as a dependent. Many clients of financial planners will have incomes that are too high to be eligible for Hope or lifetime learning credits. These high-income parents could elect *not* to claim a child as a dependent, which would probably enable the child to claim the Hope or lifetime learning tax credit. By not claiming the child, the parents lose the tax benefit of the dependency exemption, but the child gains the benefit of the tax credit. Parents can compare their tax savings from claiming the child as a dependent to the child's tax savings from the credit.

The personal exemption amount is $3,000 (in 2002), but exemptions begin to phase-out at income levels above $206,000 (in 2002) for joint returns and $137,300 for single taxpayers. Under the phase-out, a family loses 2 percent of the exemption for each $2,500 of income or fraction thereof above the threshold. If a couple has adjusted gross income above $328,500, they receive no benefit from claiming their child as a dependent. They should not claim the child, since this would allow the child to claim a tuition credit.

It sometimes pays not to claim a child as a dependent even if parents receive some benefit from the exemption. For example, suppose parents have adjusted gross income of $265,700, provide more than half their college-age son's support, and are in the 40 percent tax bracket. If they claim him, they can only take 52 percent of the $3,000 deduction, and the dependency exemption will only save them $624 in taxes [0.52 • $3,000 • 0.40]. If their son could save more than $624 in taxes by claiming the Hope or lifetime learning credit, the family would be better off by not claiming him.

Recall that the maximum lifetime learning credit is currently $1,000 *per family*. Suppose a son is in graduate school and a daughter is a senior undergraduate. If the parents do not claim their son, the parents and son are separate "families" for purposes of this credit. The parents can get a lifetime learning credit based on the daughter's qualified expenses and the son can get this credit based on his qualified expenses.

Independence

When a child provides more than half of his or her own support, the child is considered independent for tax purposes. If independent, the child can take advantage of the $4,700 standard deduction and the $3,000 personal exemption (in 2002). If independent, the child can have $7,700 in income and pay no taxes.

For example, suppose a mother gives $6,000 to her son during his sophomore year in high school. It grows to $7,000 by his first year in college. During his first year, his support for food, shelter, school, and so on totals $25,000. He obtains $7,000 from the prior gift and $8,000 from working at his mother's office. The mother provides the other $10,000. For tax purposes, the son is independent because he provided $15,000, which is more than half of his support.

Assume the son has $8,250 in income—$8,000 in wages and $250 of income on the $6,000 gift earned in this tax year. The first $7,700 is tax-free. If not for the Hope credit, he would pay $55 in taxes—10 percent of the other $550. The Hope credit, however, eliminates the tax liability. By arranging matters so he is independent, the son avoids income taxes. The family's tax savings from such an arrangement could be substantial, especially if the parents' income is too high to benefit from the dependency exemption.

For families with incomes below the income limits, the Hope and lifetime learning credits are an obvious benefit. These parents can claim the credit and get the benefit of the dependency exemption on the child. It is less clear whether parents with incomes above the income limits should claim a child as a dependent or the child should seek to be considered independent. The family should compare the overall family tax burden under three scenarios—the parents claim the child, the parents do not claim the child, and the child is independent. Their combined taxes may be lowest under one of the latter scenarios.

Analysis

In this section, we develop after-tax ending-wealth models for each education savings vehicle. Later, we present the basic structure affecting eligibility for financial aid.

Analysis of Strategies

In the spirit of Chapter 2, we develop after-tax ending-wealth models for the various college savings vehicles. Comparing these ending-wealth models shows which education savings vehicles provide the most-favored tax structures. Concerns about control, flexibility to redirect money, financial aid, and so on could be sufficiently strong to offset the tax savings addressed here.

Before proceeding, we define our notation:

i Market-based rate of return on investment
$i_{non\text{-}mkt}$ Non-market-based rate of return on investment
t Parents' federal-plus-state tax rate on ordinary income
n Number of years until redemption
t_{state} Parents' state income tax rate
t_n Parents' federal-plus-state ordinary income tax rate in effect at future time n
t_{oic} Child's federal-plus-state tax rate on ordinary income

Parent Saves in Taxable Accounts

The benchmark against which other savings vehicles are considered is saving in the parents' names in a taxable account. The ending-wealth model for ordinary bonds held in a taxable account is:

$$[1 + i \bullet (1 - t)]^n \qquad\qquad \text{(Eq. 8.1)}$$

This is the same as Equation 2.1. As with retirement savings vehicles, the models for stocks are more complicated since capital gains and dividends are taxed at different rates. However, dividends and realized capital gains are taxed each year at the parents' rates. For simplicity, we omit these models. As we shall see, other vehicles will dominate this option.

Gifting Strategies including UGMAs/UTMAs

The ending-wealth models for gifting strategies are the same as for taxable accounts, except that the applicable tax rate is the child's lower rate.

$$[1 + i \bullet (1 - t_{oic})]^n \qquad\qquad \text{(Eq. 8.2)}$$

529 Qualified Tuition Plans

Under the 2001 Tax Act, returns in 529 plans are tax-exempt. The ending-wealth model for 529 prepaid QTPs is:

$$(1 + i_{non\text{-}mkt})^n \qquad\qquad \text{(Eq. 8.3)}$$

The ending-wealth model for 529 savings QTPs is:

$$(1 + i)^n \qquad\qquad \text{(Eq. 8.4)}$$

For prepaid QTPs, the rate of return is the appropriate college tuition inflation rate (adjusted, if necessary, for any state-guaranteed minimum); this is a non-market interest rate. For savings QTPs, the rate of return is market based. It depends on the underlying rates of returns on stocks and bonds.

Some states allow state income tax deductions for contributions to in-state 529 QTPs. For these plans, the ending-wealth models are:

$$(1 + i_{\text{non-mkt}})^n / (1 - t_{\text{state}}) \qquad \text{(Eq. 8.5)}$$

and

$$(1 + i)^n / (1 - t_{\text{state}}) \qquad \text{(Eq. 8.6)}$$

For example, if the parents' state tax rate on ordinary income is 8 percent, then a \$1 after-tax contribution is like a \$1.087 before-tax contribution. The \$1.087 contribution would reduce taxes by \$0.087.

Savings Bonds

Like 529 QTPs, savings bonds are exempt from federal income tax when used for qualified expenses. The ending-wealth model is:

$$(1 + i_{\text{non-mkt}})^n \qquad \text{(Eq. 8.7)}$$

The Treasury Department sets these interest rates, usually at levels below those available from marketable Treasury securities.

Coverdell Educational Savings Accounts

This is a tax-exempt education savings vehicle. Since the underlying investments are marketable securities, the ending-wealth model is:

$$(1 + i)^n \qquad \text{(Eq. 8.8)}$$

Deductible IRAs

If used to pay qualified expenses, withdrawals from a deductible IRA are taxable at ordinary income tax rates, but the penalty tax does not apply. Considering the deduction, the ending-wealth model is:

$$[(1-t_n) / (1 - t)] \bullet (1 + i)^n \qquad \text{(Eq. 8.9)}$$

Roth IRAs

If used to pay qualified expenses, withdrawals of contributions only (or principal only) from a Roth IRA are tax-free. In addition, withdrawals after five years and after age 59½ are tax-exempt. The ending-wealth model is:

$$(1 + i)^n \qquad \text{(Eq. 8.10)}$$

If used to pay qualified expenses, the ending-wealth model for total withdrawals from a Roth IRA before age 59½ is:

$$(1 + i)^n - t_n \bullet [(1 + i)^n - 1] \qquad \text{(Eq. 8.11)}$$

TABLE 8.3 Comparison of Ending-Wealth Models for Education Savings Vehicles

Taxable Account in Parents' Names	$[1 + i \cdot (1 - t)]^n$	Eq. 8.1
UGMA/UTMA Taxable Account in Child's Name	$[1 + i \cdot (1 - t_{oic})]^n$	Eq. 8.2
529 Prepaid QTPs	$(1 + i_{non\text{-}mkt})^n$	Eq. 8.3
529 Savings QTPs	$(1 + i)^n$	Eq. 8.4
529 Prepaid QTPs with State Deduction	$(1 + i_{non\text{-}mkt})^n / (1 - t_{state})$	Eq. 8.5
529 Savings QTPs with State Deduction	$(1 + i)^n/(1 - t_{state})$	Eq. 8.6
Savings Bonds	$(1 + i_{non\text{-}mkt})^n$	Eq. 8.7
Coverdell Educational Savings Accounts	$(1 + i)^n$	Eq. 8.8
Deductible IRAs	$[(1 - t_n) / (1 - t)] \cdot (1 + i)^n$	Eq. 8.9
Roth IRAs: Withdrawal of Contributions	$(1 + i)^n$	Eq. 8.10
Roth IRAs: Total Withdrawal	$(1 + i)^n - t_n \cdot [(1 + i)^n - 1]$	Eq. 8.11

Table 8.3 compares the ending-wealth models for these education savings vehicles. Assuming the non-market rates of return arc below market-based returns—which they usually are—the best savings vehicles are state-tax-deductible 529 savings QTPs and deductible IRAs when the parents' tax rate in the withdrawal year is below their tax rate in the contribution year; that is, $t_n < t$. Few states allow contributions to be deducted for state taxes, and, when they do, they often cap the deduction at relatively low contribution levels.[8] As noted earlier, although we encourage parents to use deductible IRAs to fund their retirement, they can also use them to fund their children's education needs. In practice, we suspect that most parents' tax rates during their children's college years will be at least as high as their tax rates in the contribution year; that is, $t_n \geq t$.

Consequently, for most parents, the most tax-favored education savings vehicles are likely to be 529 savings QTPs and Coverdell Education Savings Accounts. Since Education Savings Accounts have low contribution limits, 529 savings QTPs with moderate expenses should attract the most funds among education savings vehicles. However, savings in Education Savings Accounts and other savings vehicles can provide asset-choice flexibility and complement savings in 529 savings QTPs.

At the margin, the choice between Education Savings Accounts and 529 savings QTPs depends upon costs. Each of these savings vehicles offers market-based rates of return. Table 8.2 presented a selection of low-cost 529 savings QTPs.

Financial Aid Eligibility

Our analysis has focused on tax consequences of education savings vehicles. Feldstein (1995) characterizes the financial aid calculation systems—the Federal Methodology and the College Board's Institutional Methodology—as "education taxes" with substantial disincentives for savings. We provide a brief sketch of the

Federal Methodology and discuss some implications. (The Institutional Methodology is similar.) Full consideration of the financial aid system is beyond the scope of this chapter. We are comfortable omitting financial aid in our analysis because many clients of financial professionals will have sufficiently high incomes or asset bases that they will be ineligible for need-based grants at most colleges. Ma and Fore (2002) estimate that a family with $100,000 in assets and $90,000 in income will have an expected family contribution of about $16,000; many clients will have substantially higher incomes and assets.

A key to understanding the Federal Methodology is that it treats parental income and assets differently than student income and assets. Although there are many complications and allowances, parental assets are assessed approximately 5.64 percent per year, and parental income is assessed 47 percent for middle- and upper-income parents. Retirement accounts like IRAs are not assessed. Student assets are assessed 35 percent per year and student income is assessed 50 percent. Savings and prepaid 529 QTPs deserve special note. Current rules for prepaid 529 QTPs state that they reduce financial aid dollar-for-dollar—a 100 percent assessment.[9] Savings 529 QTPs are considered account-owner (typically, parental) assets. However, the treatment of both types of QTPs is subject to change.

The financial aid rules combine to favor IRAs and savings bond strategies over Education Savings Accounts and gifting strategies like UTMA accounts. Although it potentially complicates estate planning, holding education savings assets in grandparents' names eliminates many of these financial aid considerations.

Applications

This section presents two cases that apply some of the lessons of this chapter.

Strategies for a Young Child

For the first example, consider the Hamiltons who want to finance Caroline's college education. She is two years old and their only child. Mr. and Mrs. Hamilton have professional careers and anticipate that their joint income will remain near $250,000 in today's dollars. They will be ineligible for the Hope and lifetime learning credits, above-the-line deductions, and any strategy dependent upon savings bonds.

The best education savings vehicles available to them are the 529 savings QTPs and Coverdell Educational Savings Account. From Table 8.2, they choose a low-cost 529 savings plan from another state; this plan's lower costs compared to the costs of their state's plan will likely provide a large ending wealth advantage over the long investment horizon.

The parents' income prevents them from contributing to an ESA in Caroline's name. However, subject to income tests, Caroline's grandmother can contribute the funds to Caroline's Education Savings Account. These contributions can continue until Caroline turns 18.

Funds from 529 plans and Education Savings Accounts cover tuition, books and supplies, and room and board. Consequently, the parents can set aside sufficient funds in Caroline's name to finance all of her qualified college education expenses. These funds will earn market-based, tax-exempt returns.

The parents may also consider investing in capital assets with appreciation potential. Later, they can give these appreciated assets to Caroline. She could then sell them and pay capital gains taxes at her lower tax rate. The parents can sell the assets that lose value, which will lower their taxes. In short, they realize losses in their names and shift gains to their daughter. Moreover, if the parents are worried that Caroline will not use the funds for college, they can delay giving her the assets until she is college age. At that time, there probably will be no control issue.

Strategies for an Older Child

It is April 1, 2003, and the James family is trying to finance Graham's freshman year of college. Graham is their 18-year-old son who will begin college in six months. In the absence of adjustments discussed later, the parents' adjusted gross income will consist of the father's $84,000 from his construction business. The parents' marginal tax bracket is 25 percent. Expected costs include $3,000 for full-time tuition at a state university, $5,000 for room and board, and $3,000 for books and miscellaneous items.

It is effectively too late to shift future returns into Graham's name. However, assume they can shift $3,000 into Graham's name by hiring him in the summer. This would reduce the parents' AGI to $81,000, which qualifies the family for the Hope credit. The $5,000 of tuition is allocated to the Hope credit. The Hope credit will save the family $1,500 in taxes. The $3,000 above-the-line deduction would have saved the family $750 in taxes, but taxpayers are not eligible to claim this deduction and the Hope credit in the same year for the same student.

Mr. and Mrs. James own 200 shares of stock that was acquired in March 1998. It has a $2,000 basis and current market value of $5,000. They could give the shares to Graham. If he sells the stock at $5,000, he would only owe $240 in capital gain taxes, 8 percent of the $3,000 gain. The 8 percent capital gain tax rate applies to individuals in the 10 percent or 15 percent ordinary income tax bracket who realize a capital gain on assets held at least five years. Since Graham is in one of these low tax brackets, his acquisition date is March 1998; therefore, he qualifies for the 8 percent rate.

The $5,000 from the stock sale and the $3,000 in earned income will provide the other $8,000 for Graham's freshman year. These funds can be used to finance any education expense, including miscellaneous ones.

Summary

Financial professionals can help clients choose the best education savings vehicles or best set of college savings vehicles. Many savings strategies and tax strategies will be attractive to middle- and high-income families. Helping a client choose among the savings vehicles requires the comparison of tax structures and other restrictions. However, the best vehicle is usually the one that produces the largest after-tax ending wealth—which depends primarily upon the tax structure. Thus, if expenses are minimal, the choice among savings vehicles is largely a choice among tax structures.

Among college savings strategies, we recommend the following. The 529 savings QTPs offer market-based, tax-exempt returns with few restrictions. This savings vehicle can accommodate substantial amounts of money. Coverdell Education Savings Accounts also offer market-based, tax-exempt returns, but they have low contribution limits. Savings bonds and 529 prepaid QTPs can complement these savings vehicles, but they offer non-market rates of return that are usually below market-based returns. In practice, asset restrictions on 529 savings QTPs should not prove onerous since a family can adjust its other, non-college assets to achieve the desired overall asset allocation. Families concerned about "overfunding" education savings (in case the child receives a scholarship or chooses a low-cost college) should consider savings bonds, IRAs, and waiting to gift low-basis assets. If eligible, the tax credits and above-the-line deductions are attractive. Parents in higher-income families should consider hiring their child, gifting low-basis assets, not claiming their child as a dependent, and arranging finances so the child is legally independent.

References

Feldstein, Martin. 1995. College scholarship rules and private savings. *American Economic Review,* June, 552–566.

Ma, Jennifer, and Douglas Fore. 2002. Saving for college with 529 plans and other options: An update. TIAA-CREF Institute's Research Dialogue No. 70 (http://www.tiaa-crefinstitute.org/publications/resdiags/70_1–2002.htm).

Marks, Barry, and William Reichenstein. 2000. Tax strategies for financing higher education. *Journal of Financial Planning,* May, 104–113.

Marks, Barry, and William Reichenstein. 2001. How to profit from reduced capital gain tax rates. *AAII Journal,* November, 14–17.

Publication 590: Individual retirement arrangements. 2001. Washington, DC: Department of the Treasury, Internal Revenue Service.

Publication 970: Tax benefits for higher education. 2001. Washington, DC: Department of the Treasury, Internal Revenue Service.

Notes

1. Married filing separately taxpayers are explicitly prohibited from using the Hope credit, the lifetime learning credit, the above-the-line deduction, and savings bond strategies. IRS Publication 970 is ambiguous about Education Savings Accounts; the wording can be interpreted that married filing separately taxpayers are eligible if their MAGI is below the limits for *single* taxpayers.

2. Some state plans set the prepayment prices near today's prices. Some states use other procedures—an example of which is given below. However, from the investor's perspective, the rate of return is approximately the tuition inflation rate. In Colorado's 529 prepaid plan, participants buy "units," where the price of each unit is based on the average cost of tuition at community colleges and state universities. More "units" are required to purchase one year of college at a higher-cost school than a lower-cost school. Nevertheless, the return on each unit is the average tuition inflation rate across these colleges and universities.

3. According to www.savingsbonds.gov, the interest rate is computed as Fixed rate + 2 • Semi-annual inflation rate + Semi-annual inflation rate • Fixed rate.

4. According to the March 2002 issue of *Morningstar Principia Pro Plus for Mutual Funds,* the average expense ratio is 0.76 percent on no-load government bond funds with government/agency holdings greater than 50 percent. An EE bond offering 90 percent of an average five-year yield will likely provide a larger net return than a five-year Treasury bond fund with a 0.76 percent annual expense ratio.

5. The UTMA legislation supercedes the earlier UGMA legislation. Every state has adopted the UTMA except South Carolina and Vermont (which is considering it in 2002). It is possible for South Carolina and Vermont residents to utilize a UTMA if certain conditions are met; consult an attorney. The "uniform version" of the UTMA legislation uses age 21 as the age of majority (age that UTMA custodianship terminates) even in instances when the state's non-UTMA age of majority is lower. A handful of states modified the "uniform version" of the UTMA to specify the age of majority. Alaska, California, and Nevada allow the person who sets up the custodianship to specify an age between 18 and 25. Arkansas, New Jersey, North Carolina, Oklahoma, Maine, Michigan, Virginia, and Washington, DC allow the person who sets up the custodianship to specify an age between 18 and 21. Financial advisors should confirm our interpretation of their state's implementation of UGMA and UTMA and also ensure that their state has not updated its implementation.

6. The 8 percent capital gain tax rate applies to gains on assets held for more than five years and realized by someone in the 10 percent or 15 percent ordinary income tax bracket. For this low-bracket investor, the holding period may begin before January 2001. For example, suppose parents acquired stock on January 2, 1998, and give it to their son in 2001. If the son is in the 10 percent or 15 percent ordinary income tax bracket in 2003 and he sells the stock after January 2, 2003, the 8 percent capital gain tax rate applies. In contrast, the 18 percent capital gain tax rate applies to individuals in higher ordinary income tax brackets and only for assets acquired after January 1, 2001. For further information, see Marks and Reichenstein (2001).

7. The 20 percent provision makes the lifetime learning credit different from other credits. Generally, credits are preferable to deductions—but this holds when the credit is 1:1. With the lifetime learning credit, the ratio is 1:5. Some taxpayers may prefer to take an above-the-line deduction instead of the lifetime learning credit.

8. The benefit of the state income tax deduction should be weighed against the expense level. Using the deduction in Colorado, for example, requires using the in-state 529 QTP which has higher expenses than some other plans. Breakeven analysis shows some savers—particularly those with few years until college—should opt for the deduction despite the higher expenses.

9. This is the federal interpretation. Some states, Illinois for example, assert that 529 prepaid QTPs will not affect eligibility for *in-state* universities.

Part II

A New Approach to Calculating a Family's Asset Allocation

CHAPTER

9

Calculating the Asset Allocation

Introduction

Part II of this book challenges two features of the traditional approach to calculating an individual's or family's asset allocation. First, the traditional approach weighs assets according to their market values instead of their after-tax values. Second, it ignores the value of postretirement income streams.

Table 9.1 illustrates the two changes that we advocate. It presents the family portfolio for Lisa, who is single and age 65. She has $500,000 in a stock fund held in a 403(b) plan and $500,000 in a bond fund held in a taxable account. The cost basis and market value of the bond fund are both $500,000. She recently retired from teaching and will receive $30,000 a year from the teachers' pension plan for the rest of her life. The teachers' plan is not part of the Social Security system, and Lisa does not qualify for Social Security benefits. Lisa is in the combined federal-plus-state 30 percent tax bracket for ordinary income and expects to remain there during retirement. She asks you, her financial advisor, to recommend an asset allocation. Most people's first retirement planning issue—and Lisa's only retirement planning issue—is whether she has sufficient resources to meet her retirement income needs.

According to the traditional approach to calculating a family's asset allocation, Lisa's portfolio contains $500,000 in stocks and $500,000 in bonds. It contains 50 percent stocks and 50 percent bonds. The traditional approach's first error is that it does not distinguish between the before-tax dollars in the 403(b) and the after-tax dollars in the taxable account. If she withdraws $1,000 from the pension, she pays

TABLE 9.1   Lisa's Family Portfolio

	Market Values	After-tax Values	Savings Vehicle
Financial Assets			
Bond Fund	$500,000	$500,000	Taxable Account
Stock Fund	500,000	350,000	403(b) plan
Total	$1,000,000	$850,000	
Other Assets			
Bond	$364,700	$255,000	Teachers' Pension
Total Assets			
Extended Portfolio		$1,105,000	

	Traditional Approach Asset Allocation	Recommended Approach Asset Allocation
Bonds	50.0%	31.7%
Stocks	50.0%	68.3%

$300 in taxes and can buy $700 of goods and services. If she withdraws $1,000 from the bond fund, she can buy $1,000 of goods and services. We recommend calculating the asset allocation based on after-tax values *because goods and services are purchased with after-tax dollars.*

The traditional approach's second error is that it excludes the value of the teachers' pension from Lisa's portfolio. When addressing the issue of her ability to meet her retirement needs, we believe this pension should be capitalized and viewed as a bond in her portfolio. Although we address the valuation of defined-benefit plans in detail in Chapter 13, for now we estimate its pre-tax present value as the value of a 20-year, $30,000 per-year annuity due when discounted at 6 percent per year (the life expectancy of a 65-year-old woman is about 20 years). The pre-tax value is $364,700, and its after-tax value is about $255,000 [$364,700 • (1 − 0.30)].

The traditional approach says Lisa's asset allocation is 50 percent stocks and 50 percent bonds. Our recommended approach says she has $350,000 of stocks after taxes [$500,000 • (1 − 0.30)], $500,000 of traditional bonds, and $255,000 of pension "bonds" after taxes. Thus, her extended portfolio contains $1,105,000. The asset allocation is 31.7 percent stocks [$350,000 / $1,105,000] and 68.3 percent bonds.

Obviously, a family portfolio can be substantially different when calculated using the traditional approach and our recommended approach. The first question is which is the better approach. Since goods and services are purchased with after-tax funds, we believe it is appropriate to calculate the asset mix based on after-tax funds. The traditional approach equates $1 of before-tax funds with $1 of after-tax funds. This is an apples-to-oranges comparison.

The second issue is whether retirement income streams—the teachers' pension plan in this case—should "count" as part of her portfolio. Studies that look at people's preparedness for retirement regularly count retirement income streams, while studies that calculate a family's asset allocation regularly ignore the value of these streams. This is inconsistent. When assessing Lisa's ability to satisfy her retirement needs, the pension clearly matters. We believe, therefore, that it should be capitalized and viewed as part of her portfolio when calculating her current asset allocation. In contrast, if we are assessing Lisa's potential estate taxes, the teachers' pension should not count. Notice that the decision to include or exclude the teachers' pension depends upon the issue being addressed.

Unique Features when Managing Family Portfolios

In the investment world, the big money has traditionally been in the management of institutional funds, including defined-benefit pension plans, endowments, and mutual funds. Mean-variance optimization and other asset allocation techniques were designed with these investors in mind. Therefore, it is not surprising that, when professionals approached the asset allocation decision for individuals and families, they frequently use the same techniques. These techniques, however, ignore the unique features of individual and family portfolios (henceforth, family portfolios), including the different impacts of taxes on family assets and the existence of retirement income streams.

For example, a university endowment fund might use mean-variance optimization to determine its asset allocation. The unique features of family portfolios are not present for the endowment. For the endowment, it is clear what assets belong in the portfolio and taxes are irrelevant. Input into the optimization includes expected pre-tax returns and pre-tax risks of each asset class and the correlation coefficient between each pair of asset classes.

Next, let's consider how mean-variance optimization would apply to an individual. Suppose Lisa sought advice on her asset allocation from a financial professional and he or she tries to apply mean-variance optimization. Following the traditional method, the professional would view her portfolio as worth $1 million. This method ignores the value of the teachers' pension and the distinction between the before-tax funds in the 403(b) and the after-tax funds in the taxable account. Input in the optimization would include expected pre-tax returns and pre-tax risks of each asset class and the correlation coefficient between each pair of asset classes—the same inputs as for the endowment. Suppose, based on this optimization, the financial professional recommends Lisa's current portfolio, which the professional views as containing 50 percent stocks.

This traditional method ignores the unique aspects of family portfolios. First, her extended portfolio contains $1,105,000 after taxes, and not $1,000,000 of before-tax and after-tax funds. Second, traditional mean-variance optimization only considers pre-tax returns and pre-tax risks; it ignores taxes. For example, it may state a bond's expected returns at 6 percent and its risk (standard deviation) at 10 percent. In reality, the portion of the bond's *risk* and *returns* borne by the individual investor depends upon the savings vehicle it is held in. If held in a Roth IRA, the individual bears all the bond's risk and receives all the bond's return; for the individual, expected returns are 6 percent and risk is 10 percent. If held in a taxable account, federal and state governments take 30 percent of the bond's returns, which means they also share 30 percent of its risk; for the individual, expected returns are 4.2 percent and risk is 7 percent. The individual receives 70 percent of the bond's returns and bears 70 percent of its risk. For an individual, the bond's after-tax risk and after-tax returns vary with the savings vehicle. Taxes matter! Traditional mean-variance ignores taxes and their effects on risk and returns. Nevertheless, traditional mean-variance analysis has been used, and continues to be used, to recommend asset allocations for family portfolios. Although ignoring taxes is acceptable when managing endowments and defined-benefit plans, it is not acceptable when managing family portfolios.

Another complication when managing family portfolios is the presence of retirement income streams, such as the teachers' pension. There is nothing similar to these "assets" when managing institutional funds. Therefore, it is not surprising that, until recently, professionals have ignored these family assets, including professionals who work with families. Retirement income streams are large, valuable assets; they make up 23 percent of the after-tax value of Lisa's extended family portfolio. Any method that ignores this value also ignores a substantial portion of her portfolio.

The professional inappropriately viewed Lisa's portfolio as being worth $1 million and her current asset allocation as being 50 percent stocks. Based on the expanded portfolio, her portfolio is worth $1,105,000 after taxes and her current asset allocation contains 31.6 percent stocks. If her risk tolerance dictates a 50 percent stock exposure, then the current portfolio is too conservative. Advice based on the wrong portfolio and based on asset classes' pre-tax risk and pre-tax returns will prove faulty. It is simply not possible to properly manage family portfolios without taking into consideration the unique features affecting family portfolios.

Are the Unique Features Implicitly Considered?

Some people might argue that professionals implicitly consider taxes and implicitly consider the value of retirement income streams when managing family portfolios. We find no evidence to support this position. Moreover, there may be as many ideas about what it means to implicitly consider these unique features as there are financial professionals. More important, we find strong evidence against the position that the unique features are implicitly considered.

The application of traditional mean-variance analysis to family portfolios, as previously discussed, is one example. For another example, consider *Cases in Port-*

folio Management by Peavy and Sherrerd. We use this book because it is the cap-stone book in the CFA literature and, therefore, can be considered representative of the profession's current practice. *Cases* provides analysts with the ability to "put the portfolio management process into practice" (p.1). *Cases* never distinguishes between the before-tax funds in deductible pensions and the generally after-tax funds in taxable accounts, and it never makes other adjustments for taxes. Furthermore, it never views retirement income streams as bonds in the family portfolio.

Ironically, an example in one of the cases provided the idea that, after several years of thought and development, eventually resulted in this book. In the Profit Sharing Advisory, Inc. (B) case, Mr. Williams becomes the beneficiary of a trust that is expected to pay him $50,000 of taxable income per year for 25 years. In the guide-line answer, Peavy and Sherrerd state, "Because the income stream from the trust is equivalent to a massive fixed-income investment, most of the bond fund should now be replaced with stocks." They recognized that the trust's income stream is essen-tially a bond and should be implicitly considered part of the family portfolio. Yet, they did not recognize that retirement income streams are essentially bonds, too. Of course, we argue that they should be explicitly considered in the family portfolio.

Relationship between the Book's Two Parts and an Outline

The focus of Part II of this book is on calculating a family's asset allocation. It com-plements the discussion on savings vehicles in Part I in that both halves emphasize the need to compare after-tax dollars to after-tax dollars when considering the choice of savings vehicles and when calculating the asset allocation. The finance profession routinely distinguishes the tax-exempt interest of municipal bonds from the taxable interest of corporate bonds. Yet, to date, the profession has regularly failed to distinguish before-tax and after-tax dollars when calculating the asset al-location. The two Parts complete the whole.

Part I examined the investment implications of alternative savings vehicles. These issues can be evaluated separately from the issues in Part II and, therefore, they were presented separately. For example, someone does not have to look at the asset-allocation issue in order to understand that a $1 investment of after-tax funds in a taxable account should be compared to a $1.54 investment of before-tax funds in a deductible pension. Recall that $1.54 is $1 / (1 − 0.35), where 0.35 is his or her current year's tax rate.

Again, Part II deals with asset allocation. There is wide agreement among pro-fessionals that the choice of asset allocation is an investor's most important deci-sion. Therefore, the argument that the profession has been miscalculating the asset allocation of individuals and families is, indeed, significant. In addition to pointing out problems with the traditional approach, Part II presents detailed discussion and recommended procedures to correct two problems with the profession's current method: failure to distinguish between before-tax and after-tax values and failure to consider the value of postretirement income streams. Chapter 10 discusses and critiques methods that can be used to convert assets' market values to after-tax values when the assets are held in each savings vehicle. Chapters 11 through 13 present models that can be used to estimate the present value of, respectively, Social Security, military retirement, and defined-benefit plans including teachers' retirement plans. Chapter 14 discusses the asset location issue. That is, given that some assets are held in pensions and others in taxable accounts, to the degree possible, should bonds be held in pensions and stocks in taxable accounts, or vice versa? Stated differently, given the asset allocation, does it make any difference whether bonds are *located* in pensions and stocks are *located* in taxable accounts, or vice versa?

When reading Part II, it is helpful to know how each chapter fits into the big picture. This earlier example using Lisa's portfolio illustrates the key ideas of Part II and paints the big picture. In a nutshell, that big picture is the following: If the question is a family's ability to meet its retirement income needs, the family's asset allocation should be calculated based on after-tax funds in an extended portfolio that includes the after-tax value of retirement income streams. By keeping this example in mind, professionals will be able to skip around to the material they need. For example, advisors who do not work with military retirees can avoid Chapter 12. Similarly, Chapter 13 presents and critiques models that estimate the present value of defined-benefit plans. This chapter is long due to a number of potential complications. Professionals can skip chapters and complications within chapters that do not apply to their clients.

References

Peavy, John W., III, and Katrina F. Sherrerd. 1990. *Cases in portfolio management.* Charlottesville, VA: Association for Investment Management and Research.

Conversion to After-tax Funds

Introduction

This chapter examines issues of what belongs in the family portfolio. It then examines issues surrounding the conversion of the market values of assets held in taxable accounts to after-tax values. Later, it does the same for assets held in retirement savings vehicles, including deductible pensions, non-qualified annuities, and Roth IRAs. Finally, the chapter discusses issues related to estimating the after-tax value of retirement income streams.

What Belongs in the Family Portfolio

Financial planners must decide what to include in the family portfolio. Naturally, the answer depends upon the question being asked. For example, consider two assets: a $1 million term life insurance policy and retirement income from a defined-benefit plan. If the family is concerned about estate planning, the $1 million of life insurance counts, while the income from the defined-benefit plan does not. If the family is concerned about retirement income needs, the income from the defined-benefit plan counts. It is not clear whether the term life policy should count in the family portfolio. We discuss this issue later.

What belongs in the family portfolio when the issue is retirement income needs? Scott (1995) presents a good framework for answering this question. She says the family "portfolio should consist of financial assets that you would be willing to sell for spending money or that generate some form of spending money, either now or sometime in the future" (p. 15). We use this criterion to decide whether each of the following belongs in the family portfolio: retirement income streams; life insurance, including whole life and term life; the personal residence; and the mortgage.

According to this criterion, retirement income streams belong in the family portfolio. Specifically, we recommend that the family portfolio include the *after-tax* present value of retirement income streams, and that this value be viewed as bonds in the family portfolio. Chapters 11 through 13 present models that estimate the *before-tax* present values of Social Security, military retirement, and defined-benefit plans. We discuss how to convert these before-tax values to after-tax values in this chapter instead of in each of the three chapters.

Studies that examine families' preparedness for retirement routinely consider Social Security and other retirement income streams.[1] Yet, the traditional approach to calculating a family's asset allocation excludes the values of retirement income streams. This is inconsistent. Including their value in the family portfolio removes this inconsistency.

The authors know several couples where both members retired from the military in their upper forties, and do not plan to reenter the work force. Without their inflation-adjusted military pensions, they would not be retired today. They clearly understand that retirement income streams "count" in their family portfolios. It is time for financial professionals to recognize what others already understand.

Life Insurance, Residence, and Mortgages

In this book, we do not take a strong position for including or excluding life insurance, the personal residence, or the mortgage from the family portfolio. We leave it to each financial professional to make these decisions. We will discuss these three items in turn.

Suppose a single person has a term life insurance policy that does not provide income that he can use to finance his retirement needs. It does not belong in his portfolio. In contrast, assume there is a term life policy on a couple's major breadwinner. If the breadwinner dies first, the survivor can use the insurance proceeds to satisfy his or her needs. In this case, it is less clear that the insurance should be excluded from the portfolio. Nevertheless, we recommend that term life insurance be ignored when calculating the family portfolio. This does not mean that the life insurance has no value or that life insurance needs should be ignored. Rather, these issues come up when addressing questions related to the adequacy of life insurance. We consider this to be primarily a financial-planning issue rather than a portfolio issue.

Whole life insurance is a separate issue. Suppose someone has a whole life insurance policy with a $100,000 death benefit and a cash value of $40,000. The $40,000 could be included as a bond in the family portfolio. However, if the individual or couple plans to await the death benefit, then we believe the life insurance can be left out of the portfolio—particularly for retirement-planning purposes. Again, some professionals may include the cash surrender value and others may ignore it. For most families, cash surrender value is relatively small.

The treatments of the personal residence and mortgage are more contentious and usually entail larger values. Scott excludes the home because it does not generate income that can be used to finance retirement needs. She views the residence primarily as a consumption good. She says, "Most families do not purchase homes strictly for investment purposes. Usually, if you sell a home, you must buy another one to live in. If you plan to 'downsize' at some point, you could wait until you receive the sales proceeds, and then reassess and rebalance the portfolio" (p. 17).

We agree with Scott and recommend that the personal residence not be included in the family portfolio because it generally does not create cash flows that can be used to finance retirement. In fact, with taxes and upkeep, the house requires cash expenses. If someone plans to downsize, then the funds that are expected to be freed in the process may be viewed as cash in the family portfolio.

In a 1998 article in *Financial Services Review* and a 2001 article in *Journal of Financial Planning,* Reichenstein (1998, 2001) argues that the mortgage should be viewed as a short bond position. Essentially, a family that takes out a mortgage has issued a bond. Scott does not consider the mortgage in the family portfolio. Yet, since it affects cash flows, it would appear to meet her criterion.

Suppose a couple has a $140,000 mortgage and bonds held in a taxable account worth $140,000 (the cost basis and market value of the bonds are $140,000). On Tuesday, they liquidate the taxable bond account and prepay the mortgage. On Wednesday, they take out a $140,000 mortgage and invest in bonds held in a taxable account. They are in the same financial position after Wednesday as before Tuesday. If the bonds are included in the family portfolio but the mortgage is not, the family appears to decrease its bond exposure the first day and increase it the second. It seems logically inconsistent to exclude the mortgage from the family portfolio.

Similarly, consider two retired couples with identical assets and personal residences, except one couple owes $140,000 on its home and the other owns its home debt free. The second couple has a substantially better financial position. Again, it seems logically inconsistent to exclude the mortgage. The mortgage could be considered a short bond position. (This issue is separate from the other issues addressed in this book. We excluded it from more emphasis here to concentrate attention on the other issues.)

Converting the Value of Assets Held in Taxable Accounts

For assets held in taxable accounts, one major issue when converting market values to after-tax values is the treatment of built-in capital gains and losses. For simplicity, assume a couple is 60 years old and in the combined state-plus-federal capital gain tax bracket of 25 percent before retirement; the couple expects to be in the 20 percent bracket after retirement. Before retirement, they may be living in a state that has state income taxes, but they expect to move after retirement to a state that does not have state taxes. This couple holds stock with a $10,000 cost basis and a $30,000 market value. One treatment is to assume they sell the stock today and pay capital gain taxes. The after-tax value is $25,000 [$30,000 − 0.25 • ($20,000)], where $20,000 is the built-in gain.

Other tax treatments are possible. One possibility is the stock will be sold several years later. The following example suggests that it is acceptable to view the stock's current after-tax value by deducting taxes at the expected capital gain tax rate at the anticipated sales date. Assume the stocks will be sold in five years when the couple will be retired and in the 20 percent capital gain bracket. In five years, the tax liability will be 20 percent of the capital gain at that date. A reasonable expectation may be a projected total stock return of 9 percent, including 7 percent capital gain. This implies a projected sales price of about $42,000 [$30,000 • $(1.07)^5$], which implies a projected capital gain of $32,000 and projected tax liability of $6,400, or 20 percent of the projected gain. The present value of $6,400 when discounted at 9 percent, which reflects the stock's risk, is $4,160. The $4,160 is "close" to the $4,000 tax liability if the stock is sold today. Thus, if this couple expects to sell the stock years later when they are in a lower tax bracket, they could estimate its current after-tax value by subtracting taxes as if the asset were sold today and the lower tax rate applies. That is, the following after-tax value appears reasonable: $30,000 − 0.2($20,000) or $26,000.

Other possibilities are that the couple plans to (1) give the appreciated asset to charity or (2) hold the stock until the first spouse dies, at which time the surviving spouse will liquidate the stock. If the couple gives the appreciated asset to a tax-deductible charity, it would receive the tax benefit of a $30,000 donation. The charity could sell the asset yet avoid capital gain taxes due to its charitable status. In this case, the asset's after-tax value is $30,000.

After the death of the first spouse, the surviving spouse receives the asset at a step-up in basis. If he or she lives in a community property state, the asset's new basis is $30,000 since all shares receive a step-up in basis. If he or she lives in a common-law state, the new basis is $20,000 since half the shares receive a step-up in basis. In this case, the asset's after-tax value is $28,000, 30,000 − 0.2($10,000).

In summary, there is not one "right way" to handle the tax treatment of the built-in capital gain. The client and financial advisor should discuss the issue and decide on an acceptable assumption for the specific planning goal. The financial advisor provides a valuable service by educating the client about the tax issue.

In the prior section, we argued that the personal residence should generally be excluded from the family portfolio. An exception occurs when the family expects to downsize. Suppose a retired couple bought a house several decades earlier for

$250,000, and it is worth $600,000 today (net of sales commissions and other sales expenses). They will downsize to a $200,000 home. They could include the $400,000 in freed funds as cash in the family portfolio. There would be no capital gain taxes on the sale due to a special feature of the Tax Code. A couple can exclude from taxes up to $500,000 in capital gains from the sale of a personal residence. A single person can exclude up to $250,000. To be eligible for this capital-gain exclusion, the couple must *own* and *occupy* the principal residence for an aggregate of at least two of the prior five years. The exclusion can apply to one sale or exchange every two years; this is not a once-per-lifetime exclusion.[2] Consequently, the after-tax value of freed funds is generally its market value.

Capital losses should also be considered in the portfolio. Suppose a couple has a capital asset with a cost basis of $10,000 that is worth $7,000. By realizing the loss, the couple can use the $3,000 loss to either offset an equal amount of realized gains or reduce taxable income by a like amount. If the ordinary income tax rate is 30 percent, then the $3,000 reduction in taxable income reduces taxes by $900. In this case, the after-tax value of the asset is $7,900. The Tax Code only allows the write-off of up to $3,000 per year. If a capital asset has, say, a $5,000 built-in loss, the individual could reduce taxable income by $3,000 this year by selling it, and carry forward the remaining $2,000. In this case, the value of the tax write-off is slightly less than $5,000 times t, where t is the expected marginal tax rate this year and next.

Converting the Value of Assets Held in Retirement Savings Vehicles

The tax status of funds in retirement savings vehicles dictates the method of converting assets to after-tax values. Deductible pensions contain only before-tax funds. Thus, their after-tax value is obtained by multiplying the before-tax value by $(1 - t_n)$, where t_n is the expected tax rate in the withdrawal year (or the average tax rate in withdrawal years). Suppose a couple has an ordinary income tax rate of 35 percent before retirement and expects to be in the 30 percent bracket during retirement. Each dollar in deductible pensions is worth $0.70 after taxes. Since the funds are intended to finance retirement needs, the expected tax rate during retirement is the applicable rate.

This leads to a situation that sometimes causes confusion. Suppose Joe is age 50 and just contributed $10,000 to a 401(k). He is in the 35 percent tax bracket this year. He expects to withdraw the funds in retirement when he will be in the 28 percent tax bracket. The $10,000 contribution reduces this year's consumption by only $6,500 or $10,000 • t, where t is the ordinary income tax rate. Yet, when planning for retirement, he should view it as a $7,200 investment of after-tax funds or $10,000 • $(1 - t_n)$, where t_n is the expected tax rate during retirement. The difference between $6,500 and $7,200 is due to tax timing, as defined and discussed in Chapters 2 and 3.

Suppose the family portfolio contains a non-qualified tax-deferred annuity with a market value of $50,000 and a cost basis of $30,000. The additional $20,000 is tax-deferred returns. The non-qualified annuity is a hybrid asset containing before-tax and after-tax funds. Eventually, the deferred returns will be taxed as ordinary income. The issues surrounding the treatment of the deferred returns are similar to those discussed earlier for built-in capital gains when the asset might be sold this year or several years hence. If sold this year, its after-tax value is $50,000 − $20,000 • t. If sold several years hence during retirement, its after-tax value can be estimated at $50,000 − $20,000 • t_n. As with the tax treatment of the built-in capital gain, it appears to be reasonable to reduce the asset's current market value as if taxes were paid today but at the later tax rate; that is, $50,000 − $20,000 • t_n is a reasonable estimate of the after-tax value.

The issues are the same for the tax treatment of the deferred returns in a nondeductible IRA and a non-qualified annuity. Therefore, if $4,000 has been invested in a nondeductible IRA and its current market value is $7,000, then the after-tax value can be approximated at $7,000 − $3,000 • t_n.

It is easy to understand the treatment of funds in a Roth IRA. Since distributions from a Roth IRA are generally tax-exempt, its after-tax value is identical to its market value. The only time a Roth IRA's market value would be adjusted is if the taxpayer expects to withdraw funds before the Roth IRA has been established five years or before the taxpayer reaches age 59½.

Converting the Value of Retirement Income Streams

Conceptually, it is easy to convert the before-tax values of income from Social Security, military retirement, and defined-benefit plans to after-tax values. If the before-tax value of one of these income streams is $200,000, then, in general, its after-tax value is $200,000 • $(1 − t_n)$, where t_n is the combined federal-plus-state marginal tax rate. It can be tricky trying to determine the combined federal-plus-state marginal tax rate. At the federal level, income from military retirement and defined-benefit plans are fully taxable, while up to 85 percent of income from Social Security is taxable. At the state level, however, the tax treatment of these sources of income varies considerably.

According to Baer (2001), as of 2000, only 15 states taxed Social Security income—Colorado, Connecticut, Iowa, Kansas, Minnesota, Missouri, Montana, Nebraska, New Mexico, North Dakota, Rhode Island, Utah, Vermont, West Virginia, and Wisconsin. In the other 35 states and the District of Columbia, Social Security income is only taxed at the federal level. Consequently, for retirees living in these 35 states (and the District of Columbia) and for individuals who expect to retire in these states, the marginal tax rate on Social Security income is the federal marginal tax rate. For retirees in these 35 states, if 85 percent of Social Security income is taxable and the marginal federal tax rate is 25 - percent, then the before-tax value can be converted to an after-tax value by multiplying by 0.7875 or $(1 - 0.85 \cdot 0.25)$.

According to Baer (2001), most states have an income tax exemption for at least part of the income from military retirement and defined-benefit plans. However, when it comes to income from military retirement, federal civil service, private DB plans, and public DB plans, state tax treatments differ within a state and across states. Table 10.1 summarizes the state income tax treatment of pension income from military retirement, federal civil service, private plans, and public (state and local) plans for the 41 states (and the District of Columbia) that have broad-based state taxes.

Table 10.1 excludes seven states because they have no state income taxes: Alaska, Florida, Nevada, South Dakota, Texas, Washington, and Wyoming. Baer also excludes New Hampshire and Tennessee because they have limited income taxes. In Illinois, Mississippi, and Pennsylvania, all of these sources of pension income are tax-exempt. For state income taxes, seven states fully exempt income from public pensions (military, federal civil service, state and local governments) but do not fully exempt income from private pensions. They are Alabama, Hawaii, Kansas, Louisiana, Massachusetts, Michigan, and New York. At the other extreme, California, Connecticut, Nebraska, Rhode Island, and Vermont fully tax all income that is included in federal adjusted gross income. The other states either treat public and private pensions differently or use tax credits or income limits that affect the state tax treatment of pension income. See Table 10.1 for a summary.

In practice, professionals usually know the state tax treatment of pension income in their state and in clients' states. *The relevant tax treatment, however, is for the state in which the individual expects to retire.*

The following examples may clarify the issues. Hank is single and receives $1,400 per month (or $16,800 per year) from Social Security. Although we will present and critique models in Chapter 11, for now assume that the before-tax value of Social Security is about $257,400. If the before-tax value is $257,400 and 85 percent is taxable at a 25 percent tax rate, then the after-tax value is about $202,700 [$257,400 $\cdot (1 - 0.85 \cdot 0.25)$].

Judy just retired from teaching in Nebraska and will receive $2,000 a month in retirement benefits. Suppose the before-tax value of this projected income is $270,000. Nebraska does not exempt any of this income from state taxes. If her combined federal-plus-state tax rate is 30 percent, then the after-tax value is $189,000 [$270,000 $\cdot (1 - 0.30)$]. If she will retire in Texas, which has no state income tax, then her after-tax value may be $202,500, where 25 percent is her projected federal tax rate.

TABLE 10.1 State Income Tax Treatment of Social Security Benefits and Pension Income, 2000 (single filers)

State	Is Social Security Tax-exempt?	Private Exemption	Military Exemption	Federal Exemption	State and Local Exemption	Age Minimum for Pension Exclusions?	Income Restrictions for Pension Exclusions?
Alabama	Yes	None/Full	Full	Full	Full	No	No
Arizona	Yes	None	$2,500	$2, 500	$2,500	No	No
Arkansas	Yes	$6,000	$6,000	$6,000	$6,000	No	No
California	Yes	None	None	None	None	NA	NA
Colorado	No	$24,000/$20,000	$24,000/$20,000	$24,000/$20,000	$24,000/$20,000	Yes	No
Connecticut	No	None	None	None	None	NA	NA
Delaware	Yes	$12,500/$2,000	$12,500/$2,000	$12,500/$2,000	$12,500/$2,000	No	No
District of Columbia	Yes	None	$3,000	$3,000	$3,000	Yes	No
Georgia	Yes	Full/Part	---See Georgia explanation---			Yes	No
Hawaii	Yes	None	Full	Full	Full	No	No
Idaho	Yes	None	$17,196	$17, 196	$17,196	Yes	No
Illinois	Yes	Full	Full	Full	Full	No	No
Indiana	Yes	None	$2,000	$2, 000	None	Yes	No
Iowa	No	$5,000	$5,000	$5,000	$5,000	Yes	No
Kansas	No	None	Full	Full	Full	No	No
Kentucky	Yes	$36,414	---See Kentucky explanation---		Full	Yes	No
Louisiana	Yes	$6,000	Full	Full	Full	Yes	No
Maine	Yes	$6,000	$6,000	$6,000	$6,000	No	No
Maryland	Yes	$16,500	$16,500–$19,000	$16,500	$16,500	Yes	Yes
Massachusetts	Yes	None	Full	Full	Full	No	No
Michigan	Yes	$34,920	Full	Full	Full	No	No

State							
Minnesota	No	See **Minnesota** explanation				Yes	Yes
Mississippi	Yes	Full	Full	Full	Full	No	No
Missouri	No	$4,000	$6,000	$6,000	$6,000	No	Yes
Montana	No	$3,600	$3,600	$3,600	$3,600	No	Yes
Nebraska	No	None	None	None	None	NA	NA
New Jersey	Yes	$9,375	Full	$9,375	$9,375	Yes	No
New Mexico	No	See **New Mexico** explanation				Yes	Yes
New York	Yes	$20,000	Full	Full	Full	Yes	No
North Carolina	Yes	$2,000	Full/$4,000	Full/$4,000	Full/$4,000	No	No
North Dakota	No	None	$5,000	$5,000	$5,000/None	Yes	No
Ohio	Yes	See **Ohio** explanation					
Oklahoma	Yes	$4,400	$5,500	$5,500	$5,500	Yes	Yes
Oregon	Yes	See **Oregon** explanation					
Pennsylvania	Yes	Full	Full	Full	Full	See below	No
Rhode Island	No	None	None	None	None	NA	NA
South Carolina	Yes	$3,000/$10,000	$3,000/$10,000	$3,000/$10,000	$3,000/$10,000	No	No
Utah	No	$4,800/$7,500	$4,800/$7,500	$4,800/$7,500	$4,800/$7,500	No	No
Vermont	No	None	None	None	None	NA	NA
Virginia	Yes	See **Virginia** explanation					
West Virginia	No	None	$2,000	$2,000	Full/$2,000	No	No
Wisconsin	No	None	None/Full	None/Full	None/Full	No	No

© 2001, AARP. Reprinted with permission.

NA stands for not applicable. Seven states—Alaska, Florida, Nevada, South Dakota, Texas, Washington, and Wyoming—are excluded because they have no personal income tax. Two states—New Hampshire and Tennessee—are excluded because they have limited income taxes.

Source (for Table 10.1 and accompanying explanations): Adapted from Baer, David. 2001. State taxation of Social Security and pensions in 2000. Public Policy Institute, American Association of Retired People, Issue Brief Number 55, 7–15. The author originally collected the data from state income tax forms and telephone surveys of state revenue offices.

Explanations to Table 10.1

Alabama—Private defined-benefit pensions are tax-exempt. All out-of-state government pensions are tax-exempt if they are defined-benefit plans.

Arizona—All out-of-state government pensions are fully taxed.

Arkansas—The total exemption from all pension plans cannot exceed $6,000 per taxpayer. The exemption refers to income from public or private retirement systems, plans, or programs. Distributions from Simplified Employee Pension (SEP) plans do not qualify. However, IRA distributions can be included as part of the $6,000 exemption if a taxpayer is age 59½ or older. All out-of-state government pensions also qualify for the $6,000 exemption. Persons age 65 or older who do not qualify for the $6,000 deduction qualify for a $250 tax credit per taxpayer.

California—All out-of-state government pensions are fully taxed.

Colorado—Pensioners ages 55 to 64 qualify for a $20,000 pension and annuity exemption; pensioners age 65 or older qualify for a $24,000 pension and annuity exemption. The exemptions pertain to periodic payments received as a result of personal services performed prior to retirement, contributions to retirement plans that were tax-deferred, lump-sum distributions from pension or profit-sharing plans, IRA distributions, self-employed retirement account distributions, annuities, and federally taxable Social Security benefits. All out-of-state government pensions qualify for the pension exemptions.

Delaware—Persons under age 60 receive a $2,000 pension exemption; persons age 60 or older receive a $12,500 retirement exemption. The $12,500 retirement exemption covers qualified retirement plans (such as IRA distributions, 401(k) plans, Keogh plans, and government-deferred compensation [Sec. 457] plans). In addition, the exemption covers dividends, capital gains, interest, and net rental income from real property. The total exemption from all retirement plans cannot exceed the $2,000 or $12,500 limit. Out-of-state government pensions qualify for the pension and retirement exemptions.

District of Columbia—Taxpayers age 60 or older qualify for the $3,000 exemption. The exemption covers military retired pay, annuity income, or survivor benefits from the District of Columbia government or the federal civil service. All state government pensions are fully taxed.

Georgia—Taxpayers who are age 60 or older or are totally disabled can claim retirement income exemptions (including pension income, IRA distributions, interest, dividends, alimony, and capital gains) for a maximum exemption of $13,500 per taxpayer. Taxpayers can exempt up to $4,000 of earned income toward the $13,500 exemption. All out-of-state government pensions are eligible for the $13,500 exemption. The maximum exemption increased to $14,000 in 2001.

Hawaii—Private defined-benefit pensions are exempt as are other employer-funded plans, such as profit-sharing and defined-contribution plans. Private pensions featuring employee contributions are partially taxable: only earnings attributable to employee contributions are taxable. Public pension income or annuities are exempt. All out-of-state government pensions are tax-exempt.

Idaho—Pensioners must be age 65 or older, or age 62 or older and disabled, to qualify for the public pension exemptions. Public pension exemption amounts are $17,196 (single filers) and $25,794 (married filing jointly). These amounts are adjusted annually according to the maximum worker's retirement benefit under Social Security. The exemption amounts are reduced by the amount of Social Security and Railroad Retirement benefits received. Allowable state/local pension exemptions are pensions from a city's police retirement fund or from the state's retirement fund for firefighters. Out-of-state government pensions are fully taxed.

Illinois—Exempt pension/retirement income includes qualified employee benefit plans, Simplified Employee Pension (SEP) plans, IRA distributions, 401(k) plans, government retirement or government disability plans, Railroad Retirement income, lump-sum distributions of appreciated employer securities, and early distributions from qualified plans and IRAs. All out-of-state government pensions are tax-exempt.

Indiana—Federal civil service pensioners must be age 62 or older to claim the $2,000 pension exemption, and it is offset by Social Security and Railroad Retirement benefits received. Military pensioners must be age 60 or older to claim the exemption. Out-of-state pensions are fully taxed.

Iowa—Taxpayers age 55 or older can claim an exemption of $5,000 (single filers) or $10,000 (married filing jointly) from pensions, annuities, Simplified Employee Pension (SEP) plans, and IRA distributions. Out-of-state government pensions qualify for the exemptions.

Kansas—Exempt public pension income includes federal civil service and military pensions, Kansas government pensions, and lump-sum distributions from the Kansas Public Employees Retirement System (KPERS). All out-of-state government pensions are fully taxed.

Kentucky—Kentucky state, local, and federal employees retiring before January 1, 1998, receive a full exemption of their public pensions. Those retiring after January 1, 1998, receive an exemption of their public pension based on the amount of the individual's service time prior to January 1, 1998, compared to their total service time. Public pensioners are eligible for at least a $36,414 exemption. Out-of-state government pensions are also eligible for the $36,414 exemption. Exempt public pensions are federal, Kentucky state and local pensions, Railroad Retirement benefits, and disability pension income. Exempt private pension income includes defined-benefit pensions, IRA distributions, annuities, and disability retirement income.

Louisiana—Taxpayers must be age 65 or older to qualify for the $6,000 (single filers) or $12,000 (married filing jointly with both spouses age 65 or older) private pension/retirement exemption. The private retirement exemption pertains to pensions and annuity income. Out-of-state government pensions qualify for the private pension/retirement exemption.

Maine—The $6,000 exemption is reduced by taxable and nontaxable Social Security and Railroad Retirement benefits received. Eligible qualified pension plans that are covered by the exemption include those under Internal Revenue Code Sec. 401(a) (including Savings Incentive Match Plan for Employees [SIMPLE] plans), Sec. 403 (annuities), and Sec. 457(b) (state and local government/tax-exempt organizations/eligible deferred compensation plans). Distributions from an IRA (including SIMPLE retirement accounts), a Simplified Employee Pension (SEP) plan, and benefits from ineligible deferred compensation plans do not qualify for the exemption. Out-of-state government pensions are eligible for the $6,000 exemption.

Maryland—Pensioners must be age 65 or older and/or totally disabled to qualify for up to a $16,500 exemption, which is reduced by Social Security and Federal Railroad Retirement benefits. Exempt income includes pensions, annuities, or endowment income from an employee retirement system (not including IRA distributions, Keogh plans, or deferred compensation plans). The exemption amount changes annually according to the maximum benefit received under the Social Security Act. Out-of-state government pensions do qualify for the $16,500 exemption. Military pensioners are eligible for an additional pension exemption of up to $2,500. To qualify, a pensioner must be age 55 or older, must have been an enlisted member of the military at retirement, and must have a federal adjusted gross income of $22,500 or less.

Massachusetts—Pension income from other state or local governments that do not tax pension income from Massachusetts' public employees is exempt from Massachusetts' taxable income. Other states or local governments must have a specific deduction, exclusion, or exemption for pension income that applies to Massachusetts' state or local contributory public pension plans or have no income tax.

Michigan—Private pension income is exempt up to $34,920 (single filers) or $69,840 (married filing jointly). These maximum allowable exemptions for private pensions are reduced by the amount of any public pension deduction claimed. Examples of exempt income are pension plans that define eligibility for retirement and set contribution and benefit amounts in advance, qualified retirement plans for the self-employed, IRA distributions (received after age 59½), and qualified life annuities for taxpayers age 65 or older. Taxpayers age 65 or older may deduct interest, dividends, and capital gains up to $7,785 (single filers) or $15,570 (married filing jointly). These deductions are reduced by any pension exemption taken. Michigan has reciprocal agreements with other states. That is, if another state does not tax out-of-state government pensions of former Michigan state or local government employees who are now citizens of the other state, then Michigan will not tax Michigan residents who receive public pensions from those other states. Otherwise, out-of-state government pensions qualify for the same exemptions as private pensions.

Minnesota—Taxpayers age 65 or older or permanently disabled (that are receiving federal disability income) who qualify can exempt from any income source (including taxable Social Security benefits) $9,600 (single filers) or $12,000 (married filing jointly) less the following: nontaxable Social Security benefits, Railroad Retirement benefits, nontaxable veterans' pensions, and one-half of federal adjusted gross income (AGI) of more than $14,500 (single filers or married filing jointly if one spouse is under age 65 and one is age 65 or older) or $18,000 (married filing jointly if both spouses are age 65 or older). To qualify for the above exemptions, the AGI of single filers must be less than $33,700, and Railroad Retirement benefits and nontaxable Social Security benefits must be less than $9,600. For married taxpayers filing jointly (in which both spouses are age 65 or older or disabled), the AGI must be less than $42,000, and Railroad Retirement benefits and nontaxable Social Security benefits must be less than $12,000.

Mississippi—Retirement income that qualifies for the exemption includes income from public pensions, annuities, and deferred-compensation plans. Out-of-state government pensions are tax-exempt.

Missouri—Taxpayers qualify for the $6,000 (public) or $4,000 (private) exemptions if their Missouri adjusted gross income (not including federal taxable Social Security benefits) is less than $25,000 per year (single filers) or $32,000 (married filing jointly). Exemptions are phased out for taxpayers whose income is greater than $31,000 (single filers) or $44,000 (married filing jointly, assuming both spouses are receiving pensions). Out-of-state government pensions qualify for the $6,000 exemption. Taxpayers cannot receive more than a combined exemption of $6,000 from both private and public pension income.

Montana—The $3,600 exemption pertains to qualified pensions, annuities, Keogh plans, Simplified Employee Pension (SEP) plans, deferred compensation, and IRA distributions. The exemption does not include premature distributions. Taxpayers cannot receive more than a combined exemption of $3,600 from pension and annuity income. Out-of-state government pensions qualify for the $3,600 exemption. The $3,600 exemption is reduced by $2 for every $1 that the federal AGI exceeds $30,000. The exemption is entirely phased out when income reaches $31,800 (single filers) or $33,600 (married filing jointly, when both spouses have pension income).

Nebraska—Out-of-state government pensions are fully taxed.

New Jersey—Taxpayers must be age 62 or older or disabled as defined by the Social Security Administration to qualify for *any* of the pension exemptions. For non-military pensions, the exemption amounts are up to $9,375 (single filers) or $12,500 (married filing jointly). The exemptions include taxable pensions, annuities, and IRA distributions. Since employee contributions to pensions or annuities have been taxed previously, they are not taxed when they are withdrawn. Out-of-state government pensions qualify for the $9,375 (single filers) or $12,500 (married filing jointly) exemption. Taxpayers age 62 or older who do not claim the maximum pension exclusions of $9,375 (single filers) or $12,500 (married filing jointly) are eligible to apply the unclaimed portion of their pension exclusion to other types of income if their wages, net business profits, partnership income, and S Corporation income are $3,000 or less. In addition, taxpayers age 62 or older who are unable to receive Social Security or Railroad Retirement benefits, but who would have been eligible for benefits had they been covered by either program, can deduct up to $3,000 (single filers) or $6,000 (married filing jointly) in other retirement income.

New Mexico—Taxpayers age 65 or older whose income is less than $28,500 (single filers) or $51,000 (married filing jointly) may exempt up to $8,000 from *any* income source (including Social Security benefits) depending on the level of their adjusted gross income.

New York—Taxpayers must be age 59½ or older to qualify for a $20,000 exemption from private pensions, annuities, IRA distributions, Keogh plans, and disability income. Pensions from New York state and local governments, the military, and the federal civil service are tax-exempt. Out-of-state government pensions can be deducted as part of the $20,000 exemption.

North Carolina—North Carolina state and local government retirees and federal retirees who worked for five years or more (as of August 12, 1989) can receive a full pension exemption from their defined benefit public pension plan (based on the "Bailey settlement"). This benefit also applies to the state's 401(k) and 457 plans if the retiree contributed to the plan prior to August 12, 1989. Other government retirees receive up to a $4,000 exemption per taxpayer. However, pensioners cannot claim the $4,000 exemption for the same pension income that they already claimed as a full deduction (described earlier under the "Bailey settlement"). Out-of-state government pensions also qualify for the $4,000 exemption. Total private and public pension exemptions for retirees may not exceed $4,000 per taxpayer for those who do not qualify for the full public pension exemption. Exempt private pension incomes are amounts paid by an employer to a former employee under a retirement plan to provide payments after the employee leaves.

North Dakota—All public-sector pensioners must be age 50 or older to qualify for the pension exemption. Public pension exemptions are reduced by the amount of Social Security benefits received, and pensioners must file the long tax form to qualify. Only highway patrol, city police, and city firefighters qualify to receive the $5,000 exemptions under state/local retirement pension plans. Out-of-state government pensions are fully taxed.

Ohio—Tax credits are available for retirement income (without age restrictions) as follows:

Retirement Income	Tax Credit
$500 or less	None
More than $500 but not more than $1,500	$25
More than $1,500 but not more than $3,000	$50
More than $3,000 but not more than $5,000	$80
More than $5,000 but not more than $8,000	$130
More than $8,000	$200

To qualify for the *retirement income credit,* a taxpayer must be receiving retirement benefits, annuities, or distributions from a pension, retirement, or profit-sharing plan. The income must be retirement-related and be included in Ohio adjusted gross income. Out-of-state government pensions can be applied toward the retirement income credit.

Oklahoma—The public pension exemption covers the pensions of retirees from Oklahoma state and local governments, the military, and the federal civil service.

Taxpayers age 65 or older whose adjusted gross income is $25,000 or less (single filers) or $50,000 or less (married filing jointly) are eligible for the private pension exemption. Total public and private exemptions cannot exceed $5,500 per person. Out-of-state government pensions qualify for the $4,400 exemption of private pensions.

Oregon—Federal pensioners who work prior to October 1, 1991, can deduct *part or all* of their federal pension income. Federal pensioners retiring before October 1, 1991, receive a full exemption for federal pensions. Those retiring after that date receive an exemption for their federal pension based on the amount of the individual's service time prior to October 1, 1991, compared to his or her total service time. Taxpayers age 62 or older whose household incomes are less than $22,500 (single filers) or $45,000 (married filing jointly) and who have not received more than $7,500 (single filers) or $15,000 (married filing jointly) in Social Security and Tier 1 Railroad Retirement benefits are eligible for a retirement income tax credit. This retirement income tax credit can be as much as 9 percent of retirement income depending on the level of total income, Social Security benefits, and Tier 1 Railroad Retirement benefits. The credit can be applied to the following income: public and private pensions, individual retirement plans, deferred-compensation plans, and employee annuity plans. Out-of-state government pensions can be applied toward the retirement income tax credit.

Pennsylvania—Taxpayers who receive retirement income from plans whose benefits would be subject to additional taxes under Internal Revenue Code Sec. 72(q) or 72(t) must be age 59½ or older and terminated from employment to exempt this income. Exceptions to this age requirement apply to Internal Revenue Code Sec. 72(q)(2) or 72(t)(2). Traditional defined-benefit plans have no age requirements for exempting retirement income. Exempt retirement income includes private and public pensions, annuities, Keogh plans, Simplified Employee Pension (SEP) income, deferred-compensation plans, and IRA distributions. Out-of-state government pensions are tax-exempt as long as taxpayers meet the age requirement described earlier.

Rhode Island—Out-of-state government pensions are fully taxed.

South Carolina—Retirees under the age of 65 can deduct up to $3,000 of their qualified retirement income. Retirees age 65 or older can deduct up to $10,000 of their qualified retirement income. Qualified retirement income includes all public employee retirement plans defined in Internal Revenue Code Sec. 401, 403, 408, and 457, as well as IRA distributions, Keogh plans, and military retirement. In addition to the qualified retirement exemption of $3,000 or $10,000, taxpayers age 65 or older qualify for a senior deduction of $15,000 (single filers) or $30,000 (married filing jointly if both spouses are age 65 or older) against any taxable income. However, the senior deduction is reduced by any qualified retirement exemption taken.

Utah—Taxpayers under the age of 65 may exempt up to $4,800 in pensions, annuities, and taxable Social Security benefits. Out-of-state government pensions qualify for the $4,800 exemption. Taxpayers age 65 or older may exempt up to $7,500 on *all* income sources. Exclusions for both age groups are subject to a $1 reduction for every $2 of federal AGI (plus interest on line 8b of federal form 1040 plus any lump-sum amount on line 6 of the Utah return) in excess of $25,000 (single filers) or $32,000 (married filing jointly).

Vermont—Out-of-state government pensions are fully taxed.

Virginia—Taxpayers 62 to 64 years old qualify for a $6,000 exemption from *any* income source, and those age 65 or older qualify for a $12,000 exemption from *any* income source.

West Virginia—The West Virginia Teachers' Retirement System, West Virginia Public Employees Retirement System, and federal pensions qualify for the $2,000 pension exemption. Retirees under the West Virginia state or local police, deputy sheriff's, or firefighter's retirement system receive a full pension exemption. Taxpayers who are age 65 or older or are permanently disabled qualify for up to an $8,000 exemption from any income source including taxable Social Security benefits. However, the $2,000 pension exemption, the full pension exemption for public safety officials, and interest or dividends on United States or West Virginia obligations (which are already tax-exempt from federal tax but subject to state tax) count toward the $8,000 ceiling. Out-of-state government pensions qualify for the $8,000 exemption. Starting in tax year 2001, military pensioners are eligible for an additional military retirement income exemption. The exemption will equal 2 percent multiplied by the number of years of active service multiplied by the first $30,000 of military retirement income.

Wisconsin—Only military, federal civil service, and certain state/municipal pensioners who retired prior to January 1, 1964, or became a member of the retirement system as of December 31, 1963, and then retired at a later date, qualify for a tax exemption on their pension income. For state and local government retirees, only certain Milwaukee City, Milwaukee County, and the Wisconsin teachers' retirement systems qualify for exemptions subject to the conditions discussed above. Out-of-state government pensions are fully taxed.

Retirement Income Streams as Contingent Assets

Social Security and other retirement income streams are different from financial assets. They are *contingent* income streams in that the income is contingent upon someone living (or, if married, at least one member of the couple living). Suppose Luke is single, age 62 and has a 20-year life expectancy. He receives a retirement income of $1,667 a month or $20,000 a year from a defined-benefit plan. Payments cease at his death. This is different from a *guaranteed* $20,000 a year for 20 years. Let us compare two packages of payments. The first package is expected payments from Luke's pension, where each year's expected payment is the probability that he will be alive times $20,000. Expected payment during his 62nd year is about $20,000. Expected payments during his 63rd year, 64th year, and so on slowly decrease since the probability decreases that he will still be alive. The second package is a 401(k) that contains a laddered portfolio of zero-coupon $20,000 bonds maturing each year for 20 years. Each year for 20 years, the participant withdraws

$20,000 at which time the 401(k) is exhausted. Assuming a 5 percent discount rate, both packages of payments have similar pre-tax present values of about $249,000.

The laddered portfolio has one important advantage compared to the defined-benefit plan. If Luke should die prematurely, it will continue to pay $20,000 inflation adjusted for the remainder of the 20 years, while income from his defined-benefit plan will cease at his death. Of course, his defined-benefit plan will continue to make payments for as long as he is alive, while payments from the laddered portfolio will cease after 20 years.

Suppose Luke has a daughter who needs special care. To ensure his daughter's financial needs, he may wish to guarantee the *after-tax* value of the defined-benefit plan by buying life insurance. Life insurance benefits are tax-exempt, while income from the defined-benefit plan is taxable. If he is in the 28 percent tax bracket, he could buy a $179,000 term life policy. This effectively converts the *contingent* after-tax value of the defined-benefit plan—contingent upon him living at least 20 years—into a *guaranteed* after-tax value. Through the years, he can reduce the size of the death benefit. With the exception of this important caveat, we contend that Luke should view the defined-benefit plan as a bond in his portfolio worth about $179,000 after taxes.

Despite the contingent nature of retirement income, we believe the defined-benefit plan should be considered a $179,000 bond in Luke's portfolio. However, he and his financial advisor should be aware of the distinction between its contingent value and guaranteed value. The same contingent-claims issue pertains to retirement benefits provided by military retirement and Social Security.

Summary

There are two unique issues when managing family portfolios. The first is what belongs in the family portfolio. In particular, when calculating the family's asset allocation, what should be included in the portfolio? We address this issue when the question is, "Will the family have sufficient resources to meet its retirement needs?" Our primary conclusion is that the family portfolio should include the present value of after-tax income from Social Security and other retirement income streams. These income streams are essentially bonds, and including them can dramatically affect a family's asset allocation.

The second issue involves differences in the taxation of assets. Since goods and services are purchased with after-tax funds, portfolio values should first be converted to after-tax funds, and then the asset allocation should reflect these after-tax values. We recommend methods of converting accounts' market values to after-tax values. Separate methods apply to assets held in taxable accounts, deductible pensions, non-qualified tax-deferred annuities, nondeductible IRAs, and Roth IRAs. Finally, we explain how to convert the pre-tax values of retirement income streams into after-tax values. Also, we point out that retirement income streams are contingent claims and how a contingent claim differs from guaranteed claims.

In summary, we conclude that the family portfolio should contain the after-tax value of retirement income streams plus the after-tax value of other assets. The family's current asset allocation should reflect these after-tax values.

References

Baer, David. 2001. State taxation of Social Security and pensions in 2000. Public Policy Institute, American Association of Retired People, Issue Brief Number 55, 7–15.

Kennickell, Arthur B., Martha Starr-McCluer, and Annika E. Sunden. 1997. Family finances in the U.S.: Recent evidence from the survey of consumer finances. *Federal Reserve Bulletin,* January, 1–24.

Poterba, James M., Steven F. Venti, and David A. Wise. 1994. Targeted retirement saving and the net worth of elderly Americans. *American Economic Review,* May, 180–185.

Reichenstein, William. 1998. Calculating a family's asset mix. *Financial Services Review,* Vol. 7, No. 3, 195–206.

Reichenstein, William. 2001. Rethinking the family's asset allocation. *Journal of Financial Planning,* May, 102–109.

Scott, Maria Crawford. 1995. Defining your investment portfolio: What should you include? *AAII Journal,* November, 15–17.

Tacchino, Kenn B., and Cynthia Saltzman. 2001. Should Social Security be included when projecting retirement income? *Journal of Financial Planning,* March, 98–112.

Yuh, Yoonkwung, Sherman Hanna, and Catherine Phillips Montalto. 1998. Mean and pessimistic projections of retirement adequacy. *Financial Services Review,* Vol. 7, No. 3, 175–193.

Notes

1. See Poterba, Venti, and Wise (1994); Kennickell, Starr-McCluer, and Sunden (1997); Yuh, Hanna, and Montalto (1998); and Tacchino and Saltzman (2001).
2. The capital gain exclusion is pro-rated for periods shorter than two years if the sale is due to a change in employment, health, or unforeseen circumstances. Thus, if a couple realized a $100,000 capital gain from a principal residence that they owned and occupied for 18 months, they could exclude three-fourths (18/24 months) of the gain. The $500,000 exclusion for a married couple filing jointly applies if at least one spouse satisfies the ownership test and neither spouse is ineligible for exclusion due to a sale or exchange within the prior two years.

Estimating the Value of Social Security Retirement Benefits

Introduction

What is the value of an individual's assets that can be used to satisfy retirement income needs? In addition, what is his or her current asset mix? When answering these questions, Scott (1995), Fraser, Jennings, and King (2000), and Reichenstein (1998, 2000, and 2001) conclude that individuals should estimate the present value of projected Social Security payments and include this value as a "bond" in their personal portfolios. Individuals' portfolios are usually substantially different when the value of Social Security is included than when it is excluded. When answering these questions, these authors conclude the profession has been miscalculating individuals' "true" portfolios by excluding Social Security. If individuals optimize their traditional portfolios, which exclude Social Security, then they will have excessively conservative, sub-optimal true portfolios. However, before we can calculate the true portfolios, we must be able to estimate the present value of Social Security retirement benefits.

There are three objectives of this chapter. First, we explain the current structure of Social Security retirement benefits. Professionals who advise individual investors should have knowledge of the benefits structure. With this knowledge, they can add value for clients by helping them decide when to begin receiving benefits. Second, we provide models to estimate the present value of expected Social

Security retirement benefits.[1] These models rely on the similarities between inflation-linked Treasury bonds and Social Security. Third, we demonstrate that including the value of Social Security benefits can substantially change the calculation of the current asset mix.

Social Security Retirement Benefits

We begin this section by describing retirement entitlements under Social Security that apply to most individuals. We then present the details of how the Social Security Administration calculates the level of before-tax retirement benefits for someone born in 1936. We then discuss three factors that may reduce or eliminate this level of before-tax benefits.

Description of Entitlements

This section describes Social Security entitlements that apply to most individuals. As with many government programs, there are exceptions. Additional details are available on the Social Security Administration web site at http://www.ssa.gov and in a TIAA-CREF pamphlet entitled "Making Sense of Social Security," which is available at http://www.tiaa-cref.org/wc_libser/mss/index.html.

Someone gains eligibility for Social Security benefits when he or she earns 40 work credits. A work credit is earned for each quarter that he or she has earnings subject to Social Security taxes of at least $830. Up to four credits can be earned in each year. Almost all Americans earn at least 40 credits and are entitled to Social Security benefits. Benefit payments may begin as early as age 62 or as late as age 70. The later one starts, the higher the monthly benefit payment. Once benefits begin, payments are adjusted annually with consumer prices. This cost-of-living adjustment (COLA) assures beneficiaries that payments will keep pace with inflation. Social Security may replace 60 percent of preretirement income for someone earning $15,000 a year, but only 25 percent of income for someone earning $74,000.

To repeat, Social Security benefit payments may begin as early as age 62 or as late as age 70. For someone born before 1938, the starting age for full benefits—henceforth, Full Retirement Age (FRA)—is 65. (Terms used by the Social Security Administration are capitalized, while terms defined by this chapter are not.) It is later for people born after 1937. Table 11.1 summarizes the FRA by year of birth and the adjustments that occur if someone begins receiving benefits before or after FRA. The FRA is 65 years and two months for someone born in 1938, and it then increases by two months each year. It is 66 years for people born from 1943 through 1954. It increases by two months a year beginning in 1955, and it is 67 years for people born after 1959. The reduction from full benefits is 5/9 percent for the first 36 months (6⅔ percent per year) before FRA and 5/12 percent for any additional months (5 percent per year) before FRA. Again, for someone born in 1938, the FRA is 65 years and

TABLE 11.1 Eligibility Age for Full Social Security Benefits Is Increasing: Full Retirement Age

Year of Birth*	Year Individual Turns 62	Full Retirement Age (FRA) (years/ months)	Reduction for Beginning Payments Before FRA (per month)	Benefits Fraction at Age 62 (percent of benefits at FRA)	Delayed Retirement Credits (per year)	Benefits Fraction at Age 70 (percent of benefits at FRA)
1936 or before	1998 or before	65/0	5/9%	80%	6%	130%
1937	1999	65/0	5/9%	80	6½	132½
1938	2000	65/2	5/9%/mo. for 1st 36 + 5/12%/mo. thereafter	79⅙	6½	131 5/12
1939	2001	65/4	5/9% for 36 + 5/12%/mo.	78⅓	7	132⅔
1940	2002	65/6	5/9% for 36 + 5/12%/mo.	77½	7	131½
1941	2003	65/8	5/9% for 36 + 5/12%/mo.	76⅔	7½	132½
1942	2004	65/10	5/9% for 36 + 5/12%/mo.	76⅚	7½	131¼
1943–1954	2005–2016	66/0	5/9% for 36 + 5/12%/mo.	75	8	132
1955	2017	66/2	5/9% for 36 + 5/12%/mo.	74⅙	8	130⅔
1956	2018	66/4	5/9% for 36 + 5/12%/mo.	73⅓	8	129⅓
1957	2019	66/6	5/9% for 36 + 5/12%/mo.	72½	8	128
1958	2020	66/8	5/9% for 36 + 5/12%/mo.	71⅔	8	126⅔
1959	2021	66/10	5/9% for 36 + 5/12%/mo.	70⅚	8	125⅓
1960 or later	2022 or later	67/0	5/9% for 36 + 5/12%/mo.	70	8	124

*Social Security considers people born on January 1 to have been born in the prior year.

two months. If benefits begin at age 62, the reduction is 20⅚ percent [36 • (5/9%) + 2 • (5 / 12%)], where 36 denotes the first 36 months of early retirement and 2 denotes the additional two months of early retirement; the benefits fraction at age 62 is 79⅙ percent. The way the Social Security Administration calculates the reduction period is complex. For example, suppose someone attains FRA of 66 in July 2006 and begins benefits in January 2003. His reduction period is 42 months if his birthday falls on July 1 or July 2 and 41 months if his birthday falls on July 3 through July 31. We ignore this one-month discrepancy. Individuals who delay receiving Social Security benefits until after Full Retirement Age receive Delayed Retirement Credits (DRC). If born in 1936 or before, DRC is 6 percent per year (0.5 percent per month). The DRC is larger for people born after 1936, reaching 8 percent for those born after 1942. (Although the DRC is expressed as a yearly percent, someone does not need to delay benefits for one full year to receive a DRC. Someone who delays benefits for one month receives one-twelfth of the yearly DRC.)

Social Security benefits are based on a worker's earned income that is subject to Social Security taxes. Consider Jane, whose earnings record entitles her to a certain level of monthly benefits. In addition, others may be entitled to benefits based on her earnings record, including her husband, unmarried minor or disabled children, parents (if over age 62 and her dependents), and possibly her divorced husband. Jane's current husband may receive up to 50 percent of her benefits. Dependent unmarried children under age 18 (or 19 if a full-time high-school student) are eligible for up to 50 percent of the level of her benefit. However, there is a maximum family benefit *based on her earnings,* which varies from 150 percent to 188 percent of her monthly benefits.

If Jane is married, she has a dual entitlement. She is entitled to the larger of benefits based on her earnings record or spouse's benefits based on her husband's record. If Jane is divorced, she may also be entitled to benefits based on her ex-husband's record. We defer discussion of spouse's benefits until later.

Calculation of Social Security Retirement Benefits

Suppose Anna Mathias was born January 3, 1936. She retired and began receiving payments immediately after turning 62 in 1998. Table 11.2 presents a detailed review of the calculation of Social Security benefits for someone born in 1936. The first step records her actual earnings each year of her work career, but not more than that year's maximum income subject to Social Security taxes ($84,900 in 2002). For example, if she earned $6,000 in 1958, she should record $4,200 since Social Security taxes were applied to a maximum of $4,200 that year.

The second step adjusts her earnings history for wage inflation as measured by the average national wage level. For example, if she earned at least $4,200 in 1958, her inflation-indexed earnings would be $29,610 [$4,200 • 7.05], where 7.05, the Index Factor, adjusts 1958 dollars for wage inflation. Past earnings are indexed for wage inflation through the year the person turns age 60, and actual earnings are considered thereafter. Thus, the Index Factor is 1.0 for 1996 and later years.

Steps 3 and 4 calculate her Average Indexed Monthly Earnings (AIME), the average monthly earnings for the 35 calendar years with the highest indexed earnings. If she had 25 years of earnings, AIME would include 10 years of zero earnings. In the early years, relatively little income was subject to Social Security taxes even after adjusting for wage inflation. Thus, the highest 35 years are generally the most recent years. AIME is the sum of these 35 earnings years divided by 420 [35 • 12 months]. Suppose she retires in 1998 with an AIME of $4,157; her AIME98 is $4,157.

Step 5 converts AIME98 into a corresponding Primary Insurance Amount (PIA). For someone born in 1936, the Bend Points are $477 and $2,875, and they will not change. (The definitions of the Bend Points will soon become clear.) The Bend Points are adjusted each year with inflation, so they will be higher for someone born after 1936. Anna's PIA in 1998, PIA98, is $1,388, which is the sum of three amounts (rounded down to the whole dollar): 90 percent of the first $477 of AIME, 32 percent of the next $2,398, and 15 percent of the amount over $2,875 (up to the maximum subject to Social Security tax), where $2,398 is $2,875 – $477. The multiples guarantee that retirees will receive 90 percent of the first few dollars of average monthly income but much smaller portions of higher income. Even though Anna paid the same amount of taxes on her last dollar of Social Security income as someone with average income below $477, she only receives one-sixth the benefit; if we consider taxes and benefit reductions due to earnings limits (to be discussed later), she receives even less.

The final step is to adjust her PIA for the early retirement date. Her Full Retirement Age (FRA) is 65. Since she applies for payments at age 62 and zero months, she receives 80 percent of PIA98 or $1,110.40 per month beginning in February 1998. Her reduction is 20 percent [36 • (5/9%)]. Her monthly payment is $1,110.40 in 1998, and payments will increase each year with inflation as measured by the Consumer Price Index for Urban Wage Earners and Clerical Workers (CPI-W).

Reductions and Taxation of Benefits

We need to estimate the present value of Social Security benefits, both before taxes and after taxes. As discussed in Chapters 9 and 10, Reichenstein (1998, 2000, and 2001) argues that we should first convert all asset values to after-tax dollars and then calculate the asset allocation based on after-tax funds. Some financial advisors may prefer to use the present value of before-tax benefits. This chapter provides estimates of the present value of both before-tax and after-tax benefits.

Monthly benefits may be reduced or eliminated due to three factors. The first two factors directly reduce or eliminate benefits, while the third—taxation—indirectly reduces benefits.

The first factor is an Earnings Test, which applies to individuals who begin receiving payments before reaching Full Retirement Age. In the years before reaching FRA, Social Security benefits are reduced by $1 for every $2 of *earned income* above $11,280 (in 2002). In the year someone reaches Full Retirement Age, benefits may be reduced by $1 for every $3 of earned income above $30,000 (in 2002). After reaching Full Retirement Age, individuals can receive full benefits with no limit on earnings.

TABLE 11.2   Estimating Your Social Security Retirement Benefit

Estimating Your Social Security Retirement Benefit for Workers Born in 1936

Step 1:	Enter your actual earnings in Column B, but not more than the amount shown in Column A.	$_____
Step 2:	Multiply the amounts in Column B by the "index factors" in Column C, and enter the results in Column D. This gives you your indexed earnings, or the approximate value of your earnings in current dollars.	$_____
Step 3:	Choose from Column D the 35 years with the highest amounts. Add these amounts.	$_____
Step 4:	Divide the result from Step 3 by 420 (the number of months in 35 years). This will give you your average indexed monthly earnings.	$_____
Step 5:	a. Multiply the first $477 in Step 4 by 90 percent.	$_____
	b. Multiply any amount over $477 and less than $2,875 by 32 percent.	$_____
	c. Multiply any amount over $2,875 by 15 percent.	$_____
Step 6:	Add a, b, and c from Step 5. Round down to the whole dollar. This is your estimated monthly retirement benefit at age 65.	$_____
Step 7:	Multiply the amount in Step 6 by 80 percent. This is your estimated monthly retirement benefit at age 62.	$_____

Year	A. Maximum Earnings	B. Actual Earnings	C. Index Factor	D. Indexed Earnings
1951	3,600		9.26	
1952	3,600		8.72	
1953	3,600		8.25	
1954	3,600		8.21	
1955	4,200		7.85	
1956	4,200		7.34	
1957	4,200		7.12	
1958	4,200		7.05	
1959	4,800		6.72	
1960	4,800		6.47	
1961	4,800		6.34	
1962	4,800		6.04	
1963	4,800		5.89	
1964	4,800		5.66	

1965	4,800	5.56	
1966	6,600	5.25	
1967	6,600	4.97	
1968	7,800	4.65	
1969	7,800	4.40	
1970	7,800	4.19	
1971	7,800	3.99	
1972	9,000	3.63	
1973	10,800	3.42	
1974	13,200	3.23	
1975	14,100	3.00	
1976	15,300	2.81	
1977	16,500	2.65	
1978	17,700	2.45	
1979	22,900	2.26	
1980	25,900	2.07	
1981	29,700	1.88	
1982	32,400	1.78	
1983	35,700	1.70	
1984	37,800	1.61	
1985	39,600	1.54	
1986	42,000	1.50	
1987	43,800	1.41	
1988	45,000	1.34	
1989	48,000	1.29	
1990	51,300	1.23	
1991	53,400	1.19	
1992	55,500	1.13	
1993	57,600	1.12	
1994	60,600	1.09	
1995	61,200	1.05	
1996	62,700	1.00	
1997	65,400	1.00	

Source: http://www.ssa.gov/pubs/1070-98.html.

Let's say Joe begins receiving Social Security benefits at age 62 in January 2002 and is entitled to $600 a month ($7,200 for the year). During the year, he earns $20,000, $8,720 over the $11,280 limit. Social Security would withhold $4,360 of his Social Security benefits, but he would still receive $2,840 in benefits. The $4,360 is $1 for every $2 over the limit. This is equivalent to a 61 percent "tax rate" on his benefits [$4,360 / $7,200].

Now, suppose Joe was 64 at the beginning of the year but reaches Full Retirement Age in July 2002. He earns $66,000 during the year, including $33,000 from January through June. The amount of benefits withheld would be $1,000 ($1 for every $3 earned through June above the $30,000 limit). For 2002, he would receive $6,200 in Social Security benefits. Beginning in July (when he reached Full Retirement Age), he would receive full benefits no matter how much he earned.

A third example illustrates a special rule that applies to the first year of retirement when someone retires before attaining FRA. Suppose Luke works through September of his 63rd year and then retires and begins benefits in October. (This example differs from the prior example because Joe attained FRA while Luke has not.) Luke earns $50,000 through September of 2002, at which time he retires. He begins benefits in October and takes a part-time job that pays less than $940 a month, where $940 is the 2002 yearly income limit of $11,280 divided by 12. Even though his earnings through September substantially exceeded the annual limit, he would receive his Social Security benefits for October through December as long he earns $940 or less each month. If he earns $1 more than $940 in any month after September, he will lose all benefits for that month. Beginning in 2003, only the yearly income limit will apply to him because he will be beyond his first year of retirement.

This Earnings Test is based on *earned income;* that is, wages, salary, and self-employed income. The following do not count as earned income: interest income, dividends, capital gains, withdrawals from a deductible pension, and withdrawals from non-qualified tax-deferred annuities.

Pensions from work not covered by Social Security are the second factor that may reduce or eliminate Social Security benefits. This has two aspects: a Windfall Elimination Provision that affects benefits based on the worker's earnings record and a Government Pension Offset that affects benefits based on a spouse's earnings record. The Windfall Elimination Provision applies to benefits based on the worker's earnings record when he or she also receives pension benefits from an employer that does not withhold Social Security taxes (e.g., certain federal, state, or local government agencies).

Suppose Betty receives retirement benefits from the Texas State Teachers' Retirement System, which is not part of the Social Security system. In addition, she paid Social Security taxes on "substantial" earnings for 20 years or less. In this case, when converting AIME to PIA, the 90 percent factor applied below the first Bend Point is reduced to 40 percent. If she paid Social Security taxes on "substantial" earnings for 21 to 30 (or more) years, the 90 percent factor varies by 5 percent a year from 45 percent to 90 percent. See SSA Publication No. 05–0045 for details, including definitions of "substantial" earnings.

Assume Judy receives $1,000 a month from a state agency's pension and is eligible for $300 a month from Social Security based on her earnings record. Bob, her husband, receives $1,200 a month from Social Security. Betty qualifies for the larger of (1) $300 based on her record or (2) spouse's benefits based on Bob's record. In the absence of the state agency's pension, if she has reached FRA, she would be entitled to spouse's benefits of $600 a month, half of Bob's benefit. The Government Pension Offset reduces the amount of the spouse's or widow(er)'s benefit by two-thirds of the amount of the government pension. For Judy, the off-set is $667 (two-thirds of $1,000), which eliminates her spousal benefits. Thus, she should collect $300 in Social Security benefits based on her record. (As an aside, her state pension will not affect Bob's Social Security benefits when based on his record.) For further details, see "A Pension from Work Not Covered by Social Security," SSA Pub No. 05–10045, and "Government Pension Offset," SSA Pub No. 05–10007.

Taxation of benefits is the third reduction of Social Security benefits. The Earn-ings Test, discussed previously, applies only to individuals below Full Retirement Age. The Income Test, discussed here, applies to everyone who receives Social Security benefits regardless of age. The Income Test is based on Combined Income, which is the sum of adjusted gross income plus nontaxable interest plus one-half of Social Security benefits.

A single person with Combined Income between $25,000 and $34,000 would have to pay taxes on up to 50 percent of Social Security benefits. If Combined Income exceeds $34,000, up to 85 percent of the benefits are taxable. For a couple filing jointly, the income thresholds are $32,000 and $44,000. Couples filing separately who lived together automatically pay taxes on 85 percent of their benefits.

Consider a couple filing jointly with $45,000 of adjusted gross income, $2,000 of nontaxable municipal interest, and $18,000 of Social Security payments. Combined Income is thus $56,000—the $45,000 plus $2,000 plus half of their Social Security payments. The taxable portion of Social Security payments is the minimum of three totals. The first total is the sum of 50 percent of income between $32,000 and $44,000 plus 85 percent of income above $44,000. This is $16,200. The second total is 85 percent of Social Security benefits, which is $15,300. The third total is the sum of one-half the Social Security benefits plus 85 percent of the amount above $44,000. This total is $19,200. This couple must pay taxes on 85 percent of Social Security benefits, the minimum of the three amounts. As this example shows, a couple need not be living in luxury before it has to pay taxes on 85 percent of benefits.[2]

To estimate the present value of after-tax Social Security benefits, we must consider the Earnings Test, pensions from work not covered by Social Security, and the Income Test. Practically, the Earnings Test is easy to handle since individuals affected by it will likely delay receiving benefits until reaching Full Retirement Age. The Windfall Elimination Provision and Government Pension Offset affect relatively few individuals who have pensions from work not covered by Social Security. To calculate after-tax benefits, the taxation of benefits must be reflected in the analysis. For someone in the 28 percent tax bracket during retirement, taxes effectively reduce Social Security benefits by up to 23.8 percent [0.85 • 0.28].

Estimating Social Security's Before-tax Value for Singles

To estimate the present value of Social Security benefits, we must estimate when benefits begin. Appendix 11.1 demonstrates that, for males and females with an average life expectancy, the present value of benefits is at or near its maximum when benefits begin at age 65. Also, it discusses factors that single people should consider when deciding when to begin receiving benefits. We moved this analysis to an Appendix because of its length and complexity. The next section illustrates our method of estimating the present value of before-tax benefits to single females, single males, widows, and widowers. We then discuss the adjustment for taxes. Finally, we discuss estimation issues.

Calculating Present Value of Before-tax Benefits for Singles

We begin by estimating the present value of *expected cash flows,* which is different from, and theoretically better than, the present value of *cash flows through life expectancy*. Later, we show that for singles the present value of cash flows through life expectancy is a slightly upward-biased estimate of the present value of expected cash flows. However, it is much simpler to calculate the present value of cash flows through life expectancy. Later, we present a method of estimating the value of benefits that relies on the present value of cash flows through life expectancy with an adjustment for the bias.

We begin by estimating the theoretically preferred present value of expected cash flows. This estimated present value is the product:

(benefits fraction at age 65) • (PIA) • (12 months) • (multiple) *or*   (Eq. 11.1)

(initial monthly payment) • (12 months) • (multiple) *or*

(initial annual benefits) • (multiple)

To illustrate the model, assume today is January 2004. Mary is single, was born in 1943, and turned 60 last month in December 2003. She recently received her annual *Your Social Security Statement* from the Social Security Administration. It says:

> **You have earned enough credits to qualify for benefits. At your current earnings rate, if you stop working . . .**
> at age 62, your payment would be about $750 a month
>
> **If you continue working until . . .**
> your full retirement age (66 years), your $1,000 a month
> payment would be about
> age 70, your payment would be about $1,320 a month

We assume she applies for benefits in the month she turns 65 and receives the first benefit one month later. Since she applies for benefits at age 65 and zero months, one year before reaching FRA, her benefits fraction is 0.933. PIA is $1,000, so her projected initial monthly payment is $933 a month to be received in January 2004. The "12 months" converts monthly payments to annual benefits to accommodate mortality tables. The initial annual benefits are $11,196. The multiple is the present value of Social Security payments assuming she receives an inflation-adjusted $1 each year she is alive beginning at age 65.

Table 11.3 presents the calculation of the multiple. Recall that Mary is age 60. Based on updated mortality tables, there is a 0.966657 probability that she will be alive at age 65.[3] The expected cash flow is $0.966657 in 2004 dollars. There is a 0.957274 probability that she will be alive at age 66 and will receive a second $1 payment. The expected cash flow is $0.957274 (in 2004 dollars). There is a 0.946788 probability that she will be alive at age 67, and the expected cash flow is $0.946788 (in 2004 dollars). This procedure continues until age 120 when there is a 0.000009 probability that she will receive one last $1 payment (in 2004 dollars).

Since Social Security promises a constant real benefit, we discount the expected cash flows at today's (January 2004) long-term real yield on U.S. Treasury securities. As discussed in Fraser, Jennings, and King (2000), and Jennings and Reichenstein (2002), an appropriate discount rate is today's yield on Treasury Inflation Protection Securities (TIPS) with maturity closest to her life expectancy. Like Social Security benefits, payments from TIPS are linked to consumer price inflation. Moreover, Social Security payments and TIPS are both obligations of the U.S. government. Figure 11.1 illustrates the "Treasury Bonds, Notes and Bills" table in the *Wall Street Journal* and explains how to estimate the appropriate TIPS yield.

We use the mid-year convention. For example, benefits for someone age 65 are assumed to be received at age 65.5. Discounting at a 3 percent real yield, we get the

TABLE 11.3   Calculation of the Multiple for a 60-year-old Single Female Starting Benefits at Age 65

Age	Probability of Being Alive	Real Payment	Expected Real Payment	Present Value of Expected Real Payment
65	0.966657	$1	$0.966657	$0.966657/(1.03)$^{5.5}$
66	0.957274	1	0.957274	0.957274/(1.03)$^{6.5}$
67	0.946788	1	0.946788	0.946788/(1.03)$^{7.5}$
⋮	⋮	⋮	⋮	⋮
120	0.000009	1	0.000009	0.000009/(1.03)$^{60.5}$
				Multiple = 12.32

The multiple is the present value of expected real payments, where $1 is the annual real or inflation-adjusted payment. The $1 is an annuity received at mid-year. For example, the $1 benefit for someone age 65 is received at age 65.5. The TIPS yield, discount interest rate, is 3 percent.

Treasury Bonds, Notes and Bills

May 8, 2002

Explanatory Notes

Representative Over-the-Counter quotation based on transactions of $1 million or more. Treasury bond, note and bill quotes are as of mid-afternoon. Colons in bid-and-asked quotes represent 32nds; 101:01 means 101 1/32. Net changes in 32nds. n-Treasury note. i-Inflation-Indexed issue. Treasury bill quotes in hundredths, quoted on terms of a rate of discount. Days to maturity calculated from settlement date. All yields are to maturity and based on the asked quote. Latest 13-week and 26-week bills are boldfaced. For bonds callable prior to maturity, yields are computed to the earliest call date for issues quoted above par and to the maturity date for issues below par. *When issued.

Source: eSpeed/Cantor Fitzgerald

U.S. Treasury strips as of 3 p.m. Eastern time, also based on transactions of $1 million or more. Colons in bid and asked quotes represent 32nds; 99:01 means 99 1/32. Net changes in 32nds. Yields calculated on the asked quotation. ci-stripped coupon interest. bp-Treasury bond, stripped principal. np-Treasury note, stripped principal. For bonds callable prior to maturity, yields are computed to the earliest call date for issues quoted above par and to the maturity date for issues below par.

Source: Bear, Steams & Co. via Street Software Technology Inc.

Government Bonds & Notes

RATE	MATURITY MO/YR	BID	ASKED	CHG	ASK YLD
7.500	May 02n	100:03	100:04	...	0.04
6.500	May 02n	100:08	100:09	-1	1.54
6.625	May 02n	100:09	100:10	...	1.41
6.250	Jun 02n	100:20	100:21	...	1.63
6.375	Jun 02n	100:20	100:21	-1	1.65
3.625	Jul 02i	101:11	101:12	1	0.00
6.000	Jul 02n	100:30	100:31	-1	1.66
6.250	Jul 02n	101:00	101:01	-1	1.71
6.375	Aug 02n	101:07	101:08	...	1.65
6.125	Aug 02n	101:10	101:11	...	1.74
6.250	Aug 02n	101:11	101:12	...	1.77
5.875	Sep 02n	101:18	101:19	-1	1.75
6.000	Sep 02n	101:19	101:20	-2	1.79
5.750	Oct 02n	101:26	101:27	-1	1.80
11.625	Nov 02	105:00	105:00	-1	1.82
5.625	Nov 02n	102:01	102:02	-1	1.91
5.750	Nov 02n	102:03	102:04	-1	1.89
5.125	Dec 02n	102:00	102:00	-2	1.98
5.625	Dec 02n	102:08	102:09	-3	2.01
4.750	Jan 03n	101:28	101:29	-4	2.08
5.500	Jan 03n	102:14	102:15	-3	2.07
6.250	Feb 03n	103:02	103:03	-3	2.15
10.750	Feb 03	106:17	106:18	-3	2.11
4.625	Feb 03n	101:30	101:31	-3	2.16
5.500	Feb 03n	102:20	102:21	-3	2.15
4.250	Mar 03n	101:24	101:25	-4	2.21
5.500	Mar 03n	102:27	102:28	-4	2.23
4.000	Apr 03n	101:19	101:20	-4	2.29
5.750	Apr 03n	103:09	103:10	-4	2.30
10.750	May 03	108:12	108:13	-4	2.33
4.250	May 03n	101:29	101:30	-5	2.37
5.500	May 03n	103:06	103:07	-6	2.39
3.875	Jun 03n	101:17	101:18	-5	2.46
5.375	Jun 03n	103:07	103:08	-6	2.46
3.875	Jul 03n	101:18	101:19	-5	2.55
5.250	Aug 03n	103:07	103:08	-7	2.62
5.750	Aug 03n	103:27	103:28	-6	2.63
11.125	Aug 03	110:16	110:17	-8	2.62
3.625	Aug 03n	101:06	101:07	-7	2.66
2.750	Sep 03n	100:00	100:01	-6	2.73
2.750	Oct 03n	99:28	99:29	-7	2.80
4.250	Nov 03n	101:30	101:31	-8	2.90
11.875	Nov 03	113:06	113:07	-10	2.90
3.000	Nov 03n	100:02	100:03	-8	2.93
3.250	Dec 03n	100:11	100:12	-8	3.01
3.000	Jan 04n	99:25	99:26	-10	3.10
4.750	Feb 04n	102:25	102:26	-9	3.10
5.875	Feb 04n	104:21	104:22	-10	3.12
3.000	Feb 04n	99:22	99:23	-9	3.15
3.625	Mar 04n	100:22	100:23	-10	3.22
3.375	**Apr 04n**	**100:04**	**100:05**	**-10**	**3.28**
5.250	May 04n	103:24	103:25	-10	3.30
7.250	May 04n	107:19	107:20	-11	3.30
12.375	May 04	117:17	117:18	-12	3.30
6.000	Aug 04n	105:15	105:16	-12	3.46
7.250	Aug 04n	108:04	108:05	-12	3.48
13.750	Aug 04	122:04	122:05	-15	3.50
5.875	Nov 04n	105:10	105:11	-13	3.63
7.875	Nov 04n	110:01	110:02	-14	3.65
11.625	Nov 04	118:29	118:30	-15	3.68
7.500	Feb 05n	109:24	109:25	-14	3.75
6.500	May 05n	107:10	107:11	-15	3.89
6.750	May 05n	108:00	108:00	-14	3.91
12.000	May 05	122:27	122:28	-17	3.88
6.500	Aug 05n	107:17	107:18	-16	4.00
10.750	Aug 05	120:07	120:08	-18	4.07
5.750	Nov 05n	105:06	105:07	-16	4.14
5.875	Nov 05n	105:21	105:22	-16	4.12
5.625	Feb 06n	104:26	104:27	-17	4.22
9.375	Feb 06	117:19	117:20	-18	4.26
4.625	May 06n	101:02	101:03	-17	4.33
6.875	May 06n	109:08	109:09	-18	4.33
7.000	Jul 06n	109:27	109:28	-18	4.39
6.500	Oct 06n	108:02	108:03	-20	4.46
3.500	Nov 06n	96:00	96:00	-18	4.48
3.375	Jan 07i	103:24	103:25	-6	2.51
6.250	Feb 07n	107:06	107:07	-20	4.55
6.625	May 07n	108:27	108:28	-23	4.62
4.375	**May 07n**	**99:01**	**99:02**	**...**	**4.59**
6.125	Aug 07n	106:21	106:22	-23	4.68
7.875	Nov 07	103:01	103:02	-2	1.89
3.625	Jan 08i	104:12	104:13	-10	2.78
5.500	Feb 08n	103:22	103:23	-24	4.75
5.625	May 08n	104:03	104:04	-24	4.82
8.375	Aug 08	107:00	107:00	-6	2.73
4.750	Nov 08n	99:04	99:05	-24	4.90
8.750	Nov 08	108:13	108:14	-9	3.01
3.875	Jan 09i	105:20	105:21	-11	2.94
5.500	May 09n	103:00	103:00	-28	4.99
9.125	May 09	111:03	111:04	-7	3.37
6.000	Aug 09n	105:24	105:25	-29	5.04
10.375	Nov 09	115:19	115:20	-11	3.80
4.250	Jan 10i	108:04	108:05	-9	3.05
6.500	Feb 10n	108:27	108:28	-30	5.10
11.750	Feb 10	120:08	120:09	-14	3.94
10.000	May 10	116:15	116:16	-13	4.13
5.750	Aug 10n	103:30	103:31	-31	5.15
12.750	Nov 10	127:13	127:14	-16	4.26
3.500	Jan 11i	103:02	103:03	-9	3.09
5.000	Feb 11n	98:22	98:23	-31	5.18
13.875	May 11	134:15	134:16	-20	4.41
5.000	Aug 11n	98:15	98:16	-31	5.20
14.000	Nov 11	138:08	138:09	-22	4.53
3.375	Jan 12i	102:05	102:06	-13	3.11
4.875	**Feb 12n**	**97:15**	**97:16**	**-32**	**5.20**
10.375	Nov 12	126:09	126:10	-25	4.88
12.000	Aug 13	137:07	137:08	-30	5.00
13.250	May 14	147:25	147:26	-35	5.07
12.500	Aug 14	144:11	144:12	-33	5.11
11.750	Nov 14	140:16	140:17	-34	5.17
11.250	Feb 15	151:22	151:23	-51	5.54
10.625	Aug 15	146:22	146:23	-48	5.59
9.875	Nov 15	140:00	140:00	-47	5.61
9.250	Feb 16	134:02	134:03	-47	5.65
7.250	May 16	114:26	114:27	-42	5.70
7.500	Nov 16	117:12	117:13	-44	5.72
8.750	May 17	130:07	130:08	-49	5.72
8.875	Aug 17	131:21	131:22	-50	5.73
9.125	May 18	135:00	135:01	-52	5.75
9.000	Nov 18	134:04	134:05	-52	5.77
8.875	Feb 19	132:29	132:30	-54	5.78
8.125	Aug 19	125:04	125:05	-52	5.80
8.500	Feb 20	129:19	129:20	-53	5.80
8.750	May 20	132:21	132:22	-55	5.80
8.750	Aug 20	132:27	132:28	-56	5.81
7.875	Feb 21	123:06	123:07	-53	5.82
8.125	May 21	126:08	126:09	-54	5.82
8.125	Aug 21	126:11	126:12	-55	5.83
8.000	Nov 21	125:05	125:06	-55	5.82
7.250	Aug 22	116:21	116:22	-51	5.83
7.625	Nov 22	121:09	121:10	-53	5.83
7.125	Feb 23	115:10	115:11	-51	5.84
6.250	Aug 23	104:28	104:29	-47	5.84
7.500	Nov 24	120:20	120:21	-54	5.84
7.625	Feb 25	122:08	122:09	-55	5.84
6.875	Aug 25	113:00	113:00	-52	5.84
6.000	Feb 26	101:30	101:31	-48	5.84
6.750	Aug 26	111:20	111:21	-52	5.84
6.500	Nov 26	108:13	108:14	-52	5.85
6.625	Feb 27	110:03	110:04	-53	5.84
6.375	Aug 27	106:29	106:30	-52	5.84
6.125	Nov 27	103:23	103:24	-51	5.84
3.625	Apr 28i	104:12	104:13	-13	3.37
5.500	Aug 28	95:17	95:18	-48	5.83
5.250	Nov 28	92:06	92:07	-47	5.83
5.250	Feb 29	92:08	92:09	-47	5.82
3.875	Apr 29i	108:27	108:28	-16	3.37
6.125	Aug 29	104:05	104:06	-52	5.82
6.250	May 30	106:09	106:10	-54	5.79
5.375	**Feb 31**	**95:30**	**95:31**	**-51**	**5.66**
3.375	Apr 32i	102:01	102:02	-15	3.27

U.S. Treasury Strips

MATURITY		TYPE	BID	ASKED	CHG	ASK YLD
May	02	ci	99:31	99:31	...	1.46
May	02	np	99:31	99:31	...	1.49
Aug	02	ci	99:19	99:19	...	1.54
Aug	02	np	99:17	99:17	...	1.74
Nov	02	ci	99:08	99:08	...	1.44
Feb	03	ci	98:12	98:12	-4	2.13
Feb	03	np	98:10	98:11	-3	2.19
May	03	ci	97:22	97:23	-5	2.29
Jul	03	ci	97:08	97:08	-6	2.36
Aug	03	ci	96:31	97:00	-6	2.41
Aug	03	np	96:22	96:23	-6	2.65
Nov	03	ci	96:10	96:11	-8	2.47
Nov	03	np	95:21	95:22	-8	2.94
Jan	04	ci	95:00	95:01	-8	3.06
Feb	04	ci	94:20	94:22	-9	3.12
Feb	04	np	94:19	94:20	-9	3.15
May	04	ci	93:19	93:20	-10	3.30
May	04	np	93:14	93:16	-11	3.37
Jul	04	ci	92:27	92:28	-11	3.42
Aug	04	ci	92:14	92:15	-11	3.48
Aug	04	np	92:10	92:11	-12	3.54
Nov	04	ci	91:02	91:03	-11	3.75
Nov	04	bp	90:31	91:00	-12	3.78
Nov	04	np	91:03	91:05	-12	3.72
Jan	05	ci	90:14	90:15	-12	3.76
Feb	05	ci	89:31	90:01	-12	3.84
Feb	05	np	90:01	90:02	-14	3.82
May	05	ci	88:24	88:26	-13	3.98
May	05	bp	88:23	88:24	-13	4.00
May	05	np	88:24	88:26	-13	3.98
May	05	np	88:27	88:28	-13	3.95
Jul	05	ci	88:05	88:07	-13	3.98
Aug	05	ci	87:21	87:23	-14	4.05
Aug	05	bp	87:08	87:10	-14	4.20
Aug	05	np	87:20	87:22	-14	4.06
Nov	05	ci	87:01	87:03	-15	3.97
Nov	05	np	86:10	86:12	-16	4.21
Nov	05	np	86:12	86:14	-15	4.20
Jan	06	ci	85:28	85:30	-15	4.16
Feb	06	ci	85:09	85:11	-15	4.25
Feb	06	bp	84:27	84:29	-16	4.39
Feb	06	np	85:06	85:08	-16	4.28
May	06	ci	84:02	84:04	-16	4.35
May	06	np	83:25	83:27	-16	4.44
Jul	06	ci	83:29	84:00	-17	4.22
Jul	06	np	83:03	83:05	-16	4.46
Aug	06	ci	83:09	83:12	-17	4.31
Nov	06	ci	82:01	82:03	-18	4.42
Feb	07	ci	80:16	80:18	-18	4.58
Feb	07	np	80:06	80:09	-18	4.66
May	07	ci	79:02	79:05	-19	4.72
May	07	np	78:31	79:02	-19	4.74
Aug	07	ci	78:07	78:09	-20	4.70
Aug	07	np	77:26	77:29	-19	4.80
Nov	07	ci	77:18	77:21	-20	4.64
Feb	08	ci	75:13	75:16	-20	4.93
Feb	08	np	75:24	75:26	-18	4.86
May	08	ci	74:03	74:05	-20	5.03
May	08	np	74:14	74:16	-20	4.95
Aug	08	ci	73:08	73:10	-21	5.01
Nov	08	ci	72:07	72:10	-21	5.04
Nov	08	np	72:11	72:14	-21	5.01
Feb	09	ci	70:19	70:22	-22	5.19
May	09	ci	69:16	69:19	-22	5.24
May	09	np	70:03	70:06	-22	5.11
Aug	09	ci	68:19	68:22	-23	5.23
Aug	09	np	68:28	69:00	-23	5.17
Nov	09	ci	67:17	67:20	-23	5.27
Nov	09	bp	66:09	66:12	-22	5.53
Feb	10	ci	66:08	66:12	-22	5.35
Feb	10	np	66:23	66:26	-24	5.26
May	10	ci	65:04	65:07	-23	5.40
Aug	10	ci	64:09	64:13	-23	5.39
Aug	10	np	64:27	64:31	-25	5.29
Nov	10	ci	63:16	63:20	-24	5.38
Feb	11	ci	62:02	62:05	-24	5.50
Feb	11	np	63:04	63:07	-26	5.30
May	11	ci	61:00	61:02	-24	5.55
Aug	11	ci	60:07	60:09	-24	5.54
Nov	11	ci	59:10	59:12	-25	5.56

Treasury Bills

MATURITY	DAYS TO MAT	BID	ASKED	CHG	ASK YLD
May 16 02	7	1.70	1.69	0.01	1.71
May 23 02	14	1.70	1.69	0.01	1.71
May 30 02	21	1.70	1.69	...	1.72
Jun 06 02	28	1.73	1.72	0.01	1.75
Jun 13 02	35	1.71	1.70	...	1.73
Jun 20 02	42	1.71	1.70	...	1.73
Jun 27 02	49	1.71	1.70	-0.01	1.73
Jul 05 02	57	1.71	1.70	...	1.73
Jul 11 02	63	1.71	1.70	-0.01	1.73
Jul 18 02	70	1.71	1.70	-0.01	1.73
Jul 25 02	77	1.71	1.70	...	1.73
Aug 01 02	84	1.72	1.71	-0.01	1.74
Aug 08 02	**91**	**1.73**	**1.72**	**...**	**1.75**
Aug 15 02	98	1.73	1.72	...	1.75
Aug 22 02	105	1.73	1.72	...	1.75
Aug 29 02	112	1.74	1.73	0.01	1.76
Sep 05 02	119	1.76	1.75	0.04	1.78
Sep 12 02	126	1.76	1.75	0.04	1.79
Sep 19 02	133	1.76	1.75	0.03	1.79
Sep 26 02	140	1.75	1.74	0.02	1.78
Oct 03 02	147	1.78	1.77	0.04	1.81
Oct 10 02	154	1.79	1.78	0.05	1.82
Oct 17 02	161	1.79	1.78	0.04	1.82
Oct 24 02	168	1.81	1.80	0.04	1.84
Oct 31 02	175	1.83	1.82	0.03	1.86
Nov 07 02	**182**	**1.86**	**1.85**	**0.04**	**1.89**

Inflation-Indexed Treasury Securities

RATE	MAT	BID/ASKED	CHG	*YLD	ACCR PRIN
3.625	07/02	101-11/12	1	0.000	1112
3.375	01/07	103-24/25	-6	2.514	1124
3.625	01/08	104-12/13	-10	2.781	1102
3.875	01/09	105-20/21	-11	2.936	1086
4.250	01/10	108-04/05	-9	3.051	1058
3.500	01/11	103-02/03	-9	3.091	1023
3.375	01/12	102-05/06	-13	3.111	1003
3.625	04/28	104-12/13	-13	3.369	1101
3.875	04/29	108-27/28	-16	3.371	1083
3.375	04/32	102-01/02	-15	3.266	1003

*Yield to maturity on accrued principal.

FIGURE 11.1 Reading Treasury Security Yields

The date of this issue of the *Wall Street Journal* is May 8, 2002. It contains closing prices and yields for May 7. The next-to-last entry under "Government Bonds & Notes" is highlighted in bold and begins 5.375 Feb 31. This row provides information for the 5.375 percent Treasury bond maturing in February 2031. Its coupon interest rate is 5.375 percent. On May 8, 2002, its maturity was almost 29 years. The closing bid and ask prices are expressed 95:30 and 95:31 and indicate prices of 95$\frac{30}{32}$ percent and 95$\frac{31}{32}$ percent of par. The 5.66 percent in the last column denotes the yield (sometimes called yield to maturity) based on the ask price and semi-annual bond convention; that is, the ask price is the present value of the bond's cash flows when discounted at the 2.83 percent semi-annual discount rate, [5.66 / 2]. A 2.83 percent semi-annual rate is an effective annual yield of 5.74 percent, $[(1.0283)^2 - 1]$. This is the nominal yield on the longest available (regular or non-inflation-indexed) Treasury bond.

Suppose you want the 20-year bond yield. As of May 8, 2002, the two bonds with maturity nearest to 20 years are the 8 percent bond maturing in November 2021 and the 7.25 percent bond maturing in August 2022. Since their yields are 5.82 percent and 5.83 percent, 20-year yield is about 5.82 percent. The effective annual yield is 5.90 percent, $[(1.0291)^2 - 1]$.

The last row under "Government Bonds & Notes" presents information on the 3.375 percent Treasury Inflation Protection Security (TIPS) bond maturing in April 2032; the "i" in "Apr 32i" indicates that this is an inflation-linked bond. This and the other TIPS bonds are listed under "Inflation-Indexed Treasury Securities," which is at the end of the table. Its ask price is 102$\frac{2}{32}$ percent of par. From the last column, the accrued principal for an original $1,000 par value bond is $1,003; since issue, the accrued value has been increased 0.3 percent or $3 due to inflation. Its TIPS yield is 3.266 percent when expressed using the semi-annual bond convention. Relatively few TIPS bonds have been issued. Ignoring the bond maturing in July 2002, there are original 10-year bonds maturing in 2007 through 2012 and original 30-year bonds maturing in 2028 through 2032. Suppose someone wants a 15-year TIPS yield. It is between the 3.111 percent yield on the about 10-year bond (maturing in January 2012) and the 3.369 percent yield on the about 26-year bond (maturing in 2028). Based on a weighted average, the 15-year yield is about 3.192 percent [3.111% + 5/16 • (3.369 − 3.111%)]. To date, TIPS yields vary relatively little by maturity. So, the large gap in available maturities has not been a problem.

FIGURE 11.1   *(Continued)*

present value at age 60 of expected future benefits at 12.32 times initial annual benefits. The multiple is 12.32 for a 60-year-old single female when the TIPS yield is 3 percent. The present value of Mary's expected before-tax benefits is $137,935 [0.933 • $1,000 • 12 • 12.32].

Benefit Reductions for Singles

Next, if necessary, we must adjust this before-tax present value for benefit reductions and taxes. We assume the Earnings Test does not apply.[4] Also, we assume there is no Government Pension Offset or Windfall Elimination Provision. If there is, the reduced benefits must be substituted for annual benefits. If 85 percent of Mary's benefits are taxable and she will be in the 28 percent tax bracket during retirement, the after-tax value of Social Security benefits is $105,106 [$137,935 • (1 − 0.85 • 0.28)]. When calculating her asset mix, we believe Mary should consider Social Security as a bond worth approximately $105,000 in her portfolio.

In short, the model assumes individuals begin receiving benefits when they reach age 65. The present value calculations rely on expected cash flows assuming annual benefits are paid at mid-year. It assumes no benefits reduction due to an Earnings Test, Government Pension Offset, or Windfall Elimination Provision. The discount rate is the maturity-appropriate TIPS real yield. Then, if necessary, it reduces benefits for taxes.

Properties of Multiples

To accommodate financial advisors, all tables of multiples are placed at the end of the chapter. Similarly, all tables of multiples in the chapters on military retirement and defined-benefit plans are placed at the end of those chapters.

Tables 11.4 and 11.5 present the multiples, respectively, for single females and widows and for males and widowers for TIPS yields of 2.5 percent, 3 percent, 3.5 percent, and 4 percent. In addition, they present life expectancies. The multiples exhibit bond-pricing principles since valuing Social Security is essentially like valuing an inflation-linked bond. There is a negative relationship between multiples and interest rates. As rates rise, multiples fall and vice versa.

The multiples are sensitive to the level of the TIPS yield. Moreover, this sensitivity is larger for the young than the old. At age 50, a single female's multiple is 13.2 percent larger when the TIPS yield is 2.5 percent instead of 3 percent. At age 75, the multiple is 3.7 percent larger.

The multiples exhibit the positive convexity of government bond prices. For example, consider a 60-year-old female. From Table 11.4, the multiple rises 0.96 if rates fall from 3 percent to 2.5 percent, but falls a smaller amount, 0.88, if rates rise from 3 percent to 3.5 percent. Naturally, multiples are highest at age 65 and fall through the retirement years.

The multiples fall relatively slowly through retirement years. For example, at a 3.5 percent TIPS yield, a 65-year-old male has a multiple of 12.84 and a life expectancy of 17.6 years. Ten years later, after surviving more than half the 17.6

years, the multiple is 8.77, about one-third lower. This relatively slow decline is due to two features. First (assuming he survived the 10 years), his life expectancy did not decrease from 17.6 years to 7.6 years, but only to 10.6 years. Second, the discounting process reduces the present value of expected cash flows. The more distant the cash flow, the larger the discount. As one ages, expected cash flows are much nearer. In the remainder of this section, we critique our estimation method.

Expected Cash Flows or Cash Flows through Life Expectancy

Consistent with traditional financial methods, we estimate the value of Social Security based on *expected cash flows*. An alternative approach is to estimate the value based on *cash flows through life expectancy*. For Mary of Table 11.3, each year's expected cash flow is the probability she will be alive at the beginning of that year times $11,196. In contrast, cash flow through life expectancy assumes she is certain to receive payments until her expected date of death, and certain to receive nothing thereafter. To demonstrate that the present value of cash flows through life expectancy exceeds the present value of expected cash flows, our initial estimates of the former parallels the estimate of the latter. At age 60, Mary's life expectancy (assuming average life expectancy for a female) is 24.4 years. With a 3 percent TIPS yield, the present value of an $11,196 annual annuity, beginning in five years (with payments received at mid-year) and continuing for 19.4 years is $142,586.[5] This is 3.4 percent larger than the present value of expected cash flows, $137,935.

Table 11.6 presents the bias produced from estimating Social Security's value as the present value of the initial annual benefits through life expectancy (instead of expected cash flows). (To accommodate financial advisors, Table 11.6 is located with the multiples tables at the end of the chapter.) The bias is small; in fact, the 3.4 percent bias for a 60-year-old female is the largest bias for females or males age 80 or younger. Thus, singles—females, males, widows, and widowers—can approximate Social Security's value by discounting cash flows through life expectancy.

Moreover, there are advantages to discounting cash flows through life expectancy. It better accommodates the influence of family history on life expectancy. If Mary comes from a line of long-lived ancestors, she could estimate Social Security's value based on a longer but more appropriate expected life. In addition, given a life expectancy and TIPS yield, someone only needs a financial calculator to calculate the present value; mortality tables are not needed.

Now that we have established that the bias is small when we estimate Social Security's value based on cash flows through life expectancy, we introduce a simpler method. We estimate the value as the present value of the initial monthly payment for the life expectancy and then adjust for the bias. The value of $933 a month annuity due for 232.8 months (19.4 years times 12 months) beginning in 60 months when discounted at 0.2466 percent a month $[(1.03)^{1/12} - 1]$ is $142,773.[6] Since the bias from Table 11.6 is 3.4 percent, the final estimated value is $138,078 [$142,773 / (1.034)]. This estimate is trivially different than the $137,935 estimate of present value of expected cash flows.

Other Criticisms

We have presented two estimation methods: one estimates the value of expected cash flows, while the other estimates the value of cash flows through life expectancy and then adjusts for the bias. There are at least three potential criticisms that apply to both methods. First, we assume benefits begin at age 65. Second, we assume the Earnings Test does not reduce benefits. Third, we estimate the value of projected benefits based in part on future earnings.

The Appendices that end this chapter suggest that the first assumption does not represent a serious problem. For singles and couples with average life expectancy, the present value of projected benefits is approximately the same whether benefits begin at age 62 or 63 or any age through 70. Individuals adversely affected by the Earnings Test will probably not begin receiving benefits until they attain Full Retirement Age. As we just said, the present value of cash flows assuming payments begin at FRA is close to the present value if payments begin at age 65.

The third criticism is more of a concern. The annual *Your Social Security Statement* projects benefits assuming earnings continue at the current real level until someone retires and begins benefits. For someone age 50, this *Statement* may project benefits at FRA of $1,400, while actual benefits might be $1,250 if he or she drops out of the labor force today (at age 50). Even if he or she continues to work, conservatism suggests that Social Security's *current value* should not reflect the additional retirement benefits from *future* work. We suspect that this problem will not prove severe in practice. The calculation of one's Primary Insurance Amount consists of 90 percent of the first $531 of Average Indexed Monthly Earnings (for someone who turns 62 in 2000), 32 percent of the next $2,671, and 15 percent of the remaining AIME. AIME only considers each year's income up to that year's Social Security income limit. Due to this weighting scheme, for people who have worked since their twenties and are age 50 or older, there is likely to be little difference between their PIA if they quit work today and their PIA if they continue to work. This criticism is more of a problem for individuals under age 50 and individuals who dropped out of the labor force for many years, such as some mothers.

Estimating Social Security's Before-tax Value for Couples

The couples' model estimates the present value of expected cash flows to a couple with average life expectancy. It thus follows the spirit of the singles' model. In this section, we first describe spouse's and survivor's benefits. We then illustrate the couples' model for a same-age couple. We present multiples for couples the same age and when the wife is three years younger than the husband.

Spouse's Benefits: A spouse has dual entitlements to Social Security benefits. He or she is entitled to the larger of 100 percent of benefits at Full Retirement Age based on his or her earnings record or up to 50 percent of the spouse's benefits at FRA. When someone applies for benefits, the Social Security Administration calculates his or her benefits based on that person's own earnings record and the spouse's record, and it pays the larger amount. However, someone cannot begin benefits based on his or her record and later switch to benefits based on the spouse's record, or begin benefits based on the spouse's record and later switch to benefits based on his or her own record.[7]

Consider the couple, Sara, age 63, and Max, age 66. Both have a Full Retirement Age of 66. Based on her record, Sara has a Primary Insurance Amount of $1,000. Based on his record, Max has a PIA of $1,200. Now consider Sara's Social Security benefit possibilities. Based on her record, she could begin benefits today at $800 a month; since she is 36 months short of reaching FRA, she receives 80 percent of $1,000, where 80 percent is $100\% - 5 / 9\% \cdot 36$. Alternatively, Sara may receive spouse's benefits based on Max's earnings record if this amount is larger than benefits based on her own record. The rules for spouse's benefits are more complex. If she had attained FRA, Sara would be entitled to 50 percent of his PIA or $600. Spouse's benefits are reduced by $25 / 36$ percent for each of the first 36 months that benefits are begun before reaching FRA and by $5/12$ percent for each additional month. Since she is 36 months shy of FRA, she could receive spouse's benefits of 75 percent of $600 or $450 a month, where 75 percent is $100\% - 25 / 36\% \cdot 36$. In addition, Sara can only begin spouse's benefits before she attains FRA if Max has started benefits based on his own record. Spouse's benefits do not reflect Delayed Retirement Credits. If Max postpones the beginning of benefits until age 68, two years after reaching FRA, his benefits based on his own earnings record would reflect the 16 percent Delayed Retirement Credits, but Sara's spousal benefits would not. In this example, Sara would receive benefits based on her own earnings record since this amount, $800, is larger than her spouse's benefits, $450.

Survivor's Benefits: We discuss survivor's benefits as if a male dies, but benefits are parallel if a female dies. If a male dies, the following individuals could receive survivor's benefits based on his earnings record: widow, divorced widow, unmarried minor or disabled children, and dependent parents. In this book, we focus on benefits to widows and divorced widows.

The widow has dual entitlements under Social Security. She is entitled to benefits based on her earnings record or survivor's benefits based on her deceased husband's earnings record. If the deceased had not begun benefits, the widow can wait until Full Retirement Age and receive his PIA or receive reduced benefits as early as age 60. A disabled widow can begin benefits as early as age 50. The same rules apply for divorced widows who were married to the deceased husband at least 10 years and did not remarry before age 60. For more information, see "Survivors Benefits" at http://www.ssa.gov/pubs/10084.html and "What Every Woman Should Know" at http://www.ssa.gov/pubs/10127.html.

If the deceased had not begun benefits, the widow receives a percentage of the deceased husband's PIA. If she is FRA or older, she receives 100 percent of his PIA including increases in PIA due to Delayed Retirement Credits. If she is younger than FRA, she receives between 71.5 percent and 100 percent of PIA. Regardless of the age at which the widow reaches FRA, she receives 71.5 percent of her deceased husband's PIA if she begins survivor's benefits at age 60 and 100 percent if she waits until FRA. Thus, if FRA is 65, the maximum reduction of 28.5 percent is spread over 60 months, [(65 − 60) • 12], and the monthly reduction factor is 57 / 120 percent, [28.5% / 60 months]. If FRA is 66, the maximum reduction is spread over 72 months, [(66 − 60) • 12], and the monthly reduction factor is 57 / 144 percent, [28.5% / 72 months].

Assume Jeff and Martha are both 60 with Full Retirement Ages of 66. Jeff dies before beginning benefits when his PIA is $1,000 per month. If Martha begins survivor's benefits at age 60, she is entitled to $715 per month, [$1,000 • (100% − 57 / 144 % • 72)], where 57 / 144 percent represents the monthly reduction factor for someone with FRA of 66 and 72 denotes the months until she attains FRA. If she waits until FRA to begin survivor's benefits, she will receive $1,000.

If the deceased had already begun receiving benefits, the widow faces a possible reduction in her survivor's benefits. She is entitled to the smaller of (1) her survivor's benefit calculated using the normal method detailed previously or (2) the larger of the deceased's benefit at the time of his death and 82.5 percent of his PIA.

There are two key differences between survivor's benefits and spouse's benefits. First, survivor's benefits reflect Delayed Retirement Credits, while spouse's benefits do not. Second, someone can begin benefits based on his or her own earnings record and later switch to survivor's benefits, or begin survivor's benefits and later switch to benefits based on his or her own record. In contrast, such switching strategies are not allowed between spouse's benefits and benefits based on his or her own record. Appendix 11.2 discusses these switching strategies.

Calculating Present Value of Before-tax Benefits for Couples

We estimate the present value of a couple's before-tax Social Security benefits as the product:

(benefits fraction at age 65) • (PIA of higher earner) • (12 months) • (couple multiple) or (initial monthly payment) • (12 months) • (couple multiple) or (initial annual benefits) • (couple multiple)   (Eq. 11.2)

Appendix 11.2 concludes that the present value of a same-age couple's expected benefits is at or near its maximum when benefits begin at age 65. Therefore, our model assumes each partner begins receiving benefits when he or she reaches age 65. In addition, it examines when each partner in a couple should begin receiving Social Security benefits. This is a separate but important topic. Due to its length, it is placed in Appendix 11.2.

To illustrate the model, consider Mike and Fran. They are both currently 55 years old, and their Full Retirement Age is 66. They will begin receiving benefits at age 65, and their benefits fraction at age 65 is 0.933. They recently received their annual *Your Social Security Statements*. Mike's PIA is $1,200. Fran's is $1,400. The formula inserts the higher PIA of $1,400. The 12 months converts monthly payments into annual benefits. As we shall see, the couple multiple considers the lower PIA.

The couple multiple reflects the present value of the couple's benefits per $1 of initial annual benefits paid to the higher earner. We first calculate the ratio of lower-to-higher PIAs [$1,200 / $1,400], which is 0.857. The PIA ratio is the larger of this ratio or 0.5. In this example, it is 0.857. But if Mike's benefits based on his earnings were less than his spousal benefits, which is 50 percent of her PIA when he attains FRA, the PIA ratio would be 0.5. At age 55, Mike and Fran's current age, the expected dollar benefits (in age 55 dollars) to be received at mid-year at age 65 are:

$$(0.933) \bullet (\$1,400) \bullet [p(m) \bullet p(f) \bullet (1.857) + (1 - p(m)) \bullet p(f) + p(m) \bullet (1 - p(f))]$$

(Eq. 11.3)

where $p(m)$ and $p(f)$ denote the probabilities of, respectively, the male and female being alive at age 65. Thus, for example, $(1 - p(m))$ denotes the probability of Mike being dead at age 65. Equation 11.3 says the couple will receive $1.857 (per dollar of initial annual benefits to higher earner) if both are alive, $1 (per dollar of initial annual benefits to higher earner) if one is alive, and nothing if neither is alive. Equation 11.3 already reflects the benefits fraction, 0.933, and higher PIA, $1,400. The couple multiple calculates the present value of the bracketed amount discounted at today's maturity-appropriate TIPS yield.

Each year's expected cash flow is:

$[p(m) \bullet p(f) \bullet (1.857) + (1 - p(m)) \bullet p(f) + p(m) \bullet (1 - p(f))]$ times initial annual benefits to the higher earner.

At age 55, the probabilities of Mike and Fran being alive at age 65 are, respectively, 0.933821 and 0.949715. Inserting these amounts in the bracketed term produces 1.756714. At age 55, the expected cash flow at age 65 is 1.756714 times initial annual benefits to the higher earner. The expected cash flow at age 66 is 1.738433 times this amount. The 1.738433 is slightly lower than 1.756714 because the probabilities of Mike and Fran being alive at age 66 are slightly lower. Follow the same procedure until age 120, the end of the mortality tables. The couple multiple reflects the present value of these bracketed amounts discounted back to their current age 55 at today's TIPS yield.

Table 11.7 presents information to calculate the couple multiple for this 55-year-old same-age couple. For a 3 percent TIPS yield, it presents two numbers: 12.39 and 7.38. The couple multiple is 18.71 [12.39 + 0.857 • 7.38]. This couple multiple applies to all same-age couples regardless of their Full Retirement Age.

The before-tax value of Social Security is estimated at $293,268 [0.933 • $1,400 • 12 • 18.71]. If 85 percent of payments are taxable and they are in the 28 percent tax bracket, the after-tax value is estimated at about $223,000 [$293,268 • (1 − 0.85 • 0.28)]. We argue that this couple should consider Social Security benefits as a

$223,000 bond in their portfolio.[8] Clearly, Social Security is a valuable asset and one that the profession has traditionally ignored when calculating the value of an individual's or family's portfolio.

Table 11.8 presents information to calculate the couple multiple when the wife is three years younger than the husband. For comparison with the earlier couple multiple, assume a TIPS yield of 3 percent, PIA ratio of 0.857, and the husband and wife's ages are 55 and 52, respectively. The multiple is 18.14 [13.03 + 0.857 • 5.96]. This is 0.57 lower than the couple multiple when they are both age 55 because the wife does not begin receiving payments until she reaches age 65, which is three years later. After both partners begin receiving payments, the couple multiple with the wife three years younger is larger due to the wife's longer life expectancy.

Recall that we could use the life expectancy of a single male or single female to approximate the value of Social Security retirement benefits. Unfortunately, in general, we cannot use life expectancies to approximate the value of Social Security to a couple. The exception occurs when both spouses receive the same Social Security benefits. In this case, the PIA ratio is 1.0, and the couple multiple is the sum of the comparable multiple for single women and multiple for single men.

Investment Implications

We recommend that individuals and couples include the after-tax present value of Social Security payments when calculating the value of their retirement assets and their current asset mix. When answering the following questions, we believe the individual's or family's portfolio should include the value of Social Security: Can the family satisfy its retirement income needs during its lifetime? What is its current asset mix (based on assets that can be used to satisfy retirement income needs)? When answering other questions, the family portfolio would ignore the value of Social Security. For example, Social Security should be ignored when estimating estate taxes.

Nancy and Chris are a 65-year-old financially secure couple with FRAs of 65. They have $1 million in stock funds held in 401(k) plans and $1 million in bonds held in taxable accounts. The market value and tax basis of the bonds are both $1 million. They have average life expectancies for their sex and age, and they will apply today to begin receiving Social Security payments. Chris will receive $1,483 per month, and Nancy will receive $1,335 per month. What is their current asset mix?

According to the traditional approach, they have $1 million in stocks in a $2 million total portfolio. The traditional approach ignores the value of Social Security and other retirement income streams such as military retirement and company pensions. Figure 11.2 presents their current asset mix, which contains 50 percent stocks.

If we include the present value of Social Security benefits in their portfolio, they have a different mix. The before-tax value of benefits is about $460,000. It is the product of (1.00) • ($1,483) • (12) • (25.83), where 25.83 is the couple multiple assuming a 3.5 percent long-term TIPS yield. The couple multiple is 16.13 + 0.9 •

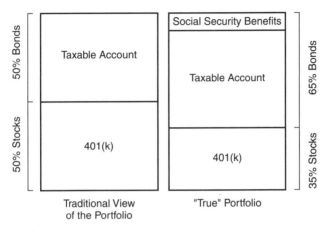

Chris and Nancy, a hypothetical retiree couple described in the text.

FIGURE 11.2   Illustrative Implications of After-tax Valuation and Retirement Benefits

10.78, where 0.9 is the PIA ratio of $1,335 / $1,483. Assuming a 28 percent tax rate during retirement and 85 percent of benefits are taxable, the after-tax value of Social Security is about $350,000 [$460,000 • (1 − 0.85 • 0.28)].

We recommend that the couple makes two adjustments to the family portfolio. First, they should adjust before-tax funds to after-tax funds and then calculate the asset mix based on after-tax funds. This is an apples-to-apples comparison. If their expected tax rate during retirement is 28 percent, the $1 million of before-tax funds in the 401(k) converts to $720,000 after taxes [$1,000,000 • (1 − 0.28)]. Figure 11.2 presents their current asset mix, which contains 35 percent stocks [$720,000 / ($720,000 + $1,000,000 + $350,000)].

By ignoring the value of Social Security benefits, they underestimate the value of assets intended to meet their retirement needs. In addition, they overestimate their current stock exposure by 15 percent. Clearly, including Social Security substantially changes the portfolio of this financially secure couple. Including Social Security would have a more dramatic affect on less secure individuals and couples.

Some of the investment implications from this chapter follow:

1. Incomes from Social Security, military retirement, and defined-benefit plans are valuable assets. They affect a family's retirement preparedness, and their value should be included in the family's extended portfolio.

2. Families that manage their traditional portfolio really have a more conservative portfolio than they think they have and should have. For example, if Nancy and Chris manage their traditional portfolio, they think they have a 50 percent stock allocation. After adding the value of Social Security and adjust-

ing for taxes, they really have a 35 percent stock allocation. Clearly, adding the values of retirement income streams—Social Security in this example—decreases their stock allocation. In addition, research indicates that most families have a heavier stock allocation in their tax-deferred retirement accounts than in the taxable portion of their traditional financial portfolio. For example, Nancy and Chris have 100 percent stocks in the 401(k) and no stocks among the other $1 million of traditional financial assets. Both factors cause the stock allocation in their extended portfolio to be smaller than the stock allocation in their traditional portfolio.

3. Everything else the same, because the values of retirement incomes are essentially bonds, families with substantial retirement incomes can invest a larger portion of their traditional financial assets in stocks. This statement applies to families that are in retirement and to those that have not yet reached retirement.

4. At the death of the first spouse, the surviving spouse should rebalance the portfolio. Suppose Sandy and Russ are 70 years old and receive, respectively, $1,300 and $900 from Social Security based on their earnings record. Assuming average life expectancies and a 3 percent TIPS yield, the value of their Social Security is about $328,000 [$1,300 • 12 months • 21]. The multiple of 21 is 14.76 + 0.69 • 9.05, where 0.69 is the PIA ratio of $900 / $1,300 and the other numbers come from Table 11.7.

   Suppose Sandy dies unexpectedly. Several things may change. First, the expected value of Social Security benefits falls to about $175,000 [$1,300 • 12 • 11.21], where 11.21 is the multiple for a single male from Table 11.5. Second, the family portfolio would lose the value of any other pension income she may have, such as income from a company pension. Third, life insurance proceeds, if any, would increase the size of the family portfolio. Thus, the portfolio changed at Sandy's death. Suppose Russ does not change his investment goals or target asset allocation. The first two changes previously listed would decrease the amount of "bonds" in the portfolio. The third would increase the cash in the portfolio. The impact on the stock allocation depends upon the relative sizes of the decrease in pension values and the increase in cash from life insurance. If the loss of pension value is larger (and his target asset allocation remains the same), Russ will need to sell stocks and buy bonds. If the cash from life insurance is larger (and his target asset allocation remains the same), he will need to use the insurance funds to buy additional stocks.

5. Return to the prior example except assume Sandy is diagnosed with terminal cancer that shortens her life expectancy to one or two years. The portfolio implications are similar. The key is that the values of retirement incomes fall sharply.

6. The decrease in Social Security's value from a sharp decline in life expectancy is different for singles and couples. Since singles do not have a current spouse, a sharp decline in life expectancies produces a dramatic

decrease in the value of Social Security. Since Social Security provides benefits to a surviving spouse, a sharp decline in one partner's life expectancy usually produces a much smaller decrease in the value of the couple's Social Security.

7. *Assuming average life expectancy,* the value of pension income declines relatively slowly. Implications 5 and 6 apply to people who experience a sharp decline in life expectancy. This implication applies to singles and couples who do not have a sharp decline in life expectancy. Rather, they remain healthy long into their retirement. For example, consider a 65-year-old single female who has an average life expectancy of about 20 years. Assuming a 3.5 percent yield, the multiples and her life expectancies are as follows:

Age	Multiple	Life Expectancy
65	14.06	20.1 years
75	10.09	12.7 years
85	6.37	7.1 years

As she ages from 65 to 75—half her original life expectancy—Social Security's value is 72 percent of its original value. As she ages from 65 to 85—her original life expectancy—its value is 45 percent of its original value. Two factors account for this slow decrease in pension value. First, each year she survives, her remaining life expectancy falls less than one year. Second, since near term payments are more valuable than distant payments, the value of the pension falls slowly. For example, at age 65 the multiple is approximately the value of $1 per year for 20 years. At age 66, it is approximately the value of $1 per year for 19 years. The decrease in value is the value of the most distant payment, which is the least valuable payment.

Future Changes in Social Security

In all likelihood, there will be future changes in the Social Security system. We suspect most changes will occur on the revenue side—increases in taxes—with relatively few changes in benefits. Furthermore, of the relatively few benefit changes, we suspect most of them will affect younger workers who have decades to adjust to the changes. As benefits change, we will need to adjust the models. Neither the expectation of future changes nor the many assumptions embedded in the models change the fundamental reality that Social Security has value. Since current practice ignores the value of Social Security when calculating a family's asset mix, it implicitly assumes its value is zero. If the value of Social Security retirement benefits should be considered a bond in the family portfolio, then the current models represent a substantial improvement over current practice.

Summary

There are three objectives to this chapter. First, we present the current structure of Social Security retirement benefits. Professionals who advise individual investors should understand the current system, including client options under this system. Appendices 11.1 and 11.2 examine factors that should influence when singles and couples begin benefits. Professionals can explain to single clients the financial implications of beginning Social Security payments before or after reaching Full Retirement Age and help them select the best time to begin receiving payments. Due to the dual entitlement system, the decision as to when each member of a couple begins receiving benefits is much more complex. Professionals can add value for clients by helping them work through the interesting alternatives.

Second, we present models that estimate the present value of Social Security retirement benefits for singles (including widows and widowers) and married couples. In addition, we discuss estimation issues, critique the models, and present examples.

Finally, we show that a family's portfolio usually looks substantially different when it includes the after-tax present value of Social Security benefits as a "bond" in that portfolio. We believe professionals should capitalize Social Security (and military retirement, company pensions, and teacher retirement) benefits and include their after-tax values in the family portfolio. Professionals who fail to consider the value of retirement income streams cannot be providing optimal advice to their clients.

TABLE 11.4 Multiples and Life Expectancy of Single Females and Widows

Age	TIPS Yield				Life Expectancy
	2.5%	3%	3.5%	4%	
30	6.06	4.86	3.90	3.14	53.0
35	6.87	5.64	4.64	3.83	48.1
40	7.80	6.56	5.53	4.67	43.2
45	8.86	7.64	6.60	5.71	38.4
50	10.09	8.91	7.89	7.00	33.6
55	11.53	10.44	9.47	8.60	28.9
60	13.28	12.32	11.44	10.65	24.4
65	15.55	14.77	14.06	13.40	20.1
70	13.16	12.60	12.08	11.59	16.2
75	10.85	10.46	10.09	9.75	12.7
80	8.66	8.40	8.16	7.93	9.7
85	6.68	6.52	6.37	6.22	7.1
90	5.10	5.00	4.91	4.82	5.2

*Source: **Social Security Singles/Female**.*

TABLE 11.5   Multiples and Life Expectancy of Single Males and Widowers

Age	TIPS Yield				Life Expectancy
	2.5%	3%	3.5%	4%	
30	5.34	4.30	3.47	2.81	50.0
35	6.06	5.00	4.14	3.43	45.1
40	6.89	5.82	4.93	4.19	40.3
45	7.84	6.79	5.90	5.13	35.5
50	8.95	7.94	7.06	6.29	30.8
55	10.26	9.33	8.50	7.76	26.2
60	11.89	11.08	10.34	9.67	21.7
65	14.06	13.43	12.84	12.30	17.6
70	11.65	11.21	10.79	10.41	13.9
75	9.33	9.04	8.77	8.51	10.6
80	7.21	7.03	6.86	6.70	7.8
85	5.41	5.30	5.20	5.10	5.5
90	4.02	3.96	3.91	3.85	3.9

Source: *Social Security Singles/Male*.

TABLE 11.6   Bias in Social Security Valuations Based on Cash Flows through Expected Life

Age	Female	Male
30	2.1%	0.1%
35	2.3	0.3
40	2.5	0.9
45	2.9	1.4
50	3.0	2.0
55	3.2	2.6
60	3.4	2.6
65	2.6	2.2
70	2.2	1.7
75	1.2	0.6
80	0.4	−1.0
85	−1.7	−4.2
90	−3.7	−7.1

Bias denotes the percent by which present value of cash flows through expected life exceeds present value of expected cash flows. All estimates assume a 3 percent TIPS yield.

TABLE 11.7   Multiples for Married Couples: Husband and Wife the Same Age

Age	2.5%		3%		3.5%		4%	
	1	F	1	F	1	F	1	F
30	7.32	4.09	5.84	3.32	4.68	2.70	3.76	2.20
35	8.29	4.65	6.78	3.86	5.56	3.22	4.57	2.68
40	9.39	5.30	7.87	4.51	6.62	3.85	5.57	3.29
45	10.65	6.05	9.15	5.28	7.88	4.62	6.80	4.04
50	12.08	6.96	10.64	6.22	9.38	5.57	8.29	5.00
55	13.74	8.06	12.39	7.38	11.19	6.77	10.13	6.22
60	15.67	9.50	14.47	8.92	13.40	8.39	12.42	7.89
65	17.98	11.63	17.01	11.19	16.13	10.78	15.31	10.39
70	15.48	9.34	14.76	9.05	14.10	8.77	13.49	8.51
75	12.93	7.25	12.43	7.07	11.96	6.90	11.52	6.73
80	10.44	5.43	10.11	5.33	9.80	5.23	9.50	5.13
85	8.15	3.93	7.94	3.88	7.74	3.82	7.55	3.77
90	6.28	2.85	6.15	2.82	6.03	2.79	5.91	2.76

This table presents two factors used to compute the couple multiple. To calculate the couple multiple, we must first calculate the PIA ratio. It is the larger of 0.5 or the ratio of lower Primary Insurance Amount to higher PIA. If the couple's PIAs are $1,200 and $1,400, then this ratio is 0.857. Assuming a 3 percent TIPS yield, the couple multiple for a 55-year-old couple is 18.71 [12.39 + 0.857 • 7.38], where 12.39 and 7.38 are under columns labeled, respectively, 1 and F.

Source: Social Security Couples/Same Age.

TABLE 11.8   Multiples for Married Couples: Wife Three Years Younger than Husband

Husband's Age	2.5%		3%		3.5%		4%	
	1	F	1	F	1	F	1	F
30	7.74	3.36	6.16	2.69	4.92	2.16	3.94	1.74
35	8.76	3.81	7.15	3.13	5.84	2.58	4.79	2.13
40	9.92	4.34	8.29	3.66	6.95	3.08	5.84	2.60
45	11.25	4.96	9.63	4.28	8.27	3.70	7.11	3.20
50	12.76	5.69	11.19	5.03	9.84	4.45	8.68	3.94
55	14.49	6.58	13.03	5.96	11.73	5.40	10.59	4.90
60	16.50	7.72	15.19	7.16	14.02	6.65	12.96	6.18
65	18.87	9.34	17.80	8.88	16.82	8.45	15.93	8.05
70	16.41	9.84	15.60	9.52	14.86	9.21	14.17	8.93
75	12.96	7.30	12.46	7.12	11.99	6.94	11.54	6.78
80	11.37	5.80	10.98	5.68	10.61	5.57	10.26	5.46
85	9.00	4.24	8.75	4.18	8.51	4.11	8.28	4.05
90	6.95	3.06	6.79	3.03	6.64	3.00	6.50	2.96

This table presents two factors used to compute the couple multiple. To calculate the couple multiple, we must first calculate the PIA ratio. It is the larger of 0.5 or the ratio of lower Primary Insurance Amount to higher PIA. If the couple's PIAs are $1,200 and $1,400, then this ratio is 0.857. (The model assumes the husband's PIA is larger, but the estimated value is similar if the wife's PIA is higher.) Assuming a 3 percent TIPS yield, the couple multiple when the husband is 55 and the wife is 52 is 18.24 [13.03 + 0.857 • 5.96], where 13.03 and 5.96 are under columns labeled, respectively, 1 and F. The model assumes that both partners begin receiving payments at age 65.
Source: **Social Security Couples/Female Three Years Younger.**

Appendix 11.1: When Should the "Average" Single Person Begin Receiving Benefits?

There are two objectives to this Appendix. The first is to determine when a single female, single male, widow, or widower *with average life expectancy* should begin receiving benefits. The second is to discuss factors that should influence when a single person should begin receiving benefits.

This Appendix demonstrates that the Social Security system is close to actuarially fair for single individuals with average life expectancies. To be more precise, assuming life expectancy is average and the Earnings Test does not apply, the present value of expected benefit payments is approximately the same whether benefits begin at age 62, 63, 64.5, or any age through 70. (For simplicity, we assume benefits begin on a full year—e.g., 62, 63, etc.—but they may begin at any time beginning at age 62.) No one should postpone the beginning of benefits beyond age 70 since there is no reward for such a delay.

Table 11.9 presents the pattern of present values at age 62 of expected before-tax benefits for single males and females with average life expectancies and Full Retirement Ages of 66 and 67. Although not shown, the pattern of present values for single individuals born before 1943 is similar to the pattern for people with FRAs of 66.

The first row labeled Female Relative denotes the present value relative of projected benefits for a female with a FRA of 66. The present value relative of 100% at age 67 indicates that the present value of her projected benefits reaches a maximum if she begins benefits at that age. The absolute level of benefits does not affect the present value relatives. If she begins benefits at age 62, the present value of projected benefits would be 97.1% of the maximum. Based on these present value relatives, the present value of projected benefits reaches a maximum when benefits begin at age 67, but the present value is within 2.9% of this maximum if benefits start at any other age.

The second row presents the present value relatives for a single male with a FRA of 66. The present value of his benefits reaches a maximum when benefits begin at age 64 or 65. The present value is 6.2% lower when benefits start at age 70. Due to his shorter life expectancy, there is a weak incentive for the average male to begin benefits at an earlier age than the average female.

The patterns of Female Relatives and Male Relatives are similar when the FRA is 67. Due to differences in life expectancies, there is a weak incentive for women to begin benefits about a year after attaining FRA, while men have a weak incentive to begin benefits between 62 and 66.

In this book, the model of present value of Social Security benefits requires us to assume an age at which benefits begin. Technically, there would be a different model for each possible starting date. To keep the analysis tractable, we assume benefits begin at age 65. Table 11.9 shows that the present value of benefits to females and males is at its maximum or within 1 percent of its maximum when benefits begin at age 65. However, even though our model assumes benefits begin at age 65, the model's estimate provides a close approximation to the present value of benefits if benefits begin at any other age.

TABLE 11.9 Relative Present Values of Benefits for Singles when Benefits Begin at Ages 62 through 70

FRA 66	62	63	64	65	66	67	68	69	70
Female Relative	97.1%	97.3%	98.8%	99.4%	99.4%	100%	99.8%	98.9%	97.3%
Male Relative	99.5%	99.1%	100%	100%	99.3%	99.1%	98.1%	96.3%	93.8%
FRA 67	**62**	**63**	**64**	**65**	**66**	**67**	**68**	**69**	**70**
Female Relative	97.6%	98.1%	98.1%	99.4%	99.8%	99.7%	100%	99.6%	98.4%
Male Relative	100%	100%	99.3%	100%	99.7%	98.8%	98.3%	97.0%	94.9%

This table compares present values of benefits at age 62 when they begin at age 62, 63, and so on through age 70. It demonstrates that, for someone with average life expectancy, the present values are similar no matter when benefits actually begin. Female Relative and Male Relative denote present value percentages relative to the maximum present value. The panels reflect singles with Full Retirement Ages of 66 and 67. Similar results prevail for other FRAs. We assume a TIPS yield of 0.25 percent per month (3 percent per year).
Source: Cook, Jennings, and Reichenstein (2002).

Table 11.9 indicates that, assuming average life expectancies and benefits are not reduced by the Earnings Test, the benefits schedule is close to actuarially fair for single males and females. Consequently, the two key factors that should influence when a single person begins receiving Social Security benefits are the applicability of the Earnings Test and the expected length of the individual's life.

As discussed previously, the Earnings Test limits or eliminates Social Security benefits for moderate- and high-income individuals. Suppose Judy applies for $1,200 per month in benefits at age 62, but she earns $35,000 in 2002. In the absence of the Earnings Test, her annual benefits would be $14,400. After this test, they are $2,540, [$14,400 − 0.5 • ($35,000 − $11,280)], where $11,280 is the earned income limit in 2002. Consequently, working singles who earn more than the earned income limit should seldom begin benefits before attaining FRA. An exception would be a single individual with a short life expectancy and with no dependents, such as a child, who will receive survivor's benefits. If Judy is terminally ill and has, say, two years to live, she should take the greatly reduced benefits instead of forfeiting benefits entirely.

The second key factor is life expectancy. In general, the shorter the life expectancy, the stronger is the incentive to begin benefits at an early age. The longer the life expectancy, the stronger is the incentive to delay the start of benefits.

In summary, we conclude that the two most important factors that influence when a single person should begin receiving payments are whether the Earnings Test applies and whether they have a shorter- or longer-than-expected life expectancy. Other decidedly weaker factors are the person's sex and levels of interest rates. Due to their shorter life expectancies, single men have a weak incentive to begin receiving payments earlier than single women. When interest rates fall, the present values of future cash flows increase. Thus, low interest rates encourage people to delay the start of benefits.

Appendix 11.2: When Should the "Average" Couple Begin Receiving Benefits?

There are two objectives to this Appendix. The first is to show that, for a couple *with average life expectancy,* the present value of expected Social Security benefits reaches a maximum or close to a maximum when benefits begin at age 65. Consequently, the model in this book assumes the couple begins benefits at age 65. The second objective is to discuss factors and strategies that should influence when each partner in a couple should begin receiving benefits. In practice, the timing of the beginning of benefits can be important to couples with shorter- or longer-than-average-age life expectancies and in many other circumstances.

In practice, the model of present value of a couple's Social Security benefits requires us to assume the age at which benefits begin. There would be a different model for each combination of starting dates for each partner. To keep the analysis tractable, we assume both partners have average life expectancies and begin benefits at the same age. This section suggests that age 65 seems to be the best assumed starting date.

Table 11.10 presents the pattern of present value relatives for same-age couples with Full Retirement Ages of 66 and 67. Most couples with earlier FRAs have already begun benefits. It assumes the Primary Insurance Amount of the couple's lower earner is 80 percent of the higher earner's PIA and a TIPS yield of 3.5 percent. It estimates present value relatives at age 62 assuming benefits begin at age 62, at age 63, and so on through age 70.

The top half of Table 11.10 presents the present value relatives for a couple with Full Retirement Ages of 66. If benefits begin at age 62, the present value relative is 99.1 percent, which indicates that it is 0.9 percent lower than the maximum present value at age 65. The last half presents the present value relatives for couples

---

TABLE 11.10 Relative Present Values of a Couple Beginning Benefits at Ages 62 through 70

FRA 66	62	63	64	65	66	67	68	69	70
PVRe165	0.991	0.988	0.998	1.000	0.995	0.995	0.988	0.973	0.952

FRA 67	62	63	64	65	66	67	68	69	70
PVRe165	0.996	0.997	0.992	1.000	1.000	0.992	0.990	0.980	0.963

This table compares present values at age 62 of benefits when they begin at age 62, age 63, and so on through age 70. It assumes a PIA ratio of 0.8 and a TIPS yield of 3.5 percent. For couples, it demonstrates that the present value of benefits is at or near its maximum when benefits begin at age 65. PVRe165 denotes the present value of benefits relative to the present value at age 65. The panels reflect couples with Full Retirement Ages of 66 and 67.
Source: Cook, Jennings, and Reichenstein (2002).

with Full Retirement Ages of 67. Present values for these couples reach a maximum when benefits begin at age 65.

The analysis suggests that age 65 is the best age for a same-age couples with average life expectancies to begin Social Security benefits. Consequently, the couple's model assumes each partner begins benefits at age 65. However, even if benefits begin at other ages, the estimated present values would be close to the estimated present value assuming benefits begin at age 65. Therefore, the model should provide good value estimates to couples with average life expectancies even if they expect to begin benefits at other ages.

The second objective of this Appendix is to discuss factors and strategies that should influence when each partner in a couple begins receiving benefits. One factor—perhaps the most important factor—is whether the Earnings Test applies. When it applies, benefits should be delayed until FRA or later. Another factor is each partner's life expectancy. However, due to the rules governing spouse's and survivor's benefits, the life expectancy of the longer-lived spouse is the critical factor.

Both partners are FRA or older: Fran and Mike are both 66, their Full Retirement Ages, and both partners have retired from the work force. Fran is entitled to $800 per month based on her earnings record, and Mike is entitled to $1,200 per month based on his record. Assuming average life expectancies, Mike will live about 17 years, but their joint life expectancy is about 24 years. Their joint life expectancy is the expected time until the last partner dies. At 24 years, it is longer than the either partner's expected life.

Table 11.11 presents payments for two strategies assuming Mike lives 17 years, his life expectancy, and Fran lives 24 years, their joint life expectancy. In Strategy A, they both begin benefits today based on their own records. They jointly receive $2,000 a month for the first year and an equivalent real amount in subsequent years until the first dies. After the first dies—it does not matter who dies first—the survivor receives $1,200 per month.

In Strategy B, Fran begins benefits today, but Mike delays the beginning of benefits for one year. In the first year, they get Fran's $800 per month. In the second and subsequent years until the first dies, they get $2,096 a month—Fran's $800 and Mike's $1,296, which is 8 percent higher than $1,200 due to the Delayed Retirement Credit. After the death of the first, the survivor receives $1,296 a month.

The Difference column presents the differences in monthly payments by year between these two strategies. In Strategy B, they jointly receive $1,200 per month less the first year and $96 per month more in subsequent years until the survivor dies. The last two columns separate the Difference column into two parts. Diff 1 presents the difference in Mike's benefits if he were single and lived 17 years, his life expectancy. He would forego $1,200 a month the first year but get $96 more per month for the next 16 years. Assuming a 3 percent TIPS yield, this is a fair tradeoff in present value terms. The last column, Diff 2, is additional benefits to the couple due to survivor's benefits. Assuming Fran lives 24 years, the couple gets an additional $96 per month in sur-

TABLE 11.11   Fran and Mike's Payoffs from Social Security

Age	Years	Strategy A	Strategy B	Difference	Diff 1	Diff 2
		Fran & Mike	Fran & Mike		If Mike was single	Survivor's benefits
66	1	$2,000 mo.	$800 mo.	–$1,200 mo.	–$1,200 mo.	
67	2	$2,000 mo.	$2,096 mo.	$96 mo.	$96 mo.	
68	3	$2,000 mo.	$2,096 mo.	$96 mo.	$96 mo.	
69	4	$2,000 mo.	$2,096 mo.	$96 mo.	$96 mo.	
70	5	$2,000 mo.	$2,096 mo.	$96 mo.	$96 mo.	
	. . .					
81	16	$2,000 mo.	$2,096 mo.	$96 mo.	$96 mo.	
82	17	$2,000 mo.	$2,096 mo.	$96 mo.	$96 mo.	
83	18	$1,200 mo.	$1,296 mo.	$96 mo.		$96 mo.
84	19	$1,200 mo.	$1,296 mo.	$96 mo.		$96 mo.
85	20	$1,200 mo.	$1,296 mo.	$96 mo.		$96 mo.
86	21	$1,200 mo.	$1,296 mo.	$96 mo.		$96 mo.
87	22	$1,200 mo.	$1,296 mo.	$96 mo.		$96 mo.
88	23	$1,200 mo.	$1,296 mo.	$96 mo.		$96 mo.
89	24	$1,200 mo.	$1,296 mo.	$96 mo.		$96 mo.

Source: Cook, Jennings, and Reichenstein (2002).

vivor's benefits for years 18 through 24. This last column is the approximate increase in present value of joint benefits if the higher earner—Mike in our example—delays the beginning of benefits based on his record by one year.

Although the structure of Social Security benefits is close to actuarially fair for singles, it does not appear to be actuarially fair for couples. Rather, it encourages the higher earners to delay the beginning of benefits. The additional value from postponing is approximately equal to the additional survivor's benefits. One lesson from Table 11.11 is that, as long as their joint life expectancy exceeds 17 years, the higher earner should delay the beginning of benefits. An extreme example emphasizes this point.

Suppose Mike is terminally ill and has one year to live, but Fran comes from a line of long-lived ancestors and has a 24-year life expectancy. By delaying benefits for one year, the couple loses $1,200 a month for the first year but will likely receive an additional $96 a month for 23 years. In this example, the costs and benefits from Mike delaying his benefits one year are the same as the Difference column in Table 11.11.

Let us examine another question that applies to married partners who have both reached FRA. Should the lower earner also delay the beginning of benefits

TABLE 11.12   Fran and Mike's Payoffs from Social Security

Age	Years	Strategy B Fran & Mike	Strategy C Fran & Mike	Difference
66	1	$800 mo.	$0 mo.	−$800 mo.
67	2	$2,096 mo.	$2,160 mo.	$64 mo.
68	3	$2,096 mo.	$2,160 mo.	$64 mo.
69	4	$2,096 mo.	$2,160 mo.	$64 mo.
Until death of 1st		$2,096 mo.	$2,160 mo.	$64 mo.
After death of 1st		$1,296 mo.	$1,296 mo.	$0 mo.

Source: Cook, Jennings, and Reichenstein (2002).

based on his or her record? Let us return to the previous example and compare two strategies. Table 11.12 compares these strategies. Strategy B was described earlier; Fran begins benefits at FRA, and Mike delays benefits one year. In Strategy C, Fran and Mike both postpone the start of benefits one year. Beginning in one year, they will receive a combined monthly benefit of $2,160—her $864 and his $1,296. The Difference column is the key column. When both partners delay benefits instead of just the higher earner, the couple loses $800 a month the first year, but gains $64 a month thereafter *until the first spouse dies*. Assuming a 3 percent annual TIPS yield, they would *both* have to live at least 17 years for Strategy C to be preferred in present value terms. Even if both Mike and Fran have average life expectancies, the probability is greater than 50 percent that one of them will die before 17 years pass. In short, the lower earner should begin benefits today. In this example, Mike should delay benefits if their joint life expectancy exceeds his 17-year life expectancy, while Fran should begin payments early if one of them is likely to die before 17 years.

Let us generalize from this example. The value added from having the higher-earning spouse postpone the start of benefits would be much greater if the lower-earning spouse is much younger and healthy. For example, if Mike was 66 but Fran was 56, he should have a strong preference to delay benefits. Each year he delays receiving benefits past FRA through age 70, his monthly payment and her survivor's payment increase by 8 percent. Due to her young age (and assumed good health), she will likely receive this additional payment for a long time.

Lesson: If they have both reached FRA, there is an advantage for the lower-earning partner to begin benefits and the higher-earning partner to delay benefits. This advantage is especially large when the lower-earning partner is healthy and much younger.

One partner depends on spouse's benefits: Some partners will receive more from spouse's benefits than from benefits based on their own earnings record. This scenario applies to a stay-at-home wife. It also fits some employees of state and local governments and some teachers because of the Government Pension Offset. This example explains a couple's strategy when one partner depends on spouse's benefits. In addition, it explains a potential reduction in survivor's benefits if the deceased spouse had already started benefits based on his or her own earnings record.

Sam and Sue are 62 with Full Retirement Ages of 66. Sam just retired from work, and Sue has not worked outside the home. Sam has a PIA of $1,000. They are deciding when to begin benefits. Although Sue qualifies for spouse's benefits, she cannot receive these benefits until Sam begins payments. If they both begin benefits at 62, he receives $750 and she receives $350 a month. His benefits fraction is 75 percent, [100 percent − 5 / 9 percent • 36 − 5 / 12 percent • 12]. Her benefits fraction is 35 percent, [50 percent • (100 percent − 25 / 36 percent • 36 − 5 / 12 percent • 12)]. If she dies, he will continue to receive $750 a month. If he dies, we assume she applies immediately for survivor's benefits. As explained in the next paragraph, if he dies at 62, she will receive $810 a month in survivor's benefits.

If Sam, the deceased, had already begun receiving benefits, Sue, the survivor, faces a possible reduction in her survivor's benefits. She is entitled to the smaller of (1) her survivor's benefit calculated using the normal method detailed previously or (2) the larger of Sam's benefit at the time of his death and 82.5 percent of his PIA. Thus, in the example above, Sue receives the smaller of (1) $810, [$1,000 • (100 percent − 57 / 144 percent • 48)], or (2) the larger of $750 and $825, [$1,000 • 82.5 percent].

If they begin benefits at age 63, he receives $800 and she receives $375 a month as long as they both live. If she dies, he will continue to receive $800 a month. If he dies at 63, she will receive survivor's benefits of $825. She receives the smaller of (1) $858, [$1,000 • (100 percent − 57 / 144 percent • 36)], or (2) the larger of $800 and $825.

If they begin benefits at FRA of 66, he receives $1,000 and she receives $500 a month as long as they both live. When the first dies, the survivor receives $1,000 a month.

If they begin benefits at age 67, he receives $1,080 and she receives $500 a month as long as they both live. His benefits reflect the delayed Retirement Credit, but her spouse's benefits do not. When the first dies, the survivor receives $1,080 a month.

Table 11.13 presents the present value relatives for such couples with average life expectancies. The maximum present value occurs when benefits begin at FRA, age 66 in this example. The key to the analysis is that reduction in spouse's benefits is severe when benefits begin before FRA. The spouse's benefits fractions at ages 62 through 65 are 70 percent, 75 percent, 83.3 percent, and 91.7 percent, while the corresponding fractions when benefits are based on one's own record are 75 percent, 80 percent, 86.7 percent, and 93.3 percent. Since the benefits fractions for personal benefits are close to actuarially fair, it follows that the reductions for spouse's beginning benefits before FRA are actuarially

TABLE 11.13   Relative Present Values of Benefits When One Partner Depends on Spouse's Benefits

AGE	62	63	64	65	66	67	68	69	70
PV Relatives	96.7%	96.4%	98.1%	99.4%	100%	99.0%	97.6%	95.7%	93.4%

We assume a TIPS yield of 0.25 percent per month (3 percent per year).
Source: Cook, Jennings, and Reichenstein (2002).

harsh. Consequently, there is an incentive to delay the beginning of the spouse's benefits until FRA.[9] However, the couple should not postpone benefits beyond FRA. Although delaying benefits beyond FRA would raise his benefits, it would not increase her spouse's benefits since spouse's benefits do not reflect Delayed Retirement Credits.

Let us change the example. Suppose Sam is 66, Sue is 62, and all other assumptions remain the same. In this case, Sam can begin benefits immediately, but Sue continues to have an incentive to delay the beginning of spouse's benefits until age 66. The reduction for beginning spouse's benefits before FRA is severe. Consequently, unless Sue has a shorter-than-average life expectancy, she should delay the beginning of her spouse's benefits until FRA.

Lesson: Assuming average life expectancies, for couples where one partner depends on the other's earnings record, the dependent partner should consider delaying the beginning of benefits until but not beyond his or her Full Retirement Age.

Switching strategies involving survivor's benefits: Jack and Beth are both 62 with Full Retirement Ages of 66. Jack has a Primary Insurance Amount of $1,000 and Beth has a PIA of $800 based on their personal earnings records. Neither partner currently receives Social Security benefits. Jack dies, and Beth decides to begin benefits today. The second and third columns of Table 11.14 present two of her options. In Strategy A, she begins reduced benefits on her own record of $600 per month today, [$800 • (100 percent − 5 / 9 percent • 36 − 5 / 12 percent • 12)], and later switches to survivor's benefits of $1,000 per month at FRA. The present value of this strategy at age 62 is $181,125. In Strategy B, she begins reduced survivor's benefits of $810 per month today, [$1,000 • (100 percent − 57 / 144 percent • 48)], and then switches to benefits of $1,056 based on her own record at age 70, [$800 • (100 percent + 32 percent)], where 32 percent represents the increase in benefits due to Delayed Retirement Credits. The present value of this option at age 62 is $189,379. Based on the average female's approximately 24-year life expectancy, Strategy B has the larger present value.

Beth can only begin survivor's benefits and later switch to her own benefits if she had not already begun benefits based on her own record. Return to the prior example but suppose they learn at age 62 that Jack has a terminal illness. Beth

TABLE 11.14 Switching Strategies between Survivor's Benefits and Benefits Based on Own Earnings Record

	Beth's Strategies		Beth's Strategies		Jack's Strategies	
	A	B	C	D	E	F
62	$600	$810				
63	$600	$810				
64	$600	$810				
65	$600	$810				
66	$1,000	$810	$1,000	$1,000	$1,000	$800
67	$1,000	$810	$1,000	$1,000	$1,000	$800
68	$1,000	$810	$1,000	$1,000	$1,000	$800
69	$1,000	$810	$1,000	$1,000	$1,000	$800
70	$1,000	$1,056	$1,000	$1,056	$1,000	$1,320
71	$1,000	$1,056	$1,000	$1,056	$1,000	$1,320
72	$1,000	$1,056	$1,000	$1,056	$1,000	$1,320
73	$1,000	$1,056	$1,000	$1,056	$1,000	$1,320
74	$1,000	$1,056	$1,000	$1,056	$1,000	$1,320
75	$1,000	$1,056	$1,000	$1,056	$1,000	$1,320
76	$1,000	$1,056	$1,000	$1,056	$1,000	$1,320
77	$1,000	$1,056	$1,000	$1,056	$1,000	$1,320
78	$1,000	$1,056	$1,000	$1,056	$1,000	$1,320
79	$1,000	$1,056	$1,000	$1,056	$1,000	$1,320
80	$1,000	$1,056	$1,000	$1,056	$1,000	$1,320
81	$1,000	$1,056	$1,000	$1,056	$1,000	$1,320
82	$1,000	$1,056	$1,000	$1,056	$1,000	$1,320
83	$1,000	$1,056	$1,000	$1,056		
84	$1,000	$1,056	$1,000	$1,056		
PV	$181,125	$189,379	$173,629	$180,822	$159,649	$187,244

We assume a TIPS yield of 0.25 percent per month (3 percent per year). In the final row of the table, the present values assume that the stream of payments for each strategy is discounted back to the year in which benefits begin. Thus, if benefits begin at age 62, we discount the payments back to age 62.
Source: Cook, Jennings, and Reichenstein (2002).

should not begin payments on her own record since this would preclude her from applying for survivor's benefits and later switching to her own benefits.

Now suppose that Jack and Beth both have attained FRA of 66. Their PIAs are still $1,000 and $800, respectively, and neither receives benefits currently. Jack dies, and Beth elects to begin benefits today. The fourth and fifth columns of Table 11.14 present two of Beth's options. In Strategy C, she begins survivor's benefits of

$1,000 per month today and continues to receive these benefits until her death. In Strategy D, she begins survivor's benefits of $1,000 per month today and later switches to benefits of $1,056 based on her own record at age 70, [$800 • (100 percent + 32 percent)]. Strategy D is clearly the better choice.

Assume the same facts as the scenario above except that Beth dies rather than Jack. Strategies E and F present two of Jack's options. In Strategy E, Jack starts payments of $1,000 on his own record and continues to receive these benefits until he dies. In Strategy F, he begins survivor's benefits of $800 today and switches at age 70 to his own benefits of $1,320, which is 32 percent more than his PIA due to Delayed Retirement Credits. Based on the average male's 17-year life expectancy, Strategy F has the much larger present value.

To understand why the advantage is substantial, consider the tradeoff if Jack was never married and was deciding whether to start benefits at age 66 (FRA) or 70. If he begins benefits at 66, he receives $1,000 a month for the rest of his life. If he begins at 70, he receives $1,320 a month for the rest of his life. By delaying until age 70, he loses $1,000 a month for four years but gains $320 a month for the rest of his life. In present value terms, this is close to a fair tradeoff. In contrast, due to survivor's benefits, when Jack delays benefits based on his own record until age 70, he still gets $800 a month in survivor's benefits for four years. This $800 a month between ages 66 and 69 is close to a pure gain in present value terms.

Finally, survivor's benefits can begin at age 60 (or at age 50 if disabled), while spouse's benefits can begin at age 62. Consequently, if one partner dies before age 62, the survivor should generally begin survivor's benefits as soon as possible and later switch at age 70 to benefits based on his or her own record. For example, repeat the scenario in Strategies A and B except assume Jack and Beth are age 60 when Jack dies. In this case, Beth could begin survivor's benefits of $715 per month at age 60 and switch to benefits based on her own record of $1,056 at age 70. Alternatively, she could receive nothing for two years, begin reduced benefits on her own record of $600 per month at age 62, and switch to survivor's benefits of $1,000 per month at FRA. The first option is clearly more valuable.

Lesson: Many individuals who are eligible for benefits as survivors and based on their own earnings records should begin survivor's benefits immediately and apply for benefits based on their own records at age 70. This strategy is usually optimal when the level of benefits based on their own records at age 70 exceeds the level of survivor's benefits.

Strategies for the divorced: Strategies for the divorced also revolve around spouse's and survivor's benefits. We will discuss situations for Fay, a divorced female, but the same rules also apply to a divorced male.

Fay is entitled to spouse's benefits if her marriage to Xavier, her ex-husband, lasted at least 10 years and she is currently unmarried. If Xavier has started benefits, Fay is entitled to the larger of spouse's benefits based on Xavier's record or benefits based on her record. If Xavier has not begun benefits but is at least age 62 and eligible for benefits, Fay may apply for spouse's benefits if they have been divorced at least two years. However, Fay may not apply for reduced spouse's benefits and later switch to unreduced benefits based on her own record.

Fay is entitled to survivor's benefits based on the deceased Xavier's record if their marriage lasted at least 10 years and she is currently unmarried.[10] In general, she should begin survivor's benefits as soon as possible and switch to benefits based on her own record at age 70.

If Fay remarries after age 60, she is entitled to the larger of (1) survivor's benefits based on Xavier's record or (2) the larger of benefits based on her own record or spouse's benefits based on her current husband's record. If she begins survivor's benefits based on Xavier's record, she may later switch to the larger of benefits based on her record or spouse's benefits based on her current husband's record. Remember that Delayed Retirement Credits apply to benefits based on her own record but not to spouse's benefits.

Summary: In summary, couples affected by the Earnings Test should seldom begin benefits before attaining Full Retirement Age. Also, a long life expectancy encourages delaying benefits. However, with a couple, the life expectancy of the longer to live is usually the key factor. In general, if *either* member of the couple has a long life expectancy, the higher-earning member should postpone the beginning of benefits based on his or her earnings record until after Full Retirement Age. Since survivor's benefits reflect Delayed Retirement Credits, it usually pays for the higher earner to delay the start of benefits beyond Full Retirement Age. The advantages from the higher earner delaying benefits are especially strong if the lower-earning partner is much younger and healthy.

In general, in couples where one partner relies on spouse's earnings record, that partner should delay the beginning of spouse's benefits until FRA. The penalty for beginning spouse's benefits before FRA is severe. Consequently, unless the lower-earning spouse has a short life expectancy, he or she should delay the start of spouse's benefits until FRA.

Someone can switch from survivor's benefits to benefits based on his or her own record or from benefits based on his or her own record to survivor's benefits. Suppose one spouse dies before the other partner begins benefits. It often pays for the widow or widower to begin survivor's benefits and then switch to benefits based on his or her record at age 70. By delaying benefits based on his or her own record until age 70, he or she maximizes the size of the Delayed Retirement Credits. Yet, he or she still receives survivor's benefits in the interim.

Individuals may be entitled to benefits based on their ex-spouse's earnings record. The strategies for divorcees revolve around spouse's and survivor's benefits. Consequently, their strategies are the same as those discussed previously.

Our analysis only examined benefits paid to single individuals and married couples. It did not consider payments to children or other dependents. In a separate study, Walsh (2002) considered benefits paid to all family members. He encourages individuals to begin benefits early if they have children under age 18 (or children age 18 or 19 who are full-time high school students). For example, it may pay a single parent to apply for benefits at age 62 if he or she has children who would receive benefits. In contrast, the children may be too old to receive benefits if the parent delays the start of benefits until FRA.

This study also ignores income tax consequences. Some taxpayers may be forced into a higher tax bracket after age 70½ due to required distributions from certain retirement accounts. They may not want to delay Social Security benefits if doing so would subject these payments to a higher tax rate. For additional information, see Batterman (1999).

Finally, Clements (2002) encouraged delaying benefits for a separate reason. He recognizes that, for someone with average life expectancy, the present value of benefits to singles is essentially the same no matter what age benefits actually begin. Yet, he suggests postponing benefits because he views Social Security payments as insurance against the risks of living too long and mismanaging the portfolio: "By delaying benefits, you are buying yourself more insurance, in case you outlive your nest egg or mismanage your retirement savings."

Appendix 11.3: Explanations of Multiple Calculations for Social Security Retirement Benefits

Appendix 11.3.1: Worksheets for Single Males, Single Females, Widowers, and Widows

An interactive version of the spreadsheet used to generate the multiples in Tables 11.4 and 11.5 is available at http://www.wiley.com/go/reichenstein. This spreadsheet, entitled *App 11.3.1 Social Security Singles,* contains worksheets that calculate multiples for Social Security retirement benefits for single males, single females, widowers, and widows. The worksheet entitled *Female* calculates multiples for single females and widows *with average life expectancies.* The worksheet entitled *Male* calculates multiples for single males and widowers *with average life expectancies.* Payments are assumed to begin at age 65, and all payments occur at mid-year. The file contains two additional worksheets, *Female Life Expectancy* and *Male Life Expectancy,* that present average life expectancies for females and males, respectively. Each worksheet contains a text box that explains its purpose and use.

Appendix 11.3.2 Worksheets for Married Couples

An interactive version of the spreadsheet used to generate the multiples in Tables 11.7 and 11.8 is available at http://www.wiley.com/go/reichenstein. This spreadsheet, entitled *App 11.3.2 Social Security Couples,* contains worksheets that calculate couple multiples for Social Security retirement benefits. The worksheet entitled *Same Age* contains calculations for married couples when the husband and wife are the same age. The worksheet entitled *Female 3 Years Younger* contains calculations for married couples when the wife is three years younger than the husband. The age in the latter worksheet denotes the husband's age. Both worksheets contain a text box that explains their purpose and use.

References

Batterman, Thomas W. 1999. Coordinating IRA Distributions with Social Security Income. *AAII Journal*, April.

Clements, Jonathan. 2002. Want a comfortable retirement? Taking Social Security early could be a mistake. *Wall Street Journal*, May 8, D1.

Cook, Kirsten A., William W. Jennings, and William Reichenstein. 2002. When should you begin receiving social security benefits? (American Association of Individual Investors) *AAII Journal,* November, 27–34.

Fraser, Steve P., William W. Jennings, and David R. King. 2000. Strategic asset allocation for individual investors: The impact of the present value of Social Security benefits. *Financial Services Review,* Winter, 295–326.

Jennings, William W., and William Reichenstein. 2002. The value of retirement income streams: The value of military retirement. *Financial Services Review,* Vol. 10, no. 1, 19–35.

Reichenstein, William. 1998. Calculating a family's asset allocation. *Financial Services Review,* Vol. 7, No. 3, 195–206.

Reichenstein, William. 2000. Calculating the asset allocation. *The Journal of Wealth Management* (previously *Journal of Private Portfolio Management*), Fall, 20–25.

Reichenstein, William. 2001. Rethinking the family's asset allocation. *Journal of Financial Planning,* May, 102–109.

Scott, Maria Crawford. 1995. Defining your investment portfolio: What should you include? *AAII Journal,* November, 15–17.

Social Security Administration. 2000a. A pension from work not covered by Social Security. SSA Pub. No. 05–10045.

Social Security Administration. 2000b. Government pension offset. SSA Pub. No. 05–10007.

Social Security Administration. 2000c. How work affects your benefits. SSA Pub. No. 05–10069.

TIAA-CREF. Making Sense of Social Security. (http://www.tiaa-cref.org/wc_libser/mss/index.html.)

Walsh, Thomas G. 2002. Electing normal retirement social security benefits versus electing early retirement social security benefits. http://www.tiaa-crefinstitute.org/Publications/wkpapers/wp 7-2002.htm.

Notes

1. The Social Security program makes payments for other reasons besides retirement. For example, it makes payments to a family if a worker becomes disabled or dies prematurely. This chapter is concerned with retirement needs and the value of Social Security retirement benefits. Although these other insurance benefits have value, estimations of their values are beyond the scope of this chapter.

2. For a single beneficiary receiving $8,000 in benefits, Combined Income of only $33,295 is needed to reach 85 percent taxation. For married couples filing jointly receiving $19,000 in benefits, Combined Income of $46,442 is needed to reach 85 percent taxation. For a good example and useful table to calculate the taxable portion, see "Making Sense of Social Security" at the Web site http://www.tiaa-cref.org/wc_lib-ser/ mss/index.html. Go to the chapter "How Tests and Taxes Affect Your Income," and click on "Do You Owe Tax on your Social Security Benefits?" at the end of the chapter.

3. See the Society of Actuaries Web site at http://www.soa.org/research. We used Tables 4.5 and 4.6, the male and female RP-2000 Rates, for "Combined Healthy."

4. If it does, she would likely delay benefits until FRA or later. Appendix 11.1 estimates that, assuming she has average life expectancy, the present value of expected cash flows if she begins receiving payments at age 66 or later is essentially the same as the present value if payments begin at age 65. Therefore, this model provides a good estimate even if the Earnings Test applies.

5. There are three parts to this calculation. To calculate the present value *of the annuity due* at age 65, insert into a financial calculator $n = 19.4$, $i = 3$ percent, PMT = $11,196, FV = $0 and compute the PV of $167,757. To move payments from the beginning of the year to mid-year, divide by $(1.03)^{0.5}$ and get $165,296. To calculate the present value at age 60, insert FV = $165,296, $n = 5$, $i = 3$ percent, PMT = $0 and compute the PV of this lump sum, which is $142,586. (Alternatively, to calculate the present value *at age 65,* you could calculate the present value of a regular annuity and then multiply by $(1.03)^{0.5}$ to move all payments to mid-year.)

6. There are two parts to this calculation. To calculate the present value *of the annuity due* at age 65, insert into a financial calculator $n = 232.8$, $i = 0.2466$ percent, PMT = $933, FV = $0 and compute the PV of $165,510. To calculate the present value at age 60, insert FV = $165,510, $n = 60$ months, $i = 0.2466$ percent, PMT = $0 and compute the PV of this lump sum, which is $142,773. A 3 percent rate compounded annually corresponds to a 0.2466 percent rate compounded monthly. If the discount (interest) rate is set at 0.25 percent per month, the present value is 0.56 percent less. This is well within estimation error. So, someone could estimate Social Security's value by setting the monthly rate at annual rate/12.

7. An exception to this rule occurs if one spouse continues to work past FRA and postpones the start of benefits based on his or her own record. Suppose that a wife elects to retire and begin benefits while her husband chooses to keep his job and delay benefits. The wife can begin benefits based on her own record and later switch to spouse's benefits when her husband retires, assuming spouse's benefits are higher.

8. Note that the "Social Security bond" has inflation-indexed bond features, including low volatility and low correlation with other assets. For a fuller discussion of the portfolio implications of these features, see Fraser, Jennings, & King (2000).

9. Due to the complex reduction rule described earlier in this section, the penalty is frequently even more severe for beginning survivor's benefits before attaining FRA. This rule encourages both partners to delay the beginning of benefits until FRA.

10. She is also entitled to survivor's benefits if she is unmarried and caring for his child, even if their marriage lasted less than 10 years. However, her benefit fraction is smaller than that of a divorced widow married at least 10 years. A divorced widow who was married less than 10 years and is receiving benefits only because she is caring for a child is limited to receiving no more than 75 percent of her deceased husband's PIA.

CHAPTER 12

Calculating the Value of Military Retirement Income

Introduction

Retirement planning is a core component of financial planning. Like Social Security income, income from pensions is considered when assessing a family's ability to meet its retirement needs. However, pension income is seldom considered when calculating the asset allocation. Again, we argue that this is inconsistent. Since both pensions and the investment portfolio generate retirement funds, both should be considered when calculating a family's asset allocation.

We argue that the finance profession makes two mistakes when calculating a family's asset allocation. First, it does not distinguish before-tax funds and after-tax funds. Before calculating the asset allocation, we should first convert accounts' market values to after-tax values. We addressed this issue in Chapter 10. Second, the family portfolio should be extended to include the after-tax present value of retirement income streams such as Social Security, company pensions, and military retirement. These income streams are essentially bonds and, as Reichenstein (1998, 2000) and Fraser, Jennings, and King (2000) demonstrate, including these bonds in the portfolio can dramatically affect the family's asset allocation.

In this chapter, we first describe the U.S. military retirement system. Approximately 2 million people receive military retirement income in this country. Financial advisors who have military personnel as clients should be familiar with the major features of the military retirement systems. Next, we examine issues surrounding, and present estimates of, the present value of military retirement income.

The military retirement system has several interesting dimensions. Service members, for example, are eligible to receive benefits after 20 years of service. Like many firefighters and police officers, military members can retire and then start a second career to earn a second pension; that is, they can "double-dip." Military retirees do not incur the severe penalty associated with mid-career job switching of employees in defined-benefit pension plans (Woerheide and Fortner, 1994) because military retirement income begins immediately after the first retirement, and the income is indexed for inflation.

This chapter incorporates military retirement benefits into the family's asset-allocation decision. Like traditional deductible IRAs and 401(k)s, funds derived from military retirement are taxable. Therefore, we must adjust the before-tax value of military retirement benefits for taxes. We use the similarities between inflation-indexed Treasury bonds and military retirement benefits to value those benefits. Cash flows from both Treasury Inflation Protection Securities (TIPS) and military retirement are linked to the Consumer Price Index (CPI), and both sets of cash flows are backed by the federal government. These similarities suggest treating the present value of military retirement benefits as bonds in the family's portfolio.

Fraser, Jennings, and King (2000) make the distinction that these real bonds differ from nominal bonds in important risk, return, and correlation characteristics. For simplicity, we ignore this distinction.

The family's extended portfolio includes financial assets and the present value of retirement income streams such as military retirement income (Scott, 1995). As Reichenstein (1998, 2000) and Fraser, Jennings, and King (2000) demonstrate, including these pseudo-bonds in the portfolio can dramatically affect the family's asset allocation. For example, suppose a family's risk tolerance calls for a 50/50 stocks/bonds asset allocation, and it allocates its financial assets—the traditional definition of the family portfolio—to meet this target asset mix. Its extended portfolio, which includes military retirement income, may be 25/75 in stocks/bonds. If the family fails to recognize that military retirement income is a bond in its portfolio, then it will miss its target asset allocation.

This chapter reviews the literature that supports our recommended changes to the traditional approach of calculating a family's asset mix. It presents details of the U.S. military retirement system. Then, it discusses issues surrounding the estimation of the present value of retirement income streams, presents our estimation method, and critiques it. It then presents an example that demonstrates the importance of including the present value of retirement income streams—in this case military retirement—in a family's portfolio. The final section concludes.

What "Counts" in the Family Portfolio?

Scott (1995), Reichenstein (1998, 2000), and Fraser, Jennings, and King (2000), among others, argue that the family portfolio should reflect the present value of retirement income streams such as Social Security, company pensions, and military retirement. Retirement income streams are traditionally included in studies of retirement preparedness (see Kennickell, Starr-McCluer, and Sunden, 1997; Poterba, Venti, and Wise, 1994; and Yuh, Hanna, and Montalto, 1998, among others), but excluded when calculating a family's asset allocation (see Peavy and Sherrerd, 1990, and Stevens, 2000, among many others). Scott's criterion for deciding whether to include an asset in the family portfolio was to include "financial assets that you would be willing to sell for spending money or that generate some form of spending money, either now or sometime in the future. . . " (1995, p. 15). She thus includes the present value of the *before-tax* Social Security payments and other retirement-income cash flows. In this chapter, we include the present value of these *after-tax* amounts. Whether someone includes before-tax or after-tax values of retirement income streams, their inclusion can dramatically affect the measurement of the family's asset allocation. Thus, the decision to include or exclude the retirement income stream is an important one whether we use before-tax or after-tax values. See Chapter 9 for more detail.

U.S. Military Retirement Systems

There are three main military retirement systems in the United States: Final Pay, High Three, and REDUX. Final Pay applies to service members who entered the military before September 8, 1980. High Three applies to service members who entered from September 8, 1980 to July 31, 1986. Service members who enter the military after July 31, 1986, must, after 15 years of service, elect either the High Three system or the REDUX system and receive a $30,000 career retention bonus. "REDUX" is suggestive of the reduction in benefits created under the 1986 Military Retirement Reform Act (see U.S. Code, Title 10, §1409). Except in unusual circumstances, service members must serve 20 years to be eligible for retirement pay. Time at service academies (such as the U.S. Air Force and Naval Academies) or on certain ROTC *scholarships* counts for determining the entry date but does not count for computing years of service. Table 12.1 summarizes the key aspects of each system.

Few military personnel can choose between the three systems since, in general, the date of entry into military service determines eligibility. The only choice is for those who entered after July 31, 1986. These personnel must choose between REDUX and High Three. While their choice will depend on individual circumstances, a quick analysis, based on the valuation multiples that we present below, suggests that only those who expect to have long military careers (e.g., 28 years or longer), attain senior ranks (e.g., to Colonel or General), or earn high real returns (e.g., greater than 8 percent) on the $30,000 bonus should remain under REDUX and take the bonus. The web site http://pay2000.dtic.mil provides a more detailed discussion of the choice for those who entered after July 31, 1986.[1]

Three key elements of each system are Base Pay Amount, Percentage, and cost-of-living adjustment. (To avoid confusion, Base Pay Amount and Percentage are

TABLE 12.1   Key Elements of U.S. Military Retirement Systems

	Final Pay	**High Three**	**REDUX**
Base Pay Amount	Final base pay, excluding bonuses	Average base pay in highest 36 months, excluding bonuses	Average base pay in highest 36 months, excluding bonuses
Percentage	50 percent + 2.5 percent (years of service − 20)	50 percent + 2.5 percent (years of service − 20)	Before age 62, 40 percent + 3.5 percent (years of service − 20). Beginning age 62, 50 percent + 2.5 percent (years of service − 20).
Cost-of-living Adjustment	Base Pay Amount increases with CPI inflation rate	Base Pay Amount increases with CPI inflation rate	Before age 62, Base Pay Amount increases with CPI inflation rate less 1 percent. At age 62, Base Pay Amount is adjusted to amount under High Three. After age 62, this adjusted Base Pay Amount increases with CPI inflation rate less 1 percent.

typed with capital letters when they refer to a key element.) Current Annual Payment is the product of Base Pay Amount and Percentage.

Under Final Pay, Base Pay Amount at retirement is the final base pay, excluding bonuses such as those for hazardous duty. Under High Three and REDUX, Base Pay Amount at retirement is the average base pay for the highest 36 months, excluding bonuses.

The Percentage for Final Pay and High Three is 50 percent + 2.5 percent • (years of service − 20). This means a retiree receives 50 percent of the Base Pay Amount after 20 years of service, and the Percentage increases by 2.5 percent a year. For example, if someone retires after 21.3 years of service, the Percentage is 53.25 percent. The Percentage for REDUX is 40 percent + 3.5 percent • (years of service − 20). This means that after 20 years a retiree receives 40 percent of the Base Pay Amount, and the Percentage increases by 3.5 percent a year. After 30 years of service, a retiree receives 75 percent of the Base Pay Amount under all three systems. Once the Percentage reaches 75 percent, it does not increase.

Unlike most private-sector defined-benefit pensions, military retirement payments receive cost-of-living adjustments (COLA). The COLA has a dramatic valuation impact and is worth considering in some detail. Under Final Pay and High Three, Base Pay Amount (and thus Current Annual Payment) increases annually with the CPI–W inflation rate, where CPI–W denotes the Consumer Price Index for Urban Wage Earners and Clerical Workers. Under REDUX, Base Pay Amount (and Current Annual Payment) increases annually by 1 percent less than the CPI–W inflation rate. No COLA is granted if CPI–W is less than 1 percent.

Under REDUX, at age 62, there is a one-time "catch-up" that adjusts retirement pay to the level it would be under High Three. This catch-up requires two adjustments: Base Pay Amount is changed to the level it would have been without the 1 percent inflation lag, and Percentage is changed to the higher Percentage under High Three. Under REDUX, after age 62, Base Pay Amount (and thus Current Annual Payment) again increases annually by 1 percent less than the CPI–W inflation rate. The Defense Finance and Accounting Service (DFAS) web site provides more detailed information about the retirement plans (see http://www.dfas.mil/money/retired).

Issues, Illustration, and Critique of Our Estimates

This section discusses issues in the estimation of the present value of military retirement income, presents and illustrates our model, and critiques our model.

Issues

Three issues must be resolved before calculating the present value of military retirement income. These include the use of before-tax or after-tax income, the appropriate discount rate, and the projected income stream.

The first two issues can be covered quickly. For reasons discussed earlier, we estimate the value of military retirement income as the present value of projected after-tax income. For present value calculations, the discount rate is the yield on the Treasury Inflation Protection Security (TIPS) with maturity closest to the length of the expected income stream. TIPS pay a fixed real rate of interest each year on principal, and the principal is increased each year based on CPI-U, the CPI inflation rate for Urban Consumers. Thus, principal and interest payments increase with the level of the CPI. They are inflation-protected securities. As such, the TIPS real yield can be used to discount the inflation-adjusted, or real, military retirement income stream. Real rates are used to discount real income, and nominal rates are used to discount nominal income.

For 1974–1999, the correlation coefficient between CPI-W and CPI-U is 0.9998, and there is a negligible difference between their long-horizon cumulative inflation rates. Consequently, use of TIPS yields, which rely on CPI-U, does not bias our estimates of military retirement income, which relies on CPI-W. Henceforth we ignore the distinction and refer to them as CPI. Fraser, Jennings, and King (2000) acknowledge the CPI difference and other caveats in using TIPS to value real income streams but conclude the usefulness of TIPS outweighs the shortcomings.

The final issue is the projected income stream. We estimate the before-tax value of military retirement income as the present value of expected before-tax income, which is the finance profession's traditional method of estimating an asset's value. As we shall see, this is different from the present value of income through someone's expected life.

Illustration

We estimate the after-tax present value of military retirement income for single males and single females as follows:

Present value after taxes = (Base Pay Amount) • (Percentage) • (multiple) • $(1 - t)$

(eq. 12.1)

or

Present value after taxes = (Current Annual Payment) • (multiple) • $(1 - t)$

where t is the expected marginal tax rate during retirement, multiples are explained below, and the other variables are described in the previous section.

Before going into the details of calculating a multiple, consider a simple demonstration of the preceding equations. Assume Luke is single and retires on his 44th birthday in either the Final Pay or the High Three system. He served 20 years, so the Percentage is 50 percent. If his Base Pay Amount is $40,000, his Current Annual Payment is $20,000. In his first year of retirement, he will receive $1,667 a month [$20,000 / 12]. As demonstrated next, assuming a 4 percent TIPS yield the multiple is 18.92. We estimate the before-tax value of Luke's military retirement income at $378,400 [$20,000 • 18.92]. Since military retirees can easily calculate their Current Annual Payment (CAP) at 12 times the current monthly check amount, multiples are always expressed as a multiple of CAP.

Table 12.2 details the calculation of a multiple under Final Pay or High Three systems. Since Luke just retired, there is a 100 percent probability that he will receive the first $1; again, multiples are expressed per $1 of Current Annual Payment. Based on updated mortality tables (Society of Actuaries, 2000), he has a 0.998603 probability of being alive at age 45 and thus receiving the second $1 real payment.[2] Since nominal payments increase with inflation, the real payments remain constant. The expected real payment the second year is thus $0.998603. There is a 0.997097 probability that he will live to age 46 and receive the third $1 real payment. This process is repeated through his 120th birthday—the end of the mortality tables—where there is a 0.0000004 probability that he will be alive and receive one last $1 real payment. We assume all payments occur at mid-year. Therefore, assuming a 4 percent TIPS yield, the present value of the first year's $1 payment is $1 / (1.04)^{0.5}$. The present value of the second expected real payment is $0.998603 / (1.04)^{1.5}$. The pre-tax mul-

TABLE 12.2   Calculation of the Multiple for a 44-year-old Single Male under the Final Pay or High Three Retirement System

Age	Probability of Being Alive	Real Payment	Expected Real Payment	Present Value of Expected Real Payment
44	1.000000	$1	$1	$1/(1.04)^{0.5}$
45	0.998603	1	0.998603	$0.99806/(1.04)^{1.5}$
46	0.997097	1	0.997097	$0.997097/(1.04)^{2.5}$
⋮	⋮	⋮	⋮	⋮
79	0.608287	1	0.608287	$0.608287/(1.04)^{35.5}$
80	0.573050	1	0.573050	$0.573050/(1.04)^{36.5}$
⋮	⋮	⋮	⋮	⋮
120	0.0000004	1	0.0000004	$0.0000004/(1.04)^{76.5}$
				Multiple = 18.92

The multiple is the present value of expected real payments, where $1 is the annual real or inflation-adjusted payment. All payments occur at mid-year. The TIPS yield, discount interest rate, is 4 percent.

tiple is the sum of the present value of each year's expected real income. Assuming a 4 percent TIPS yield, it is the sum of $1 / (1.04)^{0.5}$ + $0.998603 / (1.04)^{1.5}$ + $0.997097 / (1.04)^{2.5}$ + ... + $0.0000004 / (1.04)^{76.5}$. Figure 11.1 in the previous chapter illustrated the "Treasury Bonds, Notes and Bills" table in the *Wall Street Journal* and explained how to estimate the appropriate TIPS yield.

The before-tax value of Luke's military retirement income is $378,400 [$20,000 • 18.92]. If he expects to be in the 28 percent tax bracket, the after-tax value is about $272,400. We argue that Luke should include military retirement income in his portfolio and consider it a bond worth about $272,400 after taxes.

Critique of Our Estimates

There are at least two potential criticisms of our method of estimating the value of military retirement income. First, we calculate the value of military retirement income as the present value of *expected cash flows*. Some professionals would prefer to estimate it based on either *cash flows through life expectancy* or cash flows for a period longer than life expectancy. As we shall see, these professionals would consider our estimates too low.

Let us return to Luke, the 44-year-old single male retiree. His life expectancy is 36.5 years. The present value of a $20,000-a-year annuity for 36.5 years with payments received at mid-year when discounted at 4 percent is about $388,100.[3] This present value exceeds the present value of expected cash flows, which is $378,400. Experimentation indicates that the present value of cash flows through life expectancy is slightly larger than the present value of expected cash flows. For single retirees, estimates based on cash flows through life expectancy are approximately equal to estimates based on expected cash flows, which implies that the former estimates have merit. However, we cannot estimate the value of military retirement to a couple based on that couple's life expectancy. Suppose a military retiree and his wife have a joint life expectancy of 26 years; that is, the second to die is expected to live 26 years. The size of this couple's payment each year depends upon whether the military retiree is alive.

The fact that one present-value estimate is higher or lower than others does not determine its desirability. An estimate's desirability depends upon whether its assumptions fit the situation. For example, one goal of financial planning is to ensure that someone will not outlive his or her resources. Thus, some planners may want to value military retirement income assuming Luke will live longer, say 42 or 44 years. (There is about a one-third chance that he will live at least 42 years and about a one-fourth chance that he will live at least 44 years.) These planners would place a higher value on military retirement income than our method. We believe those interested in the average case should use the present value of expected cash flows—the finance profession's traditional method of calculation.

Retirement Income Streams as Contingent Assets

The second potential criticism concerns the difference between a *contingent* value and a *guaranteed* value. As discussed in Chapter 10, the value of military retirement income to a single male or female is contingent upon the recipient remaining alive. Should he or she die, the value ceases. The contingent value of military retirement income also falls at the death of a military retiree who is covered under the SBP plan, since the spouse receives reduced payments.

Suppose a single military retiree has a daughter who needs special care. To ensure his daughter's financial needs, he may wish to guarantee the *after-tax* value of military retirement income by buying life insurance.

In short, our method of estimating the value of military retirement is not beyond criticism. The value may be too low in that it is based on expected cash flows instead of cash flows through life expectancy or longer. Some retirees, especially those primarily concerned about the risk of outliving their resources, may want to place a higher value on military retirement income. In addition, some military retirees will want to buy life insurance to guarantee the value of this contingent income stream.

Multiples

Income multiples are always expressed as a multiple of Current Annual Payment. To accommodate financial advisors, we place the tables of multiples at the end of the chapter. Tables 12.4 through 12.9 provide multiples for military personnel under the Final Pay and High Three systems. Tables 12.10 through 12.14 provide multiples under the REDUX retirement system. Excel spreadsheets for the multiples are available for download at www.wiley.com/go/reichenstein. In addition, Appendix 12.1 explains the worksheets.

Multiples under the Final Pay and High Three Systems

Tables 12.4 through 12.9 present multiples for retirees under the Final Pay and High Three systems. Tables 12.4 and 12.5 present multiples for single males and single females, respectively. The earlier illustration presented the estimation method for single males. The same method applies to single females. Due to their longer life expectancy, single females have larger multiples than single males.

Tables 12.6 and 12.7 present income multiples under Final Pay and High Three for, respectively, married male retirees and married female retirees who choose the Survivors Benefit Plan (SBP). Most married retirees choose the SBP. In fact, the retiree must choose it unless the spouse waives the right to demand it. There are two sets of multiples in each table. One set assumes the husband and wife are the same age. The other assumes the wife is three years younger.

Suppose Luke, age 44, retires with a Base Pay Amount of $40,000 and a Percentage of 50 percent. He and his wife, who is three years younger, opt for the SBP. If single (or married and not in the SBP), his Current Annual Payment (CAP1) would be $20,000. Since he and his wife chose the SBP, the Current Annual Payment (CAP2) is $18,700 [(Base Pay Amount) • (Percentage) • $(1 - 0.065)$], where 6.5 percent is the cost of the SBP. If Luke dies first, his surviving wife receives 55 percent of CAP1 until *she reaches* age 62, and 35 percent of CAP1 thereafter. The multiples in Tables 12.5 and 12.6 are multiples of CAP2, which is 12 times their current monthly payment. The multiple calculation in Table 12.7 is analogous for a retired female service member and her husband under the SBP.

The multiple for a married male retiree in Table 12.6 is larger than the multiple for a single male retiree in Table 12.4. The married-male multiple reflects expected cash flows if the male is alive *plus* expected cash flows to his wife if he dies first. The same relationship exists between multiples for single females and married female retirees.

Full analysis of the decision to choose the Survivor Benefit Plan is beyond the scope of this chapter. However, our multiples offer some insight into whether the 6.5 percent reduction in benefits for the SBP represents the fair insurance cost of providing spousal coverage. Recall that while most retirees take SBP, it is possible to decline SBP with spousal consent. Such a decision is made at retirement. It is also possible, with spousal consent, to select less than the full SBP coverage we analyze, and it is also possible to purchase Supplemental SBP. If Luke's wife waives SBP, their pre-tax pension wealth is $378,400 [18.92 • $20,000], where 18.92 is the multiple in Table 12.4 for a 44-year-old single male when the TIPS rate is 4 percent. If Luke's wife is the same age and elects SBP, their pre-tax pension wealth is about $368,000 [19.68 • $20,000 • $(1 - 6.5\%)$]. The present value of expected cash flows is slightly higher without SBP. The same conclusion holds for female military members, instances when the female is three years younger, and with lower TIPS yields. Again, full analysis of the SBP decision (including issues of insurability, risk tolerance, individual circumstances, and so on) is beyond the scope of this chapter, but our analysis suggests that the 6.5 percent reduction in benefits for the SBP slightly exceeds its fair insurance value.

Tables 12.8 and 12.9 present the income multiples under Final Pay and High Three for, respectively, a widower and a widow, where their deceased spouse was the military retiree. Suppose Sal and Suzanne, both age 44, are married. Sal retires under Final Pay or High Three with a Base Pay Amount of $60,000 and 20 years of service. If single, he would have received $30,000 a year, which we call CAP1. If they elect the Survivors Benefit Plan, their Current Annual Payment is 6.5 percent less or $28,050 [0.50 • $60,000 • (1 − 0.065)], which we call CAP2. If Sal dies before Suzanne reaches age 62, she will receive 55 percent of CAP1. She will continue to receive 55 percent of CAP1 until she reaches age 62, and 35 percent of CAP1 thereafter. Multiples in Tables 12.8 and 12.9 are expressed relative to CAP1, which is 12 times the survivor's current monthly payment.

Multiples under the REDUX Retirement System

Military personnel began to retire under the REDUX retirement system in 2000. Nevertheless, the tables present multiples for a wide range of ages to accommodate future retirees.

Table 12.10 presents numbers that allow someone to estimate the income multiple under the REDUX retirement system for single males and females. The following example illustrates how to use this table.

Suppose Barry is 50 years old and retired at age 44 with 23 years of service.[4] His Current Annual Payment is 50.5 percent of the Base Pay Amount at age 50. Since he retired six years earlier, the real Base Pay Amount has lagged the CPI inflation rate by 1 percent a year for the last six years. At age 62, there are two adjustments. First, his Base Pay Amount increases to the level it would have been without the CPI cap; mathematically, the real Base Pay Amount at age 62 is approximately the real Base Pay Amount at age 50 times $(1.01)^6$, where six denotes the years of 1 percent inflation lag from age 44 to 50. Second, the Percentage is increased from 50.5 percent to 57.5 percent, the Percentage for someone retired after 23 years of service under High Three. Compared to his real Current Annual Payment at age 50, the real Current Annual Payment at age 62 will be almost 21 percent larger $[(1.01)^6 • (57.5 / 50.5) − 1]$. For a 4 percent TIPS yield, the present value of Barry's payments through age 61 is the product 8.97 • CAP, where CAP is the level of his Current Annual Payment at age 50. The present value of payments from age 62 and beyond is the product 7.73 • (fraction) • CAP. The fraction is 1.14 [57.5 / 50.5], where 50.5 and 57.5 are the Percentages of the Base Pay Amount that the re-

TABLE 12.3   Calculation of the Multiple for a 50-year-old Single Male under the REDUX Retirement System

Age	Probability of Being Alive	Real Base Pay Amount	Fraction	Expected Real Payment	Present Value of Expected Real Payment
50	1.000000	$1	1	$1	$1/(1.04)^{0.5}
51	0.997862	$1/(1.01)^1$	1	0.987982	$0.987982/(1.04)^{1.5}$
52	0.995418	$1/(1.01)^2$	1	0.975804	$0.975804/(1.04)^{2.5}$
⋮	⋮	⋮	⋮	⋮	⋮
61	0.957004	$1/(1.01)^{11}$	1	0.857785	$0.857785/(1.04)^{11.5}$
62	0.949658	$1(1.01)^6$	1.14	1.149212	$1.149212/(1.04)^{12.5}$
63	0.941342	$1(1.01)^5$	1.14	1.127870	$1.127870/(1.04)^{13.5}$
⋮	⋮	⋮	⋮	⋮	⋮
120	0.0000004	$1/(1.01)^{52}$	1.14	0.0000003	$0.0000003/(1.04)^{70.5}$
					Multiple = 17.78

The multiple is the sum of the present value of expected real payments, where $1 is the Current Annual Payment. All payments occur at mid-year. The discount interest rate is 4 percent. At age 62 and beyond, the fraction is 0.575/0.505, where 0.575 and 0.505 are, respectively, the Percentages of the Base Pay Amount before and after age 62. At age 62, the Real Base Pay Amount is adjusted to the level it would have been if the Base Pay Amount had been adjusted since military retirement with the CPI inflation rate instead of CPI − 1 percent. For REDUX, the military personnel is assumed to retire at age 44, except the 38- and 41-year-olds are assumed to retire at ages 38 and 41, respectively. The multiple for this 50-year-old male single retiree is 17.78 [8.97 + 1.14 • 7.73].

tiree receives before and after age 62. The pre-tax value of Barry's retirement income is thus 17.78 • CAP [(8.97 • CAP) + (7.73 • 1.14 • CAP)]. His income multiple is 17.78. Table 12.3 presents details of this calculation. The calculation of the income multiple for a single female is analogous.

Tables 12.11 and 12.12 present multiples for, respectively, married male and married female retirees who opt for the SBP. Suppose Luke, age 44, retires after 24 years of service with a Base Pay Amount of $40,000 under REDUX and his Percentage is 50 percent. He and his wife, who is three years younger, opt for the SBP. If single, his Current Annual Payment (CAP1) would be $20,000. Since he and his wife chose the SBP, the Current Annual Payment (CAP2) is $18,700, or 6.5 percent less due to the cost of the SBP. If Luke dies before he reaches age 62, his surviving wife receives 55 percent of CAP1. When he, *the military retiree*, would have reached age 62, the one-time catch-up occurs; that is, the Base Pay Amount catches up for the past years of 1 percent inflation lag, and the Percentage increases to 60 percent, the level under Final Pay and High Three. When she, *the surviving spouse*, reaches age 62, the fraction is reduced to 35 percent. In Table 12.12, the multiple calculation is analogous for a retired female and her husband under the SBP.

Tables 12.13 and 12.14 present multiples for, respectively, widowers and widows, where their deceased spouse was the military retiree and they chose the Survivors Benefit Plan. Suppose Mary is a 53-year-old widow of a military retiree. Her deceased husband was three years older. He served 20 years and retired under REDUX when he was age 44. She currently receives 55 percent of the Current Annual Payment, where the latter is the product of 40 percent—the Percentage under REDUX—and the Base Pay Amount. (After the military retiree's death, the Current Annual Payment is not reduced by 6.5 percent for SBP insurance.) The fraction is reduced from 55 percent to 35 percent when she turns 62. When he would have turned 62 (and she is age 59), the Percentage jumps to 50 percent, and his Base Pay Amount is increased to make up for the 1 percent lag to inflation since he retired at age 44. Based on a 4 percent TIPS yield, her multiple from Table 12.14 is 15.38 [7.63 + 1.25 • 6.20], where 1.25 is the ratio of Percentages before and after age 62 [0.50 / 0.40]. In Table 12.13, the multiple calculation is analogous for a male widower of a military retiree.

Properties of Multiples

Income multiples exhibit bond-pricing properties because valuing a retirement income stream is essentially like valuing a bond. Although we use multiples in Table 12.4 to demonstrate the bond-pricing properties, they are present in all multiples.

The multiples are sensitive to the level of TIPS yield. Moreover, this sensitivity is larger for younger retirees than for older retirees. At age 44, a single male's multiple is 15.6 percent larger when the TIPS yield is 3 percent instead of 4 percent. At age 74, the multiple is 6.6 percent larger. In addition, for a given change in yield, this sensitivity is larger at low yields than at high yields. For example, the 44-year-old single male's multiple increases 1.39 years when the TIPS yield falls from 4 percent to 3.5 percent and a larger 1.56 years when the yield falls from 3.5 percent to 3 percent. Finally, the size of the multiple decreases relatively slowly, especially for younger retirees. At age 44 and a TIPS yield of 4 percent, a single male has a multiple of 18.92 and a life expectancy of about 36 years. At age 62, half his life expectancy later, the multiple has only decreased about 30 percent to 13.41.

In addition to the bond-pricing properties previously noted, one's life situation affects the multiples. As noted, due to their longer life expectancy, single women have higher multiples than single men do. Similarly, widows have higher multiples than widowers do. Married retirees who opt for SBP have higher multiples than singles, widows, and widowers. This results from joint-life expectancies exceeding single-life expectancies. This effect is amplified when the retiree's spouse is younger.

Illustration of Our New Approach to Calculating the Family's Asset Mix

George, age 64, is a military retiree. Pam, age 62, is his wife. George retired from his postmilitary job three years ago, and Pam recently retired. They have $300,000 in stocks in 401(k) plans and $300,000 in bonds in taxable accounts; the cost basis and market value of the bonds are $300,000. They live in Texas, which has no state income tax, and expect to be in the 25 percent federal tax bracket during retirement. Their Current Annual Payment from military retirement is $30,000. (For simplicity, we assume that George did not earn a second defined-benefit pension that would require valuation and integration into the portfolio.) Their target asset mix is 50 percent stocks and 50 percent bonds. What is their current asset mix?

If Pam and George calculate their asset mix based on the traditional approach, they believe they have achieved the desired asset mix. Their traditional portfolio contains $300,000 in stocks and $300,000 in bonds.

Now let us examine the after-tax values of their extended portfolio, which includes their military retirement. We must first convert all assets to after-tax values. The $300,000 in the 401(k) plans is before-tax dollars, which represents $225,000 after taxes [$300,000 • (1 − 0.25)]. The $300,000 of bonds in the taxable account is after-tax funds. We must estimate their multiple. Today's TIPS yield is 4 percent. From Table 12.6, the multiple for a 65-year-old male retiree with a wife three years younger is 13.66. George is one year younger than 65, and Pam is two (not three) years younger than George. Therefore, we need to interpolate from the tables. Their multiple is 13.93 [13.66 + 0.35 − 0.08]. The 0.35 is one-third the difference between the multiples for males age 65 and age 62 with a wife three years younger [1/3 • (14.72 − 13.66)], and 0.08 is one-third the difference between the multiples for a male age 65 with a wife three years younger and a male age 65 with a wife the same age [1/3 • (13.66 − 13.43)].[5] The present value of their after-tax military retirement income is about $313,000 [$30,000 •13.93 • (1 − 0.25)].

Based on after-tax funds and including the value of military retirement, their portfolio contains $838,000 in assets. Their true asset mix consists of 27 percent stocks [$225,000 / $838,000] and 73 percent bonds, which is about half the stock portion they desire (and think they have). To achieve the desired 50 percent stock exposure, we recommend that they invest all $300,000 of the taxable account in stocks and about $119,000 of after-tax 401(k) funds (or $158,700 of before-tax 401(k) funds) in stocks. Moreover, we recommend that they either passively manage the stocks in taxable accounts or buy tax-efficient stock funds. We address this asset-location decision in Chapter 14.

To convert Pam and George's traditional asset mix to their true asset mix, we need an estimate of their marginal tax rate during retirement. In addition, the multiple reflects numerous assumptions, including the assumption that the actuarial tables reflect their unique life expectancy. Although Pam and George's true asset mix can only be estimated, we hold that it is better to rely on an estimate of their true portfolio than to rely on their traditional portfolio. By ignoring taxes, the traditional portfolio implicitly assumes their marginal tax rate will be zero. By ignoring military retirement, the traditional portfolio implicitly assumes the value of military retirement is zero. Although there may be uncertainty about Pam and George's retirement tax rate and the value of their military retirement, it is clear that the traditional approach's implicit estimates are less than optimal.

Summary

We argue that it is inconsistent to consider retirement income streams in retirement planning but ignore the value of these streams in asset allocation. We argue that the steady income provided by these pension plans makes them bond-like. In particular, we argue that the inflation-adjusted, regular payments from military pensions make them similar to Treasury Inflation Protection Securities and we value military pensions accordingly.

As the example in the previous section demonstrated, a portfolio managed with a target asset allocation can be grossly out of alignment if pension wealth is ignored. Given the relative importance of asset allocation over security selection and market timing (Brinson, Hood, and Beebower, 1986), there is a critical need to focus attention on a family's true portfolio. We build on the work of Scott (1995) and others by highlighting the importance of extending the family portfolio to include pension wealth. Given the substantial bond-like value associated with pension wealth, we recommend considering military pension wealth as a bond in a family's extended portfolio.

There are several implications to doing so. Because pension wealth can convert a seemingly stock-heavy portfolio into a bond-heavy one, excluding pension wealth can have a significant impact on investment decisions. Thinking of pension wealth as a bond creates arguments for including more stock in the financial part of the extended portfolio. Every financial advisor has experienced clients who are reluctant to hold as much stock in the financial asset portion of the total portfolio as the advisor recommends. By pointing out that their true portfolio contains the values of military retirement and Social Security benefits and that these are essentially bonds, the clients may be persuaded to increase the stock portion of financial assets.

In this framework, the client's mistake was not desiring a too-conservative risk tolerance. Rather, it was the failure to concentrate on their extended portfolio, which contains the value of retirement income streams. Given their current "bond" exposure due to the values of military retirement, Social Security, and company pensions, the rest of the portfolio should have a heavier stock exposure to satisfy their risk tolerance.

	TABLE 12.4	Multiples for Single Males under the Final Pay or High Three Retirement System		

	TIPS Yield			
Age	**2.5%**	**3%**	**3.5%**	**4%**
38	25.81	23.68	21.82	20.19
41	24.76	22.81	21.10	19.59
44	23.64	21.87	20.31	18.92
47	22.45	20.86	19.45	18.19
50	21.19	19.78	18.51	17.38
53	19.85	18.62	17.50	16.49
56	18.45	17.38	16.41	15.52
59	17.01	16.10	15.26	14.50
62	15.54	14.77	14.07	13.41
65	14.06	13.43	12.84	12.30
68	12.61	12.10	11.62	11.17
71	11.18	10.77	10.39	10.02
74	9.78	9.47	9.17	8.88
77	8.46	8.22	7.99	7.77
80	7.21	7.03	6.86	6.70
83	6.08	5.95	5.83	5.71
86	5.09	5.00	4.91	4.82
89	4.26	4.19	4.13	4.07

*Source: **Military Retirement Singles/Single Male.***

TABLE 12.5   Multiples for Single Females under the Final Pay or High Three Retirement System

| Age | TIPS Yield | | | |
	2.5%	3%	3.5%	4%
38	26.80	24.48	22.48	20.73
41	25.79	23.66	21.80	20.17
44	24.73	22.78	21.07	19.56
47	23.60	21.83	20.27	18.88
50	22.40	20.82	19.40	18.14
53	21.13	19.72	18.46	17.32
56	19.79	18.56	17.44	16.43
59	18.41	17.33	16.36	15.47
62	16.98	16.06	15.22	14.46
65	15.55	14.77	14.06	13.40
68	14.12	13.47	12.88	12.32
71	12.69	12.17	11.68	11.22
74	11.30	10.88	10.49	10.11
77	9.96	9.62	9.31	9.02
80	8.66	8.40	8.16	7.93
83	7.43	7.24	7.06	6.88
86	6.32	6.18	6.04	5.91
89	5.37	5.27	5.16	5.06

*Source: **Military Retirement Singles/Single Female.***

TABLE 12.6 Multiples for Married Male Military Retirees under the Final Pay or High Three Retirement System

Males Age	Wife Same Age TIPS Yield				Wife Three Years Younger TIPS Yield			
	2.5%	3%	3.5%	4%	2.5%	3%	3.5%	4%
38	26.93	24.61	22.60	20.84	27.15	24.78	22.73	20.95
41	25.93	23.79	21.93	20.29	26.16	23.98	22.08	20.41
44	24.86	22.91	21.19	19.68	25.11	23.11	21.36	19.81
47	23.72	21.95	20.39	19.00	23.98	22.17	20.57	19.15
50	22.50	20.92	19.51	18.25	22.78	21.16	19.71	18.41
53	21.21	19.81	18.55	17.42	21.51	20.06	18.77	17.60
56	19.86	18.63	17.52	16.51	20.17	18.89	17.75	16.71
59	18.84	17.38	16.42	15.54	18.77	17.66	16.66	15.75
62	16.99	16.09	15.26	14.50	17.32	16.38	15.51	14.72
65	15.53	14.77	14.07	13.43	15.86	15.07	14.33	13.66
68	14.06	13.44	12.86	12.32	14.40	13.74	13.13	12.56
71	12.60	12.09	11.62	11.18	12.95	12.41	11.91	11.44
74	11.15	10.75	10.37	10.02	11.51	11.07	10.67	10.29
77	9.76	9.44	9.15	8.87	10.11	9.77	9.45	9.15
80	8.42	8.19	7.96	7.75	8.77	8.51	8.26	8.03
83	7.18	7.01	6.84	6.68	7.52	7.32	7.14	6.96
86	6.08	5.95	5.83	5.71	6.39	6.24	6.11	5.97
89	5.14	5.04	4.95	4.86	5.41	5.30	5.20	5.10

Source: Military Retirement Couples/MF Same Age and Female 3 Years Younger.

TABLE 12.7   Multiples for Married Female Military Retirees under the Final Pay or High Three Retirement System

Female's Age	Husband Same Age TIPS Yield				Husband Three Years Older TIPS Yield			
	2.5%	3%	3.5%	4%	2.5%	3%	3.5%	4%
38	27.53	25.10	22.99	21.16	27.38	24.98	22.90	21.09
41	26.56	24.31	22.36	20.64	26.40	24.19	22.25	20.56
44	25.53	23.47	21.66	20.07	25.36	23.33	21.54	19.97
47	24.43	22.55	20.90	19.43	24.25	22.40	20.77	19.32
50	23.70	21.95	20.40	19.01	23.07	21.40	19.92	18.60
53	22.01	20.50	19.15	17.94	21.81	20.33	19.00	17.81
56	20.69	19.36	18.16	17.08	20.49	19.18	18.01	16.94
59	19.32	18.15	17.10	16.15	19.11	17.97	16.94	16.01
62	17.90	16.90	15.99	15.16	15.87	15.07	14.34	13.66
65	16.46	15.61	14.83	14.16	14.41	13.75	13.14	12.57
68	15.01	14.30	13.65	13.04	12.96	12.42	11.91	11.45
71	13.55	12.97	12.43	11.93	11.52	11.09	10.68	10.30
74	12.10	11.64	11.20	10.79	10.12	9.79	9.47	9.17
77	10.69	10.33	9.98	9.65	8.79	8.53	8.29	8.05
80	9.33	9.04	8.77	8.52	7.55	7.36	7.17	6.99
83	8.03	7.82	7.61	7.42	8.09	7.88	7.67	7.48
86	6.85	6.69	6.53	6.39	5.47	5.36	5.26	5.16
89	5.83	5.71	5.60	5.49	4.69	4.61	4.53	4.46

*Source: **Military Retirement Couples/FM Same Age** and **Male 3 Years Older.***

TABLE 12.8   Multiples for Male Widowers of Military Retirees under the Final Pay or High Three Retirement System

	TIPS Yield			
Male's Age	**2.5%**	**3%**	**3.5%**	**4%**
38	22.89	21.21	19.73	18.41
41	21.61	20.11	18.77	17.58
44	20.23	18.91	17.72	16.66
47	18.77	17.61	16.57	15.63
50	17.20	16.20	15.30	14.48
53	15.52	14.68	13.91	13.21
56	13.75	13.04	12.39	11.80
59	11.87	11.28	10.74	10.25
62	15.54	14.77	14.07	13.41
65	14.06	13.43	12.84	12.30
68	12.61	12.10	11.62	11.17
71	11.18	10.77	10.39	10.02
74	9.78	9.47	9.17	8.88
77	8.46	8.22	7.99	7.77
80	7.21	7.03	6.86	6.70
83	6.08	5.95	5.83	5.71
86	5.09	5.00	4.91	4.82
89	4.26	4.19	4.13	4.07

*Source: **Military Retirement Singles/Widower.***

TABLE 12.9   Multiples for Female Widows of Military Retirees under the Final Pay or High Three Retirement System

	TIPS Yield			
Female's Age	2.5%	3%	3.5%	4%
38	23.55	21.75	20.17	18.78
41	22.29	20.67	19.24	17.97
44	20.95	19.51	18.22	17.08
47	19.52	18.24	17.11	16.09
50	17.98	16.87	15.88	14.98
53	16.35	15.39	14.53	13.75
56	14.61	13.79	13.05	12.38
59	12.76	12.07	11.44	10.87
62	16.98	16.06	15.22	14.46
65	15.55	14.77	14.06	13.40
68	14.12	13.47	12.88	12.32
71	12.69	12.17	11.68	11.22
74	11.30	10.88	10.49	10.11
77	9.96	9.62	9.31	9.02
80	8.66	8.40	8.16	7.93
83	7.43	7.24	7.06	6.88
86	6.32	6.18	6.04	5.91
89	5.37	5.27	5.16	5.06

Source: Military Retirement Singles/Widow.

TABLE 12.10 Multiples for Single Males and Females under the REDUX
Retirement System

Age		Male TIPS Yield				Female TIPS Yield			
		2.5%	3%	3.5%	4%	2.5%	3%	3.5%	4%
38	Before 62	16.11	15.33	14.61	13.94	16.18	5.40	14.67	14.00
	After 62	7.28	6.18	5.25	4.47	8.02	6.77	5.73	4.86
41	Before 62	14.74	14.11	13.51	12.95	14.81	14.16	13.57	13.01
	After 62	7.86	6.77	5.84	5.04	8.65	7.41	6.37	5.48
44	Before 62	13.23	12.73	12.26	11.81	13.29	12.78	12.31	11.86
	After 62	8.50	7.42	6.50	5.69	9.34	8.12	7.08	6.18
47	Before 62	11.56	11.19	10.83	10.49	11.61	11.23	10.87	10.53
	After 62	9.47	8.40	7.45	6.63	10.40	9.17	8.11	7.19
50	Before 62	9.71	9.45	9.20	8.97	9.75	9.49	9.24	9.00
	After 62	10.57	9.50	8.56	7.73	11.59	10.37	9.31	8.37
53	Before 62	7.66	7.50	7.35	7.20	7.69	7.53	7.38	7.23
	After 62	11.81	10.78	9.85	9.02	12.93	11.74	10.69	9.75
56	Before 62	5.38	5.31	5.23	5.16	5.40	5.32	5.25	5.18
	After 62	13.24	12.25	11.36	10.56	14.45	13.32	12.30	11.38
59	Before 62	2.85	2.83	2.81	2.79	2.85	2.83	2.81	2.79
	After 62	14.89	13.99	13.17	12.41	16.20	15.15	14.20	13.33
62		14.10	13.44	12.83	12.27	15.26	14.48	13.77	13.12
65		12.88	12.33	11.82	11.34	14.10	13.43	12.82	12.25
68		11.65	11.20	10.77	10.38	12.91	12.35	11.84	11.35
71		10.42	10.05	9.71	9.39	11.71	11.25	10.82	10.41
74		9.20	8.91	8.64	8.38	10.52	10.14	9.79	9.46
77		8.01	7.79	7.58	7.38	9.34	9.04	8.76	8.49
80		6.89	6.72	6.56	6.41	8.19	7.96	7.73	7.52
83		5.85	5.73	5.61	5.50	7.08	6.91	6.74	6.57
86		4.93	4.84	4.76	4.67	6.06	5.93	5.80	5.68
89		4.15	4.08	4.02	3.96	5.18	5.08	4.99	4.89

For REDUX, the multiples assume the military personnel retired at age 44, except for
the multiples for ages 38 and 41 that assume retirement at, respectively, ages 38 and 41.
*Source: **Military Retirement Singles/Single Male** and **Single Female**.*

TABLE 12.11   Multiples for Married Male Retirees under the REDUX
Retirement System

Male's Age		Wife Same Age TIPS Yield				Wife Three Years Younger TIPS Yield			
		2.5%	3%	3.5%	4%	2.5%	3%	3.5%	4%
38	Before 62	16.26	15.47	14.74	14.07	16.26	15.48	14.75	14.07
	After 62	8.07	6.82	5.78	4.90	8.24	6.96	5.89	4.99
41	Before 62	14.89	14.24	13.64	13.07	14.89	14.24	13.64	13.07
	After 62	8.71	7.47	6.42	5.53	8.89	7.61	6.54	5.63
44	Before 62	13.36	12.85	12.37	11.92	13.36	12.85	12.37	11.92
	After 62	9.40	8.18	7.13	6.23	10.18	8.83	7.67	6.68
47	Before 62	11.67	11.29	10.93	10.59	11.67	11.29	10.93	10.59
	After 62	10.46	9.24	8.17	7.25	11.32	9.96	8.78	7.76
50	Before 62	9.80	9.54	9.29	9.05	9.80	9.54	9.29	9.05
	After 62	11.65	10.44	9.37	8.43	12.60	11.25	10.06	9.02
53	Before 62	7.72	7.56	7.41	7.26	7.72	7.57	7.41	7.26
	After 62	12.99	11.81	10.76	9.82	14.03	12.71	11.54	10.49
56	Before 62	5.42	5.34	5.27	5.20	5.42	5.34	5.27	5.20
	After 62	14.52	13.39	12.38	11.46	15.64	14.38	13.24	12.22
59	Before 62	2.86	2.84	2.82	2.80	2.86	2.84	2.82	2.80
	After 62	16.26	15.23	14.28	13.41	17.47	16.30	15.23	14.26
62		15.30	14.53	13.83	13.18	15.55	14.75	14.02	13.35
65		14.11	13.46	12.85	12.29	14.37	13.69	13.06	12.48
68		12.89	12.35	11.84	11.37	13.17	12.59	12.06	11.56
71		11.65	11.21	10.79	10.39	11.94	11.47	11.02	10.61
74		10.41	10.05	9.71	9.39	10.70	10.32	9.96	9.62
77		9.18	8.90	8.63	8.38	9.48	9.18	8.89	8.62
80		7.99	7.77	7.57	7.37	8.29	8.06	7.83	7.62
83		6.87	6.70	6.55	6.40	7.16	6.98	6.81	6.65
86		5.85	5.73	5.61	5.50	6.13	6.00	5.87	5.74
89		4.97	4.88	4.80	4.71	5.22	5.12	5.02	4.93

For REDUX, the multiples assume the military personnel retired at age 44, except for
the multiples for ages 38 and 41 that assume retirement at, respectively, ages 38 and 41.
Source: Military Retirement Couples/MF Same Age and Female 3 Years Younger.

TABLE 12.12   Multiples for Married Female Retirees under the REDUX Retirement System

Female's Age		Husband Same Age TIPS Yield				Husband Three Years Older TIPS Yield			
		2.5%	3%	3.5%	4%	2.5%	3%	3.5%	4%
38	Before 62	16.29	15.50	14.77	14.09	16.28	15.49	14.76	14.08
	After 62	8.53	7.19	6.08	5.15	8.42	7.11	6.01	5.10
41	Before 62	14.91	14.27	13.66	13.09	14.90	14.25	13.65	13.08
	After 62	9.20	7.87	6.75	5.80	9.09	7.78	6.68	5.74
44	Before 62	13.38	12.87	12.39	11.94	13.37	12.86	12.38	11.93
	After 62	9.92	8.62	7.50	6.54	9.80	8.52	7.42	6.47
47	Before 62	11.69	11.31	10.95	10.61	11.68	11.30	10.94	10.60
	After 62	11.04	9.73	8.59	7.60	10.91	9.61	8.49	7.52
50	Before 62	9.82	9.55	9.30	9.06	9.80	9.54	9.29	9.05
	After 62	12.29	10.98	9.84	8.83	12.14	10.86	9.74	8.74
53	Before 62	7.73	7.58	7.42	7.28	7.72	7.57	7.41	7.27
	After 62	13.69	12.42	11.29	10.28	13.53	12.28	11.17	10.18
56	Before 62	5.42	5.35	5.27	5.20	5.42	5.34	5.27	5.19
	After 62	15.27	14.06	12.96	11.98	15.10	13.91	12.83	11.86
59	Before 62	2.86	2.84	2.82	2.80	2.86	2.84	2.82	2.80
	After 62	17.08	15.95	14.92	13.99	16.89	15.79	14.78	13.86
62		16.02	15.18	14.41	13.71	14.37	13.69	13.06	12.48
65		14.87	14.15	13.48	12.87	13.17	12.60	12.07	11.57
68		13.68	13.07	12.50	11.98	11.95	11.48	11.03	10.62
71		12.46	11.96	11.48	11.04	10.72	10.33	9.97	9.63
74		11.24	10.82	10.43	10.07	9.50	9.19	8.91	8.63
77		10.01	9.68	9.37	9.07	8.32	8.08	7.86	7.64
80		8.80	8.54	8.30	8.07	7.20	7.02	6.85	6.68
83		7.64	7.44	7.25	7.07	7.70	7.50	7.31	7.13
86		6.56	6.41	6.27	6.13	5.28	5.18	5.08	4.99
89		5.62	5.51	5.40	5.30	4.55	4.48	4.40	4.33

For REDUX, the multiples assume the military personnel retired at age 44, except for the multiples for ages 38 and 41 that assume retirement at, respectively, ages 38 and 41.
Source: Military Retirement Couples/FM Same Age and *Male 3 Years Older.*

TABLE 12.13   Multiples for Male Widowers of Military Retirees under the REDUX Retirement System

Male's Age		Male and Female Same Age TIPS Yield				Male Three Years Older TIPS Yield			
		2.5%	3%	3.5%	4%	2.5%	3%	3.5%	4%
38	Before 62	16.11	15.33	14.61	13.94	16.11	15.33	14.61	13.94
	After 62	4.63	3.93	3.34	2.84	4.55	3.85	3.26	2.77
41	Before 62	14.74	14.11	13.51	12.95	14.74	14.11	13.51	12.95
	After 62	5.00	4.31	3.71	3.21	4.64	3.94	3.36	2.86
44	Before 62	13.23	12.73	12.26	11.81	13.23	12.73	12.26	11.81
	After 62	5.41	4.72	4.13	3.62	5.36	4.67	4.08	3.57
47	Before 62	11.56	11.19	10.83	10.49	11.56	11.19	10.83	10.49
	After 62	5.85	5.19	4.60	4.09	5.98	5.29	4.69	4.16
50	Before 62	9.71	9.45	9.20	8.97	9.71	9.45	9.20	8.97
	After 62	6.34	5.70	5.13	4.63	6.67	5.99	5.38	4.85
53	Before 62	7.66	7.50	7.35	7.20	7.66	7.50	7.35	7.20
	After 62	6.87	6.27	5.73	5.25	7.45	6.79	6.19	5.66
56	Before 62	5.38	5.31	5.23	5.16	5.38	5.31	5.23	5.16
	After 62	7.47	6.92	6.42	5.96	8.35	7.72	7.14	6.63
59	Before 62	2.85	2.83	2.81	2.79	2.85	2.83	2.81	2.79
	After 62	8.16	7.67	7.22	6.80	9.39	8.81	8.28	7.79
62		14.10	13.44	12.83	12.27	16.72	15.91	15.17	14.48
65		12.88	12.33	11.82	11.34	12.88	12.33	11.82	11.34
68		11.65	11.20	10.77	10.38	11.65	11.20	10.77	10.38
71		10.42	10.05	9.71	9.39	10.42	10.05	9.71	9.39
74		9.20	8.91	8.64	8.38	9.20	8.91	8.64	8.38
77		8.01	7.79	7.58	7.38	8.01	7.79	7.58	7.38
80		6.89	6.72	6.56	6.41	6.89	6.72	6.56	6.41
83		5.85	5.73	5.61	5.50	5.85	5.73	5.61	5.50
86		4.93	4.84	4.76	4.67	4.93	4.84	4.76	4.67
89		4.15	4.08	4.02	3.96	4.15	4.08	4.02	3.96

For REDUX, the multiples assume the military personnel retired at age 44, except for the multiples for ages 38 and 41 that assume retirement at, respectively, ages 38 and 41.
Source: Military Retirement Singles/Widower.

TABLE 12.14 Multiples for Female Widows of Military Retirees under the REDUX Retirement System

Female's Age		Male and Female Same Age TIPS Yield				Male Three Years Older TIPS Yield			
		2.5%	3%	3.5%	4%	2.5%	3%	3.5%	4%
38	Before 62	16.18	15.40	14.67	14.00	16.49	15.68	14.92	14.22
	After 62	5.10	4.31	3.65	3.09	4.95	4.18	3.54	3.00
41	Before 62	14.81	14.16	13.57	13.01	15.10	14.43	13.81	13.22
	After 62	5.50	4.72	4.05	3.49	5.34	4.58	3.93	3.39
44	Before 62	13.29	12.78	12.31	11.86	13.61	13.08	12.58	12.11
	After 62	5.94	5.17	4.50	3.93	5.94	5.17	4.50	3.93
47	Before 62	11.61	11.23	10.87	10.53	11.97	11.57	11.19	10.83
	After 62	6.42	5.67	5.01	4.44	6.62	5.84	5.16	4.57
50	Before 62	9.75	9.49	9.24	9.00	10.15	9.87	9.60	9.35
	After 62	6.95	6.22	5.58	5.02	7.37	6.60	5.92	5.32
53	Before 62	7.69	7.53	7.38	7.23	8.13	7.96	7.79	7.63
	After 62	7.52	6.83	6.22	5.67	8.23	7.47	6.80	6.20
56	Before 62	5.40	5.32	5.25	5.18	5.90	5.81	5.73	5.64
	After 62	8.16	7.52	6.95	6.43	9.19	8.48	7.83	7.24
59	Before 62	2.85	2.83	2.81	2.79	2.85	2.83	2.81	2.79
	After 62	8.88	8.31	7.78	7.31	8.62	8.06	7.55	7.09
62		15.26	14.48	13.77	13.12	15.26	14.48	13.77	13.12
65		14.10	13.43	12.82	12.25	14.10	13.43	12.82	12.25
68		12.91	12.35	11.84	11.35	12.91	12.35	11.84	11.35
71		11.71	11.25	10.82	10.41	11.71	11.25	10.82	10.41
74		10.52	10.14	9.79	9.46	10.52	10.14	9.79	9.46
77		9.34	9.04	8.76	8.49	9.34	9.04	8.76	8.49
80		8.19	7.96	7.73	7.52	8.19	7.96	7.73	7.52
83		7.08	6.91	6.74	6.57	7.08	6.91	6.74	6.57
86		6.06	5.93	5.80	5.68	6.06	5.93	5.80	5.68
89		5.18	5.08	4.99	4.89	5.18	5.08	4.99	4.89

For REDUX, the multiples assume the military personnel retired at age 44, except for the multiples for ages 38 and 41 that assume retirement at, respectively, ages 38 and 41. *Source: Military Retirement Singles/Widow.*

Appendix 12.1: Explanations of Multiple Calculations for Military Retirement Benefits

Appendix 12.1.1: Worksheets for Single Males, Single Females, Widowers, and Widows

An interactive version of the spreadsheet used to generate the multiples in Tables 12.4, 12.5, 12.8, 12.9, 12.10, 12.13, and 12.14 is available at http://www.wiley.com/go/reichenstein. This spreadsheet, entitled *App 12.1.1 Military Retirement Singles,* contains worksheets that calculate multiples for military retirement benefits for single males, single females, widowers, and widows under Final Pay or High Three and under REDUX. Each worksheet contains a text box that explains its purpose and use and a yellow box that summarizes the multiples.

Appendix 12.1.2: Worksheets for Married Couples

An interactive version of the spreadsheet used to generate the multiples in Tables 12.6, 12.7, 12.11, and 12.12 is available at http://www.wiley.com/go/reichenstein. This spreadsheet, entitled *App 12.1.2 Military Retirement Couples,* contains worksheets that calculate multiples for military retirement benefits under REDUX. The worksheet *MF Same Age* calculates multiples for married male military retirees with wife the same age under each system. The worksheet *FM Same Age* calculates the corresponding multiples for married female military retirees with husband the same age. The worksheets *Female 3 Years Younger* and *Male 3 Years Older* calculate corresponding multiples for married male military retirees with wife three years younger and married female military retirees with husband three years older, respectively. Each worksheet contains a text box that explains its purpose and use and a yellow box that summarizes the multiples.

References

Brinson, G.P., L.R. Hood, and G.L. Beebower. 1986. Determinants of portfolio performance. *Financial Analysts Journal,* July/August, 39–44.

Defense Finance and Accounting Service. Retired and annuitant pay. (http://www.dfas.mil/money/retired).

Fraser, Steve P., William W. Jennings, and David R. King. 2000. Strategic asset allocation for individual investors: The impact of the present value of Social Security benefits. *Financial Services Review,* Winter, 295–326.

Kennickell, Arthur B., Martha Starr-McCluer, and Annika E. Sunden. 1997. Family finances in the U.S.: Recent evidence from the survey of consumer finances. *Federal Reserve Bulletin,* January, 1–24.

Office of the Secretary of Defense. Military compensation. (http://pay2000.dtic.mil).

Peavy, John W., III, and Katrina F. Sherrerd. 1990. *Cases in portfolio management.* Charlottesville, VA: Association for Investment Management and Research.

Poterba, James M., Steven F. Venti, and David A. Wise. 1994. Targeted retirement saving and the net worth of elderly Americans. *American Economic Review*, May, 180–185.

Reichenstein, William. 1998. Calculating a family's asset allocation. *Financial Services Review*, Vol. 7, No. 3, 195–206.

Reichenstein, William. 2000. Calculating the asset allocation. *The Journal of Wealth Management* (previously *Journal of Private Portfolio Management*), Fall, 20–25.

Reichenstein, William. 2001. Rethinking the family's asset allocation. *Journal of Financial Planning*, May, 102–109.

Scott, Maria Crawford. 1995. Defining your investment portfolio: What should you include?" *AAII Journal*, November, 15–17.

Society of Actuaries. Table 4–5 Male RP–2000 Rates for "Combined Healthy" and Table 4–6 Female RP–2000 Rates for "Combined Healthy." (http://www.soa.org/research).

Stevens, Sue. 2000. Top 10 retirement-planning pitfalls, Part 2. *Morningstar*, March 30.

Woerheide, Walt, and Rich Fortner. 1994. The pension penalty associated with changing employers. *Financial Counseling and Planning*, Vol. 5, 101–116.

Yuh, Yoonkwung, Sherman Hanna, and Catherine Phillips Montalto. 1998. Mean and pessimistic projections of retirement adequacy. *Financial Services Review*, Vol. 7, No. 3, 175–193.

Notes

1. Some assumptions in the analysis on the Web site http://pay2000.dtic.mil do not match our assumptions.
2. See the Society of Actuaries Web site at http://www.soa.org/research. For males, we used Table 4–5 Male RP–2000 Rates for "Combined Healthy." For females, we used Table 4–6 Female RP–2000 Rates for "Combined Healthy."
3. Insert into a financial calculator, $n = 36.5$, $i = 4$ percent, PMT = \$20,000, FV = \$0 and calculate PV of an annuity of \$380,532. Then, multiplying this amount by $(1 + i)^{0.5}$ to move all payments up to mid-year, we get about \$388,100.
4. The multiples assume the military personnel retired at age 44, except for the 38- and 41-year-olds. They assume the 38- and 41-year-olds retired at ages 38 and 41, respectively.
5. Suppose the TIPS yield was 3.9 percent. Their multiple would be about 0.13 higher or about one-fifth the difference between the multiples for a male age 65 with a wife three years younger with TIPS yields of 3 percent and 3.5 percent.

CHAPTER 13

Calculating the Value of Defined-benefit Plans: Company Pensions, Teachers', Firefighters', and Police Officers' Pensions

Introduction

The goal of this chapter is to help a financial professional estimate the present value of retirement income in defined-benefit (DB) plans. Despite the proliferation of defined-contribution plans, DB plans remain popular, especially in the public sector and at medium or large private establishments. A complete treatment of this chapter's goal requires discussion of several topics: (1) retirement-income formulas, (2) reductions in benefits, if any, due to integration of defined-benefit payments with Social Security payments, (3) automatic and discretionary increases in postretirement benefits, and (4) assessments of default risk associated with promised benefits. In addition, the value of a DB plan's retirement income to a particular plan participant depends upon individual-specific estimates,

Three Key Estimates

	Initial Level of Benefits	Growth Rate	Discount Rate
Current Retiree	Known	Benefits formula	Treasury yield and perhaps more
Current Worker	Benefits formula Expected retirement age Payout option	Benefits formula	Treasury yield and perhaps more

FIGURE 13.1   Three Key Estimates for Projected Retirement Income

including the age at which he or she will retire and the payout option that he or she will select.

In practice, we can usually obtain a reasonable estimate of the present value of income from a DB plan with three key estimates. Figure 13.1 illustrates the three key estimates. The first is the current level of retirement benefits for a current retiree or the estimated beginning level of benefits for a current worker. For current retirees, the current level of benefits is known. For current workers, the beginning level of benefits must be estimated. It can be estimated from the DB plan's benefits formula and from estimates of when the worker will retire and which payout option he or she will select. The second key estimate is the growth rate in the level of postretirement benefits. The benefits formula specifies this growth rate. Most plans do not provide automatic postretirement increases, so the growth rate is zero. In some plans, benefits grow at a fixed percent per year, while other plans automatically raise benefits to keep pace with inflation. The third key estimate is the discount rate that is used to reduce future benefits to their present value. In most cases, future benefits are essentially default risk-free, and the discount rate can be estimated based on a current Treasury yield.

This chapter provides a background discussion of defined-benefit plans, including public-sector and private-sector plans. It then discusses estimation issues associated with (1) benefit formulas, (2) integration of DB plan benefits with Social Security benefits, (3) participant's selection of payout options, (4) potential adjustments in the level of postretirement benefits, and (5) setting the discount rate. The chapter ends by presenting examples that value the retirement income from several common designs of DB plans.

Background Discussion of Defined-benefit Plans

State and local governments usually sponsor public plans. Typically, participants in these plans have a benefits formula based on earnings, do not pay into the Social

TABLE 13.1   Public and Private Defined-benefit Pension Plan Design Features

	Public	Private
Benefit Formulas		
Dollar Amount Basis	13%	22%
Earnings Basis	82	75
Other Basis	5	3
Benefits Integrated with SS	32	63
Postretirement Increase		
Automatic	50	Rare
Full CPI	27	Rare

Source: Adapted from Mitchell, Olivia S., and Roderick Carr. 1997. State and local pension plans. Appendix Three. *Pension planning: Pension, profit-sharing, and other deferred compensation plans,* 8th ed. Edited by Everett T. Allen, Joseph J. Melone, Jerry S. Rosenbloom, and Jack L. VanDerhei. Boston: Irwin McGraw-Hill, 504–510.

Security system, and have a benefits formula that is not integrated with Social Security benefits. About half of these participants receive automatic increases in postretirement payments, with about half of those tied to inflation.

In contrast, private businesses establish private plans. The Employment Retirement Income Security Act (ERISA) governs these plans. Typically, participants in these plans have a benefits formula based on earnings, are part of the Social Security system, and have a benefits formula that is integrated with Social Security payments. These plans rarely provide automatic increases in postretirement benefits.

Table 13.1 summarizes information on the distribution of benefits formulas and other details for full-time pension plan participants at public and private defined-benefit plans.

Benefit Formulas

Benefit formulas are usually based on earnings for participants in both public and private plans. Among public plans, the benefit formulas are earnings based for 82 percent of full-time pension plan participants, while at private plans 75 percent are earnings based (Mitchell and Carr, 1997). Benefit formulas based on dollar amounts prevail for 22 percent of private plan participants.

The most popular structure of earnings-based formulas promises payments equal to a percent times years of service times average salary during the last few years of service. For example, the initial annual benefits level may equal 1.5 percent of average annual salary over the highest three years multiplied by years of service. If the average salary during the highest three years is $60,000, then someone with 30 years of service will receive initial benefits of $27,000 a year [0.015 • 30 • $60,000].

The DB plan's percent—1.5 percent in the previous example—tends to be smaller at plans whose participants also contribute to Social Security than at plans where they do not. At these plans, employees pay Social Security taxes and are entitled to Social Security benefits. Since they receive retirement income from the DB plan and Social Security, the DB plan needs to replace a smaller portion of preretirement income. These DB plan's benefits tend to be relatively small, say 1 percent to 1.5 percent times average salary times years of service. In addition, their benefit formula is likely to be integrated with Social Security payments, which means the structure of Social Security benefits and DB-plan benefits are integrated. This integration is discussed later.

The DB plan's percent is usually 2 percent or larger for participants at public plans that are not part of the Social Security system. At these plans, employees do not pay Social Security taxes. Therefore, the DB plan's percent tends to be larger so these benefits can replace a larger fraction of preretirement income. In addition, these public plans are more likely to provide automatic increases in postretirement income with the increases often tied to the inflation rate—like Social Security. Typically, their benefit formula will not be integrated with Social Security payments.

The less typical dollar-amount formula may specify a set dollar amount per month times years of service. For example, the initial annual benefits level may equal $30 per month times months of service. If the worker has 25 years of service (300 months), then initial benefits will be $9,000 a year. The dollar payment does not vary with the participant's income. These plans are popular in unionized industries.

Integration with Social Security

Only 32 percent of participants at public plans have benefits explicitly integrated with Social Security benefits, while 63 percent of participants at private plans have benefits explicitly integrated. When integrated with Social Security, DB-plan benefits are reduced. This reduction is designed to reduce the employer's costs for paying its share of the employee's Social Security taxes. Social Security replaces up to 90 percent of earned income for a low-wage employee but a much smaller fraction of earned income for a high-income employee. Integration may be designed to reduce this tilt in benefits toward low-wage employees.

There are two types of integration: offset and step-rate. The offset approach may reduce DB benefits by up to half of initial Social Security benefits. In fact, employers that adopt this type of integration frequently set the offset at 50 percent.

To illustrate an offset, assume a DB plan specifies a formula that sets initial benefits at 1.5 percent of the average earnings during the highest five years of service times years of service, and then reduces this product by 50 percent of the initial level of Social Security benefits. If this level of average income is $60,000 and the participant has 30 years of service, then his initial benefits level before integration is $27,000. If the level of initial Social Security benefits were $14,000, the employer would pay annual benefits of $20,000. In his first year of retirement, he would receive $20,000 from the employer plus $14,000 from Social Security. Although

Social Security benefits increase each year with a CPI, the reduction in DB benefits remains at $7,000, half of the initial level of Social Security benefits.

Next, consider a step-rate approach to integration, which is sometimes called an excess-earnings approach. This approach specifies two percentages in its benefits formula. For example, a base rate may be 1.25 percent for income up to an integration level and an excess rate of 2 percent for income above the integration level. The maximum allowable integration level is Social Security's maximum tax-able earnings base ($84,900 in 2002), and plans that adopt this type of integration approach frequently set the integration level at this maximum. The difference between the base rate and excess rate is called the disparity. If the base rate is at least 0.75 percent, then the maximum permitted disparity is 0.75 percent. If the base rate is set below 0.75 percent, then the maximum permitted disparity is the base rate.

Assume that the earnings base is $84,900, and a DB plan specifies an earnings-based formula that sets initial benefits at 1 percent of final pay times years of service up to the earnings base plus 1.5 percent of final pay for income above that amount. If an employee had final pay of $100,000 and 30 years of service, she would receive $32,265 in DB benefits during her first year of retirement [0.01 • 30 • $84,900 + 0.015 • 30 • $15,100]. If she were entitled to $15,000 in Social Security benefits, then she would receive $47,265 in combined income from the two retirement pro-grams during her first year of retirement.

Table 13.1 indicates that 63 percent of participants at private plans receive ben-efits that are integrated with Social Security, while only 32 percent of participants at public plans receive integrated benefits. These statistics can be somewhat misleading in that it appears that participants in integrated plans receive reduced benefits, while participants in nonintegrated plans do not. Clearly, participants in integrated plans typically receive reduced benefits from their DB plans. However, participants in nonintegrated DB plans often receive reduced benefits from Social Security due to the Windfall Elimination Provision (see Chapter 11). Thus, in practice, the combined retirement income from DB plans and Social Security are usually integrated through either the DB plan's integration feature or Social Security's Windfall Elimination Provision.

Automatic and Discretionary Adjustments

About half of the participants in public plans receive an automatic increase in postretirement benefits. A little over half of these participants receive benefit increases to fully reflect inflation as measured by a Consumer Price Index. This cost-of-living adjustment is the same as the COLA adjustment in Social Security benefits. Other plans adjust benefits by a set percentage per year, perhaps 2 percent. These plans provide partial protection against inflation but do not provide complete protection against a high level of inflation.

Private plans rarely provide automatic increases in postretirement benefits. However, some plans have provided discretionary increases when the firm's financial health permits. To be conservative, we recommend that financial professionals assume their clients' initial levels of benefits will not be subject to discretionary increases during retirement. Resulting estimates of the present value of income from these plans will be downward biased in firms that subsequently provide *ad hoc* increases in postretirement benefits.

Estimation Issues

Figure 13.1 presents an illustration that separates many of the issues into three estimates. First, what is the initial level of retirement income? Second, what is the growth rate in this initial level of income? Third, what is the appropriate discount rate?

The current retiree in Figure 13.1 knows the level of annual retirement income that she is entitled to receive during the next year. The current worker must estimate the initial level of annual retirement income. This estimate depends upon, among other things, the benefits formula, estimated retirement age, and selection of payout option. The plan's benefits formula is known, but the retirement age and choice of payout options are individual choices.

The growth rate depends upon increases in postretirement income. Do benefits increase at all? Do they increase with inflation, some function of inflation, or at a constant rate? To be conservative in our valuation, we incorporate into valuation models the automatic increases that are built into the DB plan and assume that there will be no *ad hoc* postretirement increases.

The third estimate is the discount rate that should be used to reduce future income to a present value. An appropriate discount rate begins with a base risk-free rate, and then makes adjustments as necessary.

The remainder of this section discusses estimation issues related to the initial level of retirement income, increases in postretirement income, an appropriate discount rate, and the distinction between two present value estimates.

Estimate of Initial Level of Retirement Income

Unlike a current retiree who knows his level of retirement income, a current worker must estimate the level of retirement income during the first year of retirement. It depends upon (1) the benefits formula (and the average salary and years of service to use in that formula), (2) the expected retirement age, and (3) the choice of payout options.

The plan specifies the benefits formula. For discussion purposes, consider Sue, a 62-year-old teacher with 17 years of service and an average salary during the highest three years of $40,000. Her benefits formula calls for annual payments at her normal retirement age of 2 percent times years of service times average salary over the highest three years. Normal retirement age is specified in the defined-benefit plan as any combination of age plus years of service totaling 80. Sue expects to retire in four years at age 66 at which time she will have attained normal retirement age ($66 + 21 = 87$). We recommend that the estimate of initial level of retirement income reflect her current average salary and current years of service, but disregard the fact that she has not yet attained normal retirement age. That is, we would project her initial annual retirement income as $13,600 [2% • 17 • $40,000]. In four years, she will have 21 years of service and an average salary of perhaps $44,000, which translates into an initial annual retirement income of $18,480. However, because we view the present value of retirement income as bonds in the family's portfolio, we recommend that the $13,600 be used in computing the present value of retirement income instead of the $18,480. The $4,880 of additional retirement income is the benefit of future work, and it is generally inappropriate to consider the rewards of future work when calculating the family's current asset mix.

There are at least two potential objections to our recommended approach to estimating the initial level of retirement income. First, it seems to suggest that the present value of her projected retirement benefits is larger if she retires earlier. For example, if she retires at age 63 instead of 66, then it suggests that she will receive the $13,600 beginning three years earlier. A financial advisor can illustrate the likely trade-off between stopping work at, say, age 63 or at age 66. From the prior example, suppose Mary could retire with full benefits at age 63 or age 66. Further suppose her estimated levels of retirement benefits would be $14,760 [2% • 18 • $41,000] at age 62 or $18,480 [2% • 21 • $44,000] at age 66. By working three more years, the expected benefits level rises 25.2 percent. Mathematically, $1.252 = 1.167 • 1.073$, where $18,480 / $14,760 is 1.252, 21 / 18 is 1.167, and $44,000 / $41,000 is 1.073. By continuing to work, the level of benefits grows by the compound growth rates in years of service and salary. Due to this compound effect, DB plans are especially valuable to workers who have long careers at the same firm. Woerheide and Fortner (1994) provide an analysis of the penalty associated with changing jobs that results in changing from one DB plan to another.

The second potential objection is that we assume the payout associated with normal retirement age even though she has yet to attain that status. Many defined-benefit plans have steep penalties for retiring before attaining normal retirement age. For example, the Teachers' Retirement System of Texas has the normal retirement age previously described—any combination of age plus years of service totaling 80. If Sue retired at age 62 with 17 years of service ($62 + 17 = 79$), she would receive 67 percent of normal retirement income. That is, she would receive $9,112 [$13,600 • 0.67]. The expected benefits should reflect the planned retirement age including penalties, if any.

In making the distinction between accrued benefits and projected benefits, we are somewhat conservative. Our approach is akin to the Generally Accepted Accounting Principles' (GAAP) treatment of corporations' pension liabilities known as the *accrued benefit obligation*, which is reflected on the balance sheet. The accrued benefit obligation relies on current wages and current tenure; it is a smaller (and, thus, potentially more conservative) estimate of a pension's liability than the GAAP *projected benefit obligation,* which is based on numerous projections like salary growth.

As previously noted, a current worker must estimate his or her retirement date. This estimate should reflect the expected retirement date and not a desired retirement date. A 45-year-old worker with no life savings may say that he *hopes* to retire at age 60, but the reality may be far different. Determining the feasibility of such goals is part of the financial planner's duties.

The initial level of annual benefits also depends on the choice of payout options. To continue with the previous example, the $13,600 per year assumes Sue selects the lifetime income option with no guaranteed minimum payout period. That is, the plan, which has no automatic increases in postretirement income, would pay her $13,600 per year for the rest of her life. In most plans, Sue has several different payout options. Some of them may include the following:

- Lifetime income with payments guaranteed for 10 years: This payout would pay her a monthly income for the rest of her life and, should she die before receiving 120 monthly payments, her beneficiary would receive the remainder of the 120 payments. There also may be lifetime income options with 5-, 15-, or 20-year guarantees. These options are sometimes called "years certain" or "term certain."

- Lifetime income with 75 percent to primary beneficiary—usually the spouse: This promises Sue a lifetime income and, should she die first, it would pay her primary beneficiary 75 percent of that amount for the rest of his or her life. There also may be joint-life income options with 50 percent or 100 percent of benefits payable to the primary beneficiary.

- Hybrids of the two options just described. There may be one or more joint beneficiary options with a guaranteed minimum years payout.

Many DB plans provide annual statements that provide projected levels of benefits under available payout options. Upon written request, private plans must provide a statement of benefits. The statement may provide benefit levels for each payout option assuming Sue continues to earn $40,000 a year and continues to work until age 66. We recommend that her projected benefits be based on current years of service. However, the ratio of projected benefits can be used to estimate the reduction in benefits associated with alternative payout options. For example, Sue's annual statement may project benefits at age 66 of $16,800 [2% • 21 • $40,000] if she selects the standard annuity, or $15,456 if she selects a joint-life annuity with 75 percent spousal benefits. The ratio $15,456 / $16,800 or 0.92 can be used to estimate the reduction in benefits for this joint-life annuity. Based on 17 years of current service and the joint-life annuity with 75 percent spousal benefits payout, her projected annual benefits are $12,512 [2% • 17 • $40,000 • 0.92].

Married participants usually select a joint-payout option that promises payments for as long as the participant or his or her spouse is alive. Unless the spouse waives the right in writing, in many plans the participant *must* select a joint-payout option. In practice, participants, perhaps with the help of a financial professional, can select the best expected payout option.

Before leaving this topic, we wish to make one more point. In practice, financial advisors often will estimate the initial level of retirement income from the client/participant's annual estimate-of-benefits statement. If so, the advisor should make sure he or she understands the assumptions embedded in the estimate. In particular, is the estimate of initial income based on service to date or projected service through normal retirement age, and is it based on current income or the assumption that income will rise? If based on projected years of service or projected income, then the estimate-of-benefits statement exaggerates the present value of retirement income based on service to date and current income.

Postretirement Increases in Retirement Income

As previously noted, private plans rarely give automatic increases, while about half of the public plans give automatic increases. If postretirement income will increase with a Consumer Price Index, then the plan promises a constant real income, and we can discount the constant real income by an appropriate real interest rate. If the income will increase by a fixed percent each year, then we can reduce the appropriate nominal discount rate by the same fixed percent. For example, if a plan increases postretirement income by 2 percent a year, then the nominal discount rate should be 2 percent lower than if it promised a constant retirement income. These adjustments are discussed in more detail later.

A few state and local plans boost postretirement income by other formulas. Unfortunately, it is not always easy to accommodate these adjustments. For example, New York adjusts retirement income by 50 percent of inflation as measured by the CPI on the first $18,000 of retirement income, but the increase is restricted to the range 1 percent to 3 percent. If actual inflation is 1 percent to 2 percent, then the increase is 1 percent on the first $18,000. If it is 2 percent to 6 percent, then the increase is 50 percent of inflation on the first $18,000. If actual inflation is more than 6 percent, the increase is 3 percent on the first $18,000.

Private and public plans sometimes make *ad hoc* adjustments to postretirement benefits. Unless the financial advisor has good reason to expect a discretionary increase, we would encourage the advisor to assume that there will be no discretionary increases. In the spirit of conservatism, the resulting estimates may be downward biased.

Estimate of Discount Rate

A model of the appropriate discount rate is $k = Rf - g + RP$, where k is the discount rate, Rf denotes the risk-free rate, g is the annual percent increase in postretirement income, and RP is the default risk premium. We will now discuss each of these components.

A major problem in all social sciences, like financial *economics,* is how to find an empirical measure of a concept. We must find measures of the risk-free rate of return and the default risk premium. Like most financial economists, we recommend that the risk-free rate be measured by a Treasury yield. To be specific, we recommend that the risk-free rate be the adjusted Treasury yield on the bond with maturity closest to the participant's life expectancy.

Consider a 50-year-old woman with a life expectancy exceeding 30 years. We suggest that she use the 30-year Treasury bond yield, the longest Treasury bond available.[1] Suppose it is 6 percent. Treasury yields reflect the semi-annual bond convention. That is, this bond's price is the present value of future cash flows discounted at 3 percent per semi-annual period. The effective annual yield is thus 6.09 percent $[(1.03)^2 - 1]$. We recommend that this 6.09 percent rate be used as the risk-free rate.

There are potential criticisms to any estimate of Rf, and this adjusted Treasury yield is no exception. For example, interest on Treasury debt is tax-exempt at the state and local level, which potentially biased the *observed value.* Others may argue that the discount rate used to value DB postretirement benefits should be higher because there is no secondary market for postretirement benefits. Clearly, there is no secondary market, and postretirement benefits are thus illiquid. However, we do not believe the absence of a secondary market is relevant when answering the issue of whether someone has sufficient financial resources to meet his or her retirement needs. We are not interested in the "fair market value," which would reflect illiquidity, but rather in the individual-specific investment valuation (see Fraser, Jennings, and King, 2000, for further discussion). In short, despite potential criticisms, we recommend that financial advisors use an adjusted Treasury yield to measure the risk-free rate, Rf.

As noted earlier, if postretirement income increases each year by g percent then the discount rate is $(Rf - g)$ percent, assuming the default risk premium is zero. If postretirement income is indexed each year with inflation, then $Rf - g$ can be estimated by the yield on the maturity-appropriate (adjusted) Treasury Inflation Protection Security (TIPS). If this TIPS yield is 3.4 percent, then the discount rate would be 3.43 percent $[(1.017)^2 - 1]$. Figure 11.1 illustrates the "Treasury Bonds, Notes and Bills" table in the *Wall Street Journal* and explains how to estimate the appropriate TIPS yield.

The last estimate is the size of the default risk premium, RP. There is negligible default risk on the promises of most DB plans. For these plans, the default risk premium is zero, and the appropriate discount rate is $Rf - g$.

To assess a plan's default risk, financial professionals should look at the layers of protection backing the plan's promises. For private plans, there are three layers. The first layer is pension assets. ERISA governs private plans. Plans must report their funding ratio, defined as the ratio of pension assets/Projected Benefits Obligation, where the latter is a measure of the present value of projected benefits. The second layer of protection is corporate assets and the firm's ability to contribute funds. The federal Pension Benefit Guarantee Corporation (PBGC) provides the third layer. The PBGC guarantees most private-plan benefits of up to $40,705 a year (in 2001) for each participant.[2] Some private plans are excluded; for example, plans usually are not insured when offered by small professional service firms or by church groups. Some benefits are excluded; for example, benefits resulting from plan enhancements within five years of termination are not covered. Similarly, COLA increases are not covered. Overall, however, the PBGC guarantee is broad and strong. In addition to having a pool of funds accumulated from its insurance premiums to back this guarantee, the PBGC also has a priority claim in bankruptcy. Retirement income of private plans appears secure, especially retirement income up to the PBGC limit; the default risk on private plans is negligible.[3]

There are two layers of protection backing the promises of public plans. The first layer is pension assets, or funds already set aside to meet the liabilities. The second layer is the ability of the state or local government to contribute funds. Most participants in public plans are in large state plans. They are usually well-funded with funding ratios exceeding 90 percent. In addition, they offer the second layer of protection in that the state will likely make good on any projected shortfall. The major difficulty comes in assessing the default risk of underfunded plans, especially underfunded plans of local governments. If pension assets are insufficient, then the ability of the local government to raise funds through debt issues or taxation becomes important. For public plans, the capability of meeting unfunded pension obligations can be roughly assessed from the state or local government's credit rating. Moody's and Standard & Poor's provide credit ratings. If the government's credit rating is Baa2, then $Rf + RP$ can be estimated at the maturity-appropriate yield on Baa2 *corporate bonds;* the *risk premium, RP,* is the difference between this Baa2 yield and the Treasury yield with the same maturity.

The municipal debt has a lower yield than corporate debt due to the federal tax-exempt status of its interest payments. The tax-exempt municipal yield is not the appropriate discount rate for a participant since pension distributions are subject to income taxes. Thus, same-risk *corporate bonds* are used as the discount rate.

Two Present Values

Table 13.2 distinguishes between the present value of cash flows and the present value of cash flows through life expectancy. It illustrates the calculations of the two present values for Mary, a 60-year-old woman who is entitled to receive a constant $14,400 per year for the rest of her life beginning at age 66 when the discount rate is 5.37 percent. In the valuation models, we assume all payments occur at mid-year. That is, we adopt the mid-year convention.

The present value of expected cash flows calculates each year's expected cash flow as the product of probability that the participant will be alive (assuming average life expectancy) and the annual payment. There is a 0.957274 probability that she will be alive at age 66 and receive the first $14,400 payment. The expected dollar payment is $13,784.75 [0.957274 • $14,400]. There is a 0.946788 probabil-

TABLE 13.2   Calculations of Present Values of Expected Cash Flows and Cash Flows through Life Expectancy for a 60-year-old Single Female Beginning Benefits at Age 66

Age	Probability of Being Alive	Expected Cash Flows	Present Value of Expected Cash Flows	Present Value of Cash Flows through Life Expectancy
66	0.957274	$13,784.75	$13,784.76/(1.0537)^{6.5}$	$14,400/(1.0537)^{6.5}$
67	0.946788	13,633.75	$13,633.75/(1.0537)^{7.5}$	$14,400/(1.0537)^{7.5}$
⋮	⋮	⋮	⋮	⋮
83	0.586627	8,447.43	$8,447.43/(1.0537)^{23.5}$	$14,400/(1.0537)^{23.5}$
84	0.549959	7,919.41	$7,919.41/(1.0537)^{24.5}$	$5,760/(1.0537)^{24.5}$
85	0.511728	7,368.88	$7,368.88/(1.0537)^{25.5}$	0
⋮	⋮	⋮	⋮	⋮
120	0.000009	0.13	$0.13/(1.0537)^{60.5}$	0
			$116,496	$124,299

The discount interest rate is 5.37 percent. All payments are assumed to occur at mid-year. In this example, the present value of cash flows through life expectancy has a 6.7 percent upward bias compared to the present value of expected cash flows.

ity that Mary will be alive at age 67 and receive the second payment. The expected dollar payment is $13,633.75. This process continues through year 120, which is the end of the mortality tables. We discount the expected cash flows that occur at ages 66.5 through 120.5 back to age 60 at 5.37 percent. This present value is $116,496.

The far right-hand column of Table 13.2 illustrates the calculation of the present value of cash flows through life expectancy. Assuming average life expectancy, at age 60, Mary is expected to live 24.4 years. This present value assumes that she will receive $14,400 per year for 18.4 years beginning at age 66; she will receive $5,760 [0.4 • $14,400] in the 19th year. When discounted at 5.37 percent, this present value is $124,299.

In financial economics, an asset's value is traditionally estimated based on expected cash flows. However, it is usually easier to estimate the value of a defined-benefit plan based on cash flows through expected life. Also, it is easier to explain this valuation to a client. The cash-flows-through-expected-life method has the additional advantage that it accommodates situations where the client's life expectancy is either shorter or longer than average. Experimentation suggests that the present value of cash flows through life expectancy provides a slightly upward-biased estimate of the present value of expected cash flows. Since the two estimates are close, many financial professionals will prefer to calculate the present value of cash flows through life expectancy and then make an adjustment for its slight upward bias.

In the previous example, the bias is 6.7 percent. End-of-chapter tables present the bias for singles when the discount rate before and after retirement is 6 percent.

Although the size of the bias tends to increase with the size of the discount rate, the bias when the discount rate is 6 percent should prove useful to financial professionals who prefer to estimate the present value of cash flows through life expectancy and then adjust for the bias.

Examples of Estimates

This section presents several examples that estimate the before-tax present value of defined-benefit plan retirement income. The first part presents examples for single participants, while the second part presents examples for participants who select a joint-payout option.

Numerous end-of-chapter tables present estimated multiples. There are separate sets of multiples and thus separate tables for (1) single males, single females, and couples and (2) when postretirement benefits remain constant or increase. For example, Table 13.4 presents multiples for males with average life expectancy when postretirement benefits remain constant and, thus, the preretirement and postretirement discount rates are the same. Tables 13.5 and 13.6 present multiples for males when the postretirement discount rate is, respectively, 3 percent and 4 percent. Tables 13.7 through 13.9 present the corresponding tables for females with average life expectancy.

In addition, there are numerous tables of multiples for couples. Tables 13.10 through 13.12 present multiples for a married male with a same-age, joint-beneficiary wife when, respectively, postretirement benefits remain constant, the postretirement discount rate is 3 percent, and the postretirement discount rate is 4 percent. Tables 13.13 through 13.15 present the corresponding multiples for a male with a wife three years younger. Tables 13.16 through 13.21 present the corresponding multiples to Tables 13.10 through 13.15 except they are for a female with a joint-beneficiary husband. So financial professionals can easily access the tables of multiples, they are placed together at the end of the chapter.

Single Participants

Example S1, simple case: This example corresponds to Table 13.2. Mary is a single participant in a plan with no automatic increases in retirement benefits and no integration with Social Security benefits. She is 60 years old with 18 years of service and an average high income during the highest three years of $40,000. She expects to retire and begin receiving benefits at age 66 and to select the lifetime income option with no guaranteed payment period. Although she has not attained normal retirement age—here, any combination of age plus years of service totaling 80— she will have attained it by her expected retirement date. The benefit formula is 2 percent times years of service times average salary in the highest three years.

We project retirement income of $14,400 [2% • 18 • $40,000], beginning in six years. The present value of retirement income is the value at age 60 of benefits of $14,400 a year (or $1,200 a month) to begin at age 66 and to continue for the rest of her life. As previously discussed, the level of expected benefits reflects current years of service and current salary, but it is not reduced to reflect the fact that Mary has not yet attained normal retirement age.

This state-funded DB plan is well-funded and, although a shortfall is not anticipated, it is strongly expected that the state would back any shortfall in assets. Benefits, once begun, will remain constant. We use the 25-year Treasury bond yield of 5.3 percent to estimate the risk-free rate. The 5.3 percent Treasury yield is based on the semi-annual bond convention. As previously discussed, the 5.3 percent yield represents an effective annual yield of 5.37 percent $[(1.0265)^2 - 1]$.

Bond rates are based on a semi-annual coupon payment convention. A 5.3 percent yield based on semi-annual bond convention is a 5.37 percent effective annual yield. We value the DB pension assuming monthly payments are received as one lump-sum payment at mid-year, and we discount at the effective annual yield.

There are two estimation methods. The first method estimates the present value of expected future cash flows. The second estimates the present value of cash flows through her expected life.

Table 13.7, at the end of the chapter, presents multiples for females based on *expected future cash flows,* assuming the level of payments will remain constant.[4] The present value of benefits is the product of the multiple and \$14,400, the annual benefits level. Based on the model with 5.37 percent discount rates ($k_1 = k_2 = 0.0537$), the actual multiple is 8.09. This model is available for download at www.wiley.com/go/reichenstein. In Appendix 13.1.1, see the female worksheet. The present value of expected cash flows is \$116,496. Alternatively, this multiple can be estimated from interpolation. From Table 13.7, the multiples for a 60-year-old female when the discount rates are 5 percent and 6 percent are, respectively, 8.53 and 7.41. Using linear interpolation, the estimated multiple for 5.37 percent is 8.12 [8.53 − 0.37 • (8.53 − 7.41)], and the value is \$116,928.

Now, let us calculate the present value of cash flow through life expectancy. At age 60 and assuming average life expectancy, Mary will live 24.4 years. (Tables 11.4 and 11.5 present average life expectancies for females and males.) Inserting into a financial calculator $n = 18.4$ (she expects to receive payments for 18.4 years beginning six years hence), $i = 5.37$ percent, PMT = \$14,400 gives a present value at age 66 of an ordinary annuity of \$165,734. In an ordinary annuity, payments occur at the end of the year. To repeat, we adopt the mid-year convention, which assumes the payment occurs at mid-year. Therefore, the \$165,734 amount assumes the first payment occurs the day before she turns 67, the second payment occurs the day before she turns 68, and so on. Multiplying \$165,734 by 1.0265 (i.e., 1 + semi-annual yield or, for a 5.3 percent Treasury yield, 1 + 0.0265) moves all payments up half a year to mid-year and gives a value of \$170,126. Discounting \$170,126 at 5.37 percent for six years gives a present value at age 60 of \$124,299; insert FV = \$170,126, $i = 5.37$ percent, $n = 6$, and PMT = 0, and calculate present value.

Recall that the present value of cash flows through life expectancy is an upward-biased estimate of the present value of expected cash flows. Some professionals will want to reduce the \$124,299 estimate for this bias. From Table 13.7, when the discount rate is 6 percent, the bias is 7.3 percent. This implies an estimated value of $115,843 [$124,299 / (1.073)]. (As shown in Table 13.2, the actual bias at 5.37 percent is 6.7 percent [($124,299 − $116,496) / $116,496]. The bias tends to decrease as the discount rate falls.)

In addition, we could have estimated the present value of cash flows through life expectancy using the monthly payment of $1,200, and the estimated value would have been similar.

The present value *at age 66* of $1,200 a month for 220.8 months (18.4 times 12 months) when discounted at 0.4367 percent per month or $(1.0537)^{1/12} − 1$ is $169,798, and discounting this amount by the same interest rate for 72 months (or six years) gives a present value *at age 60* of about $124,073.

Therefore, in practice, financial professionals can estimate the pre-tax value of a DB plan using several methods. Since the profession currently values DB plans at zero when calculating a family's asset allocation, any estimate is a substantial improvement over existing methods.

The before-tax value of the DB plan varies with the estimation method, but it varies within a relatively narrow range. Present value estimates are:

PV Estimates	Method
$116,496	Expected cash flows (Multiple from model)
$116,928	Expected cash flows (Multiple from extrapolation)
$124,299	Cash flows through life expectancy (no adjustment for bias)
$115,843	Cash flows through life expectancy (adjusted for bias at 6 percent)
$124,073	Cash flows through life expectancy (monthly approach)

Example S2, term certain: Consider a slightly different example. Mary has the same years of service, average salary, and so on, except she selects a lifetime payout option with a 10-year guarantee. She names her niece the beneficiary. The benefits payment is now $14,052 per year with the reduction reflecting the term-certain guarantee. We would estimate the present value of retirement benefits in the same manner as previously shown. Using the model, the estimate based on expected cash flows is about $114,000 [$14,052 • 8.09]. The present value would be 97.583 percent of the level of the previous estimate, where 97.583 percent is $14,052 / $14,400. This estimate represents the value of retirement benefits that *will likely be available to finance Mary's retirement needs.* In addition, Mary's retirement plan may make payments to her niece, but these payments are not payments to finance Mary's retirement needs. That is, we ignore the guarantee. In essence, if Mary opts for the 10-year guarantee, then she is willing to reduce her monthly benefits to $1,171 so she can give a contingent inheritance to her niece.

Example S3, automatic fixed-percent increases: Mary has the same years of service, average salary, and so on. She will receive $14,400 per year beginning in six years at age 66, but postretirement benefits will increase at 2 percent a year. The appropriate discount rate is 6 percent before retirement and 4 percent after retirement, where 4 percent is 6 percent less the 2 percent postretirement growth rate.[5] From Table 13.9, shown at the end of the chapter, the multiple is 8.80. Therefore, the present value is about $127,000 [8.80 • $14,400]. The higher valuation reflects the increasing retirement benefits.

To estimate the value based on the cash-flows-through-life-expectancy method, first calculate the present value of $14,400 per year for 18.4 years when discounted at 4 percent. This is $185,060. Multiplying this amount by 1.0198 [$(1.04)^{0.5}$] adjusts for the mid-year convention and produces a value of $188,724. Then, to estimate the value at age 60, discount this value back at 6 percent for six years. The value before any adjustment for bias is $133,043. In this example, the cash-flows-through-life-expectancy method produces a valuation that is about 5 percent higher than the valuation based on expected cash flows.

Example S4, COLA increases: Mary has the same years of service, average salary, and so on. She will receive $14,400 per year beginning in six years at age 66, but postretirement benefits will increase with inflation. The discount rate is 6 percent before retirement and, based on the real yield on long-term inflation-indexed Treasuries, it is 3 percent after retirement; in essence, postretirement benefits are expected to increase by 3 percent, 6 percent less the 3 percent adjusted TIPS yield. From Table 13.8, the multiple is 9.68. The estimated value is $139,392.

To estimate the value based on cash flows through life expectancy, first calculate the present value of $14,400 per year for 18.4 years when discounted at 3 percent. Multiply this amount by 1.0149 [$(1.03)^{0.5}$], and then discount this new amount back at 6 percent for six years. The value before adjustment for bias is $144,069. The $144,069 is about 3.4 percent higher than the $139,392; the bias tends to decrease when the discount rate decreases.

Example S5, integration with Social Security: John is single, age 62, and expects to retire at age 66. He currently has 30 years of service. His benefits formula is integrated with Social Security using the step-rate approach. It promises 1.25 percent times years of service times average salary during the highest consecutive five years up to the maximum Social Security wage base, and 2 percent times years of service times average salary above that wage base. The maximum wage base is $84,900 (in 2002), and his average salary during his highest five years is $100,000. There are no automatic adjustments in this private DB plan. He selects the lifetime annuity option. Based on his current average salary and current wage base, he will receive $40,897.50 per year [1.25% • 30 • $84,900 + 2% • 30 • $15,100]. Assuming a 6 percent discount rate, the present value of expected cash flow is about $322,000 [$40,897.50 • 7.87]; the 7.87 is interpolated from multiples in Table 13.4 of 6.79 at age 60 and 9.50 at age 65, [6.79 + 0.4(9.50 − 6.79)].

Next, we calculate the present value of cash flows through life expectancy. The life expectancy of a 62-year-old man in average health is about 20 years. The present value of $40,897.50 per year for 16 years beginning in four years is about $337,000. Insert into a financial calculator $n = 16$, $i = 6$ percent, PMT = $40,897.50, FV = 0 and calculate the present value of an ordinary annuity at age 66 of $413,306. Multiplying this amount by $1.0296\ [(1.06)^{0.5}]$ moves all payments to mid-year, and gives a present value at age 66 of $425,540. Insert $425,540 as the FV, set $n = 4$, $i = 6$ percent, and PMT $= 0$ and calculate the present value at age 62 of about $337,000. The present value of cash flows through life expectancy is about 4.7 percent higher than the present value of expected cash flows.

Example S6, short life expectancy: Return to the previous example, but assume John has a lower than average life expectancy, perhaps due to smoking or family history. To aid comparison, we ignore the fact that, if his current life expectancy is 15 years, then he may wish to retire before age 66. If his expected retirement date is age 66, then we could estimate the present value at age 62 as the present value of $40,897.50 a year for 11 years beginning in four years; the 11 represents the number of years he will receive benefits if he begins benefits in four years and dies after 15 years. This value (before any adjustment for bias) is about $263,000.[6] This example demonstrates one important benefit of estimates based on the cash flows through life expectancy: They accommodate individuals whose life expectancies are shorter or longer than average.

Example S7, automatic fixed percent increases: Joan is covered by Colorado's state plan that promises retirement income equal to 2.5 percent times years of service times average salary in the highest consecutive 36 months within the last 10 years. It is not part of the Social Security system, and its payments are not integrated with Social Security. It promises to increase *postretirement income* by 3.5 percent a year. She has 20 years of service under this plan and an average salary of $80,000 a year. She is 58 years old and expects to retire and begin receiving benefits at age 66. Based on her current average salary and years of service, she will be entitled to $40,000 a year [2.5% • 20 • $80,000]. The present value at age 58 is the value of $40,000 beginning in eight years and increasing by 3.5 percent per year thereafter. If the nominal discount rate is 6.5 percent then the postretirement discount rate, k_2, is 3 percent and the preretirement discount rate, k_1, is 6.5 percent. The k_2 discount rate of 3 percent is the 6.5 percent nominal rate less the 3.5 percent automatic adjustment. Since the $40,000 grows at 3.5 percent a year, we can discount a constant real $40,000 per year by a discount rate that is 3.5 percent below the nominal rate.[7]

We present three estimates of this present value. From the present-value-of-expected-cash-flows model with $k_2 = 0.03$ and $k_1 = 0.065$, the multiples for 55-and 60-year-old females are 6.75 and 9.41, respectively. This model is available for download at www.wiley.com/go/reichenstein, and is described in Appendix 13.1. Based on a weighted-average of these values, the multiple for a 58-year-old female is 8.35. The present value of expected cash flows is thus $334,000 [$40,000 • 8.35].

Alternatively, from Table 13.8, the multiple for a 60-year-old female when k_1 is 6 percent and k_2 is 3 percent is 9.68. Using interpolation, the multiple for a 58-year-old when k_1 is 6.5 percent is about 8.38. The 8.38 is $9.68 - 0.5 • (9.68 - 9.15) - 0.4 • (9.68 - 7.10)$, where the adjustments are 0.5 of the difference between the multiples at $k_1 = 6$ percent and 7 percent at age 60 and 0.4 of the difference between the multiples at ages 55 and 60 with k_1 = 6 percent. The estimated present value is about $335,000.

We can also estimate the present value of cash flows through life expectancy. Assuming normal life expectancy, she is expected to live 26.2 more years and receive benefits for 18.2 years. To find the present value of an ordinary annuity at age 66, insert into a financial calculator n = 18.2, i = 3 percent, PMT = $40,000, FV = 0 and the PV at age 66 is $554,757. Multiplying this amount by 1.0149 $[(1.03)^{0.5}]$ provides the present value at age 66 using the mid-year convention of $563,023. The present value at age 58 of $563,023 to be received at age 66 is about $340,000. Insert n = 8, i = 6.5 percent, PMT = 0, FV = $571,400 and calculate the present value of about $340,000. As usual, the present value of cash flows through life expectancy is a slightly upward-biased estimate of the present value of expected cash flows. However, it is easier to calculate and easier to explain to clients than the present value of expected cash flows, and many financial professionals will view the slight bias to be insignificant.

Example S8, automatic fixed-percent increases: Assume Joan is currently 66 years old and receives $40,000 a year, an amount that will increase by 3.5 percent per year. Her life expectancy at age 66 is 19.3 years. If the nominal discount rate is 6.5 percent, then the postretirement discount rate is 3 percent; that is, k_2 = 0.03. We first estimate the present value of cash flows through life expectancy. Insert into a financial calculator n = 19.3, i = 3 percent, PMT = $40,000, FV = 0 and calculate the PV of $579,665. To adjust this ordinary annuity for the mid-year convention, multiply by $(1.03)^{0.5}$, which moves all payments from the end of the year to mid-year. The present value is about $588,300. Since this is likely a slightly upward-biased forecast of present value of expected cash flows, we reduce this amount by, say, 4 percent and estimate the value of the defined-benefit payments at $565,000.

Alternatively, the present value can be estimated based on a multiple from a table. Table 13.8 best fits this case. For nominal preretirement discount rates of 6 percent and 7 percent (and postretirement discount rate of 3%), the multiples at age 65 are 13.40 and 13.27. By interpolation, the multiple for 6.5 percent is about 13.33. Unfortunately, it is not appropriate to use linear interpolation to estimate multiples between ages 65 through 70. The multiple reaches a maximum in the first year of retirement at age 66 and decreases thereafter. Therefore, linear interpolation is inappropriate. To roughly estimate the multiple at age 66, someone can multiply the age-65 multiple of 13.33 by 1.065 or $(1 + k_1)$. In essence, the multiplication moves each expected cash flow one year closer. This estimated multiple is 14.2, [13.33 • 1.065]. This estimation procedure is not precise, since each year's expected cash flow also depends upon the probability of being alive. The present value is estimated at $568,000, [14.2 • $14,400]. The inability to use linear extrapolation between ages 65 and 70 is another advantage of deriving estimates based on the cash-flows-through-life-expectancy method.

Example S9, COLA increases: Mike is covered by a plan that promises 1.5 percent times years of service times average salary over the highest five years. In addition, it guarantees postretirement payments will increase with inflation as measured by a cost-of-living index. Mike is 60 with 27 years of service and an average salary of $50,000, and expects to retire at age 66. Based on current years of service and average salary, he will receive $20,250 when he retires at age 66 and an equivalent inflation-adjusted or real amount each year thereafter for the rest of his life. At the time of this writing, the nominal yield on a 21.6-year Treasury bond is 5.2 percent, while the TIPS yield on the bond closest to this maturity is 3.2 percent. These correspond to equivalent annual rates of 5.27 percent $[(1.026)^2 - 1]$ and 3.23 percent $[(1.016)^2 - 1]$, respectively. That is, $k_1 = 0.0527$, and $k_2 = 0.0323$. From the model, the multiple at age 60 is 8.83. This present value is about $179,000 [$20,250 • 8.83].

Alternatively, from Table 13.5, shown at the end of the chapter, the multiple for a 60-year-old male when k_1 is 5 percent is 9.15. Using interpolation, the multiple when k_1 is 5.27 percent and k_2 is 3.23 percent is about 8.84. The 8.84 is $9.15 - 0.27 • (9.15 - 8.64) - 0.23 • (9.15 - 8.40)$. The first adjustment is 0.27 of the difference between multiples at 5 percent and 6 percent, while the second is 0.23 of the difference between age-60 multiples at $k_1 = 5$ percent when k_2 is 3 percent (in Table 13.5) and at $k_1 = 5$ percent when k_2 is 4 percent (in Table 13.6). This present value is about $179,000 [$20,250 • 8.84].

The present value of cash flows through life expectancy is slightly higher. His life expectancy is 21.7 years, so he expects to receive benefits for 15.7 years. The present value of an ordinary annuity at age 66 of a constant real $20,250 per year for 15.7 years when discounted at the 3.23 percent TIPS yield is $246,334; insert into a financial calculator $n = 15.7$, $i = 3.23$ percent, PMT = $20,250, FV = 0 and calculate the present value. To reflect the mid-year convention, we multiply this amount by 1.016 and get $250,276. The present value at age 60 of $250,276 to be received six years hence when discounted at 5.27 percent is about $184,000; insert $n = 6$, $i = 5.27$ percent, PMT = 0, FV = $250,276 and calculate the present value.

Example S10, retirement age other than 66: The present-value-of-expected-cash-flows tables assume retirement at age 66. Unfortunately, different tables exist for other retirement ages. We set the assumed retirement age at 66 because it is the Social Security Full Retirement Age for a large portion of baby boomers and because we suspect that 66 will be a representative retirement age going forward.

The tables can be used for people who will retire around age 66. If retirement is at age 65, one year earlier, the multiple can be estimated by adding $1 / (1 + k_1)^{65.5 - n}$, where n is the participant's age today. In essence, the multiple increases by approximately the present value of $1 to be received at age mid-year 65.

If retirement is n-years later (where n is small, say 1), the multiple can be approximated by subtracting $1 / (1 + k_1)^{66.5 - n}$, where n is the participants' age today. In essence, the multiple decreases by approximately the present value of $1 to be received at mid-year 66. These adjustments produce multiples that are only approximately correct. The actual multiples depend upon mortality tables.

Suppose Jack is age 40 and, based on current work experience and salary, he expects a constant annual retirement income of $20,000 per year beginning at age

67 from his DB plan. His Social Security Full Retirement Age is also 67. The $20,000 will not increase in postretirement years. The discount rate is 6 percent. From Table 13.4, the age-40 multiple assuming retirement at age 66 is 2.01. Assuming retirement at age 67, the multiple is about 1.90 [2.10 − 0.21], where 0.21 is the present value of $1 at age 40 to be received at age 66.5. The present value of expected cash flows is about $38,000, [1.90 • $20,000].

The present-value-of-cash-flows-through-expected-life method can easily handle a different retirement age. An average 40-year-old male has a life expectancy of 40.3 years. The present value *at age 67* of $20,000 per year for 13.3 years when discounted at 6 percent is $179,762; the 13.3 years is the expected death at age 80.3 less the retirement age of 67. Multiplying this amount by $(1.06)^{0.5}$ adjusts for the mid-year convention and gives a value at age 67 of $185,076. Discounting this amount at 6 percent for 27 years then gives a present value at age 40 of $38,379. This estimate is near the expected-cash-flows estimate. The cash-flows-through-life-expectancy method has several advantages: (1) It requires only a financial calculator, (2) it accommodates clients with life expectancies that differ from the average, and (3) it accommodates different retirement ages.

Example S11, default risk: Suppose Bret is 60 years old and expects to retire from his job as police chief of the city of Blightsville. Based on current years of service and average salary, he will receive $35,000 when he retires at age 66. For simplicity, assume there are no automatic increases in postretirement income. Blightsville's finances have steadily declined over the last decade. The municipal pension plan is substantially underfunded. In addition, the tax base has declined to the point that the credit agencies consider Blightsville's bonds to be below investment grade—in short, junk bonds. Recall from our previous discussion that public pensions have only two layers of guarantee; PBGC guarantees do not apply.[8] In Blightsville's case, both layers of protection are weak, so adjusting the discount rate for default risk is appropriate.

Suppose Blightsville's senior general obligation bonds are rated BB+ and yield 6 percent. Corporate BB+ bonds yield 9 percent. Since this pension fund is fully backed by the municipality, the relevant rating is that of the municipality's general obligation bonds. Because retirement income is not tax-exempt like municipal bond coupon payments, we use the yield on same-risk corporate bonds. From Table 13.4, the 9 percent multiple is 4.68, which gives a present value of retirement benefits of $163,800. Comparing this value with that obtained with a risk-free rate of, say, 6 percent—$237,650 in this case—demonstrates the sensitivity of the pension's value to the discount rate.

Married Participants Who Select a Joint-life Option

This section covers examples that apply to married participants who name their spouse (or someone else in their generation) in a joint-life payout option. In these options, if a participant retiree dies before his or her spouse, the surviving spouse continues to receive benefits for the rest of his or her life. The surviving spouse may receive 50 percent, 75 percent, or 100 percent of the monthly benefits received before the death of the participant retiree.

Before we present examples that estimate the value of retirement benefits based on joint-life tables, we will first discuss a situation where we believe these tables should not be used. Suppose a wife (with the permission of her husband) names their son as the joint-life beneficiary. The son may have special needs, and both spouses agree to name their son as the joint survivor. The participant retiree—the wife in this example—is willing to accept a much lower monthly retirement income benefit in order to provide an income stream for the life of the son. In such cases, we encourage financial advisors to estimate the present value of the retirement income as if the wife were single and to use this value when considering the retirement preparedness of the husband and wife. The relevant retirement-planning question is, "What is the value of retirement income that can be used to meet the couple's retirement needs?" The fact that the defined-benefit plan will likely make years of payments to the son after the wife dies is irrelevant when assessing this couple's ability to meet their retirement needs.

Example M1, male participant with same-age wife: John and Betty are married and both are age 62. John expects to retire at age 66. His DB plan promises annual payments of 1.75 percent times years of service times average salary over the highest five years. Currently, he has 25 years of service and an average salary of $70,000. The plan is a private plan, which makes no guarantee of postretirement increases in the level of benefits. They plan to select the 50 percent joint-life payout option. It would pay him a constant amount per month and, should he die first, it would pay Betty 50 percent of that amount for the rest of her life. If John were single and selected the simple lifetime income option, he would receive $30,625 a year (or $2,552 a month) for the rest of his life [1.75% • 25 • $70,000]. Because he will select the joint-life option, it will pay $28,800 per year (or $2,400 per month) for the rest of his life and half that amount for the rest of Betty's life.

Table 13.3 illustrates the method of estimating the present value of expected cash flows on this retirement income stream. Assuming normal life prospects, the probabilities that John and Betty will be alive in four years are 0.957891 and 0.967765, respectively. Per dollar of annual retirement income, the expected first-year payment is $1 • 0.957891 + $0.50 • [(1 − 0.957891) • 0.967765]. There is a 0.957891 probability that John will be alive and they will receive $1 and a (1 − 0.957891) • 0.967765 probability that John will not be alive but Betty will be alive and they will receive $0.50. To calculate the present value at age 62 of this expected cash flow to be received at age 66.5 (mid-year of age 66), we discount by k_2 for 0.5 years (back to age 66) and then discount by k_1 for four years (back to age 62).

As their age increases, the expected annual cash flow decreases since the probabilities decrease that John and Betty will still be alive. We calculate the present value of each year's expected payment through age 120—the end of the mortality tables. The multiple is the sum of the present value of each year's expected cash flow from age 66 through age 120. From Table 13.10, shown at the end of the chap-

TABLE 13.3 Calculation of the Multiple for a 62-year-old Male Whose Same-age Wife is a 50 Percent Joint-life Beneficiary: Benefits Begin at Age 66

Age	Probability of Male Being Alive	Probability of Female Being Alive	Expected Payment	Present Value of Expected Payment
66	0.957891	0.967765	$1(0.957891) + $0.50(0.967765)	Exp. Pay. / $[(1 + k_2)^{0.5}(1 + k_1)^4]$
67	0.944089	0.957164	$1(0.944089) + $0.50(0.957164)	Exp. Pay. / $[(1 + k_2)^{1.5}(1 + k_1)^4]$
120	0.0000004	0.000009	$1(0000004) + $0.50(0.000009)	Exp. Pay. / $[(1 + k_2)^{54.5}(1 + k_1)^4]$
				Multiple = 8.73

The multiple is the present value of expected payments, where $1 is the annual payment. The $1 is an annuity received at mid-year. For example, the $1 benefit for someone age 66 is received at age 66.5. The discount interest rates are k_2 from payment date back to the retirement age (age 66 in this example) and k_1 from retirement date back to today (age 62 in this example). When k_1 and k_2 are 6 percent, the multiple is 8.73.

ter, assuming a 6 percent discount rate, this multiple is 8.73. Therefore, the before-tax present value of the DB benefits is about $251,000 [$28,800 • 8.73].

Recall that we could estimate the value of a single-person's DB benefits using either expected cash flows or cash flows through life expectancy. Except when the participant selects 100 percent survivor's benefits, the value of DB benefits cannot be estimated using cash flows through joint-life expectancy. To explain why, assume Betty will receive 50 percent survivor's benefits. Although actuarial tables indicate that their joint-life expectancy is about 27 years, this does not tell us how much they will receive each year. Each year's cash flow depends upon who is alive. While John is alive, they receive $28,800 per year. After his death, Betty receives half that amount if still alive. Consequently, knowledge of their joint-life expectancy does not indicate the amount of cash received each year. The exception is when the payout option pays the survivor 100 percent after the death of the participant. In this case, the payment is the same each year that either is alive and the last payment is expected to occur 27 years hence.

Example M2, male participant with a younger wife: Consider the same situation as above except assume Betty is age 59, three years younger than John. From Table 13.13, at the end of the chapter, the multiple is 8.90, which is slightly higher than before because his wife is three years younger and will likely receive payments for more years. The present value is about $256,000 [$28,800 • 8.90].

Example M3, married female participant: Suppose Betty is the participant, and Betty and John are both age 62. Betty will receive $28,800 per year while alive, and she expects to begin benefits at age 66. John is entitled to 50 percent survivor's benefits.

As before, k_1 and k_2 are 6 percent. From Table 13.16, the multiple is 9.07. This exceeds the multiple of 8.73 when John was the participant because, due to women's longer life prospects, they will likely receive the full $28,800 for a longer period. The estimated value is about $261,000 [$28,800 • 9.07].

Example M4, female participant with an older husband: Suppose Betty is the participant and she is 62, while John is three years older at 65. From Table 13.19, at the end of the chapter, the multiple is 8.94, which is less than the prior multiple of 9.07 due to John being three years older. The present value is about $257,000.

Example M5, interpolation: The tables provide estimates for every three years—age 62, 65, 68, and so on—and for select discount rates. In practice, professionals usually will have to use interpolation. Suppose Mike, the participant, is age 62, and Paula, his wife, is age 60. Mike expects to begin receiving benefits at age 66. Based on the benefits formula and current years of service, Mike will receive $30,000 a year. He will select a payout option that pays him 100 percent through his lifetime and, should he die first, would pay Paula 75 percent of that amount through the rest of her life. The discount rate is 5.3 percent. We present two estimates.

The professional can estimate the multiple by using the model in Appendix 13.1. It is available for download at www.wiley.com/go/reichenstein. Each worksheet contains a text box that explains the model and its use. Inserting a 5.3 percent discount rate, $k_1 = k_2 = 0.053$, into the spreadsheet and surviving spousal benefit of 75 percent, the multiples for a 62-year-old male recipient with a wife, respectively, three years younger and the same age are 10.37 and 10.06. Since Paula is two years younger than Mike, the multiple is estimated with interpolation. It is estimated at 10.27 [10.37 − 0.33 • (10.37 − 10.06)], where we subtract from 10.37 one-third the difference in multiples.

Alternatively, the multiple can be interpolated from the tables. The nearest multiple is 10.08, which is in Table 13.13. It applies to a male age 62 (who expects to begin benefits at age 66) with a wife three years younger when the spouse receives 50 percent of benefits and the discount rate is 5 percent. The interpolation makes the following adjustments: 10.08 − 0.33 • (10.08 − 9.86) − 0.3 • (10.08 − 8.90) + 0.5 • (11.49 − 10.08) = 10.36. We subtracted one-third (or 0.33) of the difference between multiples for male participants age 62 with a wife three years younger and with a wife the same age; 9.86 comes from Table 13.10. We subtracted 0.3 of the difference between the multiples at 5 percent and 6 percent discount rates for a male participant with a wife three years younger; both numbers come from Table 13.13. We added half of the difference between the multiples for 50 percent and 100 percent surviving spousal benefits.

The difference between 10.36 and the better estimate of 10.27 is primarily due to the convexity of a bond's price-yield relationship. In reality, the multiple falls faster than suggested by linear interpolation as the discount rate rises from 5 percent to 6 percent. The multiple rises slower than suggested by linear interpolation as the discount rate falls.

Example M6, automatic fixed-percent increases: Some defined-benefit plans provide automatic increases in postretirement benefits. Suppose, for example, that

Judy, age 59, plans to retire from teaching at age 66, and she will select the joint-life payout option with 100 percent survivor's benefits. Based on her current years of service and average salary, the plan will make initial benefit payments to her or Tom, her husband, of $30,000 a year (or $2,500 a month) for as long as either is alive. Judy and Tom are both age 59. The DB plan calls for postretirement benefits to increase by 3 percent, a year. The nominal discount rate is 6 percent. So, k_1 is 6 percent and k_2 is 3 percent, or 6 percent less the 3 percent automatic annual increase. From Table 13.17, shown at the end of the chapter, the multiple is 10.80, and the before-tax present value of the DB benefits is $324,000.

Since the survivor receives 100 percent of the benefits, we can also estimate the present value of expected cash flows with their joint-life expectancy of about 29.5 years. The present value at age 66 of a $1 regular annuity for 22.5 years—29.5 years less seven years until retirement—when discounted at 3 percent is $16.19. Multiplying by $(1.03)^{0.5}$ moves all payments to mid-year and raises the value to $16.43. The present value at age 59 of $16.43 to be received in seven years when discounted at 6 percent is $10.93. The multiple is 10.93. The before-tax present value of DB benefits is about $328,000.

Example M7, automatic fixed-percent increases: Return to the previous example but assume postretirement income increased at 3.5 percent a year, so k_2 is 2.5 percent. The value of DB benefits could be estimated three ways. First, from the model, the multiple is 11.39 when k_1 is 6 percent, k_2 is 2.5 percent, and spousal benefits are 100 percent. The present value is thus about $342,000. Second, the multiple can be estimated by extrapolation. From Tables 13.18 and 13.17 (when k_1 is 6 percent and survivor's benefits are 100 percent), the multiples when k_2 is 3 percent and 4 percent are, respectively, 10.80 and 9.76. From extrapolation, the multiple for k_2 of 2.5 percent is about 11.32 [$10.80 + 0.5 \cdot (10.80 - 9.76)$]. The present value is about $340,000. Finally, since the spousal benefits are 100 percent, the value can be estimated based on cash flows through life expectancy. To calculate the multiple for their 29.5-year life expectancy, we first calculate the present value at age 66 as the value of a $1 regular annuity for 22.5 years when discounted at 2.5 percent. It is $17.05. Multiplying by $(1.025)^{0.5}$ to adjust payments to mid-year produces a value of $17.26. The present value at age 59 of $17.26 when discounted at 6 percent for seven years is $11.48. This before-tax value is about $344,000.

Example M8, retiring earlier: Continue with Example 7 except assume Judy plans to retire at age 64. The multiple rises if she retires earlier because it is based on her current average salary and current years of service. We developed models that assume she will retire at age 62 and age 66. The multiple assuming she retires at age 64 can be estimated using linear interpolation based on the multiples assuming retirement at ages 62 and 66. From the model with k_1 of 6 percent and k_2 of 2.5 percent, the multiples are 16.22 and 11.39, respectively. The multiple assuming she retires at age 64 is thus about 13.81, and the present value is estimated at about $414,000.

Example M9, COLA increases: Assume Russell is 62 and Sandy, his wife, is 59. Russell expects to retire at age 66. The initial annual benefit formula is 1.5 percent times years of service times average salary during the highest consecutive five years. In addition, this state plan promises to increase postretirement benefits with inflation as measured by a Consumer Price Index. Currently, he has 20 years of service and an average salary of $40,000. He expects to select a joint-life payout option that, should he die first, would pay Sandy 75 percent of the level of retirement income he would receive if he was still alive. The initial level of benefits based on current years of service and average salary is $11,700.

The professional advisor goes to the Treasury securities section of the *Wall Street Journal* to determine appropriate discount rates on this secure plan. Since Sandy has a life expectancy of about 25 years, the advisor looks up the yield on a 25-year Treasury bond. It is 5.43 percent. Adjusting for the semi-annual compounding, the effective annual yield is about 5.5 percent $[(1.02715)^2 - 1]$, where 5.43% / 2 is 0.02715. The postretirement discount rate, k_2, is based on the current 25-year TIPS yield of 3.17 percent. Adjusting for semi-annual bond convention, this translates into an annual yield of 3.2 percent, $[(1.01585)^2 - 1]$. Inserting k_1 of 0.055, k_2 of 0.032, and spousal percent of 0.75 into the model for a male participant with a spouse three years younger produces a multiple of 12.65. The before-tax present value of retirement income is about $148,000 [$11,700 • 12.65].

Alternatively, the multiple can be estimated by interpolation from Tables 13.14 and 13.15. From Table 13.14, the multiple for k_1 of 5 percent and k_2 of 3 percent and spousal benefits of 50 percent is 12.19. The estimated multiple is 12.71 [12.19 − 0.5 • (12.19 − 11.73) + 0.5 • (14.14 − 12.19) − 0.2 • (12.19 − 11.05)]. The first adjustment is 0.5 of the difference between multiples at k_1 of 5 percent and 6 percent (in Table 13.14). The second is 0.5 of the difference between multiples at 50 percent and 100 percent spousal benefits in Table 13.14. The third is 0.2 of the difference between the multiples at k_1 of 5 percent and k_2 of, respectively, 3 percent in Table 13.14 and 4 percent in Table 13.15. The value of retirement income is about $149,000.

Conversion to After-tax Values

So far, we have presented two models that estimate the before-tax present value of income from defined-benefit plans. As discussed in Chapter 10, we recommend that the family portfolio be expanded to include the after-tax present value of income from Social Security and defined-benefit plans, including military retirement. To convert a before-tax value to an after-tax value, we multiply the before-tax value by $(1 - t_n)$, where t_n is the combined federal-plus-state marginal tax rate on pension income during retirement.

Retirement Income Streams as Contingent Assets

Defined-benefit plans provide a contingent income stream. The income is contingent upon someone living (or, if married, at least one member of the couple living). Suppose Luke is single, age 62 and has a 20-year life expectancy. He receives a retirement income of $1,667 a month or $20,000 a year from a defined-benefit plan. Payments cease at his death. This is different from a *guaranteed* $20,000 a year for 20 years.

Suppose Luke has a daughter who needs special care. As discussed in Chapter 10, to ensure his daughter's financial needs he may wish to guarantee the *after-tax* value of the defined-benefit plan by buying life insurance. This effectively converts the *contingent* after-tax value of the defined-benefit plan—contingent upon him living at least 20 years—into a *guaranteed* after-tax value. Through the years, he can reduce the size of the death benefit as the amount of his daughter's needs decreases. With the exception of this important caveat, we contend that Luke should view the defined-benefit plan as a bond in his portfolio.

Summary

The goal of this chapter has been to help a financial professional estimate the present value of retirement income in defined-benefit (DB) plans. We began with a discussion of several topics that can affect retirement income in DB plans. They include retirement-income formulas, integration of defined-benefit payments with Social Security payments, and automatic and discretionary increases in postretirement benefits.

In practice, we can usually obtain a reasonable estimate of the present value of a DB plan with three key estimates. For someone who has yet to retire, the first estimate is the level of retirement benefits (based on current years of service and current salary) during the first year of retirement. For a current retiree, the corresponding amount is the current level of retirement benefits, which is known. The second key estimate is the growth rate in the level of postretirement benefits. The defined-benefit plan specifies if there is any automatic increase in postretirement benefits and, if so, whether those increases are at a fixed percent, based on inflation, or on some other formula. The third key estimate is the discount rates that are used to reduce future benefits to their present value. In most plans, future benefits are essentially default risk-free. Therefore, discount rates can be estimated based on current Treasury yield, with adjustments if the level of postretirement benefits increases automatically.

This chapter discussed issues associated with the three key estimates. In addition, it distinguished between two estimation methods: one based on present value of expected cash flows and the other on present value of cash flows through life expectancy. For singles and couples that select 100 percent spousal benefits, the method based on cash flows through life expectancy has important advantages, including ease of calculation, ease of explaining the method to clients, and the abilities to accommodate nonstandard life expectancies and different retirement ages. This chapter also presents numerous examples that cover most issues that may arise when estimating the value of a defined-benefit plan.

Finally, we acknowledge that it is impossible to cover all possible complications that can arise when valuing DB benefits. Since the profession currently ignores the value of the DB plan when calculating a family's asset allocation, it places an implicit value of zero on these benefits. The good news is that, even if it is impossible to obtain a precise estimate of the DB plan's value, it is easy to improve upon the profession's implicit valuation of zero.

TABLE 13.4   Multiples for Single Males: No Automatic Increase in
Postretirement Income

Age	4%	5%	6%	7%	9%	Expected Life	Bias at 6%
35	3.15	2.16	1.49	1.04	0.51	45.1	5.7%
40	3.85	2.77	2.01	1.46	0.79	40.3	6.2
45	4.72	3.56	2.70	2.07	1.23	35.5	6.5
50	5.79	4.58	3.65	2.92	1.90	30.8	6.9
55	7.14	5.93	4.95	4.16	2.97	26.2	7.3
60	8.90	7.75	6.79	5.97	4.68	21.7	6.9
65	11.32	10.34	9.50	8.75	7.53	17.6	5.7
70	10.41	9.70	9.07	8.51	7.56	13.9	5.0
75	8.51	8.02	7.59	7.19	6.51	10.6	4.2
80	6.70	6.39	6.11	5.85	5.39	7.8	2.6
85	5.10	4.92	4.75	4.59	4.30	5.5	−0.9
90	3.85	3.74	3.64	3.54	3.37	3.9	−4.2

Assumptions: Retirement at age 66, preretirement and postretirement discount rate are the same.
The multiples are for discount rates of 5 percent to 9 percent.
*Source: **Defined Benefits Singles/Male** with $k_1 = k_2$.*

TABLE 13.5   Multiples for Single Males: Postretirement Discount Rate at 3%

Age	4%	5%	6%	7%	9%	Expected Life	Bias at 6%
35	3.43	2.55	1.90	1.42	0.80	45.1	−0.5%
40	4.20	3.27	2.56	2.00	1.24	40.3	0.2
45	5.14	4.20	3.44	2.83	1.92	35.5	0.7
50	6.31	5.41	4.65	4.00	2.98	30.8	1.5
55	7.78	7.00	6.31	5.69	4.64	26.2	2.3
60	9.69	9.15	8.64	8.17	7.31	21.7	2.5
65	12.33	12.21	12.09	11.98	11.76	17.6	2.3
70	11.21	11.21	11.21	11.21	11.21	13.9	1.7
75	9.04	9.04	9.04	9.04	9.04	10.6	0.6
80	7.03	7.03	7.03	7.03	7.03	7.8	−1.0
85	5.30	5.30	5.30	5.30	5.30	5.5	−4.2
90	3.96	3.96	3.96	3.96	3.96	3.9	−7.1

Assumptions: Retirement at age 66, postretirement discount rate at 3 percent. The multiples are
for preretirement discount rates of 5 percent to 9 percent.
*Source: **Defined Benefits Singles/Male** with $k_2 = 3$ percent.*

TABLE 13.6   Multiples for Single Males: Postretirement Discount Rate at 4%

Age	4%	5%	6%	7%	9%	Expected Life	Bias at 6%
35	3.15	2.34	1.75	1.31	0.74	45.1	1.8%
40	3.85	3.01	2.35	1.84	1.14	40.3	2.4
45	4.72	3.86	3.16	2.60	1.76	35.5	2.8
50	5.79	4.97	4.27	3.67	2.73	30.8	3.5
55	7.14	6.43	5.79	5.22	4.26	26.2	4.2
60	8.90	8.40	7.94	7.50	6.71	21.7	4.1
65	11.32	11.21	11.10	11.00	10.80	17.6	3.6
70	10.41	10.41	10.41	10.41	10.41	13.9	3.0
75	8.51	8.51	8.51	8.51	8.51	10.6	2.0
80	6.70	6.70	6.70	6.70	6.70	7.8	0.3
85	5.10	5.10	5.10	5.10	5.10	5.5	−3.1
90	3.85	3.85	3.85	3.85	3.85	3.9	−6.1

Assumptions: Retirement at age 66, postretirement discount rate at 4 percent. The multiples are for preretirement discount rates of 5 percent to 9 percent.
*Source: **Defined Benefits Singles/Male** with k_2 = 4 percent.*

TABLE 13.7   Multiples for Single Females: No Automatic Increase in Postretirement Income

Age	4%	5%	6%	7%	9%	Expected Life	Bias at 6%
35	3.55	2.42	1.66	1.14	0.56	48.1	7.3%
40	4.33	3.09	2.22	1.61	0.86	43.2	7.4
45	5.29	3.96	2.99	2.27	1.33	38.4	7.6
50	6.48	5.09	4.03	3.20	2.06	33.6	7.6
55	7.97	6.56	5.44	4.54	3.21	28.9	7.6
60	9.87	8.53	7.41	6.48	5.02	24.4	7.3
65	12.42	11.26	10.26	9.40	7.99	20.1	5.9
70	11.59	10.71	9.94	9.26	8.13	16.2	5.5
75	9.75	9.12	8.55	8.05	7.19	12.7	4.9
80	7.93	7.50	7.12	6.77	6.15	9.7	4.1
85	6.22	5.95	5.70	5.47	5.06	7.1	2.0
90	4.82	4.65	4.49	4.34	4.07	5.2	−0.1

Assumptions: Retirement at age 66, preretirement and postretirement discount rates are the same. The multiples are for preretirement discount rates of 5 percent to 9 percent.
*Source: **Defined Benefits Singles/Female** with $k_1 = k_2$.*

TABLE 13.8   Multiples for Single Females: Postretirement Discount Rate at 3%

Age	4%	5%	6%	7%	9%	Expected Life	Bias at 6%
35	3.90	2.90	2.16	1.62	0.91	48.1	1.9%
40	4.76	3.71	2.90	2.27	1.40	43.2	2.1
45	5.82	4.76	3.90	3.20	2.17	38.4	2.6
50	7.13	6.12	5.25	4.52	3.36	33.6	2.8
55	8.76	7.89	7.10	6.41	5.23	28.9	3.1
60	10.85	10.24	9.68	9.15	8.18	24.4	3.4
65	13.65	13.52	13.40	13.27	13.03	20.1	2.8
70	12.60	12.60	12.60	12.60	12.60	16.2	2.2
75	10.46	10.46	10.46	10.46	10.46	12.7	1.2
80	8.40	8.40	8.40	8.40	8.40	9.7	0.4
85	6.52	6.52	6.52	6.52	6.52	7.1	−1.7
90	5.00	5.00	5.00	5.00	5.00	5.2	−3.7

Assumptions: Retirement at age 66, postretirement discount rate at 3 percent. The multiples are for preretirement discount rates of 5 percent to 9 percent.
Source: **Defined Benefits Singles/Female** with k_2 = 3 percent.

TABLE 13.9   Multiples for Single Females: Postretirement Discount Rate at 4%

Age	4%	5%	6%	7%	9%	Expected Life	Bias at 6%
35	3.55	2.64	1.97	1.47	0.83	48.1	4.0%
40	4.33	3.38	2.64	2.07	1.28	43.2	4.1
45	5.29	4.33	3.55	2.91	1.97	38.4	4.5
50	6.48	5.56	4.78	4.11	3.06	33.6	4.7
55	7.97	7.17	6.46	5.83	4.75	28.9	4.8
60	9.87	9.32	8.80	8.32	7.45	24.4	4.9
65	12.42	12.30	12.19	12.07	11.85	20.1	4.0
70	11.59	11.59	11.59	11.59	11.59	16.2	3.5
75	9.75	9.75	9.75	9.75	9.75	12.7	2.6
80	7.93	7.93	7.93	7.93	7.93	9.7	1.7
85	6.22	6.22	6.22	6.22	6.22	7.1	−0.4
90	4.82	4.82	4.82	4.82	4.82	5.2	−2.4

Assumptions: Retirement at age 66, postretirement discount rate at 4 percent. The multiples are for preretirement discount rates of 5 percent to 9 percent.
Source: **Defined Benefits Singles/Female** with k_2 = 4 percent.

TABLE 13.10 Joint-survivor Multiples for Married Males with Wife the Same Age: No Automatic Increase in Postretirement Income

Age	4%		5%		6%		7%		9%		Expected Life
	50%	100%	50%	100%	50%	100%	50%	100%	50%	100%	
38	4.18	4.81	2.93	3.35	2.07	2.35	1.47	1.66	0.76	0.85	50.0
41	4.72	5.42	3.40	3.88	2.47	2.80	1.80	2.04	0.98	1.10	47.0
44	5.32	6.10	3.94	4.50	2.94	3.34	2.21	2.50	1.28	1.43	44.0
47	6.00	6.88	4.58	5.22	3.52	3.99	2.72	3.07	1.66	1.85	41.1
50	6.77	7.75	5.32	6.05	4.20	4.76	3.34	3.76	2.15	2.40	38.1
53	7.65	8.74	6.18	7.02	5.03	5.68	4.11	4.62	2.80	3.11	35.2
56	8.66	9.87	7.20	8.15	6.02	6.78	5.07	5.68	3.65	4.05	32.3
59	9.83	11.15	8.41	9.48	7.24	8.11	6.26	6.98	4.76	5.26	29.4
62	11.19	12.63	9.86	11.05	8.73	9.72	7.77	8.61	6.24	6.85	26.6
65	12.83	14.33	11.62	12.90	10.59	11.68	9.69	10.63	8.23	8.93	23.9
68	12.95	14.52	11.97	13.32	11.11	12.29	10.35	11.39	9.10	9.91	21.2
71	11.79	13.36	10.98	12.36	10.26	11.48	9.62	10.70	8.55	9.42	18.7
74	10.61	12.16	9.95	11.33	9.36	10.60	8.84	9.95	7.94	8.85	16.3
77	9.42	10.93	8.90	10.26	8.44	9.67	8.01	9.14	7.28	8.23	14.0
80	8.26	9.69	7.86	9.17	7.50	8.70	7.16	8.27	6.58	7.53	11.9
83	7.15	8.47	6.85	8.08	6.57	7.72	6.32	7.38	5.87	6.80	10.0
86	6.13	7.33	5.90	7.04	5.70	6.76	5.51	6.51	5.17	6.06	8.3
89	5.23	6.32	5.07	6.10	4.92	5.90	4.78	5.70	4.52	5.36	6.9

*The 50% and 100% denote the levels of benefits received by the surviving spouse after the death of the participant retiree.

Assumptions: Retirement at age 66, preretirement and postretirement discount rates are the same.

*Source: **Defined Benefits Couples/MF Same Age** with $k_1 = k_2$.*

TABLE 13.11   Joint-survivor Multiples for Married Males with a Wife the Same Age: Postretirement Discount Rate at 3 percent

| | 4% | | 5% | | 6% | | 7% | | 9% | | Expected |
Age	50%	100%	50%	100%	50%	100%	50%	100%	50%	100%	Life
38	4.60	5.32	3.52	4.07	2.70	3.12	2.07	2.40	1.23	1.43	50.0
41	5.18	5.99	4.08	4.72	3.22	3.72	2.55	2.94	1.60	1.85	47.0
44	5.84	6.75	4.73	5.47	3.84	4.44	3.13	3.61	2.08	2.40	44.0
47	6.59	7.61	5.49	6.34	4.59	5.30	3.84	4.43	2.70	3.12	41.1
50	7.44	8.57	6.38	7.36	5.49	6.32	4.72	5.44	3.51	4.04	38.1
53	8.41	9.67	7.42	8.54	6.56	7.55	5.81	6.68	4.57	5.25	35.2
56	9.52	10.92	8.65	9.92	7.87	9.02	7.16	8.21	5.95	6.82	32.3
59	10.80	12.34	10.10	11.54	9.45	10.80	8.85	10.11	7.77	8.88	29.4
62	12.30	13.98	11.84	13.45	11.40	12.95	10.98	12.47	10.20	11.58	26.6
65	14.10	15.87	13.97	15.72	13.83	15.57	13.71	15.43	13.45	15.15	23.9
68	14.09	15.91	14.09	15.91	14.09	15.91	14.09	15.91	14.09	15.91	21.2
71	12.72	14.52	12.72	14.52	12.72	14.52	12.72	14.52	12.72	14.52	18.7
74	11.35	13.09	11.35	13.09	11.35	13.09	11.35	13.09	11.35	13.09	16.3
77	10.00	11.67	10.00	11.67	10.00	11.67	10.00	11.67	10.00	11.67	14.0
80	8.70	10.26	8.70	10.26	8.70	10.26	8.70	10.26	8.70	10.26	11.9
83	7.47	8.91	7.47	8.91	7.47	8.91	7.47	8.91	7.47	8.91	10.0
86	6.36	7.66	6.36	7.66	6.36	7.66	6.36	7.66	6.36	7.66	8.3
89	5.41	6.56	5.41	6.56	5.41	6.56	5.41	6.56	5.41	6.56	6.9

*The 50% and 100% denote the levels of benefits received by the surviving spouse after the death of the participant retiree.
Assumptions: Retirement at age 66, postretirement discount rate at 3 percent.
Source: Defined Benefits Couples/MF Same Age with $k_2 = 3$ percent.

TABLE 13.12   Joint-survivor Multiples for Married Males with a Wife the Same Age: Postretirement Discount Rate at 4 percent

Age	4%		5%		6%		7%		9%		Expected Life
	50%	100%	50%	100%	50%	100%	50%	100%	50%	100%	
38	4.18	4.81	3.20	3.68	2.45	2.82	1.89	2.17	1.12	1.29	50.0
41	4.72	5.42	3.71	4.27	2.93	3.37	2.32	2.66	1.46	1.68	47.0
44	5.32	6.10	4.31	4.94	3.50	4.01	2.84	3.26	1.89	2.17	44.0
47	6.00	6.88	5.00	5.73	4.18	4.79	3.49	4.01	2.46	2.82	41.1
50	6.77	7.75	5.81	6.65	4.99	5.71	4.30	4.92	3.19	3.66	38.1
53	7.65	8.74	6.76	7.72	5.97	6.82	5.29	6.04	4.16	4.75	35.2
56	8.66	9.87	7.87	8.97	7.16	8.15	6.52	7.42	5.41	6.17	32.3
59	9.83	11.15	9.19	10.43	8.60	9.76	8.05	9.14	7.07	8.03	29.4
62	11.19	12.63	10.77	12.15	10.37	11.70	9.99	11.27	9.28	10.46	26.6
65	12.83	14.33	12.70	14.20	12.58	14.06	12.47	13.93	12.24	13.68	23.9
68	12.95	14.52	12.95	14.52	12.95	14.52	12.95	14.52	12.95	14.52	21.2
71	11.79	13.36	11.79	13.36	11.79	13.36	11.79	13.36	11.79	13.36	18.7
74	10.61	12.16	10.61	12.16	10.61	12.16	10.61	12.16	10.61	12.16	16.3
77	9.42	10.93	9.42	10.93	9.42	10.93	9.42	10.93	9.42	10.93	14.0
80	8.26	9.69	8.26	9.69	8.26	9.69	8.26	9.69	8.26	9.69	11.9
83	7.15	8.47	7.15	8.47	7.15	8.47	7.15	8.47	7.15	8.47	10.0
86	6.13	7.33	6.13	7.33	6.13	7.33	6.13	7.33	6.13	7.33	8.3
89	5.23	6.32	5.23	6.32	5.23	6.32	5.23	6.32	5.23	6.32	6.9

*The 50% and 100% denote the levels of benefits received by the surviving spouse after the death of the participant retiree.

Assumptions: Retirement at age 66, postretirement discount rate at 4 percent.

*Source: **Defined Benefits Couples/MF Same Age** with k_2 = 4 percent.

TABLE 13.13   Joint-survivor Multiples for Married Males with a Wife Three Years Younger: No Automatic Increase in Postretirement Income

Males' Age	4% 50%	4% 100%	5% 50%	5% 100%	6% 50%	6% 100%	7% 50%	7% 100%	9% 50%	9% 100%	Expected Life
38	4.31	5.06	3.01	3.50	2.11	2.44	1.50	1.72	0.77	0.87	51.8
41	4.85	5.69	3.48	4.05	2.52	2.91	1.84	2.11	1.00	1.13	48.8
44	5.47	6.41	4.04	4.70	3.01	3.47	2.26	2.59	1.30	1.47	45.9
47	6.17	7.22	4.69	5.45	3.60	4.41	2.77	3.17	1.68	1.90	42.9
50	6.96	8.13	5.45	6.31	4.30	4.94	3.41	3.89	2.19	2.47	40.0
53	7.86	9.17	6.34	7.32	5.14	5.90	4.19	4.78	2.84	3.20	37.0
56	8.90	10.34	7.37	8.50	6.15	7.04	5.17	5.87	3.70	4.15	34.1
59	10.09	11.67	8.61	9.87	7.39	8.41	6.38	7.21	4.83	5.40	31.2
62	11.48	13.20	10.08	11.49	8.90	10.06	7.90	8.87	6.33	7.02	28.4
65	13.66	15.55	12.46	14.05	11.43	12.79	10.53	11.70	9.08	9.96	25.6
68	13.03	14.89	11.94	13.53	11.00	12.36	10.18	11.36	8.84	9.73	22.9
71	11.91	13.80	11.00	12.63	10.20	11.62	9.50	10.75	8.33	9.30	20.3
74	10.76	12.64	10.01	11.67	9.35	10.81	8.76	10.06	7.77	8.80	17.8
77	9.61	11.46	9.01	10.66	8.47	9.95	7.98	9.31	7.15	8.24	15.4
80	8.48	10.25	8.00	9.61	7.57	9.03	7.18	8.51	6.51	7.62	13.2
83	7.38	9.06	7.01	8.55	6.68	8.09	6.37	7.67	5.84	6.95	11.2
86	6.36	7.90	6.08	7.51	5.83	7.15	5.59	6.82	5.17	6.25	9.4
89	5.44	6.82	5.24	6.53	5.04	6.25	4.86	6.00	4.54	5.55	7.8

*The 50% and 100% denote the levels of benefits received by the surviving spouse after the death of the participant retiree.
Assumptions: Retirement at age 66, preretirement and postretirement discount rates are the same.
Source: Defined Benefits Couples/Female 3 Years Younger with $k_1 = k_2$.

TABLE 13.14   Joint-survivor Multiples for Married Males with a Wife Three Years Younger: Postretirement Discount Rate at 3 percent

Males' Age	4% 50%	4% 100%	5% 50%	5% 100%	6% 50%	6% 100%	7% 50%	7% 100%	9% 50%	9% 100%	Expected Life
38	4.75	5.62	3.63	4.30	2.79	3.30	2.14	2.54	1.28	1.51	51.8
41	5.35	6.33	4.21	4.98	3.32	3.93	2.63	3.11	1.65	1.96	48.8
44	6.03	7.13	4.89	5.78	3.97	4.69	3.23	3.81	2.15	2.54	45.9
47	6.80	8.03	5.67	6.70	4.74	5.59	3.96	4.68	2.79	3.29	42.9
50	7.68	9.05	6.59	7.77	5.66	6.67	4.87	5.74	3.62	4.27	40.0
53	8.67	10.20	7.66	9.01	6.77	7.96	5.99	7.05	4.71	5.54	37.0
56	9.81	11.51	8.92	10.46	8.11	9.51	7.38	8.66	6.14	7.20	34.1
59	11.13	12.99	10.41	12.15	9.74	11.37	9.12	10.65	8.01	9.35	31.2
62	12.66	14.69	12.19	14.14	11.73	13.62	11.30	13.11	10.49	12.18	28.4
65	15.07	17.32	15.07	17.32	15.07	17.32	15.07	17.32	15.07	17.32	25.6

TABLE 13.14 (*Continued*)

Males' Age	4%		5%		6%		7%		9%		Expected Life
	50%	100%	50%	100%	50%	100%	50%	100%	50%	100%	
68	14.30	16.50	14.30	16.50	14.30	16.50	14.30	16.50	14.30	16.50	22.9
71	12.96	15.15	12.96	15.15	12.96	15.15	12.96	15.15	12.96	15.15	20.3
74	11.61	13.76	11.61	13.76	11.61	13.76	11.61	13.76	11.61	13.76	17.8
77	10.29	12.37	10.29	12.37	10.29	12.37	10.29	12.37	10.29	12.37	15.4
80	9.01	10.98	9.01	10.98	9.01	10.98	9.01	10.98	9.01	10.98	13.2
83	7.78	9.62	7.78	9.62	7.78	9.62	7.78	9.62	7.78	9.62	11.2
86	6.66	8.33	6.66	8.33	6.66	8.33	6.66	8.33	6.66	8.33	9.4
89	5.67	7.15	5.67	7.15	5.67	7.15	5.67	7.15	5.67	7.15	7.8

*The 50% and 100% denote the levels of benefits received by the surviving spouse after the death of the participant retiree.
Assumptions: Retirement at age 66, postretirement discount rate at 3 percent.
Source: Defined Benefits Couples/Female 3 Years Younger with k_2 = 3 percent.

TABLE 13.15 Joint-survivor Multiples for Married Males with a Wife Three Years Younger: Postretirement Discount Rate at 4 percent

Males' Age	4%		5%		6%		7%		9%		Expected Life
	50%	100%	50%	100%	50%	100%	50%	100%	50%	100%	
38	4.31	5.06	3.29	3.87	2.53	2.97	1.94	2.28	1.16	1.36	51.8
41	4.85	5.69	3.82	4.48	3.01	3.54	2.38	2.80	1.50	1.76	48.8
44	5.47	6.41	4.43	5.19	3.60	4.21	2.93	3.43	1.95	2.28	45.9
47	6.17	7.22	5.14	6.02	4.30	5.03	3.59	4.21	2.53	2.96	42.9
50	6.96	8.13	5.97	6.98	5.13	6.00	4.42	5.16	3.28	3.84	40.0
53	7.86	9.17	6.94	8.10	6.14	7.16	5.43	6.33	4.27	4.98	37.0
56	8.90	10.34	8.08	9.40	7.35	8.55	6.69	7.78	5.56	6.47	34.1
59	10.09	11.67	9.43	10.92	8.83	10.22	8.27	9.57	7.26	8.40	31.2
62	11.48	13.20	11.05	12.70	10.64	12.23	10.25	11.78	9.51	10.94	28.4
65	13.66	15.55	13.66	15.55	13.66	15.55	13.66	15.55	13.66	15.55	25.6
68	13.03	14.89	13.03	14.89	13.03	14.89	13.03	14.89	13.03	14.89	22.9
71	11.91	13.80	11.91	13.80	11.91	13.80	11.91	13.80	11.91	13.80	20.3
74	10.76	12.64	10.76	12.64	10.76	12.64	10.76	12.64	10.76	12.64	17.8
77	9.61	11.46	9.61	11.46	9.61	11.46	9.61	11.46	9.61	11.46	15.4
80	8.48	10.25	8.48	10.25	8.48	10.25	8.48	10.25	8.48	10.25	13.2
83	7.38	9.06	7.38	9.06	7.38	9.06	7.38	9.06	7.38	9.06	11.2
86	6.36	7.90	6.36	7.90	6.36	7.90	6.36	7.90	6.36	7.90	9.4
89	5.44	6.82	5.44	6.82	5.44	6.82	5.44	6.82	5.44	6.82	7.8

*The 50% and 100% denote the levels of benefits received by the surviving spouse after the death of the participant retiree.
Assumptions: Retirement at age 66, postretirement discount rate at 4 percent.
Source: Defined Benefits Couples/Female 3 Years Younger with k_2 = 4 percent.

TABLE 13.16   Joint-survivor Multiples for Married Females with a Husband the Same Age: No Automatic Increase in Postretirement Income

	4%		5%		6%		7%		9%		Expected
Age	50%	100%	50%	100%	50%	100%	50%	100%	50%	100%	Life
38	4.41	4.81	3.08	3.35	2.16	2.35	1.53	1.66	0.79	0.85	50.0
41	4.96	5.42	3.56	3.88	2.58	2.80	1.88	2.04	1.02	1.10	47.0
44	5.59	6.10	4.13	4.50	3.08	3.34	2.31	2.50	1.32	1.43	44.0
47	6.31	6.88	4.80	5.22	3.68	3.99	2.83	3.07	1.72	1.85	41.1
50	7.12	7.75	5.57	6.05	4.39	4.76	3.48	3.76	2.23	2.40	38.1
53	8.04	8.74	6.47	7.02	5.25	5.68	4.28	4.62	2.90	3.11	35.2
56	9.09	9.87	7.53	8.15	6.28	6.78	5.27	5.68	3.77	4.05	32.3
59	10.30	11.15	8.78	9.48	7.54	8.11	6.51	6.98	4.92	5.26	29.4
62	11.71	12.63	10.28	11.05	9.07	9.72	8.05	8.61	6.44	6.85	26.6
65	13.38	14.33	12.08	12.90	10.97	11.68	10.01	10.63	8.46	8.93	23.9
68	13.54	14.52	12.47	13.32	11.53	12.29	10.72	11.39	9.38	9.91	21.2
71	12.40	13.36	11.50	12.36	10.72	11.48	10.02	10.70	8.86	9.42	18.7
74	11.24	12.16	10.50	11.33	9.85	10.60	9.27	9.95	8.28	8.85	16.3
77	10.06	10.93	9.47	10.26	8.95	9.67	8.47	9.14	7.66	8.23	14.0
80	8.89	9.69	8.43	9.17	8.01	8.70	7.64	8.27	6.98	7.53	11.9
83	7.75	8.47	7.40	8.08	7.08	7.72	6.79	7.38	6.27	6.80	10.0
86	6.68	7.33	6.42	7.04	6.18	6.76	5.96	6.51	5.56	6.06	8.3
89	5.74	6.32	5.55	6.10	5.37	5.90	5.20	5.70	4.90	5.36	6.9

*The 50% and 100% denote the levels of benefits received by the surviving spouse after the death of the participant retiree.
Assumptions: Retirement at age 66, preretirement and postretirement discount rates are the same.
*Source: **Defined Benefits Couples/FM Same Age** with $k_1 = k_2$.*

TABLE 13.17   Joint-survivor Multiples for Married Females with a Husband the Same Age: Postretirement Discount Rate at 3 percent

	4%		5%		6%		7%		9%		Expected
Age	50%	100%	50%	100%	50%	100%	50%	100%	50%	100%	Life
38	4.86	5.32	3.72	4.07	2.85	3.12	2.19	2.40	1.31	1.43	50.0
41	5.47	5.99	4.31	4.72	3.40	3.72	2.69	2.94	1.69	1.85	47.0
44	6.17	6.75	5.00	5.47	4.06	4.44	3.30	3.61	2.20	2.40	44.0
47	6.96	7.61	5.80	6.34	4.84	5.30	4.05	4.43	2.85	3.12	41.1
50	7.85	8.57	6.74	7.36	5.79	6.32	4.98	5.44	3.70	4.04	38.1
53	8.87	9.67	7.83	8.54	6.92	7.55	6.13	6.68	4.82	5.25	35.2
56	10.03	10.92	9.11	9.92	8.29	9.02	7.54	8.21	6.27	6.82	32.3
59	11.36	12.34	10.63	11.54	9.94	10.80	9.31	10.11	8.18	8.88	29.4
62	12.92	13.98	12.43	13.45	11.97	12.95	11.53	12.47	10.71	11.58	26.6
65	14.76	15.87	14.62	15.72	14.49	15.57	14.35	15.43	14.09	15.15	23.9

TABLE 13.17   (Continued)

Age	4% 50%	4% 100%	5% 50%	5% 100%	6% 50%	6% 100%	7% 50%	7% 100%	9% 50%	9% 100%	Expected Life
68	14.79	15.91	14.79	15.91	14.79	15.91	14.79	15.91	14.79	15.91	21.2
71	13.43	14.52	13.43	14.52	13.43	14.52	13.43	14.52	13.43	14.52	18.7
74	12.07	13.09	12.07	13.09	12.07	13.09	12.07	13.09	12.07	13.09	16.3
77	10.72	11.67	10.72	11.67	10.72	11.67	10.72	11.67	10.72	11.67	14.0
80	9.40	10.26	9.40	10.26	9.40	10.26	9.40	10.26	9.40	10.26	11.9
83	8.13	8.91	8.13	8.91	8.13	8.91	8.13	8.91	8.13	8.91	10.0
86	6.96	7.66	6.96	7.66	6.96	7.66	6.96	7.66	6.96	7.66	8.3
89	5.95	6.56	5.95	6.56	5.95	6.56	5.95	6.56	5.95	6.56	6.9

*The 50% and 100% denote the levels of benefits received by the surviving spouse after the death of the participant retiree.
Assumptions: Retirement at age 66, postretirement discount rate at 3 percent.
*Source: **Defined Benefits Couples/FM Same Age** with k_2 = 3 percent.*

TABLE 13.18   Joint-survivor Multiples for Married Females with a Husband the Same Age: Postretirement Discount Rate at 4 percent

Age	4% 50%	4% 100%	5% 50%	5% 100%	6% 50%	6% 100%	7% 50%	7% 100%	9% 50%	9% 100%	Expected Life
38	4.41	4.81	3.37	3.68	2.59	2.82	1.99	2.17	1.18	1.29	50.0
41	4.96	5.42	3.91	4.27	3.08	3.37	2.44	2.66	1.53	1.68	47.0
44	5.59	6.10	4.53	4.94	3.68	4.01	2.99	3.26	1.99	2.17	44.0
47	6.31	6.88	5.26	5.73	4.39	4.79	3.67	4.01	2.58	2.82	41.1
50	7.12	7.75	6.11	6.65	5.25	5.71	4.52	4.92	3.36	3.66	38.1
53	8.04	8.74	7.10	7.72	6.27	6.82	5.55	6.04	4.37	4.75	35.2
56	9.09	9.87	8.26	8.97	7.51	8.15	6.84	7.42	5.68	6.17	32.3
59	10.30	11.15	9.63	10.43	9.01	9.76	8.44	9.14	7.41	8.03	29.4
62	11.71	12.63	11.27	12.15	10.85	11.70	10.45	11.27	9.70	10.46	26.6
65	13.38	14.33	13.25	14.20	13.13	14.06	13.00	13.93	12.76	13.68	23.9
68	13.54	14.52	13.54	14.52	13.54	14.52	13.54	14.52	13.54	14.52	21.2
71	12.40	13.36	12.40	13.36	12.40	13.36	12.40	13.36	12.40	13.36	18.7
74	11.24	12.16	11.24	12.16	11.24	12.16	11.24	12.16	11.24	12.16	16.3
77	10.06	10.93	10.06	10.93	10.06	10.93	10.06	10.93	10.06	10.93	14.0
80	8.89	9.69	8.89	9.69	8.89	9.69	8.89	9.69	8.89	9.69	11.9
83	7.75	8.47	7.75	8.47	7.75	8.47	7.75	8.47	7.75	8.47	10.0
86	6.68	7.33	6.68	7.33	6.68	7.33	6.68	7.33	6.68	7.33	8.3
89	5.74	6.32	5.74	6.32	5.74	6.32	5.74	6.32	5.74	6.32	6.9

*The 50% and 100% denote the levels of benefits received by the surviving spouse after the death of the participant retiree.
Assumptions: Retirement at age 66, postretirement discount rate at 4 percent.
*Source: **Defined Benefits Couples/FM Same Age** with k_2 = 4 percent.*

TABLE 13.19 Joint-survivor Multiples for Married Females with a Husband Three Years Older: No Automatic Increase in Postretirement Income

Females' Age	4%		5%		6%		7%		9%		Expected Life
	50%	100%	50%	100%	50%	100%	50%	100%	50%	100%	
38	5.00	5.37	3.62	3.88	2.64	2.83	1.94	2.07	1.06	1.13	48.8
41	4.87	5.22	3.50	3.75	2.54	2.72	1.85	1.98	1.01	1.07	45.9
44	5.48	5.88	4.06	4.35	3.03	3.24	2.27	2.43	1.31	1.39	42.9
47	6.19	6.63	4.71	5.04	3.61	3.86	2.79	2.98	1.70	1.81	40.0
50	6.98	7.48	5.47	5.85	4.32	4.61	3.43	3.66	2.20	2.34	37.0
53	7.89	8.44	6.36	6.79	5.16	5.51	4.22	4.49	2.86	3.04	34.1
56	8.92	9.53	7.40	7.90	6.19	6.59	5.20	5.53	3.73	3.95	31.2
59	10.12	10.78	8.64	9.19	7.43	7.89	6.42	6.81	4.87	5.15	28.4
62	11.51	12.23	10.12	10.73	8.94	9.47	7.95	8.40	6.37	6.71	25.6
65	13.17	13.91	11.91	12.55	10.83	11.39	9.90	10.39	8.38	8.77	22.9
68	11.04	12.22	10.13	11.02	9.36	10.05	8.71	9.24	7.65	7.98	20.3
71	9.63	10.70	8.94	9.72	8.35	8.93	7.83	8.28	6.97	7.26	17.8
74	8.46	9.45	7.92	8.65	7.44	8.01	7.03	7.48	6.33	6.62	15.4
77	7.35	8.28	6.92	7.63	6.55	7.11	6.22	6.67	5.66	5.97	13.2
80	6.29	7.15	5.97	6.64	5.68	6.22	5.42	5.87	4.98	5.29	11.2
83	5.32	6.07	5.08	5.68	4.87	5.35	4.67	5.08	4.34	4.63	9.4
86	4.47	5.08	4.29	4.79	4.13	4.55	3.99	4.34	3.74	3.99	7.8
89	3.78	4.24	3.65	4.03	3.53	3.86	3.43	3.70	3.24	3.45	5.8

*The 50% and 100% denote the levels of benefits received by the surviving spouse after the death of the participant retiree.
Assumptions: Retirement at age 66, preretirement and postretirement discount rates are the same.
*Source: **Defined Benefits Couples/Male 3 Years Older** with $k_1 = k_2$.*

TABLE 13.20 Joint-survivor Multiples for Married Females with Husband Three Years Older: Postretirement Discount Rate at 3 percent

Females' Age	4%		5%		6%		7%		9%		Expected Life
	50%	100%	50%	100%	50%	100%	50%	100%	50%	100%	
38	5.51	5.93	4.37	4.70	3.47	3.74	2.77	2.98	1.77	1.90	48.8
41	5.36	5.76	4.22	4.53	3.33	3.58	2.63	2.83	1.66	1.78	45.9
44	6.04	6.49	4.89	5.26	3.97	4.27	3.23	3.47	2.15	2.31	42.9
47	6.81	7.31	5.68	6.10	4.74	5.09	3.97	4.26	2.79	3.00	40.0
50	7.69	8.24	6.59	7.07	5.67	6.08	4.88	5.23	3.63	3.89	37.0
53	8.68	9.30	7.67	8.22	6.78	7.26	6.00	6.45	4.72	5.05	34.1
56	9.82	10.51	8.93	9.55	8.12	8.69	7.39	7.91	6.14	6.57	31.2
59	11.14	11.89	10.42	11.12	9.75	10.41	9.13	9.75	8.02	8.56	28.4
62	12.68	13.49	12.20	12.99	11.75	12.50	11.32	12.04	10.51	11.18	25.6
65	14.51	15.36	14.37	15.21	14.23	15.07	14.10	14.93	13.84	14.66	22.9

TABLE 13.20 *(Continued)*

Females' Age	4% 50%	100%	5% 50%	100%	6% 50%	100%	7% 50%	100%	9% 50%	100%	Expected Life
68	12.12	13.71	12.11	13.68	12.10	13.65	12.08	13.63	12.06	13.58	20.3
71	10.46	11.95	10.45	11.94	10.45	11.94	10.45	11.93	10.45	11.91	17.8
74	9.10	10.48	9.10	10.47	9.10	10.47	9.10	10.47	9.10	10.46	15.4
77	7.84	9.11	7.84	9.11	7.84	9.10	7.84	9.10	7.84	9.10	13.2
80	6.66	7.80	6.66	7.80	6.66	7.80	6.66	7.80	6.66	7.80	11.2
83	5.59	6.57	5.59	6.57	5.59	6.57	5.59	6.57	5.59	6.57	9.4
86	4.66	5.45	4.66	5.45	4.66	5.45	4.66	5.45	4.66	5.45	7.8
89	3.92	4.50	3.92	4.50	3.92	4.50	3.92	4.50	3.92	4.50	5.8

*The 50% and 100% denote the levels of benefits received by the surviving spouse after the death of the participant retiree.
Assumptions: Retirement at age 66, postretirement discount rate at 3 percent.
Source: Defined Benefits Couples/Male 3 Years Older with k_2 = 3 percent.

TABLE 13.21 Joint-survivor Multiples for Married Females with a Husband Three Years Older: Postretirement Discount Rate at 4 percent

Females' Age	4% 50%	100%	5% 50%	100%	6% 50%	100%	7% 50%	100%	9% 50%	100%	Expected Life
38	5.00	5.37	3.96	4.26	3.15	3.39	2.51	2.70	1.60	1.72	48.8
41	4.87	5.22	3.83	4.11	3.02	3.24	2.39	2.57	1.50	1.61	45.9
44	5.48	5.88	4.44	4.77	3.61	3.87	2.93	3.15	1.95	2.09	42.9
47	6.19	6.63	5.16	5.53	4.31	4.62	3.60	3.86	2.53	2.72	40.0
50	6.98	7.48	5.99	6.42	5.15	5.51	4.43	4.74	3.29	3.53	37.0
53	7.89	8.44	6.96	7.45	6.16	6.59	5.45	5.83	4.28	4.58	34.1
56	8.92	9.53	8.11	8.66	7.37	7.88	6.71	7.17	5.58	5.96	31.2
59	10.12	10.78	9.46	10.08	8.85	9.44	8.29	8.84	7.28	7.76	28.4
62	11.51	12.23	11.08	11.77	10.67	11.33	10.27	10.91	9.54	10.13	25.6
65	13.17	13.91	13.04	13.78	12.92	13.65	12.80	13.52	12.56	13.27	22.9
68	11.04	12.22	11.03	12.20	11.02	12.18	11.01	12.16	10.99	12.12	20.3
71	9.63	10.70	9.63	10.69	9.63	10.69	9.63	10.68	9.63	10.67	17.8
74	8.46	9.45	8.46	9.44	8.46	9.44	8.46	9.44	8.46	9.44	15.4
77	7.35	8.28	7.35	8.28	7.35	8.27	7.35	8.27	7.35	8.27	13.2
80	6.29	7.15	6.29	7.15	6.29	7.15	6.29	7.15	6.29	7.14	11.2
83	5.32	6.07	5.32	6.07	5.32	6.07	5.32	6.07	5.32	6.07	9.4
86	4.47	5.08	4.47	5.08	4.47	5.08	4.47	5.08	4.47	5.08	7.8
89	3.78	4.24	3.78	4.24	3.78	4.24	3.78	4.24	3.78	4.24	5.8

*The 50% and 100% denote the levels of benefits received by the surviving spouse after the death of the participant retiree.
Assumptions: Retirement at age 66, postretirement discount rate at 4 percent.
Source: Defined Benefits Couples/Male 3 Years Older with k_2 = 4 percent.

Appendix 13.1: Explanations of Multiple Calculations for Defined-Benefit Plans

Appendix 13.1.1: Worksheets for Single Males and Single Females

An interactive version of the spreadsheet used to generate the multiples in Tables 13.4 through 13.9 is available at http://www.wiley.com/go/reichenstein. This spreadsheet, entitled *App 13.1.1 Defined Benefit Singles,* contains worksheets that calculate multiples for defined-benefits for single males and single females. The worksheet entitled *Female* contains multiple calculations for both the present value of expected cash flows and the present value of cash flows through life expectancy for females. The worksheet entitled *Male* contains the corresponding multiple calculations for males. Each worksheet contains a text box that explains its purpose and use.

Appendix 13.1.2: Worksheets for Married Couples

An interactive version of the spreadsheet used to generate the multiples in Tables 13.10 through 13.21 is available at http://www.wiley.com/go/reichenstein. This spreadsheet, entitled *App 13.1.2 Defined Benefit Couples,* contains worksheets that calculate multiples for defined-benefit plan benefits for married couples. The worksheet entitled *MF Same Age* contains calculations for a male participant with wife the same age. *Female 3 Years Younger* contains calculations for a male participant with wife three years younger. *FM Same Age* and *Male 3 Years Older* contain calculations for a female participant with husband, respectively, same age and three years older. The age in the worksheets denotes the participant's age. Each worksheet contains a text box that explains its purpose and use.

References

Baer, David. 2001. State taxation of Social Security and pensions in 2000. Public Policy Institute, American Association of Retired People, Issue Brief Number 55, 7–15.

Fraser, Steve P., William W. Jennings, and David R. King. 2000. Strategic asset allocation for individual investors: The impact of the present value of Social Security benefits. *Financial Services Review,* Winter, 295–326.

McLeod, R.W., S. Moody, and A. Phillips. 1993. The risks of pension plans. *Financial Services Review,* Vol. 2, No. 2, 131–156.

Mitchell, Olivia S., and Roderick Carr. 1997. State and local pension plans. Appendix Three. *Pension planning: Pension, profit-sharing, and other deferred compensation plans,* 8th ed. Edited by Everett T. Allen, Joseph J. Melone, Jerry S. Rosenbloom, and Jack L. VanDerhei. Boston: Irwin McGraw-Hill: 504–510.

Pension Benefit Guarantee Corporation. 1999. *Pension insurance data book 1999.* Washington, DC: PBGC.

Reichenstein, William. 2001. The investment implications of lower stock return prospects. *AAII Journal,* October, 4–7.

Reichenstein, William. 2002. What do past stock market returns tell us about the future? *Journal of Financial Planning,* July.

Woerheide, Walt, and Rich Fortner. 1994. The pension penalty associated with changing employers. *Financial Counseling and Planning,* Vol. 5, 101–116.

Zorn, Paul. 1994. *Survey of state and local government employee retirement systems.* Government Finance Officers Association.

Notes

1. We are aware that the Treasury Department has suspended offering these bonds and that pricing of the bonds may reflect demand imbalances. Financial professionals might, accordingly, prefer to use the yield on the longest Treasury bond that appears unaffected by such imbalances.

2. In 2001, the guaranteed level was $40,705 for single-employer plans. Those who retire before age 65 receive a reduced guarantee. The amount increases with the Social Security contribution-and-benefit base. (The guarantee level increases; benefits of those under PBGC-terminated plans do not increase with inflation.) As might be expected, the limitation applies to individuals with high salaries and long tenure, especially those in generous pension plans. In a PBGC (1999) study, six in seven of those affected by the benefits maximum were airline pilots; less than 6 percent of plan participants were affected by the maximum, but they lost 16 percent of benefits. McLeod, Moody, and Phillips (1993) characterize the pension payoffs with a PBGC guarantee as an option-like collar—with a floor at the PBGC guarantee level and a cap at the promised benefit level. The PBGC (1999) study suggests that the floor guarantee is most relevant in default.

3. McLeod, Moody, and Phillips (1993) present a taxonomy of pension risk that includes both investment-related and pension-specific risks. Investment risks include inflation, liquidity, marketability, portfolio, reinvestment, and default. Additional risks include plan type, funding level, asset mix, regulatory noncompliance, and plan modifications under plan termination. We subsume all of these risks in the default risk premium.

4. The DB multiples developed in this chapter exhibit the bond-pricing properties similar to those described in the military retirement chapter.

5. Recall from our discussion of the PBGC guarantee that the PBGC does not guarantee automatic or inflation adjustments to pensions. In this chapter we assume the other layers of protection are sufficient to pay the pension benefits, and that no default risk premium is necessary in the automatic- or inflation-adjustment examples. Separately, we consider a default risk premium in Example S11. Valuing an automatic- or inflation-adjustment scenario with a default risk premium is substantially more complex because of the partial PBGC guarantee.

6. Insert into a financial calculator $n = 11$, $i = 6$ percent, PMT $= \$40,897.50$, FV $= 0$ and calculate the present value of an ordinary annuity of $322,553. Multiplying this amount by 1.0296 (or $1.06^{0.5}$) gives the present value assuming the mid-year convention of $332,101. The present value of $332,101 when discounted at 6 percent for four years is about $263,000.

7. The logic is the same as for the constant-growth dividend discount model. If dividends grow at a constant rate of g percent per year, then the denominator is $k - g$, where k is

the nominal discount rate and g is the growth rate. The present value of a cash flow that is growing at g percent per year when discounted at k percent is the same as the present value of a constant cash flow when discounted at $k - g$ percent per year.

8. If the PBGC guarantee applied to a private plan with default risk and the expected benefits exceeded the guarantee level, valuation would be slightly more complex. The pension promise could be bifurcated. Someone could value the PBGC-guaranteed portion, assuming there is no default risk premium. The excess portion could be valued using the risky-pension methods described here. McLeod, Moody, and Phillips (1993, Figures 2 and 3) characterize the pension payoffs with a PBGC guarantee as an option-like collar—with a floor at the PBGC guarantee level and a cap at the promised benefit level.

Asset Allocation and Asset-location Decisions

Introduction

Let us go back to the basics, but this time introduce taxes.[1] There are two assets: a stock fund and a bond fund. Each asset can be held in taxable accounts, deductible pensions, or both, where deductible pensions include 401(k), 403(b), Keogh, SEP-IRA, and so on.[2] An individual investor has some assets in taxable accounts and others in deductible pensions. He asks his financial professional to do three things: calculate his portfolio's current asset allocation, recommend an optimal asset allocation, and recommend an optimal asset location (that is, to the degree possible, should he locate stocks or bonds in tax-sheltered pensions?).

This chapter applies mean-variance optimization to determine an individual's optimal asset allocation and asset location. The individual has some assets in taxable accounts and others in deductible pensions. The portion of each asset's risk and return borne by the investor depend upon whether it is held in a taxable account or a deductible pension. As we shall show, if held in deductible pensions, the individual investor bears all of the asset's risk and receives all of its returns. In the taxable account, governments share in the asset's risk and returns.

Prior asset-location research, including that of Reichenstein (2000), one of this book's authors, considers the impact of the asset-allocation decision on returns but ignores its impact on risk. The prior research concludes active stock investors should have a strong preference to hold stocks in deductible pensions (and other retirement accounts) and bonds in taxable accounts, while passive investors should probably have a slight preference to hold stocks in taxable accounts. Optimization considers the asset-allocation decision's impact on both returns and risk. It implies active and passive investors should locate bonds in pensions and stocks in taxable accounts. Moreover, it suggests active investors should not have a strong asset-location preference, but passive investors should have a strong preference to locate stocks in taxable accounts.

Separately, we recognize that some investors make the asset-location decision first and the asset-allocation decision second. Optimizations reveal that their optimal asset allocation varies predictably and strongly with their asset-location decision. The optimal asset allocation calls for a much larger exposure to the assets held in taxable accounts.

Measuring an Individual's Asset Allocation

This section begins with a discussion of the importance of distinguishing between before-tax and after-tax funds when calculating the asset mix. It then demonstrates that, from an individual investor's perspective, an asset's risk and returns depend upon the savings vehicle it is held in.

Three Portfolios

In Chapters 9 and 10, we argued that the profession must first convert before-tax funds to after-tax funds, and then calculate the asset allocation based on after-tax funds. We need to revisit this issue in order to set up the optimizations.

Mark just retired at age 65. His assets will be used to meet his retirement income needs. Suppose his portfolio is the one presented in Portfolio A of Table 14.1. He has $100,000 in a stock fund held in a taxable account and $100,000 in a bond fund held in a taxable account. The book and market values are $100,000 for both the stock fund and the bond fund. What is his current asset allocation? On this question, we all agree. His portfolio contains 50 percent stocks and 50 percent bonds.

Suppose Mark's portfolio is Portfolio B of Table 14.1. It contains $100,000 in a stock fund held in a Roth IRA and $100,000 in a bond fund held in a taxable account. The book value and market value of the bond fund are $100,000. What is his current asset allocation? Again, we all agree. The portfolio contains 50 percent stocks and 50 percent bonds.

Portfolio C presents a third portfolio. It contains $153,800 in a stock fund held in a deductible pension and $100,000 in a bond fund held in a taxable account. The market and book values of the bond fund are $100,000. Mark is in the combined federal-plus-state ordinary income tax bracket of 35 percent, and will remain there. What is his asset mix? According to the traditional approach to calculating the asset mix, his portfolio contains 61 percent stocks [$153,800 / $253,800] and 39 percent bonds.

We contend his portfolio contains 50 percent stocks and 50 percent bonds, the same as for Portfolios A and B. In Portfolios A and B, he could withdraw $1,000 from the stock fund and buy $1,000 of goods and services. In Portfolio C, he must withdraw $1,538 from the stock fund held in a deductible pension to buy $1,000

TABLE 14.1   Asset Allocation for Three Portfolios

Asset	Market Value	Savings Vehicle	Stock Allocation	
			Traditional Approach	After-tax Approach
Portfolio A				
Stock Fund	$100,000	Taxable account	50%	50%
Bond Fund	$100,000	Taxable account		
Portfolio B				
Stock Fund	$100,000	Roth IRA	50%	50%
Bond Fund	$100,000	Taxable account		
Portfolio C				
Stock Fund	$153,800	Deductible pension	61%	50%
Bond Fund	$100,000	Taxable account		

of goods and services; taxes consume the other $538. The deductible pension contains before-tax funds, and before-tax funds buy fewer goods and services than the same amount of after-tax funds. Since Mark intends to use the funds to meet his retirement income needs, we can convert the $153,800 of before-tax funds to after-tax funds by multiplying by $(1 - t)$, where t is his expected tax rate during retirement. The deductible pension represents $100,000 of after-tax funds [$153,800 • $(1 - 0.35)$].

Any acceptable method of calculating an individual's asset mix must distinguish between before-tax and after-tax funds because goods and services are purchased with after-tax funds. Before calculating the asset allocation, we should first convert all account values to after-tax values. In so doing, we compare after-tax funds to after-tax funds. The same principle applies to investments in other savings vehicles (e.g., nondeductible IRA, non-qualified tax-deferred annuity, and taxable account). The asset allocation should reflect accounts' after-tax values because goods and services are purchased with after-tax funds.[3]

Risk and Returns across Savings Vehicles

Properly measured, Portfolios A, B, and C contain 50 percent stocks and 50 percent bonds; the current asset allocation should reflect current after-tax values. However, these three portfolios are not equally desirable. Mark should prefer Portfolios B and C to Portfolio A, because assets held in Roth IRAs and deductible pensions receive more favorable tax treatment than assets held in taxable accounts. In Part I of this book, we thoroughly discussed the implications of investing in alternative savings vehicles—taxable accounts, deductible pensions, Roth IRAs, nondeductible IRAs, and non-qualified tax-deferred annuities.

Let us first compare Portfolios B and C. Portfolio B contains $100,000 of stocks in a Roth IRA, while Portfolio C contains $153,800 of stocks in a deductible pension. They are equally desirable.[4] Mark could withdraw say $1,000 from the Roth IRA today and buy $1,000 of goods and services. Alternatively, he could withdraw $1,538 from the deductible pension and, after paying taxes, buy $1,000 of goods and services. The $1,000 in a Roth IRA is equivalent to $1,538 in a deductible pension.

Mark could also invest the funds in stocks that earn i percent for n years. After n years, today's $1,000 in a Roth IRA would buy $1,000 \cdot (1 + i)^n$ of goods and services. Alternatively, after n years, today's $1,538 in a deductible pension would buy $1,538 \cdot (1 + i)^n \cdot (1 - 0.35)$ or $1,000 \cdot (1 + i)^n$ of goods and services. Again, $1,000 in a Roth IRA is equivalent to $1,538 in a deductible pension.

The $1,000 in the Roth IRA buys $1,000 today or $1,000 \cdot (1 + i)^n$ of goods and services in n years. The $1,538 in the deductible pension buys $1,000 today or $1,000 \cdot (1 + i)^n$ of goods and services in n years. In both a Roth IRA and deductible pension, the individual bears all investment risk and receives all investment returns; in both, the effective tax rate is zero.

These examples illustrate that an acceptable method of calculating Mark's asset allocation must treat $1,000 in a Roth IRA as equivalent to $1,538 in a deductible pension. The traditional approach violates this requirement.

In Portfolio A, the stock fund is held in a taxable account, so governments share in its *returns and risk*. Mark does not bear all of the asset's risk nor receive all of its returns.

Most professional investors would consider Portfolios A and B to be virtually the same and Portfolio C to be different than the others. In reality, Portfolios B and C are the same, while Portfolio A is different. All three portfolios have the same current asset allocation. However, because the stock portion of the Portfolios is held in different savings vehicles, the individual bears different portions of its risk and returns. In Portfolios B and C, the individual bears all of the stocks' risk and receives all of its returns, while in Portfolio A, governments share in the stocks' risk and returns.

Table 14.2 presents the risk and returns on bonds and stocks when held in pensions and taxable accounts, where pensions include deductible pensions and Roth IRAs. Assume bonds offer 6 percent pre-tax expected returns and 10 percent pre-tax standard deviation. Stocks offer 11 percent pre-tax expected returns and 15 percent pre-tax standard deviation. Stock returns consist of 2 percent dividend yield plus 9 percent expected capital gain. Mark, the individual investor, is in a combined federal-plus-state ordinary tax bracket of 35 percent and combined capital gain tax bracket of 27 percent.

When an asset is held in pensions, Mark bears all the risk and receives all the returns. When held in a taxable account, Mark bears 65 percent of the bonds' risk and receives 65 percent of the returns; the after-tax risk (standard deviation) and returns are 6.5 percent and 3.9 percent, respectively.

TABLE 14.2   Expected Returns and Risk in Pensions and Taxable Accounts*

	Expected Returns	Standard Deviation
Trader		
1. Stocks in Pensions	11.00%	15.00%
2. Bonds in Pensions	6.00	10.00
3. Stocks in Taxable Accounts	7.15	9.75
4. Bonds in Taxable Accounts	3.90	6.50
Active Investor		
1. Stocks in Pensions	11.00	15.00
2. Bonds in Pensions	6.00	10.00
3. Stocks in Taxable Accounts	7.87	10.95
4. Bonds in Taxable Accounts	3.90	6.50
Passive Investor		
1. Stocks in Pensions	11.00	15.00
2. Bonds in Pensions	6.00	10.00
3. Stocks in Taxable Accounts	10.30	15.00
4. Bonds in Taxable Accounts	3.90	6.50

* Pensions include Roth IRA and deductible pensions such as 401(k), 403(b), Keogh, deductible IRA, SEP-IRA, and so on. We assume a federal-plus-state 35 percent ordinary income tax rate and 27% capital gain tax rate.

When stocks are held in a taxable account, the individual's risk depends upon his or her investment management practices. We define three hypothetical individual investors. The *trader* realizes all gains as short-term gains each year and pays taxes at the ordinary income tax rate. The *active investor* realizes all gains in one year and one day and pays taxes at the capital gain tax rate. An active investor is someone who actively manages his or her own funds or invests in an active stock fund. The *passive investor* buys and holds stocks and never pays capital gain taxes. He may give appreciated assets to charity or await the step-up in cost basis at the owner's death. He pays taxes annually on interest and dividends. This passive investor is someone who passively manages his own funds or buys and holds a passive stock fund.

The trader who holds stocks in a taxable account bears 65 percent of its risk and takes 65 percent of its returns; governments share 35 percent of the risk and returns. For this trader, stocks' after-tax expected returns and risk are 7.15 percent and 9.75 percent.

For the active investor who holds stocks in a taxable account, the after-tax expected return is 7.87 percent, $[2\% \cdot (1 - 0.35) + 9\% \cdot (1 - 0.27)]$ and the after-tax standard deviation is 10.95 percent. The dividend yield provides a certain 1.3 percent after-tax return. The return uncertainty (and thus risk) involves the size of the capital gain or loss. Since the applicable tax rate for this portion of return is

27 percent, governments only bear 27 percent of the stocks' risk. For this active investor, governments take 28.5 percent of the returns but only bear 27 percent of the risk. Moreover, the spread between the return-sharing percentage and the risk-sharing percentage increases with the spread between the ordinary income tax rate and capital gain tax rate. For someone in the 39.6 percent ordinary income tax bracket and 20 percent capital gain tax bracket, the government takes 23.6 percent of the stock returns but only bears 20 percent of its risk.

For the passive investor who holds stocks in taxable accounts, after-tax expected returns and standard deviation are 10.3 percent and 15 percent, respectively. The return is 11 percent less the 0.7 percent annual tax on dividends. The standard deviation is 15 percent, the same as for stocks held in pensions. As before, the uncertainty involves only the size of the capital gain, so it has the same risk as for a tax-exempt investor. The passive investor receives about 94 percent of stocks' returns and bears all its risk.

In summary, from an individual investor's perspective, an asset's risk and returns depend upon whether it is held in a pension or taxable account. When held in a pension, the individual bears all risk and receives all returns. When held in a taxable account, the individual bears $(1 - t)$ percent of bonds' risk and returns, where t is the marginal tax rate. When held in a taxable account, the individual's share of stocks' risk and returns depend upon his or her investment management practices. The trader bears $(1 - t)$ percent of stocks' risk and returns. The active investor and passive investor bear a larger fraction of stocks' risk than returns.

Optimization with Taxable and Retirement Accounts

Each individual investor, perhaps with the help of his or her financial advisor, must choose an asset allocation and asset location. Asset allocation refers to the allocation of after-tax funds across asset classes—stocks and bonds in our two-asset world. Asset location refers to the decision to place, insofar as the asset allocation allows, stocks in pensions and bonds in taxable accounts or vice versa.

Mean-variance optimization traditionally ignores taxes and relies on before-tax risk and expected returns. When applied to individuals, it requires recognition that a portion of the individual's after-tax funds is held in taxable accounts and the remainder in pensions. There are two assets—stocks and bonds—and two savings vehicles—taxable accounts and pensions. For optimization, there are thus effectively four "assets": stocks in pensions, bonds in pensions, stocks in taxable accounts, and bonds in taxable accounts.

This chapter applies mean-variance optimization to individual portfolios. It adjusts portfolio weights to reflect after-tax values (e.g., $1,000 of after-tax funds in a taxable account counts the same as $1,000 / (1 - t)$ in a deductible pension) and it uses the risk and returns that the individual bears in taxable accounts and pensions. Brunel (1998) discusses two shortcomings of mean-variance analysis when applied to individuals. It ignores the tax costs of, first, shifting to a new target asset allocation and, second, rebalancing to an existing one. These shortcomings apply to this chapter, except to the degree that the portfolio adjustments involve movement of retirement funds or the allocation of new funds.

There are three investors: trader, active investor, and passive investor. They each must make an asset-allocation decision and an asset-location decision. Table 14.3 summarizes one optimization for the active investor. He allocates funds among the four "assets" such that he maximizes utility. The study examines two utility

TABLE 14.3   Expected Returns and Risk in Pensions and Taxable Accounts[*]

	After-tax Expected Returns	After-tax Standard Deviation	$r_{1,j}$	$r_{2,j}$	$r_{3,j}$	$r_{4,j}$
1. Stocks in Pensions	11.00%	15.00%	1.0			
2. Bonds in Pensions	6.00	10.00	0.2	1.0		
3. Stocks in Taxable Account	7.87	10.95	1.0	0.2	1.0	
4. Bonds in Taxable Account	3.90	6.50	0.2	1.0	0.2	1.0

Maximize Utility $= ER - SD/RT$ or Utility $= ER - SD^2/RT$
$ER = Wsp\ (11\%) + Wbp\ (6\%) + Wst\ (7.87\%) + Wbt\ (3.9\%)$
Constraints
$Wsp \geq 0$
$Wbp \geq 0$
$Wst \geq 0$
$Wbt \geq 0$
$Wsp + Wbp = 0.5$
$Wsp + Wbp + Wst + Wbt = 1.0$

ER is the portfolio after-tax expected returns. SD is the portfolio after-tax standard deviation. RT is the investor's risk tolerance.

$r_{i,j}$ denotes the correlation coefficient between asset i and asset j. Wsp denotes the weight of stocks in pensions. Wbp, Wst, and Wbt denote the weights of bonds in pensions, stocks in taxable accounts, and bonds in taxable accounts. $Wsp + Wbp = 0.5$ restricts pension assets to 50 percent of total after-tax funds.

Pensions include the Roth IRA and all deductible pensions (e.g., 401(k), 403(b), Keogh, deductible IRA, and so on).

*The values reflect an active investor in the combined federal-plus-state 35 percent ordinary income tax bracket and combined 27 percent capital gain tax bracket. Stocks earn 2 percent dividend yield plus short-term capital gain and 9 percent long-term capital gain. This active stock investor realizes all capital gains each year or, technically, in one year and one day.

functions: $U = ER - SD / RT$ and $U = ER - SD^2 / RT$. U denotes utility; also, it is the portfolio's certainty-equivalent return, meaning it is the risk-free return that would provide the same utility as the portfolio. ER is the portfolio's after-tax expected returns. SD is after-tax standard deviation. RT denotes the investor's risk tolerance.

The usual portfolio constraints apply. There is no short selling. In addition, we assume half of the after-tax funds in Mark's portfolio are in pensions and half are in taxable accounts. The correlation coefficient between the bond and stock returns is 0.2. The risk tolerance for the first utility function is set at 2. It is set at 40 for the second utility function.[5] Table 14.4 summarizes the results of the optimizations.

Trader

For the trader, there are at least three optimal portfolios, and each of these produces identical portfolio risk, portfolio returns, and utility. Portfolios 1 through 3 present the optimal portfolios for the first utility function. Portfolio 1 allocates 24.9 percent of after-tax funds in stocks in pensions, 25.1 percent in bonds in pensions, and 50 percent in stocks in taxable accounts. The utility or certainty-equivalent return is 3.10 percent. The overall stock allocation is 74.9 percent and, to the degree possible, bonds are located in pensions.

Portfolios 1, 2, and 3 provide identical portfolios (in terms of portfolio risk, portfolio expected returns, and utility). Yet, they have different asset allocations and asset locations. The overall stock allocations in Portfolios 1 through 3 are 74.9 percent, 70.1 percent, and 61.4 percent, respectively. To the degree possible, Portfolio 1 locates bonds in pensions, Portfolio 3 locates stocks in pensions, and Portfolio 2 locates both bonds and stocks in pensions. *The surprising conclusion is that there is more than one optimal portfolio at a given risk level.*

Similarly, Portfolios 4 through 6 present the optimal portfolios for the second utility function. Again, there is more than one optimal portfolio.

Most scholars appear to have approached the two decisions in a sequential fashion: decide the asset-allocation decision first and the asset-location decision second.[6] Based on the specific input in this example, there is not an optimal asset allocation for the trader. Based on several examples (not reported), we conclude that traders have more than one optimal portfolio, and each optimal portfolio reflects a different asset allocation and asset location. If governments share equally in assets' risk and returns, identical portfolios (in terms of utility, portfolio risk, and portfolio expected returns) can be obtained with different asset-allocation and asset-location decisions. For traders, the two-step procedure will not work; the asset-allocation and asset-location decisions must be solved jointly.

Given an asset-location decision, there is one optimal asset allocation. For example, given the decision to locate as many bonds as possible in pensions, Portfolio 1 is the optimal allocation, and it contains 74.9 percent stock. Given the

TABLE 14.4   Asset Allocation, Asset Location, and Utility

Trader					Portfolio			
	Wsp	*Wbp*	*Wst*	*Wbt*	Stk	Utility	*ER*	*SD*
Utility = $ER - SD/RT$								
1	24.9%	25.1%	50%	0%	74.9%	3.10%	7.82%	9.44%
2	33.8	16.2	36.3	13.7	70.1	3.10	7.82	9.44
3	50.0	0	11.4	38.6	61.4	3.10	7.82	9.44
					utility loss = 0 percent			
Utility = $ER - SD^2/RT$								
4	27.0%	23.0%	50%	0%	77.0%	5.60%	7.93%	9.65%
5	35.6	14.4	36.9	13.1	72.5	5.60	7.93	9.65
6	50.0	0	14.7	35.3	64.7	5.60	7.93	9.65
					utility loss = 0 percent			

Active Investor					Portfolio			
	Wsp	*Wbp*	*Wst*	*Wbt*	Stk	Utility	*ER*	*SD*
Utility = $ER - SD/RT$								
7	23.7%	26.3%	50%	0%	73.7%	3.17%	8.12%	9.90%
8	50.0	0	23.7	26.3	73.7	3.11	8.39	10.57
9	50.0	0	15	35	65.0	3.12	8.05	9.85
					utility loss = 0.05 percent			
Utility = $ER - SD^2/RT$								
10	24.1%	25.9%	50%	0%	74.1%	5.67%	8.14%	9.94%
11	50.0	0	24.1	25.9	74.1	5.60	8.41	10.60
12	50.0	0	16	34	66.0	5.62	8.09	9.93
					utility loss = 0.05 percent			

Passive Investor					Portfolio			
	Wsp	*Wbp*	*Wst*	*Wbt*	Stk	Utility	*ER*	*SD*
Utility = $ER - SD/RT$								
13	19.6%	30.4%	50%	0%	69.6%	3.41%	9.13%	11.44%
14	50.0	0	19.6	30.4	69.6	3.20	8.70	11.01
15	50.0	0	27	33	77.0	3.21	9.18	11.94
					utility loss = 0.20 percent			
Utility = $ER - SD^2/RT$								
16	14.2%	35.8%	50%	0%	64.2%	5.88%	8.86%	10.92%
17	50.0	0	14.2	35.8	64.2	5.68	8.36	10.35
18	50.0	0	16	34	66.0	5.68	8.41	10.45
					utility loss = 0.20 percent			

Wsp, Wbp, Wst, and *Wbt* denote the weights of stocks in pensions, bonds in pensions, stocks in taxable accounts, and bonds in taxable accounts.

decision to locate stocks in pensions, Portfolio 3 is the optimal asset allocation, and it contains 61.4 percent stocks. This 13.5 percent difference is not minor. A frequently used rule-of-thumb says that an investor should maintain each asset-class weight within 10 percent of the target weight. Suppose the target weight calls for 75 percent stocks. This rule-of-thumb would say Portfolio 3 deviates too far from the target portfolio, and its stock allocation should be increased. Yet, in reality, Portfolios 1 and 3 provide identical portfolio risk and portfolio expected returns. In short, the rule-of-thumb is inadequate.

Given an asset-location decision, the optimal asset allocation varies predictably with the location decision. This statement remains valid for all three investors —traders, active, and passive. The optimal asset allocation calls for a relatively large exposure to the asset held in taxable accounts. Moreover, there is an easy explanation of this investment implication.

For the trader, governments share 35 percent of taxable assets' risk and returns. We can thus think of taxable assets as belonging 35 percent to the government and 65 percent to the individual investor. After making this adjustment, for every $100 in Portfolio 1, the individual effectively has stocks in pensions of $24.90, bonds in pensions of $25.10, and stocks in taxable accounts of $32.50 [0.65 • $50]. His effective overall asset allocation has $57.40 in stocks and $25.10 in bonds. The individual's effective overall allocations for Portfolios 2 and 3 are the same. For example, the individual in Portfolio 3 effectively has stocks in pensions of $50, stocks in taxable accounts of $7.41, and bonds in taxable accounts of $25.11. Her effective overall asset allocation is $57.41 in stocks and $25.11 in bonds, which (except for rounding error) is identical to Portfolio 1. It follows from this shared ownership that the optimal asset allocation calls for a relatively large exposure to the asset held in taxable accounts.

Active Investor

Most individuals are active investors. They either actively manage their stock portfolio or invest in active stock funds.[7] For the active investor, there is an optimal asset allocation and asset location. Portfolio 7 presents the optimal portfolio for the first utility function. The overall stock allocation is 73.7 percent. To the degree possible, bonds are located in pensions.

This asset-location decision appears to be relatively insensitive to the particular assumptions. For example, this decision calls for bonds in pensions when each of the following values is changed, holding everything else constant. The correlation is set at 0.0 or 0.4. Stocks' pre-tax expected return is set at 9 percent or 13 percent. Its pre-tax standard deviation is set at 12 percent or 20 percent. Bond's pre-tax return is set at 4 percent or 8 percent. Its pre-tax standard deviation is set at 8 percent or 12 percent. The level of risk tolerance is set at levels from 1.75 to 2.5. Finally, the asset-location decision remains the same whether we maximize $U = ER - SD/RT$

or $U = ER - SD^2 / RT$. For the latter utility function, we allowed RT to vary from 35 to 50. In addition, we allowed the correlation coefficient, expected returns, and standard deviations to vary in the same range as before.

Shoven (1999), Shoven and Sialm (1998), and Reichenstein (2000), among others, have examined the asset-location decision for active investors. (Chapter 4 is a shortened version of Reichenstein (2000d), but Chapter 4 dropped the section in Reichenstein (2000d) about asset location.) They each approach portfolio optimization as a two-step procedure: first determine the optimal asset allocation and then determine the optimal asset location. Each study concludes that active stock investors should locate stocks in pensions and bonds in taxable accounts because this decision provides larger expected ending wealth—that is, higher expected returns—than the decision to locate bonds in pensions.

In Reichenstein (2000d), he used the following logic. Individuals expect to save more in taxes (that is, lose less in returns) from holding stocks in pensions than from holding bonds in pensions. From Table 14.2 for the active investor, stocks' after-tax expected returns are 3.13 percent lower if held in taxable accounts instead of pensions, while the bonds' returns are 2.1 percent lower. He thus concluded active investors should shelter stocks' returns by holding them in pensions; this strategy would provide higher expected returns and, he presumed incorrectly, the same risk. Comparing Portfolios 7 and 8 (or Portfolios 10 and 11) confirms that, for a given asset allocation, locating stocks in pensions provides higher expected returns. For example, Portfolio 8 (stocks in pensions) provides 0.27 percent higher expected returns than Portfolio 7 (bonds in pensions), while both portfolios contain 73.7 percent stock allocation. These three studies considered the impact of the asset-location decision on returns but not risk.

Reichenstein tried to hold portfolio risk constant by rebalancing the portfolio back to the target asset allocation at the end of each year. He assumed, incorrectly, that portfolio risk is the same as long as the overall asset allocation is the same. In reality, Portfolios 7 and 8 (or Portfolios 10 and 11) have the same asset allocation, but Portfolio 8 (or 11) has more risk. He did not recognize that the asset-location decision affects portfolio risk. Because the investor bears all the risk from holding stocks in the pension, the portfolio risk is higher in Portfolio 8 than in Portfolio 7. Optimization requires us to consider the consequences of asset-location decisions on portfolio *returns and risk*. His analysis neglected the asset-location decision's impact on portfolio risk.

Portfolios 7 through 9 (or Portfolios 10 through 12) demonstrate that the asset-allocation and asset-location decisions must be solved jointly. From Portfolio 7, the optimal portfolio contains 73.7 percent stocks, and bonds are located in pensions. Portfolio 8 has this same asset allocation but, to the degree possible, locates stocks in pensions. Portfolio 9 presents the optimal asset allocation *if someone insists on locating stocks in pensions.*[8] As before, if someone insists on locating stocks in pensions, the optimal stock allocation is lower than when bonds are located in pensions.

The levels of utility are also levels of certainty-equivalent return. A comparison of Portfolio 7 and 9's utilities suggests that the asset-location decision is of relatively little importance to active investors. Portfolio 7, the optimal portfolio, provides a certainty-equivalent return of 3.17 percent. If someone insists on locating stocks in pensions, he could select Portfolio 9, which provides a 0.05 percent lower certainty-equivalent return; the utility loss is 0.05 percent. Portfolios 10 and 12 demonstrate that the utility loss is also 0.05 percent when the utility function is $U = ER - SD^2 / RT$. In short, for the active investor, the optimal asset allocation calls for bonds in pensions, but the opposite strategy appears to be only slightly less desirable.

Passive Investor

For the passive investor, there is an optimal asset allocation and asset location. Portfolio 13, the optimal portfolio, contains 19.6 percent stocks in pensions, 30.4 percent bonds in pensions, and 50 percent stocks in taxable accounts. The optimal portfolio contains 69.4 percent stocks, and it locates bonds in pensions and stocks in taxable accounts. The asset-allocation and asset-location decisions must be solved jointly. Moreover, this asset-location decision appears to be relatively insensitive to particular assumptions.

Portfolios 13 and 14 (and 16 and 17) contain the same asset allocations but opposite asset locations. Stocks are equally risky whether held in taxable accounts or pensions, and their after-tax return is similar in both savings vehicles. Therefore, passively holding stocks in pensions is a poor use of pensions' tax-favored status. In contrast, bonds are much more desirable when held in pensions, and they are thus the pension assets of choice.

A comparison of levels of utility reveals the importance of the asset-location decision, which is most important to the passive investor. Portfolio 13, the optimal portfolio, provides a certainty-equivalent return of 3.41 percent. If someone insists on locating stocks in pensions, he could select Portfolio 15, which provides a 0.20 percent lower certainty-equivalent return; the utility loss is 0.20 percent. Portfolios 16 and 18 demonstrate that the utility loss is also 0.20 percent when the utility function is $U = ER - SD^2 / RT$. In short, for this passive investor, the optimal asset allocation calls for bonds in pensions and stocks in taxable accounts, and the opposite asset-location strategy appears to be much less desirable.

Calculating Mark's Optimal Asset Mix: Traditional versus After-tax Approach

It is instructive to compare the optimal asset mix based on the traditional and after-tax approaches. Let us assume Mark is an active investor, because most investors are active. Mark's portfolio contains $153,800 in deductible pensions and $100,000 in taxable accounts. (The market value and book value of the taxable accounts are $100,000.) Cheryl, his financial advisor, determines that Mark's risk tolerance is 2,

TABLE 14.5 Optimal Asset Allocations Based on Traditional and After-tax Approaches

| | Traditional Approach | | After-tax Approach | | |
	Dollars	Percent	Dollars	Percent	Dollar Reallocation
Stocks in Pensions	$153,800	60.6%	$72,900	23.7%	−$80,900
Bonds in Pensions	0	0	80,900	26.3	+$80,900
Stocks in Taxable Accounts	22,800	9.0	100,000	50.0	+$77,200
Bonds in Taxable Accounts	77,200	30.4	0	0	$77,200

and the first utility function applies. The traditional approach says he has $253,800 of assets—that is, it ignores the difference between before-tax and after-tax funds. The traditional mean-variance optimization ignores taxes; based on assets' before-tax risk and returns, the optimal asset mix contains 69.6 percent stocks. Following recent professional advice, Cheryl recommends that stocks should be located in pensions to the degree possible. Table 14.5 presents his optimal portfolio, which contains $176,600 in stocks [69.6% • $253,800], including $153,800 in pensions and $22,800 in taxable accounts. The remaining $77,200 of taxable accounts should contain bonds.

The next two columns indicate Mark's optimal asset mix based on the after-tax approach. From Portfolio 7 in Table 14.4, the true optimal mix contains 73.7 percent stocks including 23.7 percent in pensions and 50 percent in taxable accounts. In dollars, it contains $72,900 in stocks in pensions, $80,900 in bonds in pensions, and $100,000 in stocks in taxable accounts.[9]

The last column indicates the portfolio adjustments necessary to move from the asset allocation recommended by the traditional approach to the allocation recommended by the after-tax approach. In pensions, $80,900 of stocks must be moved to bonds. In taxable accounts, $77,200 of bonds must be moved to stocks. The traditional approach and after-tax approach recommend substantially different portfolios.

Relative Importance of Investment Management Strategy and Asset Location

Jeffrey and Arnott (1993) and Ghee and Reichenstein (1996) conclude that, when stocks are held in taxable accounts, it is difficult for a stock manager to add enough value through active trading to pay for the additional taxes associated with that trading. The utility levels in Table 14.4 allow us to compare the utility loss that taxable investors bear from being in the "wrong" investment management

TABLE 14.6   Loss in Utility from "Wrong" Investment Management Strategy and "Wrong" Asset Location

	Loss in Utility	
	U1	*U2*
Trader:		
Wrong Management Strategy	0.31%	0.28%
Wrong Asset Location	0.00	0.00
Active Investor: Stocks in Taxable Accounts		
Wrong Management Strategy	0.24%	0.21%
Wrong Asset Location	0.05	0.05
Passive Investor: Stocks in Taxable Accounts		
Wrong Management Strategy	NA	NA
Wrong Asset Location	0.20%	0.20%

$U1$ is the utility function: $U = ER - SD/RT$, where ER is the expected portfolio return, SD is standard deviation, and RT is risk tolerance.
$U2$ is the utility function: $U = ER - SD^2/RT$.
NA denotes not applicable, since the passive manager uses the "correct" management strategy.

strategy—that is, not being a passive manager—and from a "wrong" asset-location decision. Table 14.6 presents the results.

Based on the first utility function, the trader loses 0.31 percent in utility from being a trader instead of a passive investor; the 0.31 percent is the utility of Portfolio 13 in Table 14.4 less the utility of Portfolio 1, 2, or 3. He loses 0.28 percent according to the second utility function. Since the trader does not have an optimal asset location, he suffers no additional loss in utility from making the wrong asset-location decision. The location decision is, nonetheless, important in that the optimal asset allocation is different when bonds are located in the pension instead of stocks. In short, the loss from choosing the wrong management strategy is substantial, while the loss from choosing the wrong asset location is nil.

Based on the first and second utility functions, the active investor loses, respectively, 0.24 percent and 0.21 percent in utility from being an active investor instead of a passive investor. This is about three-fourths as large as the utility loss for the trader. He loses an additional 0.05 percent if he locates stocks instead of bonds in pensions. The loss of utility from choosing the wrong management strategy is four to five times larger than the loss from choosing the wrong asset to locate in pensions. Moreover, the active investor's loss from choosing the wrong management strategy is only about one-fourth smaller than the loss for the trader.

By definition, the passive investor chose the "right" management strategy. He loses 0.20 percent if he makes the wrong asset-location decision. The loss from making the wrong location decision is larger for the passive investor than for the trader or active investor. Admittedly, we suspect few passive investors will make the mistake of locating stocks in pensions. Nevertheless, the evidence suggests that this decision would be costly.

In summary, the optimizations suggest that traders and active stock investors can benefit more from changing to a passive-management strategy than they can by changing their asset-location strategy. Ideally, investors pick the best investment management strategy and asset-location strategy.

Tax Losses and the Asset-location Decision

This chapter's mean-variance-optimization framework understates the advantage of locating stocks in taxable accounts and bonds in pensions instead of the opposite asset-location strategy. By locating stocks in taxable accounts, individuals are better able to recognize capital losses and use these losses to reduce current taxes (or, at a minimum, reduce capital gain taxes). Currently, individuals can use realized losses to reduce taxable income of up to $3,000 per year. For someone in the 35 percent tax bracket, the government in essence redeems $1,050 of the $3,000 loss.

It is hard to quantify the size of this advantage. In another setting, Milevsky and Panyagometh (2001) examined its value and concluded that it is substantial.[10] Clearly, since stocks are more volatile than bonds, the advantage is larger when stocks are held in taxable accounts instead of bonds. The advantage is also larger when the taxable account contains individual stocks instead of stock funds or exchange-traded funds. In a rising market, the individual who buys a broad-based mutual fund will have an unrecognized gain and no ability to reduce taxable income. In contrast, the individual who buys individual stocks can sell the losers while allowing the gains to grow unharvested. Some tax-managed mutual funds behave similarly. After a decade or longer, the investor who buys individual securities may have a portfolio with relatively large weights in prior winning stocks; that is, the portfolio will have less-than-optimal diversification. Due to the government's sharing of losses, this individual's portfolio would likely be larger but less diversified than the portfolio of a passive investor in a broad-based stock index fund. However, this trade-off may be worthwhile to many individual investors.

Even passive individual investors who buy broad-based stock funds can benefit from tax-loss selling. Suppose, in early 2000, a couple invested $20,000 in a stock index fund held in a taxable account. They had already fully funded Roth IRAs, deductible pensions, and, if desired, contributions to 529 plans. The $20,000 in the index fund was above and beyond investments in these more-favored savings vehicles, and they planned to passively hold it. If the market increased, they anticipated paying no capital gains since they would await the step-up in basis at death or use the appreciated asset for their charitable contribution. Due to the bear market, the stock index fund was worth $14,000 in 2002. They could sell this fund and immediately buy a similar index fund. These transactions would not necessarily violate wash sale rules. They could use the $6,000 realized loss to reduce taxes in 2002 and 2003. If they were in the 35 percent tax bracket, the government would, in essence, pay for $2,100 of the loss.

To repeat, this ability to reduce taxes through capital-loss realization means that the prior analysis in this chapter underestimates the advantage of locating stocks in taxable accounts and bonds in pensions.

Summary

First, we conclude that the profession has been miscalculating an individual's asset allocation, and the measurement error can be substantial. Asset allocation should reflect after-tax funds because goods and services are purchased with after-tax funds.

Second, for an individual investor, an asset's risk and expected returns depend upon the savings vehicle in which it is held. In deductible pensions or Roth IRAs, the individual bears all asset risk and receives all returns. For taxable accounts, the individual and governments share its risk and returns. With taxable *stock* investments, the risk sharing and returns sharing varies with the investor's management practices. Traders bear less risk and receive less returns than long-term passive investors. Like those holding assets in pensions, long-term passive investors essentially bear all asset risk and receive all returns. Active stock investors, who trade annually but take advantage of long-term capital gain tax rates, bear a larger portion of stock's risk than expected returns.

We perform mean-variance optimization where some assets are held in taxable accounts and others in pensions—that is, Roth IRA or deductible pensions such as 401(k). Each investor—trader, active investor, or passive investor—must decide the optimal asset allocation and the optimal asset location.

For traders, there is not an optimal asset allocation or optimal asset location. Identical portfolios (in terms of utility, portfolio expected returns, and portfolio risk) can be obtained with more than one asset allocation. Moreover, one optimal portfolio locates stocks in pensions, and another locates bonds in pensions. Since governments share the risk and returns of the taxable account's asset, governments effectively "own" part of these assets. It follows that an individual's optimal asset mix calls for a relatively large exposure to the asset held in taxable accounts.

For active investors, there is an optimal asset allocation and asset location. To the degree possible without violating the asset allocation, bonds should be located in pensions and stocks in taxable accounts. However, the opposite strategy appears to produce only a small loss in utility. In short, either asset-location decision can produce portfolios that are almost equally desirable. When individuals locate stocks in taxable accounts, the optimal asset mix calls for a relatively large overall stock allocation. Similarly, when individuals locate bonds in taxable accounts, the optimal asset mix calls for a relatively large overall bond allocation.

For passive investors, there is an optimal asset allocation and asset location. Bonds should be located in pensions and stocks in taxable accounts. Since capital gains are eventually tax-exempt in a taxable account, it is a virtual waste of the tax shelter to locate stocks in pensions.

This study rejects the two-step procedure of, first, setting the optimal asset allocation and, second, choosing the asset location. These two decisions must be made jointly. Moreover, if anyone makes the asset location decision first, then his or her optimal asset allocation depends upon that location decision; the optimal asset allocation calls for a relatively large exposure to the asset located in taxable accounts.

Although this chapter's optimizations encourage individuals to locate stocks in taxable accounts, they understate the advantage of doing so. By locating stocks in taxable accounts, individual investors can maximize the opportunity to reduce their taxes by realizing capital losses. In essence, governments refund part of these losses.

References

Brunel, Jean. 1998. Why should taxable investors be cautious when using traditional efficient frontier tools? *Journal of Private Portfolio Management* (since renamed, *Journal of Wealth Management*), Winter, 35–50.

Ghee, William, and William Reichenstein. 1996. The after-tax returns from different savings vehicles. *Financial Analysts Journal,* July/August, 16–19.

Jeffrey, Robert H., and Robert D. Arnott. 1993. Is your alpha big enough to cover its taxes? *Journal of Portfolio Management,* Spring, 15–25.

Milevsky, Moshe Arye, & Kamphol Panyagometh. 2001. Variable annuities versus mutual funds: A Monte-Carlo analysis of the options. *Financial Services Review,* Vol. 10, 145–161.

Reichenstein, William. 1998. Calculating a family's asset mix. *Financial Services Review,* Vol. 7, No. 3, 195–206.

Reichenstein, William. 1999. Savings vehicles and the taxation of individual investors. *Journal of Private Portfolio Management* (since renamed, *Journal of Wealth Management*), Winter, 15–26.

Reichenstein, William. 2000. Frequently asked questions about savings vehicles. *Journal of Private Portfolio Management* (since renamed, *Journal of Wealth Management*), Summer, 66–81.

Reichenstein, William. 2001. Rethinking the family's asset allocation. *Journal of Financial Planning,* May, 102–109.

Shoven, John B. 1999. The location and allocation of assets in pension and conventional savings accounts. *National Bureau of Economic Research.* Working Paper No. 7007, March.

Shoven, John B., and Clemens Sialm. 1998. Long run asset allocation for retirement savings. *Journal of Private Portfolio Management* (since renamed, *Journal of Wealth Management*), Summer, 13–26.

Notes

1. A slightly different version of this chapter was published as "Asset Allocation and Asset Location Revisited," *Journal of Wealth Management,* Summer 2001, 6–26.
2. Deductible pensions include all savings vehicles where the investment contribution is tax deductible in the contribution year, returns accumulate tax deferred, and all withdrawals are taxed at the ordinary income tax rate.
3. In Chapter 9, we argue that an individual's portfolio should be broadened to include, at a minimum, the value of retirement income streams (i.e., Social Security, defined-benefit plans, and military retirement). These income streams are essentially "bonds," and including them substantially changes the individual's asset allocation. The decision about what to include in an individual's portfolio is a separate question and is not addressed in this chapter. See Chapter 9, and Reichenstein (1998 and 2001) for additional discussion.
4. In this analysis, we ignore differences such as the lack of minimum withdrawal requirements on the Roth IRA.
5. We take as a given that the investor would prefer to save in a Roth IRA or deductible pension than a taxable account. This implies that the risk tolerance must exceed 1.67 in the first utility function. That is, $6\% - 10\% / RT > 3.9\% - 6.5\% / RT$. Also, it implies the risk tolerance must exceed 33.6 in the second function. That is, $11\% - (15\%)^2 / RT > 7.87\% - (10.95)^2 / RT$.
6. This two-step procedure certainly reflects the prior thought of Reichenstein, one of this book's authors. Also, he believes it reflects the thought in Shoven (1999) and Shoven and Sialm (1998).
7. Chapter 3 shows that there is little benefit to deferring taxes for a few years. Many active investors typically realize capital gains within a few years. So, even though the active-investor model assumes all capital gains are realized each year, it adequately represents most active investors.
8. This is the optimal portfolio based on 1 percent increments. Thus, Portfolio 9 had a slightly larger utility than portfolios with 14 percent or 16 percent stocks in taxable accounts. The 1 percent increment is used in similar optimizations.
9. Stocks in pensions are about $72,900, which is 23.7 percent of $200,000 in after-tax funds divided by 0.65 or $(1 - t)$, with t denoting the marginal tax rate. Similarly, bonds in pensions are about $80,900 or $(0.263) \bullet (\$200,000) / 0.65$.
10. Milevsky and Panyagometh (2001) compared the ending after-tax wealth from a taxable stock fund and a non-qualified variable annuity. They concluded that the ability to recognize losses in taxable accounts substantially increased the breakeven period before a non-qualified variable annuity beats the taxable mutual fund. See Chapter 5 for more details.

Case Studies

Introduction

In this chapter, we present integrated case studies and guideline answers. They provide the opportunity to integrate insights from throughout the book.

Case 1

Cecilia is a retired 70-year-old widow. She has a traditional portfolio worth $600,000. It consists of $100,000 in a bond fund held in a Roth IRA, $300,000 in a diversified stock fund held in a 403(b), $100,000 in an active stock fund held in a taxable account, and $100,000 in bank CDs. She is an active investor. Since she recently bought the active stock fund, both its market value and cost basis are $100,000. Cecilia has an average life expectancy for a woman her age. She receives $1,200 per month from Social Security that, of course, increases each year with inflation. Also, she receives $2,000 per month from a defined-benefit plan, but this payment is not expected to increase. The appropriate discount rates for her Social Security and defined-benefit plan benefits are 3.5 percent and 7 percent, respectively. She is in the 25 percent tax bracket, and 85 percent of Social Security income is taxable. Since the traditional method of calculating her asset allocation says she has a 67 percent stock allocation [$400,000 / $600,000], she fears that she is overexposed to stocks. Calculate the current asset allocation of her extended portfolio. Based on your calculations, does she appear to be overexposed to stocks?

Guideline Answer to Case 1

Table 15.1 presents Cecilia's extended portfolio. The $300,000 of before-tax funds in the 403(b) is worth $225,000 after paying taxes at 25 percent. The before-tax and after-tax values are the same for the Roth IRA and taxable accounts. The $24,000

Account or Savings Vehicle	Asset	Before-tax Value	After-tax Value
Roth IRA	Bonds	$100,000	$100,000
403(b)	Stocks	300,000	225,000
Taxable Account	Stocks	100,000	100,000
Taxable Account	Bonds	100,000	100,000
Defined-benefit Plan	Bonds	222,000	167,000
Social Security	Bonds	174,000	133,000
Total			$825,000

TABLE 15.1   Cecilia's Family Portfolio

per year from the defined-benefit plan is worth about $222,000 before taxes, where the multiple from Table 13.7 is 9.26 for a single female age 70 when the discount rate is 7 percent. The after-tax value is about $167,000. The Social Security benefits are worth about $174,000 before taxes [$1,200 • 12 months • 12.08], where 12.08 is the multiple from Table 11.4 for a 70-year-old female when the discount rate is 3.5 percent. The after-tax value is about $133,000 [$174,000 • (1 − 0.85 • 0.28)].

We should manage her family or extended portfolio that includes the present values of her defined-benefit plan and Social Security benefits. The stock allocation of her family portfolio is 39 percent, [$325,000 / $825,000], which is much lower than the 67 percent stock allocation based on the traditional calculation method. Since she has substantial income from her defined-benefit plan and Social Security, her family portfolio has a much lower stock allocation. Based on the extended portfolio and her risk tolerance, Cecilia is not overexposed to stocks. When her financial advisor explains that income from her defined-benefit plan and Social Security are essentially bonds, she will likely feel more comfortable with her current portfolio.

Recall that Cecilia is an active investor. She has an active stock fund in a taxable account. In Chapter 8, we state that an active stock fund held in a taxable account must overcome three burdens compared to a passive index fund: higher expenses, higher transaction costs, and higher taxes. These are steep burdens, indeed. Although we believe Cecilia would benefit from passively managing stocks in the taxable account, in this case, we suspect that she will not passively manage stocks. The analysis in Chapter 14 implies that the asset-location decision is not particularly important for an active investor. Consequently, our recommended portfolio ignores the asset-location issue. In fact, taxable accounts contain both stocks and bonds, and tax-deferred retirement accounts contain both stocks and bonds. *If we thought she would passively manage stocks* (or do so for a portion of her portfolio), we would have recommended that she buy a tax-efficient fund with the $100,000 in stocks in the taxable account. In addition, we would have recommended that she hold as little cash and bonds in her taxable accounts as necessary for liquidity and transfer the rest to passive stocks with an offsetting increase in bonds within tax-deferred retirement accounts.

Case 2, Part 1

John is single and 50 years old; he was born in 1953. He works for a firm that has a defined-benefit plan. This well-funded plan will pay him, upon retirement at normal retirement age, an annual payment equal to 1 percent of his income up to $60,000 plus 1.75 percent above $60,000 times years of service times average salary over the highest five years. Benefit levels are not expected to increase during retirement. His average salary over the highest five years is currently $80,000, and he has 15 years of service. He expects to retire at age 66 at which time he will have attained normal retirement age. He has an average life expectancy, and the risk-appropriate discount rate is 6 percent for these benefits.

He recently received his annual Social Security statement that says he can expect to receive a monthly payment of $1,250 (in current dollars) assuming his real income remains constant until retirement at his Full Retirement Age of 66. The longest-term TIPS yield is 3 percent.

He has been fully funding his 401(k) account. Although he is now 50 and can make additional catch-up contributions each year to the 401(k), he does not plan on making these additional contributions. In addition, although he qualifies for Roth IRA contributions, he has not made them.

His 401(k) contains $300,000 in an S&P 500 index fund. He holds an active stock fund in a taxable account that has a market value of $150,000 and a cost basis of $145,000. In addition, he has a bank savings account worth $50,000. He is currently in the 28 percent tax bracket but expects to be in the 25 percent bracket during retirement. His long-term capital gain tax rate is 20 percent. His risk tolerance is moderate, and his target asset allocation is 60 percent stocks and 40 percent fixed income. He hires you to help him assess and arrange his financial matters. As part of that process, answer the following questions:

1. Estimate the current value of the defined-benefit plan.
2. Estimate the before-tax present value of Social Security retirement benefits.
3. Provide advice concerning his planned use, or lack thereof, of the 401(k) catch-up contributions and Roth IRA contributions.
4. Estimate the current asset allocation of his family portfolio.
5. Provide advice concerning asset location in his portfolio.
6. Recommend portfolio changes to achieve his target stock allocation of 60 percent.

Guideline Answer to Case 2, Part 1

1. The current before-tax value of the defined-benefit plan is about $52,000. Based on current average salary and current years of service, he is entitled to $14,250 in annual retirement benefits [0.01 • 15 • $60,000 + 0.0175 • 15 • $20,000]. The multiple for a 50-year-old single male with average life expectancy is 3.65 when the discount rate is 6 percent. The before-tax value is thus about $52,000 [$14,250 • 3.65].

2. The before-tax value of Social Security is about $111,000. Although he plans to begin receiving benefits at age 66, we can use the fact that, for people with average life expectancy, the present value of benefits begun at age 66 is about equal to the present value of benefits begun at age 65. The tables in Chapter 11 assume that benefits begin at age 65; therefore, we estimate the value as if he begins benefits at age 65 and use this estimate even though he plans to retire one year later. Since he was born in 1953, his benefits fraction at age 65 is 0.933. The level of initial annual benefits is $13,995 [0.933 • $1,250 •12 months], where $1,250 is the Primary Insurance Amount. From Table 11.5, the multiple is 7.94 for a 50-year-old male with an average life expectancy when the TIPS yield is 3 percent. Therefore, the before-tax value is about $111,000 [$13,995 • 7.94].

3. The financial advisor should strongly recommend that John invest all he can in the 401(k) and Roth IRA savings vehicles. He should take advantage of the catch-up contributions within the 401(k) and the regular and catch-up contributions within the Roth IRA. If necessary, he could "finance" the additional monthly contributions by withdrawing funds from a taxable account to meet current income needs. However, since he has relatively little saved for retirement, the better strategy is to save more of his current income and use these savings to finance the contributions. Most clients think the advisor will add value to their portfolio by recommending market-beating stock funds. As experienced financial advisors know, this is a difficult task. By convincing John to maximize contributions to these tax-favored savings vehicles, the advisor can add more value than he can from trying to select particular stock funds. The value added to John's account by trying to select an index-beating stock fund is relatively small and uncertain. The value added from making sure John takes advantage of the Tax Code is relatively large and certain.

4. Table 15.2 presents the current asset allocation of his family portfolio.

The active stock fund in the taxable account has a market (or before-tax) value of $150,000, a cost basis of $145,000, and an after-tax value assuming a 20 percent capital gain tax rate of $149,000. The bank savings account contains $50,000 of after-tax funds; its before-tax and after-tax values are the same. The after-tax value of the defined-benefit plan is $39,000 [$52,000 • (1 − 0.25)], where 0.25 is the anticipated marginal tax rate during retirement. Assuming 85 percent of Social Security benefits are taxable, the after-tax value is about $87,000 [$111,000 • (1 −

TABLE 15.2   John's Family Portfolio

Account or Savings Vehicle	Asset	Before-tax Value	After-tax Value
401(k)	Stocks	$300,000	$225,000
Taxable Account	Stocks	150,000	149,000
Taxable Account	Bonds	50,000	50,000
Defined-benefit Plan	Bonds	52,000	39,000
Social Security	Bonds	111,000	87,000
Total			$550,000

0.85 • 0.25)]. The after-tax value of the 401(k) is $225,000 [$300,000 • (1 − 0.25)]. John's family portfolio is worth $550,000 after taxes. Based on after-tax values, his current stock-bond allocation is 68 percent stocks [$374,000 / $550,000] and 32 percent bonds. (This asset allocation lumps cash and bonds together as fixed income or bonds. Others may wish to separate the two.)

5. Actively managed stocks should be held in the tax-deferred 401(k), and passively managed stocks should be held in the taxable account. In the taxable account, he should sell the active stock fund and replace it with the S&P 500 index fund (or another passive, tax-efficient stock fund). Table 3.3 shows that passive investors are expected to outperform active investors by more than enough to offset the $1,000 in capital gain taxes from liquidating stocks in the taxable account. If he wants to actively manage stocks, he should do so in tax-deferred retirement accounts—the 401(k) in this example. The active stock fund realizes capital gains each year, and it must distribute these gains. If held in a taxable account, these gains are taxable in the distribution year, while, if held in a 401(k), the gains are tax deferred. The capital-gain distributions in the active stock fund will accumulate tax deferred in the 401(k), while they would be taxed in the distribution year if held in the taxable account. Meanwhile, since there are minimal capital-gain distributions in the passive fund, its unrealized capital gains will grow virtually unharvested in a taxable account.

6. John's target asset allocation is 60 percent stocks and 40 percent bonds. From the previous table, his current stock allocation is about 68 percent [($225,000 + $149,000) / $550,000]. We assume he already moved $149,000 of passive stocks into the taxable account. In addition, we assume the other $50,000 in a taxable account will remain in cash or short-term bonds to provide liquidity. To obtain the 60 percent target, he could move some 401(k) funds into bonds. Table 15.3 presents the family portfolio after adjustments.

Case 2, Part 2

John's uncle died and left him an inheritance of $100,000 after taxes. He approached a sales representative who recommended that he buy a non-qualified

TABLE 15.3 John's Family Portfolio after Adjustments

Account or Savings Vehicle	Asset	Before-tax Value	After-tax Value
401(k)	Stocks	$99,000	$74,000
401(k)	Bonds	201,000	151,000
Taxable Account	Stocks	150,000	149,000
Taxable Account	Bonds	50,000	50,000
Defined-benefit Plan	Bonds	52,000	39,000
Social Security	Bonds	111,000	87,000
Total			$550,000

variable annuity and place the funds in a stock fund that is benchmarked against the Russell 3000, which is an index of the entire U.S. stock market. This mutual fund subaccount has a total expense ratio of 2.3 percent and a surrender fee of 7 percent in the first year, with the surrender fee falling by 1 percent per year.

1. Recommend another non-qualified annuity that would be better for John (the client).

2. Assume John will passively manage these funds and wants the investment to follow the total U.S. stock market. Recommend another investment for the $100,000.

Guideline Answer to Case 2, Part 2

1. The financial advisor could recommend a low-cost variable annuity. From Table 5.4, the Stock Index and Social Choice Equity mutual funds (also called subaccounts) in the TIAA-CREF Life Variable Annuity contract benchmark the Russell 3000 stock index. The Stock Index buys (virtually) every stock in the Russell 3000 index, while Social Choice Equity holds (virtually) every stock that meets its social criteria. Both funds will produce total returns that follow the index. Naturally, the expected tracking error is larger on Social Choice Equity.

2. From Table 8.2, Fidelity, Schwab, and Vanguard each offer a low-cost index fund that targets either the Russell 3000 or Wilshire 5000. (The Wilshire 5000 is another total U.S. stock market index.) From Chapter 5, a low-cost stock index fund is expected to provide a slightly larger ending after-tax wealth than a low-cost annuity. Furthermore, this slight advantage assumes the passive index fund will eventually be sold and capital gain taxes paid. If the index fund is held until death or used to finance charitable contributions, then the index fund's advantage would be larger. However, if the investor will not passively manage the index fund, then the low-cost annuity will fare better. Both choices are good ones for the investor. The better choice depends, in part, upon investor-specific factors.

Case 2, Part 3

Assume that, one year ago, John purchased the Fidelity Spartan Total Market Index fund with the $100,000 of inherited funds. During the past year, the stock market fell and the account is now worth $91,000. What would you recommend?

Guideline Answer to Case 2, Part 3

John could sell the Fidelity fund and buy the Vanguard Total Stock Market Index fund (or any other tax-efficient total-stock-market fund). Since the Fidelity fund is held in a taxable account, its sale generates a $9,000 capital loss. These transactions do not likely violate the wash sale rules even though the Fidelity and Vanguard funds have almost identical portfolios. Meanwhile, each year for the next three years, John can reduce his taxable income by $3,000, which will reduce his taxes by $840 each year [$3,000 • 0.28]. (This assumes he has no other capital gains or losses.) One advantage of the taxable mutual fund is that losses can be realized, and, in essence, the government funds part of the loss. Due to the surrender fee, such loss harvesting is not practical in a non-qualified annuity. In addition, withdrawals from the annuity before age 59½ are usually subject to a 10 percent penalty tax. As discussed in Chapter 5, this benefit is not modeled in the comparison of low-cost annuity and low-cost passive stock funds, but it clearly has value.

Case 3

Bob and Gillian, a married couple, are both 40 years old in 2003. They are prolific savers—partially because they are not covered by a defined-benefit pension plan. This year, each spouse will contribute the maximum $12,000 to a 401(k) and $3,000 to a nondeductible IRA. Their joint income prevents them from contributing to a Roth IRA. In addition, they save about $14,000 in taxable accounts. They plan to continue to save at approximately this level for the next several years. They prefer tax-advantaged savings since their combined federal-plus-state tax rate is 40 percent. They expect to be in the 40 percent bracket before retirement and in a lower bracket during retirement—perhaps 35 percent. Their combined capital gain tax rate is 25 percent.

Their portfolio includes $500,000 in 401(k)s in actively managed U.S. stock funds. Each spouse has $130,000 in a nondeductible IRA. Gillian invested in an international stock fund, while more conservative Bob invested in a bond fund. They have $40,000 in a joint money market fund, $60,000 in a bond fund, and $140,000 in a taxable Russell 2000 index fund that they purchased in the last two years. (The Russell 2000 is a small-cap index fund.) The cost basis of the bond fund is $60,000, while the basis of the Russell 2000 index fund is $130,000. The most recent Social Security statement for each partner projected a Primary Insurance Amount (PIA) of $1,400 assuming they work until their FRA of 67. The longest-term TIPS yield is 3.5 percent.

They decided to seek professional advice because of a recent milestone—adoption of a healthy two-year-old girl. In conversations, you learn that Gillian is comfortable with an aggressive portfolio (e.g., 70–85 percent stocks), while Bob prefers a less-risky portfolio (e.g., 55–70 percent stocks). In addition, they expect major changes in the Social Security system and have generally ignored these hard-to-value benefits.

1. Calculate the current asset allocation of their family portfolio.
2. Since contributions are not deductible, do you recommend that they continue to fund the nondeductible IRA?
3. Family friends recently liquidated U.S. savings bonds, and the interest was tax-exempt since the funds were used to finance their son's college education.

Bob and Gillian ask if the purchase of savings bonds is a good way to finance their daughter's college education. In addition, recommend at least one other savings vehicle that would be more appropriate to fund their daughter's education needs.

4. Bob and Gillian bought the Russell 2000 index fund for their taxable account because they heard on a talk radio show that index funds are tax efficient. Discuss the tax efficiency of a small-cap index fund, and recommend a more tax-efficient fund.

Guideline Answer to Case 3

1. The appropriate assets to include in a portfolio depend upon the question being asked. For example, in estate planning, the value of Social Security should be ignored. However, when assessing the couple's ability to meet their retirement income needs, it should be included. Furthermore, we need to distinguish between before-tax and after-tax funds. Table 15.4 presents Bob and Gillian's family portfolio, which has a 68 percent stock allocation [$547,000 / $801,500].

The 401(k) is worth $325,000 after adjusting for anticipated taxes during retirement [$500,000 • (1 − 0.35)]. Each nondeductible IRA is worth $84,500 after taxes. The money market fund and bond fund already contain after-tax dollars. The $10,000 built-in capital gain in the Russell 2000 fund makes this fund's after-tax value $2,500 lower than its before-tax value [$10,000 • 0.25].

The couple model estimates the before-tax value of Social Security benefits as the product: (benefits fraction at age 65) • (PIA of higher earner) • (12 months) • (couple multiple). Assuming Bob and Gillian have average life expectancies, the value is similar whether benefits begin at age 65 or any other age. The before-tax present value is estimated at about $153,000 [0.867 • 12 • $1,400 • 10.47], where the final number is the couple multiple [6.62 + 1 • 3.85]. The 6.62 and 3.85 come from Table 11.7.

However, this estimate has two potential biases. It is based on Social Security's current structure, and the PIA is their initial monthly payment *assuming they*

TABLE 15.4　Bob and Gillian's Family Portfolio

Account or Savings Vehicle	Asset	Before-tax Value	After-tax Value
401(k)s	Stocks	$500,000	$325,000
His Nondeductible IRA	Bonds	130,000	84,500
Her Nondeductible IRA	Stocks	130,000	84,500
Taxable Money Market	Bonds	40,000	40,000
Taxable Bond Fund	Bonds	60,000	60,000
Taxable Russell 2000 Index Fund	Stocks	140,000	137,500
Social Security	Bonds	100,000	70,000
Total			$801,500

continue to earn their current real earnings (or, at least, the maximum income subject to Social Security taxes) *until age 67*. The model gives current credit for future work. Based on their earnings history to date, they would be entitled to lower retirement payments. This bias tends to be small for individuals age 50 and older, but it is larger for younger individuals such as Bob and Gillian. Given this couple's concerns, the likely reduction in Social Security benefits for financially secure individuals, and the bias previously discussed, the financial professional reduces her estimate of Social Security's before-tax value to $100,000. This is a conservative valuation, which should satisfy Bob and Gillian. Although the level of Social Security's future benefits is uncertain, it is highly unlikely that there will be no benefits. Assuming 85 percent of benefits will be taxable, their after-tax value is about $70,000 [$100,000 • (1 − 0.85 • 0.35)].

To repeat, Gillian prefers an aggressive portfolio, while Bob is more conservative. The couple must come to some agreement about their desired asset allocation. If they compromise, the current portfolio appears reasonable.

2. Yes, Bob and Gillian should continue to contribute to their nondeductible IRAs. Their nondeductible IRA contributions should benefit from tax deferral and tax timing. Tax deferral is a major benefit, especially to the young. (If Bob and Gillian spend the funds in the nondeductible IRAs roughly evenly between ages 70 to 90, the funds will be invested for, on average, 40 more years.) In addition, the nondeductible IRAs will benefit from tax timing if, as expected, they are in a lower tax bracket during retirement. One drawback to nondeductible IRAs is the accounting paperwork needed to calculate the taxable portion of withdrawals. However, since they already have a nondeductible IRA, this factor should not influence future contributions.

3. Unless their income falls dramatically, when the bonds are liquidated, the interest from U.S. savings bonds would be fully taxable at the federal level; their income is too high to qualify for the tax exemption of interest when funding qualified education expenses. A 529 savings Qualified Tuition Plan is a better savings vehicle to fund their daughter's education needs. They could save abundantly within one or more of these plans. Table 8.2 lists several low-cost 529 savings Qualified Tuition Plans. In addition, the Coverdell Education Savings Account provides the opportunity to earn tax-exempt, market-based returns. However, the maximum annual contribution to their daughter's ESA from all donors is $2,000 per year, and the parents' income would prevent them from being the donor.

4. The Russell 2000 stock index fund will not be tax efficient. It consists of 2000 small-firm stocks. The most successful of these stocks will rise into the mid-cap range, which will force the index manager to sell these stocks and realize the gains. For tax efficiency, the index fund should try to replicate the return on a large-cap index or a total-stock-market index. Alternatively, there are several tax-managed stock funds that should provide tax-efficient returns. Table 7.2 provides a list of tax-efficient stock funds.

Glossary

Chapter 2

10-percent penalty tax This is a fine imposed on most withdrawals before age 59½ from annuities, deductible pensions, Roth IRAs, and nondeductible IRAs (see Sec. 72(t) of the Internal Revenue Code).

death benefit At the annuity owner's death (if the annuity has not been annuitized), the death benefit guarantees that the beneficiary will receive a minimum value. Often, the guaranteed amount is the larger of the ending investment value and the original investment amount (reduced for subsequent withdrawals).

deductible IRA This is a traditional IRA where the amount of money contributed is deductible on the taxpayer's return. It is one type of deductible pension.

deductible pension This is any savings vehicle in which an individual invests before-tax dollars that grow tax deferred until withdrawal. Upon withdrawal, the principal and earnings are fully taxable at the individual's ordinary income tax rate. Examples include 401(k) plans, 403(b) plans, Keogh plans, and deductible IRAs.

nondeductible IRA This is a traditional IRA where the amount of money contributed is not deductible on the taxpayer's return.

non-qualified tax-deferred annuity This is a savings vehicle in which an individual invests after-tax dollars that grow tax deferred until withdrawal. Upon withdrawal, the earnings are fully taxable at the individual's ordinary income tax rate.

retirement savings vehicle This is a savings vehicle established by Congress and intended to be used for retirement savings. Examples include annuities, deductible pensions, Roth IRAs, and nondeductible IRAs.

Roth IRA This is a savings vehicle in which an individual invests after-tax dollars that generally grow tax-exempt and are not taxed upon withdrawal.

savings vehicle This is an entire legal structure within which an individual saves, including applicable tax structure, liquidity restrictions, and other restrictions. Examples include non-qualified tax-deferred annuities and Roth IRAs.

stepped-up basis At an individual's death, his beneficiary receives certain assets held in taxable accounts. The stepped-up basis refers to the increase in the assets' basis to their fair market values on the decedent's date of death or an alternate valuation date six months later.

tax timing This refers to the ability to withdraw funds in retirement when the investor may be in a lower tax bracket.

traditional IRA The traditional IRA includes both the deductible and nondeductible IRAs.

Chapter 4

conversion (or rollover) This refers to the direct transfer of funds from the trustee of a non-Roth IRA to the trustee of a Roth IRA or the redesignation of a non-Roth IRA as a Roth IRA maintained by the same trustee.

Chapter 5

annuitization This is the process of exchanging an annuity for a lifetime monthly income. When an annuity is annuitized, the contract owner exchanges the annuity for a guaranteed monthly income for the rest of his or her life or, more commonly, the rest of the contract owner and his or her spouse's lives.

contract charge This is an annual, fixed-dollar fee on annuities.

guaranteed minimum death benefit This is a type of death benefit promising that, upon the investor's involuntary death, the beneficiary will receive the larger of the ending investment value and the original investment amount (reduced for subsequent withdrawals).

insurance expense This is the sum of the mortality and expense (M&E) fee plus all other administrative and distribution expenses on annuities.

mortality and expense fee This is an annual percentage fee charged by the insurance firm against subaccount assets to cover the cost of the death benefit and other insurance costs.

non-qualified annuity This is an annuity in which the original investment contributions are not tax deferred. In other words, the individual invests after-tax dollars.

qualified annuity   This is an annuity in which the original investment contributions are tax deferred. In other words, the individual invests before-tax dollars.

surrender fee   This refers to a percentage penalty assessed on withdrawals in the early years of an annuity. A typical surrender fee is 6 percent of withdrawals beyond the free-withdrawal amount in the first year of the contract, with the penalty rate decreasing 1 percent per year.

Chapter 7

community property state   This is a state in which each spouse owns a one-half interest in all assets acquired after marriage unless the assets are acquired by gift or inheritance.

common law state   This is a state in which all assets acquired after marriage are owned solely by the acquiring spouse.

Exchange Traded Funds (ETFs)   An ETF is, in essence, a mutual fund traded on an exchange like individual stocks. Unlike traditional mutual funds, ETFs can be bought and sold during the trading day. Their values rise and fall with the value of a set of securities, such as stocks in the S&P 500.

Standard & Poors' Depository Receipts (SPDRs)   These are examples of exchange traded funds. SPDRs are units in a trust that holds the stocks in the S&P 500 in proportion to their index weight.

Chapter 10

family extended portfolio   This is a set of assets held by an individual or family that includes financial assets such as stocks and bonds as well as the present value of incomes from Social Security, military retirement plans, and defined-benefit plans.

Chapter 11

Average Indexed Monthly Earnings (AIME)   This is an individual's average monthly earnings for the 35 calendar years with the highest inflation-adjusted earnings. AIME is used in the calculation of Social Security retirement benefits.

bend points   The Social Security Administration uses bend points to translate someone's Average Indexed Monthly Earnings into an initial monthly benefits amount. For example, someone born in 1936 who retired at Full Retirement Age received initial monthly benefits equal to 90 percent of the first $477 of AIME plus 32 percent of additional AIME up to $2,875 plus 15 percent of additional AIME. The bend points are $477 and $2,875.

combined income   This is the sum of adjusted gross income, nontaxable interest, and one-half of Social Security benefits.

Cost-of-Living Adjustment (COLA)   This is the annual increase in retirement benefits that keeps these benefits in pace with inflation.

Delayed Retirement Credits (DRC)   These credits provide a higher level of initial Social Security benefits if these benefits are begun after attaining Full Retirement Age. For example, these credits may increase the initial level of benefits by 8 percent per year for each year these benefits are delayed.

Full Retirement Age (FRA)   This is the age at which an individual can begin benefits and receive full Social Security benefits.

Primary Insurance Amount (PIA)   This is the level of Social Security benefits that a person receives if he elects to begin receiving these benefits at Full Retirement Age. PIA is the sum of three separate percentages of portions of Average Indexed Monthly Earnings.

Chapter 12

base pay amount   Under the Final Pay military retirement system, this is a service member's final base pay, excluding bonuses. Under the High Three and REDUX military retirement systems, this is the average base pay for the highest 36 months, excluding bonuses.

current annual payment   This is the product of Base Pay Amount and Percentage.

Final Pay   This is the military retirement system that applies to service members who entered the military before September 8, 1980.

High Three   This is the military retirement system that applies to service members who entered the military after September 8, 1980.

percentage   A military retiree's Current Annual Payment is the product of Base Pay Amount and Percentage. Under the Final Pay and High Three military retirement systems, Percentage is set at 50 percent plus 2.5 percent times a service member's years of service minus 20 years [50% + 2.5% • (years of service − 20)]. Under the REDUX military retirement system, Percentage is set at 40 percent plus 3.5 percent times a service member's years of service minus 20 years [40% + 3.5% • (years of service − 20)].

REDUX   This is the military retirement system that applies to service members who entered the military after July 31, 1986. Service members eligible for the REDUX system may also select the High Three system.

Survivor Benefit Plan (SBP)   Under the SBP, a military retiree receives a reduced level of benefits, but, after the retiree's death, his or her surviving spouse is entitled to a portion of the level of retirement benefits.

Chapter 13

accrued benefit obligation   This is a measure of an employer's pension plan liability that includes benefits for vested and nonvested employees at current compensation levels.

benefits formula   This describes the method of calculating retirement benefits for defined-benefit plan participants.

defined-benefit plan   This is a pension plan in which an employer contributes amounts to a central account for all participating employees. These contributions are determined by actuarial techniques and are used to fund retirement payments for plan participants.

defined-contribution plan   This is a pension plan in which an employer contributes amounts to individual employees' accounts based on a specific formula such as a fixed percentage of compensation. Retirement benefits are based on the value of each employee's account.

integration level   *See* step-rate approach to integration.

joint-payout option   This is a type of defined-benefit plan payout option available to married couples that promises payments for as long as the participant or his or her spouse is alive. In a joint and 75 percent survivor payout, the surviving spouse receives 75 percent of the level of benefits received while the retired participant was alive. Other common percentages are 50 percent and 100 percent for the surviving spouse.

offset approach to integration   This integration approach reduces pension plan benefits by a fixed percentage of Social Security retirement benefits.

projected benefit obligation   This is a measure of an employer's pension plan liability that includes benefits for vested and nonvested employees at projected future compensation levels.

step-rate approach to integration   This integration approach sets the level of pension plan benefits as the product of a lower fixed percentage (the base rate) times the integration level of income plus the product of a higher percentage (the excess rate) times income above the integration level.

Chapter 14

asset location   This refers to the decision to locate or place assets. For example, should stocks be placed in taxable accounts and bonds in tax-deferred accounts or vice versa?

mean-variance optimization   This is a quantitative technique that finds an optimal portfolio given certain inputs. These inputs include expected return and standard deviation for each asset, correlation coefficient between each pair of assets, and a utility function to reflect the investor's risk-return trade-off.

utility   This is a measure of an investor's economic satisfaction. It allows the investor to choose between a lower risk and return asset or a higher risk and return asset.

Index